Lecture Notes in Computer Science 4748

Commenced Publication in 1973
Founding and Former Series Editors:
Gerhard Goos, Juris Hartmanis, and Jan van Leeuwen

Katinka Wolter (Ed.)

Formal Methods
and Stochastic Models
for Performance Evaluation

Fourth European Performance Engineering Workshop, EPEW 2007
Berlin, Germany, September 2007
Proceedings

 Springer

Volume Editor

Katinka Wolter
Humboldt Universität Berlin
Institut für Informatik
Unter den Linden 6, 10099 Berlin, Germany
E-mail: wolter@informatik.hu-berlin.de

Library of Congress Control Number: 2007935135

CR Subject Classification (1998): D.2.4, C.2.4, F.3, D.4, C.4

LNCS Sublibrary: SL 2 – Programming and Software Engineering

ISSN   0302-9743
ISBN-10   3-540-75210-2 Springer Berlin Heidelberg New York
ISBN-13   978-3-540-75210-3 Springer Berlin Heidelberg New York

Springer is a part of Springer Science+Business Media

springer.com

© Springer-Verlag Berlin Heidelberg 2007
Printed in Germany

Typesetting: Camera-ready by author, data conversion by Scientific Publishing Services, Chennai, India
Printed on acid-free paper   SPIN: 12164042   06/3180   5 4 3 2 1 0

Preface

This volume contains the papers presented at the 4th European Performance Engineering Workshop held during September 27–28 in Berlin.

There were 53 submissions. Each submission was reviewed by at least three Programme Committee members. From these, the committee decided to accept 20 papers.

We were very happy to have Isi Mitrani from Newcastle University give a keynote lecture on his recent work and future challenges in applied queueing theory.

The submitted papers cover all areas of performance engineering. We were able to compose an interesting program in six sessions, including sessions on theoretical work in performance engineering techniques as well as sessions presenting applications of performance engineering techniques. The final workshop program, as well as this volume, comprises the thematic sessions:

- Markov Chains
- Process Algebra
- Wireless Networks
- Queueing Theory and Applications of Queueing
- Benchmarking and Bounding
- Grid and Peer-to-Peer Systems

The volume includes very theoretical papers on topics such as bounds in stochastic ordering, canonical representation of phase-type-distributions and algorithms to solve closed queueing networks. Some papers study properties of numerical solution algorithms, other contributions evaluate hardware or software design and propose benchmarks. On the application side there are, furthermore, evaluations of wireless protocols, simulation studies of distributed systems and performance evaluation of system monitoring tools. We hope that this volume will provide a reference for fundamental work in performance engineering.

The success of the workshop is due to many helping hands. First of all, the members of the Program Committee were very cooperative, spent much time on reading and evaluating the submitted papers and gave advice where needed. Luckily, Miklos Telek passed on his experience after organizing last year's workshop.

Thanks to Levente Bodrog from Budapest the workshop had a professionally designed Web site. The EasyChair conference management software eased the administration of the PC meeting and composition of this volume. We thank the publisher for his support and continuity.

Last, but not least, I would like to thank the local organizers Johannes Zapotoczky and Steffen Tschirpke. Philipp Reinecke derserves special thanks for his help at all times.

July 2007   Katinka Wolter

Conference Organization

Programme Chair

Katinka Wolter

Programme Committee

Jeremy Bradley	Imperial College, London (UK)
Mario Bravetti	University of Bologna (Italy)
Lucy Cherkasova	HP Labs (USA)
Lucia Cloth	University of Twente (Netherlands)
Michel Cukier	University of Maryland (USA)
Tadeusz Czachorski	IITiS PAN, Gliwice (Poland)
Jean-Michel Fourneau	Université de Versailles (France)
Stephen Gilmore	University of Edinburgh (UK)
Armin Heindl	University of Erlangen-Nürnberg (Germany)
András Horváth	University of Torino (Italy)
Carlos Juiz	University Illes Balears (Spain)
Tomáš Kalibera	Charles University in Prague (Czech Republic)
Helen Karatza	Aristotle University of Thessaloniki (Greece)
Leïla Kloul	Université de Versailles (France)
Kim G. Larsen	University of Aalborg (Denmark)
Hermann de Meer	Passau University (Germany)
Aad van Moorsel	Newcastle University (UK)
Manuel Nunez	University Complutense de Madrid (Spain)
Fernando L. Pelayo	University Castilla-La Mancha (Spain)
Brigitte Plateau	Polytechnical Institute of Grenoble, LIG, (France)
Rob Pooley	Heriot-Watt University, Edinburgh (UK)
Marina Ribaudo	University of Genova (Italy)
Marco Scarpa	University of Messina (Italy)
Markus Siegle	University of the Federal Armed Forces, Munich (Germany)
Mark Squillante	IBM T.J. Watson Research Center, NY (USA)
Ann Tai	IA Tech, Inc. (USA)
Miklós Telek	Technical University of Budapest (Hungary)
Nigel Thomas	Newcastle University (UK)
Lisa Wells	University of Aarhus (Denmark)
Katinka Wolter	Humboldt University Berlin (Germany)
Armin Zimmermann	Technical University Berlin (Germany)
Wlodek M. Zuberek	Memorial University (Canada)

Local Organization

Steffen Tschirpke
Philipp Reinecke
Johannes Zapotoczky

External Reviewers

Ashok Argent-Katwala
Leonardo Brenner
Matteo Dell'Amico
Salvatore Distefano
Marco Ferrante
David de Frutos Escrig
Gabor Horvath
Douglas de Jager
Mehdi Khouja
Harini Kulatunga
Luis Llana
Natalia Lopez

Mercedes G. Merayo
Nihal Pekergin
Antonio Puliafito
Philipp Reinecke
Martin Riedl
Afonso Sales
Pere P. Sancho
Johann Schuster
Giuseppe Scionti
Antonio Sola
Valentin Valero
Maria Vigliotti

Table of Contents

Keynote

Optimization Problems in Service Provisioning Systems 1
  Isi Mitrani

Markov Chains

Untold Horrors About Steady-State Probabilities: What Reward-Based
Measures Won't Tell About the Equilibrium Distribution 2
  Alexander Bell and Boudewijn R. Haverkort

Compositionality for Markov Reward Chains with Fast Transitions 18
  Jasen Markovski, Ana Sokolova, Nikola Trčka, and Erik P. de Vink

Closed Form Absorption Time Bounds 33
  Ana Bušić and Nihal Pekergin

A Canonical Representation of Order 3 Phase Type Distributions 48
  Gábor Horváth and Miklós Telek

Process Algebras and State Machines

SPAMR: Extending PAMR with Stochastic Time 63
  Natalia López, Manuel Núñez, and Ismael Rodríguez

Faster SPDL Model Checking Through Property-Driven State Space
Generation 80
  Matthias Kuntz and Boudewijn R. Haverkort

Testing Finite State Machines Presenting Stochastic Time and
Timeouts 97
  Mercedes G. Merayo, Manuel Núñez, and Ismael Rodríguez

Grid and Peer-to-Peer Systems

Evaluation of P2P Search Algorithms for Discovering Trust Paths 112
  Emerson Ribeiro de Mello, Aad van Moorsel, and Joni da Silva Fraga

Building Online Performance Models of Grid Middleware with
Fine-Grained Load-Balancing: A Globus Toolkit Case Study 125
  Ramon Nou, Samuel Kounev, and Jordi Torres

Performance Measuring Framework for Grid Market Middleware   141
Felix Freitag, Pablo Chacin, Isaac Chao, Rene Brunner,
Leandro Navarro, and Oscar Ardaiz

Queueing Theory and Applications of Queueing

A Fixed-Point Algorithm for Closed Queueing Networks   154
Ramin Sadre, Boudewijn R. Haverkort, and Patrick Reinelt

A Framework for Automated Generation of Architectural Feedback
from Software Performance Analysis   171
Vittorio Cortellessa and Laurento Frittella

Optimal Dynamic Server Allocation in Systems with On/Off Sources . . .   186
Joris Slegers, Isi Mitrani, and Nigel Thomas

Towards an Automatic Modeling Tool for Observed System Behavior . . .   200
Thomas Begin, Alexandre Brandwajn,
Bruno Baynat, Bernd E. Wolfinger, and Serge Fdida

Benchmarking and Bounding

Censoring Markov Chains and Stochastic Bounds   213
Jean-Michel Fourneau, Nihal Pekergin, and Sana Younès

Workload Characterization of the SPECjms2007 Benchmark   228
Kai Sachs, Samuel Kounev, Jean Bacon, and Alejandro Buchmann

Resource Sharing in Performance Models   245
Vlastimil Babka, Martin Děcký, and Petr Tůma

Exploiting Commodity Hard-Disk Geometry to Efficiently Preserve
Data Consistency   260
Alessandro Di Marco

Wireless Networks

An Efficient Counter-Based Broadcast Scheme for Mobile Ad Hoc
Networks   275
Aminu Mohammed, Mohamed Ould-Khaoua, and Lewis Mackenzie

The Effect of Mobility on Local Service Discovery in the Ahoy Ad-Hoc
Network System   284
Patrick Goering, Geert Heijenk, Boudewijn Haverkort, and
Robbert Haarman

Author Index   301

Optimization Problems in Service Provisioning Systems

Isi Mitrani

School of Computing Science
Newcastle University
Newcastle upon Tyne
United Kingdom
isi.mitrani@ncl.ac.uk

A service provisioning system typically contains a number of servers which may be distributed, heterogeneous and intermittently unavailable. They are used by the host in order to offer different services to a community of users. There may or may not be Service-Level Agreements involving Quality of Service constraints. In this context, there are several areas where dynamic optimisation problems arise quite naturally. These are (a) Routing and load-balancing: Where should an incoming request be sent for execution? If some queues grow large while others are short, can something be gained by transferring jobs among them? (b) Resource allocation: If different servers are dedicated to different types of service, how many should be assigned to each? When should a server be switched from one type of service to another? (c) Revenue maximisation: How are resource allocation and job admission policies affected by economic considerations? In particular, if service-level agreements specify payments for serving jobs and penalties for failing to provide a given quality of service, how many servers should be assigned to each type of service and when should jobs of that type be accepted?

The talk will describe models that address the above problems and will discuss routing, allocation and admission policies that may be adopted in practical systems.

K. Wolter (Ed.): EPEW 2007, LNCS 4748, p. 1, 2007.
© Springer-Verlag Berlin Heidelberg 2007

Untold Horrors About Steady-State Probabilities: What Reward-Based Measures Won't Tell About the Equilibrium Distribution*

Alexander Bell and Boudewijn R. Haverkort

University of Twente
Dept. Electrical Engineering, Mathematics and Computer Science
P.O. Box 217, 7500 AE Enschede, the Netherlands
a.bell@math.utwente.nl, brh@cs.utwente.nl

Abstract. These days, parallel and distributed state-space generation algorithms allow us to generate Markov chains with hundreds of millions of states. In order to solve such Markov chains for their steady-state behaviour, we typically use iterative algorithms, either on a single machine, or on a cluster of workstations. When dealing with such huge Markov chains, the accuracy of the computed probability vectors becomes a critical issue.

In this paper we report on experimental studies of, among others, the impact of different iterative solution techniques, erratic and stagnating convergence, the impact of the state-space ordering, the influence of the processor architecture chosen and the accuracy of the measure of interest, in relation to the accuracy of the individual state probabilities.

To say the least, the paper shows that the results from analysing extremely large Markov chains should be "appreciated with care", and, in fact, questions the feasibility of the ambitious "5 nines programs" that some companies have recently started.

1 Introduction

With the advent of high-level description languages for Markovian models, such as those based on stochastic Petri nets or stochastic process algebras, it has become easy to specify extremely large Markovian models. Also, the deployment of structured and symbolic approaches towards state space generation, such as those using Kronecker algebra and those based on, for instance, multi-terminal binary decision diagrams, has made Markovian models with thousands of millions of states a reality. However, describing and generating state spaces is one thing, solving the Markov chains associated with these enormous state spaces is another issue. The largest Markovian models we are aware of that have been solved numerically have close to a billion states [2] (using an explicit state space representation and a disk-based parallel solver). Clearly, currently the solution step is lagging behind.

---

* The title of this paper has been inspired by [11].

K. Wolter (Ed.): EPEW 2007, LNCS 4748, pp. 2–17, 2007.
© Springer-Verlag Berlin Heidelberg 2007

In this paper we address the question of 1 how much confidence one actually can have in performance and dependability measures derived from numerical steady-state solutions of such extremely large Markov chains. What can we actually say about the accuracy of the computed probabilities? When we have so many states, can we still compute the state probabilities accurately enough? And how do the numerical algorithms "react" on such very small probabilities? Furthermore, if we employ parallel algorithms for the solution of the steady-state probabilities, does the way in which we distribute the state space over the nodes or the timing of information-exchange between the nodes (non-determinism) affect the accuracy of the measures we compute?

In order to illustrate our thoughts with experimental data, we present results for a generalised stochastic Petri net (GSPN) that has been used by many researchers in the past, the Flexible Manufacturing System (FMS) model [3]. This choice also gives us the ability to compare results computed at four different sites, i.e., at the RWTH Aachen, at the College of William and Mary, at Imperial College, and, most recently, at the University of Twente.

The result of our paper is not so much a recipe for obtaining steady-state probabilities that are always accurate enough. Instead, the aim of the paper merely is to show how difficult it is to actually obtain accurate results, and shows pitfalls and problems that will be all around. In doing so, it actually shows that determining very accurate performance and dependability measures, like needed in the "5 nines programs" of some industrial research laboratories (implying to determine, in a model-based fashion, that the system long-term availability is at least equal to 0.99999, which coincides with a downtime of, roughly, only 5 minutes per year), is far from trivial. In fact, the practical feasibility of such endeavours must be seriously questioned.

The rest of this paper is organised as follows. Section 2 addresses specific issues related to the employed numerical algorithms, and in Section 3 we present experimental results based on our computations and compare them to other published results. Finally, Section 4 concludes the paper with a summary and outlook.

2   Iterative Solvers for Markov Chains

For the solution of very large Markov chains, only iterative solutions can be employed; their background is rehearsed in Section 2.1 (for more details on iterative methods for Markov chains, see [10]). Since these iterative methods only produce approximations of the solution, we discuss in Section 2.2 how to make sure that a certain accuracy has been achieved. Section 2.3 gives background on the usually employed floating point number representation. Because the computed state probabilities often differ by several orders of magnitude, we address the problem caused by summing large numbers of such values in Section 2.4.

2.1   Background

During the computation of the steady-state distribution for a CTMC with generator matrix Q iterative linear equation solvers compute a sequence of approximations $\pi^{(0)}, \pi^{(1)}, \pi^{(2)}, \cdots$ for the solution vector π of the linear system $0 = \pi Q$ (which we may rewrite as $Q^{\mathrm{T}} \pi^{\mathrm{T}} = 0$ to correspond to the more general representation of linear systems $Ax = b$). Any iterative solver computes the next approximation $\pi^{(i+1)}$ by the iteration $\pi^{(i+1)} = H \cdot \pi^{(i)} + c$, where H is called the iteration matrix. Clearly, one iteration step "costs" one matrix-vector product (MVP). The number of iterations k required for an accuracy ϵ can be approximated from the spectral radius ρ of the iteration matrix H as $k = \frac{\log \epsilon}{\log \rho}$ (see: [1,10]). Instead of the spectral radius the magnitude of the sub-dominant eigenvalue can be used. Although this result looks very attractive it is of little use in practice as the computation of the eigenvalues of H requires approximately the same effort as the computation of the steady-state solution. Hence, other methods to detect convergence and hence to limit the number of iterations k have to be used, as will be discussed below.

An important issue to address is the number of solution vectors that needs to be stored at any point in time during the iterative solution process. Using double precision floating point numbers, a single solution vector (which is non-sparse) costs 8 megabyte per 1 million states. On a machine with 1 gigabyte of main memory, roughly speaking, the solution vector for a Markov chain with 100 million states can be stored, provided only a single iteration vector is required, such as is the case for Gauss-Seidel. For the Jacobi method, already two vectors are required, thus limiting the number of states to roughly 50 million. For Conjugate Gradient Squared (CGS), even more vectors are required. In all these cases, it is assumed that the matrix Q is either stored very compactly, recomputed on the fly, or stored on disk. We note that whereas for the serial solution of the steady-state probabilities methods like Gauss-Seidel, SOR, Jacobi and the CGS can be employed, parallel implementations tend to use only the Jacobi and CGS method as they can be parallelised more easily and efficiently.

2.2 Stopping Criteria

The simplest properties that can be used as stopping criteria are either to limit the maximum number of iterations or the time spent computing them. This surely limits the iteration count k but can not guarantee that the remaining error $e^{(k)} = \pi^{(k)} - \pi$ is smaller than some chosen limit. Better, but still traditional stopping criteria are based on the norm of the difference of successive iterates $e^{(k)} = ||\pi^{(k)} - \pi^{(k-1)}||$, cf. [10], where the iteration is stopped if this norm falls below $\delta > 0$. Although any norm will do, the most popular choice is the maximum norm $||x||_\infty = \max_i |x_i|$, as it requires the fewest floating point operations to perform and no underflows or overflows can occur with it. This consideration applies to all norms we will use in this section. This approach has several problems, though. First of all, it does not take into account the magnitude of the (largest) elements of the solution vector, which, indeed, may all be very small if the probability vectors consist of several hundreds of millions of entries. This problem can be overcome by either scaling $\pi^{(k)}$ in a way that the largest element of $\pi^{(k)}$ equals 1 or by using the criterion $e^{(k)} = \max_i \left(\frac{|\pi_i^{(k)} - \pi_i^{(k-1)}|}{|\pi_i^{(k)}|} \right) \leq \delta$, which computes the relative error between two successive approximations.

Secondly, it may falsely detect convergence if the iteration process converges very slowly, hence, the difference between two successive approximations is smaller then δ, even though an appropriate solution would require far more iterations. Stewart [10] suggests to check the differences of non-successive approximations resulting in a stopping criterion $e^{(k)} = \max_i \left(\frac{|\pi_i^{(k)} - \pi_i^{(k-m)}|}{|\pi_i^{(k)}|} \right) \leq \delta$, where approximations lying m iterations apart are compared. Note that m is not required to be constant, but may be chosen as a function of the convergence rate or the iteration count. An obvious disadvantage of this criterion is the fact that an additional old approximation has to be stored whereas the comparison of two successive approximations can be done on-the-fly even for a Gauss-Seidel iteration using only a single vector.

The stopping criteria discussed above can only be used if the successive approximations get better during each iteration step. If the method exhibits so-called erratic convergence (see the example in Section 3.3 for the CGS method [9]), then no conclusions about the achieved accuracy can be drawn from the comparison of two successive (or m-step apart) approximations. Hence, stopping criteria based on the residual $r^{(k)} = \pi^{(k)} Q$ should be used in conjunction with the CGS method [2,6]. Of course, these can also be applied in combination with the methods of Jacobi and Gauss-Seidel. The quality of an approximation is better the closer the residual is to zero. Note that the standard definition of the residual of a linear system $Ax = b$ is $r = Ax^{(k)} - b$. As before, the absolute magnitude of the entries in the residual vector can only be interpreted meaningfully if we compare them to the magnitude of the (sought for) elements in the solution vector. Hence, the most common stopping criterion based on the residual is $e^{(k)} = \frac{||r^{(k)}||}{||\pi^{(k)}||} \leq \delta$. Again, any norm will do, but the maximum norm is the most common choice. If we use it and rewrite the stopping criterion as $||r^{(k)}||_\infty \leq \delta ||\pi^{(k)}||_\infty$ we see that the largest entry in the residual, which should be as close to zero as possible, is at most δ times the largest entry in the approximation vector $\pi^{(k)}$. For the rest of this paper, if not mentioned otherwise, we will use this relative residual criterion as the stopping criterion. Note that the residual can be computed at no additional cost during Jacobi and CGS iterations [7].

A stopping criterion not based on the achieved accuracy but on the speed of convergence can be applied to methods like Jacobi and Gauss-Seidel that typically exhibit nearly monotone linear convergence up to a certain accuracy. If this accuracy is achieved, often no further progress will be made. One can observe this point by analysing the fraction of two successive error approximations $\frac{e^{(k-1)}}{e^{(k)}}$. An example where this point is reached will be given in Section 3.2. Note that this criterion can also be used for approximations that are more than just one iteration apart without the need to store the iteration vectors.

2.3   The IEEE 754 Floating-Point Standard

During the computation of performance measures for a system modelled as a
GSPN, errors can arise at several stages. Often forgotten is the fact that computers work with floating-point numbers which can only represent real numbers
up to a certain precision. Today the IEEE 754 floating point standard [5] is most
commonly used. It defines floating point number codes for single (32 bit), double (64 bit), and double-extended (79 bit) precision, where the latter is typically
used for processor-internal computations and not employed for the storage of
data. Only single and double precision are currently supported by the majority
of processors on the hardware side, and by programming languages on the software side. The standard does not only cover the representation of floating-point
numbers but also the handling of underflows, overflows and other exceptional
conditions. As we will see later, single precision is not an option for our problems, therefore we will focus on the double precision here.

A double precision floating point number x is represented in the form $x_s =
(-1)^S \cdot 2^{E-1023} \cdot (1.M)$, where S is the sign bit (1 bit), E is the exponent (11 bit,
stored in excess-1023 code) and M is the mantissa (52 bit, always normalised)
Adding two floating point numbers is typically done by adjusting the exponent
and the mantissa of the smaller number to match the exponent of the larger
number (resulting in a non-normalised floating point number) and then adding
the mantissas. Obviously, accuracy of the smaller number might be lost as the
rightmost digits of its mantissa are lost. The machine precision, ϵ, is the smallest
number that, if added to 1.0, produces a number different from 1.0. The IEEE
floating-point representation induces machine precisions of $\epsilon_d = 2^{-52} = 2.22 \cdot
10^{-16}$ for double precision and $\epsilon_s = 2^{-23} = 1.19 \cdot 10^{-7}$ for single precision
arithmetic. Hence, double precision offers 15 significant decimal digits whereas
single precision only features 6. Note that the machine precision is not the same
as the smallest number that can be represented using that format, as this number
depends on the size of the exponent.

2.4   Summation Problems

Once the steady-state probabilities π have been computed, measures of interest are typically computed as a weighted sum over a subset of states, e.g.,
measure $= \sum_i \rho_i \pi_i$, where π_i is the steady-state probability for state i and ρ_i is
a reward) associated with that same state. Due to the fact that the probabilities
might differ by several orders of magnitude, which might be aggravated by the
multiplication with the rewards, performing the summation might induce severe
round-off error. As we saw in Section 2.3, a number that is smaller by a factor of
the machine precision ϵ_m will have no impact when added to a larger number.

Even worse, the addition of floating point numbers is not even associative.
Consider the case where we add several thousands of numbers in the magnitude
of the machine precision ϵ_m one after the other to a larger number. This results in
a different sum than in case we first sum all the small numbers and subsequently
add the result to the larger number.

One possibility to overcome this problem is to sort the numbers to be added by their magnitude and add them, starting from the smallest. In practice the computational effort for a complete sorting cannot be justified, however, one could add the numbers in groups, that is, by using "sub-sums" for different ranges of values to be added. For example, if we have to add numbers in the range of 10^{-24} to 10^{-4}, we can compute the overall sum using five groups, summing the numbers smaller than 10^{-20}, 10^{-16}, 10^{-12} and 10^{-8}, respectively, and finally all up to 10^{-4}.

Another problem is the fact that all errors sum up. If we compute the sum of a vector comprising N entries, each entry has a round-off error of the magnitude of the machine precision. If these errors follow a Normal distribution to both smaller and larger results, the overall error will be $\sqrt{N} \cdot \epsilon_m$ [8]. However, in the worst case, if all errors tend to the same direction, we obtain an error of $N \cdot \epsilon_m$ [8].

Considering the largest Markov chain we solved (consisting of 724 million states) using double precision floating-point numbers with a machine precision of $\epsilon_d = 2.22 \cdot 10^{-16}$, the sum of a solution vector will have an error of $5.9 \cdot 10^{-12}$ for normally distributed roundoff errors and an error of $1.6 \cdot 10^{-7}$ in the worst case. This means that even if we computed the steady-state solution as precisely as possible, a performance measure can only be accurate up to 10^{-12} and might have an error up to 10^{-7} produced only by the summation. If the individual state probabilities differ in their order of magnitude, not even this accuracy can be achieved.

In the above example, if we use single precision arithmetic, the errors would lie in the range of $3.2 \cdot 10^{-3}$ and $8.6 \cdot 10$, respectively! From this example, it becomes obvious that single precision floating point arithmetic is of no use for large Markov chains and even the accuracy of double precision floating points can be a problem, depending on the measures of interest.

3 Experiments

In this section we report on our experiments. In Section 3.1 we present the employed model and the measure of interest, followed by a discussion on stagnating convergence and erratic convergence in Section 3.2 and Section 3.3, respectively. We then discuss a special phenomenon we have observed when using CGS in Section 3.4, and compare various solution techniques and their impact on accuracy in Section 3.5. We present results on different state-space orderings in Section 3.6, on different system architectures (hardware) in Section 3.7. Section 3.8 discusses the accuracy of the obtained *measure*, in contrast to the accuracy of the obtained steady-state probabilities. Finally, Section 3.9 discusses the influence of the number of processors on the accuracy obtained when using a parallel/distributed algorithm.

3.1 Model and Measure of Interest

We present experimental results for the well-known flexible manufacturing system (FMS) model, cf. [3]. The model describes a production line comprising

Table 1. Statistics for the FMS-model

k	n	a	$\sqrt{n} \cdot \epsilon_d$	$n \cdot \epsilon_d$
1	54	155	$1.616 \cdot 10^{-15}$	$1.188 \cdot 10^{-14}$
2	810	3 699	$6.261 \cdot 10^{-15}$	$1.782 \cdot 10^{-13}$
3	6 520	37 394	$1.776 \cdot 10^{-14}$	$1.434 \cdot 10^{-12}$
4	35 910	237 120	$4.168 \cdot 10^{-14}$	$7.900 \cdot 10^{-12}$
5	152 712	1 111 482	$8.597 \cdot 10^{-14}$	$3.357 \cdot 10^{-11}$
6	537 768	4 205 670	$1.613 \cdot 10^{-13}$	$1.183 \cdot 10^{-10}$
7	1 639 440	13 552 968	$2.816 \cdot 10^{-13}$	$3.607 \cdot 10^{-10}$
8	4 459 455	38 533 968	$4.645 \cdot 10^{-13}$	$9.811 \cdot 10^{-10}$
9	11 058 190	99 075 405	$7.315 \cdot 10^{-13}$	$2.433 \cdot 10^{-9}$
10	25 397 658	234 523 289	$1.108 \cdot 10^{-12}$	$5.587 \cdot 10^{-9}$
11	54 682 992	518 030 370	$1.626 \cdot 10^{-12}$	$1.203 \cdot 10^{-8}$
12	111 414 940	1 078 917 632	$2.322 \cdot 10^{-12}$	$2.451 \cdot 10^{-8}$
13	216 427 680	2 611 411 257	$3.236 \cdot 10^{-12}$	$4.761 \cdot 10^{-8}$
14	403 259 040	4 980 958 020	$4.417 \cdot 10^{-12}$	$8.872 \cdot 10^{-8}$
15	724 284 864	9 134 355 680	$5.920 \cdot 10^{-12}$	$1.593 \cdot 10^{-7}$
20	8 831 321 730	—	$2.067 \cdot 10^{-11}$	$1.943 \cdot 10^{-6}$
25	65 075 507 406	—	$5.612 \cdot 10^{-11}$	$1.432 \cdot 10^{-5}$

three machines, which process different kinds of work items that are transported through the system on pallets. The capacity of the overall system depends on the number of pallets that is used to transport the work items between the machines. The number of available pallets is modelled by a parameter k.

Table 1 illustrates the growth of the state space and the reachability graph as a function of k, which is given in the first column. Column two lists the resulting number of reachable tangible markings n and the number of non-zeroes a in the generator matrix of the underlying CTMC. State space sizes for $k = 20$ and 25 are just given to illustrate the further growth of the state space; we are currently not aware of any numerical solution for models that size. The expected magnitude of the errors induced by summing n entries using double precision arithmetic is given in columns 4 and 5 for normally distributed errors and worst case errors, respectively (see Section 2.4).

In addition to the results we computed using the PARSECS tool [2,4] for $k = 1, \ldots, 15$, we use results published by Ciardo [3] for $k = 1, \ldots, 5$, and by Knottenbelt [6] for $k = 1, \ldots, 11$. In each case the measure of interest is the so-called productivity ψ of the FMS, expressed as a reward-based measure in [3] as $\psi = 400\phi_1 + 600\phi_2 + 100\phi_3 + 1100\phi_{12}$, where ϕ_l indicates the throughput of transition t_{Pl}. Whenever we refer to some accuracy criterion in this section we use the residual criterion $||r||_\infty / ||\pi||_\infty$. The same criterion was used by Knottenbelt, whereas Ciardo does not comment on which criterion was used.

3.2 Stagnating Convergence

During our experiments we faced the effect of stagnating convergence, i.e., the fact that the solution converged nearly linearly up to a certain δ (measured by some convergence criterion) and after that, no real progress was made.

As an example of this, we present the convergence behaviour for different numerical methods (Jacobi (J), Gauss-Seidel (GS), and Conjugate Gradient Squared (CGS)) of the FMS model with $k = 8$ in Figure 1(a). The figure shows the reached accuracy, measured by the residual criterion $||r||_\infty/||\pi||_\infty$, as a function of the required number of matrix-vector products (MVPs) for the solution. The data presented in this subsection was computed using the serial version of the PARSECS solver. Note that each CGS step requires two MVPs (this has been accounted for in the figure) and that the y-axis is logarithmically scaled. For the CGS method we mark the points at which a certain accuracy is achieved for the first time; in contrast to the Jacobi and Gauss-Seidel methods the convergence for CGS is not as smooth as suggested by the connecting lines (see also the next section).

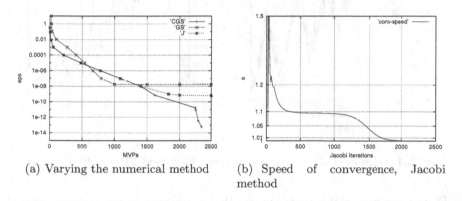

(a) Varying the numerical method   (b) Speed of convergence, Jacobi method

Fig. 1. Convergence behaviour, FMS model $k = 8$

For the method of Jacobi we computed up to 5000 iterations and no better accuracy than $\frac{||r||_\infty}{||\pi||_\infty} = 6.16 \cdot 10^{-10}$ was reached. A possible approach to detect the point where the convergence stagnates is the analysis of the speed of convergence $s = \frac{e^{(i-l)}}{e^{(i)}}$, where $e^{(i)}$ indicates the accuracy reached at iteration i and l is a parameter that decides how many iterations the compared accuracies lie apart (l for "lag"). Figure 1(b) shows the speed of convergence $s = \frac{e^{(i-10)}}{e^{(i)}}$ as a function of the number of Jacobi iterations. Note that the y-axis is logarithmically scaled. One can identify 4 phases: during the first 50 iterations the speed of convergence is irregular, after that there are roughly 200 iterations during which the speed of convergence decreases rapidly. Between iterations 250 and 1700 the speed of convergence s lies between 1.1 and 1.01, hence the convergence behaviour can be considered nearly linear. After that, the speed of convergence decreases again and reaches 1.0001 at iteration count 2200. After that no real progress is made. Actually, after roughly 3100 iterations the speed of convergence s drops below 1.0 frequently and after 4160 iterations it is constantly 1.0 (within the limits of the machine precision).

3.3 Erratic Convergence

Whereas classical iterative methods normally generate better approximations in every step, i.e., the measure used as the convergence criterion gets smaller after every iteration step, this is not generally true for Krylov subspace based methods and hence, especially not for the CGS method. In Figure 2(a) we show the development of the residual criterion $\frac{\|r\|_\infty}{\|\pi\|_\infty}$ (denoted as $|r|/|x|$ on the logarithmically scaled y-axis) during the solution of the FMS model for $k = 8$ using 16 processors up to an accuracy of $6 \cdot 10^{-16}$, which lies in the order of magnitude of the machine precision. Figure 2(b) zooms in on the first 200 iterations.

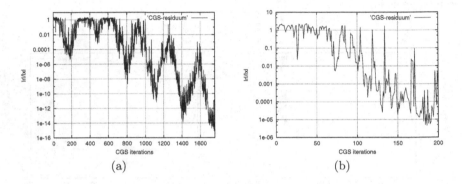

(a)   (b)

Fig. 2. Development of the residual criterion, FMS model $k = 8$, 16 processors

From these figures it is quite evident that a comparison of successive approximation vectors (or approximations lying l iterations apart) does not make sense, hence, it is also not possible to detect effects like stagnating convergence as discussed in the previous section.

3.4 Negative Elements in CGS Solutions

A numerical anomaly we experienced when using the CGS method was the appearance of negative elements in the solution vector. Whereas these cannot appear using the methods of Jacobi or Gauss-Seidel, the CGS-method computes a result which minimises the residual norm. For the FMS model with $k = 8$ (4459455 states) we found 763562 entries (or 17%!) of the entries of the solution vector to be negative for an accuracy (residual criterion) of $\delta = 10^{-15}$. Figure 3 shows an histogram of the magnitude of the positive and negative values of the solution vector, where a box for the value m on the x-axis shows the number of positive and negative values which lie in the interval $[10^{-(m+1)}, 10^{-m}]$ and $[-10^{-m}, -(10^{-(m+1)})]$, respectively.

As one can observe, the first negative entries are smaller by several orders of magnitude (the largest by magnitude start at 10^{-7}), but nevertheless annoying. Our approach to deal with these negative entries is to set them to zero.

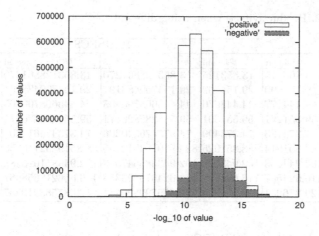

Fig. 3. Histogram of positive and negative entries in the solution vector, FMS, $k = 8$

We denote results for which we did so as being computed by the "CGS-corrected" method. It is important to note that by doing so we cannot expect our results to have more (correct) significant digits than the difference in order of magnitude between the largest positive and negative entries.

We also experimented with two other strategies to post-process the results obtained from the CGS solver:

– Obviously, negative elements are not valid in a probability vector. If we set them to zero we accept to ignore values smaller than $\min_i x_i$. This leads to the idea to ignore all values for which $|x_i| < |\min_j x_j|$, i.e., to also set all positive entries which are smaller than the absolute value of the smallest negative entry to zero. Of course, we renormalised the result afterwards.
– We did some Jacobi iterations on the result obtained via CGS including the negative elements and on the vector in which we set them to zero. For the first variant the negative elements vanished after 10–50 iterations, for the second, as expected, no negative elements were noticed.

For both approaches the results differ at the 6th or 7th significant digit, but no clear preference for either of these two post-processing options seems to be justifiable. Sometimes the results are further away from the Jacobi results, sometimes they approach them.

3.5   Different Solution Methods

Table 2 shows results for the productivity ψ computed using different numerical methods, as well as results published by others. All results are of course dependent on the parameter k given in the first column. In the second column we give the results published by Ciardo [3], which were computed using the SOR method. Results from Knottenbelt [6] are given in column 3. These results were computed using the CGS method with an accuracy of $\delta = 10^{-10}$. Results from

Table 2. Productivity ψ when using different methods, for $k = 1, \cdots, 9$

k	ψ_{Ciardo}	$\psi_{\text{Knottenbelt}}$	ψ_{Jacobi}	PARSECS ψ_{CGS}	$\psi_{\text{CGS-corrected}}$	#negative
1	13.853148	13.867015	13.853125	13.853128861270	13.853128861270	0
2	29.154731	29.154690	29.154702	29.154700488191	29.154700488191	0
3	44.443713	44.444877	44.443676	44.443668700805	44.443668700805	0
4	59.551361	59.551291	59.551301	59.551285826171	59.551285826171	0
5	74.373573	74.374123	74.373499	74.373476540306	74.373476612305	160
6	—	88.851914	88.851925	88.8519184712736	88.8519362140353	17169
7	—	102.944053	102.943746	102.943383547317	102.943811015488	118052
8	—	116.624587	116.624599	116.624678593358	116.656218658967	763562
9	—	129.876031	129.875824	129.875799826211	129.87583212267	1176422

the serial version of the PARSECS tool are given in the remaining columns, where we used Jacobi (column 4) and CGS (column 5 and 6) for the solution of the linear system. The achieved accuracy was $\delta = 10^{-9}$ for Jacobi and $\delta = 10^{-15}$ for CGS. The number of actually occurring negative elements in the solution is given in column 7.

Although these results agree to some degree, one observes several discrepancies. First of all, we note that, except for $k = 1$, the results coincide for at least 4 significant digits. While Knottenbelt, who also compared his results to those of Ciardo attributes this poor agreement to the low accuracy used by Ciardo, this argument does not hold for the results calculated using PARSECS. The differences might be influenced by the chosen state-space ordering, a theory supported by the fact that the PARSECS results for different state space generation orderings show a better agreement; we will discuss this point in the next section. Perhaps the differences are hardware dependent, but this is a speculation inspired by the fact that Knottenbelt used SPARC processors, whereas the PARSECS results were computed using Pentium processors; see Section 3.7 for details on this issue.

Another important point to mention is the fact that the "CGS-corrected" results are worse than the uncorrected results when compared to the results calculated using the Jacobi method. Thus, the fact that CGS-generated negative entries cannot be ignored and should be further investigated.

3.6   Different State Space Orderings

In contrast to the method of Jacobi, results calculated with the CGS method depend on the ordering of states, even given exact arithmetic. Using floating point numbers, results may also vary for the Jacobi method when a different state space ordering is used, as floating point operations are not associative. In this section we compare two state space orderings resulting from different search strategies during the state space generation process, namely breadth-first and depth-first search [4], for the Jacobi as well as for the CGS method. Table 3 shows the obtained results, where the first column is the parameter k of the

Table 3. Comparison of different state space orderings

	Jacobi		CGS	
k	depth first	breadth first	depth first	breadth first
3	44.4436760978369	44.4436760978368	44.4436687008048	44.4436763915087
4	59.5513008017580	59.5513008017581	59.5512858261705	59.5512869588266
5	74.3734986181677	74.3734986181672	74.3734765403062	74.3734824461310
6	88.8519252150780	88.8519252150777	88.8519521810466	88.8518434238192
7	102.943746367005	102.943746367010	102.943383547317	102.943719597266
8	116.624599210045	116.624599210081	116.624678593358	116.624569675295
9	129.875824499348	129.875824499685	129.875799826211	129.875805550217

FMS model. Columns two and three show the productivity computed using the Jacobi method up to an accuracy of 10^{-9} using either depth-first or breadth-first search during the state space generation. The corresponding results for the CGS method can be found in columns four and five where the used accuracy was set to 10^{-15}. All results were obtained using the serial version of the PARSECS state space generator and solvers.

As expected, the results for the method of Jacobi only differ in the very last digits; e.g., digit 14 and 15 differ for the case $k = 8$. Notice that we can not expect a better agreement in this case due to the summation problem discussed in Section 2.4. In fact, if we compute the one-norm of the (already normalised) solution vector the result is 0.999999999999818 which lies in the expected order of magnitude for normally distributed errors (see Table 1). Re-normalising the solution vector a second time results in a productivity of 116.624599210102.

Looking at the results for the CGS method, one observes significant differences for the computed productivity of the FMS model. In case $k = 6$, for example, the obtained performance measures only coincide for the first five significant digits, a discrepancy that cannot be accounted for by summation problems; the expected range of error due to summation problems would guarantee at least 9 correct significant digits, even for the worst case estimate (cf. Table 1, last column, row "$k = 6$"). On the other hand the observed differences lie in the range of the differences found at different sites (see Table 2).

From these results we conclude that, for the Jacobi method, the ordering of states has no impact on the obtained results (other than the expected deviations introduced by the order of summation). For the CGS method, the state space ordering has a non-negligible influence on the computed measures. Comparing both results one observes that as far as the significant digits obtained for the different state space orderings using the CGS method coincide, they also do so compared to the Jacobi results. How far one can trust results obtained using the CGS method has to be investigated in the future.

3.7   Varying the Processor Architecture

In this section we compare results obtained using the PARSECS tool on different processor architectures, namely for the Intel Pentium III (32 Bit) and the Intel

Itanium 2 (64 Bit). All performance measures were computed serially using binaries compiled from the same source code. The steady state distributions were calculated up to an accuracy of 10^{-9} for the Jacobi method and 10^{-15} for the CGS method. Table 4 shows the resulting productivity of the FMS model where the first column gives the cycling number of pallets in the system, columns two and three show the results calculated on the Pentium III for the Jacobi and CGS method, and columns four and five present these for an Itanium 2 based system.

Table 4. Productivity ψ when using different processors, for $k = 1, \cdots, 9$

	Pentium III		Itanium 2	
k	ψ_{Jacobi}	ψ_{CGS}	ψ_{Jacobi}	ψ_{CGS}
1	13.8531254	13.853128861270	13.8531249	13.853129279525
2	29.1547023	29.154700488191	29.1547460	29.154698779308
3	44.4436761	44.443668700805	44.4437592	44.443654932162
4	59.5513080	59.551285826171	59.5514280	59.551253901135
5	74.3734986	74.373476540306	74.3736730	74.373480164208
6	88.8519225	88.851918471274	88.8521326	88.851904272438
7	102.9437464	102.943383547317	102.9439671	102.94370328374
8	116.6245992	116.624678593358	116.6248367	116.62462174883
9	129.8758245	129.875799826211	129.8759381	129.87579235691

A quick look at this table reveals that the used processor has a larger impact on the performance measure than the chosen state space ordering. For the method of Jacobi we experience differences at the 5th digit for $k = 6$. These differences cannot be attributed to summation problems and require further investigation. We note that the observed differences between the two processor architectures lie in the same order of magnitude as those observed when comparing to Knottenbelt's results in Section 3.5.

3.8   Measure of Interest in Dependence of Accuracy

In this section we present the value for the productivity ψ as a function of the chosen accuracy. The first experiments were done for $k = 5$ (152712 states) and we used the methods of Jacobi and CGS as before. The results computed serially using the PARSECS tool are given in Table 5. The first column lists the accuracy δ, whereas columns two to four list the computed productivity for Jacobi, CGS, and CGS-corrected. The last column gives the number of negative elements in the solution vector. The smallest δ that produced reasonable results was 10^{-2}. We only give 6 digits of the solution here, as higher accuracies will rarely make sense for the chosen measure of interests (as we saw previously, the 6th digit already differs for the values published by Knottenbelt and Ciardo). For $\delta = 10^{-9}$ all three values coincide. Note that the value of ψ_{CGS}, rounded to 6 significant digits, does not change any more even if we compute up to $\delta = 10^{-15}$ (cf. Table 2). If we were content with just 4 significant digits, even an accuracy of $\delta = 10^{-7}$ would suffice.

Table 5. Measure of interest as a function of the chosen accuracy

δ	ψ_{Jacobi}	ψ_{CGS}	$\psi_{\text{CGS-corrected}}$	#negative
10^{-2}	76.1147	76.2969	81.0329	37952
10^{-3}	80.1650	74.4024	76.7539	40677
10^{-4}	75.7882	74.3778	74.3829	10543
10^{-5}	74.5597	74.3735	74.3742	7359
10^{-6}	74.3927	74.3735	74.3735	719
10^{-7}	74.3754	74.3734	74.3734	10
10^{-8}	74.3736	74.3735	74.3735	4
10^{-9}	74.3735	74.3735	74.3735	0

The largest example for which we have a result from the literature is $k = 11$, corresponding to 54 million states. Knottenbelt published a productivity $\psi = 155.046937$ for this case using an accuracy of $\delta = 10^{-10}$. Figure 4 shows the development of the productivity as a function of δ; these values were computed in parallel using the CGS method on 16 processors. Note that the x-axis is logarithmically scaled and that the y-axis comprises only the interval $[154.9, 155.1]$. The topmost grid-line corresponds to the result given by Knottenbelt. The most useful insight this figure gives, is the fact that for accuracies smaller than 10^{-6}, that is, from 10^{-6} to the left, a change in the measure of interest can not visually be recognised despite the narrow interval depicted on the y-axis.

3.9   Varying the Number of Processors

Finally, Figure 5 shows the influence of different number of processors on the computed productivity. The x-axis shows the number of employed processors, where one processor corresponds to the serial solution. In all cases the achieved accuracy (according to the used residual criterion) was 10^{-15}. We note that for this accuracy no negative entries were observed in the CGS solution vectors. As one can observe, the number of processors influences the 6th most significant

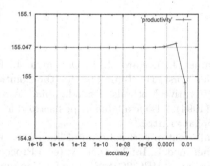

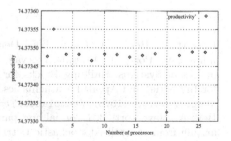

Fig. 4. Development of the net productivity as a function of the chosen accuracy, FMS model $k = 11$, 16 processors

Fig. 5. Varying the used number of processors, FMS model $k = 5$ using CGS, $\delta = 10^{-15}$

digit. Although most results are in the interval [74.37345, 74.37355], the results for 2 and 20 processors differ noticeably.

4   Conclusion

In this paper we discussed the influence of a variety of factors on the accuracy of performance and dependability measures computed from the steady-state solution of extremely large CTMCs. After discussing a number of issues that should be done very carefully in this context, we report on numerical experiments from which a number of "mini conclusions" can be drawn.

First of all, we saw that changing the numerical solver and/or the number of processors in a parallel setting can result in only 5 matching significant digits, even though the steady-state solution was computed up to a convergence criterion of 10^{-15}. On the other hand, for the FMS example, an accuracy of 10^{-6} was enough to yield 4 significant digits for the measure of interest. >From this point of view one could argue that having a stopping criterion that takes into account the measure of interest could be very effective.

Secondly, our paper also sheds light on the use of different stopping criteria; especially for the CGS method, residual-based stopping criteria seem to be preferable, in order to avoid problems due to erratic convergence. The CGS method also seems to be particularly sensitive towards the state space ordering.

Stated differently, for the extremely large Markov chains we addressed, it seems that we do need not to compute the steady-state solution using an accuracy better than about 10^{-6} or 10^{-7}, since other factors, such as the fact that we computed reward-based performance measures using very long additive series, dominate the accuracy for the derived performance measures.

It might be argued that the differences between the measures computed with the various methods are too minor to be taken seriously. This is, however, not true in general. For dependability type of measures, the measures of interest lie in the order of 0.99999, for which our considerations are important. In fact, our findings questions the feasibility of ambitious "5 nines programs" that some companies have recently started.

References

1. Barrett, R., Berry, M., Chan, T.F., Demmel, J., Donato, J.M., Dongarra, J., Eijkhout, V., Pozo, R., Romine, C., van der Vorst, H.: Templates for the Solution of Linear Systems: Building Blocks for Iterative Methods. Philadalphia: Society for Industrial and Applied Mathematics (1994), Also available as postscript file on http://www.netlib.org/templates/Templates.html
2. Bell, A., Haverkort, B.R.: Serial and parallel out-of-core solution of linear systems arising from generalised stochastic Petri net models. In: Tentner, A. (ed.) Proceedings High Performance Computing Symposium — HPC 2001. Society for Computer Simulation, pp. 242–247 (2001)
3. Ciardo, G., Trivedi, K.S.: A decomposition approach for stochastic reward net models. Performance Evaluation 18(3), 37–59 (1993)

4. Haverkort, B.R., Bell, A., Bohnenkamp, H.: On the efficient sequential and distributed generation of very large Markov chains from stochastic Petri nets. In: Proceedings of the 8th International Workshop on Petri Nets and Performance Models, pp. 12–21. IEEE Computer Society Press, Los Alamitos (1999)
5. IEEE standard 754: http://grouper.ieee.org/groups/754/
6. Knottenbelt, W.J.: Parallel Performance Analysis of Large Markov Models. PhD thesis, University of London, Imperial College of Science, Technology and Medicine (1999)
7. Knottenbelt, W.J., Harrison, P.G.: Distributed disk-based solution techniques for large Markov models. In: Proceedings of the 3rd International Meeting on the Numerical Solution of Markov Chains, September 1999, pp. 58–75 (1999)
8. Press, W.H., Teukolsky, S.A., Vetterling, W.T., Flannery, B.P.: Numerical Recipes in C. Cambridge University Press, Cambridge (1993)
9. Sonneveld, P.: CGS, a fast lanczos-type solver for nonsymmetric linear systems. SIAM Journal on Scientific and Statistical Computing 10(1), 36–52 (1989)
10. Stewart, W.J.: Introduction to the Numerical Solution of Markov Chains. Princeton University Press (1994)
11. Whitt, W.: Untold horrors of the waiting room: What the equilibrium distribution will never tell about the queue-length process. Management Science 29(4), 395–408 (1983)

Compositionality for
Markov Reward Chains with Fast Transitions

J. Markovski[1,*], A. Sokolova[2,**], N. Trčka[1,***], and E.P. de Vink[1]

[1] Technische Universiteit Eindhoven, Formal Methods Group
Den Dolech 2, 5612 AZ, Eindhoven, The Netherlands
j.markovski@tue.nl
[2] University of Salzburg, Computational Systems Group
Jakob-Haringer-Straße 2, 5020 Salzburg, Austria

Abstract. A parallel composition is defined for Markov reward chains with fast transitions and for discontinuous Markov reward chains. In this setting, compositionality with respect to the relevant aggregation preorders is established. For Markov reward chains with fast transitions the preorders are τ-lumping and τ-reduction. Discontinuous Markov reward chains are 'limits' of Markov reward chains with fast transitions, and have related notions of lumping and reduction. In total, four compositionality results are shown. In addition, the two parallel operators are related by a continuity property.

Keywords: discontinuous Markov reward chains, Markov reward chains with fast transitions, parallel composition, compositionality, lumpability, reduction, Kronecker product and sum.

1 Introduction

Compositionality is a central issue in the theory of concurrent processes. Discussing compositionality requires three ingredients: (1) a class of processes or models; (2) a composition operation on the processes; and (3) a notion of behaviour, usually given by a semantic preorder or equivalence relation on the class of processes. For the purpose of this paper, we will have semantic preorders and the parallel composition as operation. Therefore, the compositionality result can be stated as:

$$P_1 \geq \overline{P}_1, \ P_2 \geq \overline{P}_2 \implies P_1 \parallel P_2 \geq \overline{P}_1 \parallel \overline{P}_2$$

where P_1, P_2, $\overline{P}_1$ and $\overline{P}_2$ are arbitrary processes, $\parallel$ and $\geq$ denote their parallel composition and the semantic preorder relation. Hence, compositionality enables the narrowing of a parallel composition by composing simplifications of its components, thus avoiding the construction of the actual parallel system. In this paper, we study compositionality for augmented types of Markov chains.

---

* Corresponding author., Supported by Bsik-project BRICKS AFM 3.2.
** Supported by the Austrian Science Fund (FWF) project P18913.
*** Supported by the Netherlands Organization for Scientific Research (NWO) project 612.064.205.

K. Wolter (Ed.): EPEW 2007, LNCS 4748, pp. 18–32, 2007.
© Springer-Verlag Berlin Heidelberg 2007

Homogeneous continuous-time Markov chains, Markov chains for short, are among the most important and wide-spread analytical performance models. A Markov chain is given by a graph with nodes representing states and outgoing arrows determining the stochastic behavior of each state. An initial probability vector indicates which states may act as starting ones. Markov chains often come equipped with rewards that are used to measure their performance (e.g., throughput, utilization, etc.) [1]. In this paper, we focus on state rewards only, and we refer to a Markov Chain with rewards as a Markov Reward Chain.

To cope with the ever growing complexity of the systems, several performance modeling techniques have been developed to support the compositional generation of Markov Reward Chains. Such are stochastic process algebras [2,3], (generalized) stochastic Petri nets [4,5], probabilistic I/O automata [6], stochastic automata networks [7], etc. The compositional modeling enables composing a bigger system from several smaller components. The size of the state space of the resulting system is in the range of the product of the sizes of the constituent state spaces. Hence, compositional modeling usually suffers from state space explosion.

In the process of compositional modeling, performance evaluation techniques produce intermediate constructs that are typically extensions of Markov Chains featuring transitions with communication labels. In the final modeling phase, all labels are discarded and communication transitions are assigned instantaneous behavior. Previous work [8,9,10] gave an account of handling these models by using Markov chains with fast transitions, which present extension of the standard Markov Reward Chains with transitions decorated with a real-valued linear parameter. To capture the intuition that the labeled transitions are instantaneous, a limit for the parameter to infinity is taken. The resulting process is a generalization of the standard Markov chain that can perform infinitely many transitions in a finite amount of time. This model was initially studied in [11,12] without rewards, and is called a Discontinuous Markov Reward Chain. The process exhibits stochastic discontinuity and it is often considered as pathological. However, as shown in [12,13,5], it proves very useful for explanation of results. Here, we consider Discontinuous Markov Reward Chains and Markov Reward Chains with Fast Transitions. These two models are intimately related: Markov Reward Chains with Fast Transitions are used for modeling, but the notions for these processes are expressed asymptotically in terms of Discontinuous Markov Reward Chains. We define parallel composition of both models in vein of standard Markov Reward Chains [14] using Kronecker products and sums.

As already mentioned, compositional modeling may lead to state space explosion. Current analytical and numerical methods can handle Markov Reward Chains with millions of states efficiently. However, they only alleviate the problem and many real world problems still cannot be feasibly solved. Several aggregation techniques have been proposed to reduce the state space of Markov Reward Chains. Ordinary lumping is the most prominent one [15,14]. The method partitions the state space into partition classes. In each class, the states exhibit equivalent behavior for transiting to other classes, i.e. the cumulative probability of transiting to another class is the same for every state of the class. If non-trivial lumping exists, i.e. at least one partition contains more than one state, then the method produces a smaller Markov Chain that retains the performance characteristics of the original one. For example, the total reward gained in a given amount of time is the same for the original as for the reduced, so-called lumped, process. Another lumping-based method is exact lumping [14]. This method requires that each partition class of states has the same cumulative probability of transiting to every state of another class and also each state in the class has the same initial probability. The gain of exact lumping is that the probabilities of the original process can be computed for a special class of initial probability vectors by using the lumped Markov Reward Chain only.

A preliminary treatment of relational properties of lumping-based aggregations of Markov chains has been given in [16]. It has been shown that the notion of exact lumping is not transitive, i.e., there are processes which have exactly lumped versions that can be non-trivially exactly lumped again, but the original process cannot be exactly lumped directly to the resulting process. On the other hand, ordinary lumping of Markov Reward Chains is transitive and, moreover, it has a property of strict confluence. Strict confluence means that whenever a process can be lumped using two different partitions, there is always a smaller process to which the lumped processes can lump to. Coming back to our models of interest, ordinary lumping is defined for Discontinuous Markov Reward Chains in [8,9,10]. Also, so-called τ-lumping is proposed for Markov Reward Chains with Fast Transitions in [8,9,10]. The situation can be pictured as follows:

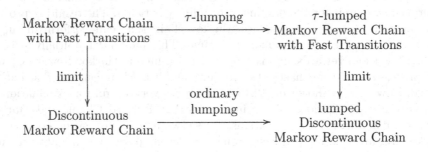

In addition, the same papers [9,10] provide an aggregation method by reduction that eliminates the stochastic discontinuity and reduces a Discontinuous Markov Reward Chain to a Markov Reward Chain. The reduction method is an extension of the method described in [17]. It is based on the elimination of stochastic discontinuity that arises in the context of instantaneous probabilistic transitions. The method is well-known in perturbation theory. Its advantage is the ability to split states. The lumping method, in contrast, provides more flexibility: also states that do not exhibit discontinuous behavior can be aggregated. The reduction-based aggregation straightforwardly extends to τ-reduction of Markov Reward Chains with Fast Transitions. Therefore, we have the following situation.

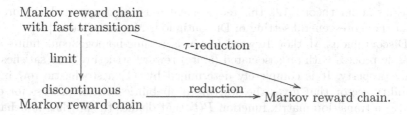

Both the lumping aggregation method and the reduction method induce semantic preorders. Namely, for two processes P and $\overline{P}$ we say that $P \geq \overline{P}$ if $\overline{P}$ is an aggregated version of P. The compositionality is very important as it allows us to aggregate the smaller parallel components first, and then combine them into the aggregated complete system. We show that the relations induced by the lumping and reduction methods indeed define preorders, i.e., reflexive and transitive relations. Having all the ingredients in place, we show the compositionality of the aggregation preorders with respect to the defined parallel composition(s). We also show continuity of the parallel composition(s). In short, the parallel operators preserve the two diagrams above.

The structure of the rest of the paper is as follows. We start by defining the first model, discontinuous Markov reward chains, in Section 2, together with its notions of lumping and reduction. Section 3 focuses on the second model, Markov reward chains with fast transitions, and introduces τ-lumping and τ-reduction. In Section 4, we show that the aggregation methods define preorders on the models. Section 5 contains the main results of the paper, compositionality of the new parallel operator for each type of Markov chains with respect to both aggregation preorders. Section 6 wraps-up with conclusions.

Notation. All vectors are column vectors if not indicated otherwise. By $\mathbf{1}^n$ we denote the vector of n 1's; by $\mathbf{0}^{n \times m}$ the $n \times m$ zero matrix; by I^n the $n \times n$ identity matrix. We omit the dimensions n and m when they are clear from the context. By $A[i,j]$ we denote an element of the matrix $A \in \mathbb{R}^{m \times n}$ assuming $1 \leq i \leq m$ and $1 \leq j \leq n$. We write $A \geq 0$ when all elements of A are nonnegative. The matrix A is called *stochastic* if $A \geq 0$ and $A \cdot \mathbf{1} = \mathbf{1}$. By A^T we denote the transpose of A.

Let $\mathcal{S}$ be a set. A set $\mathcal{P} = \{S_1, \ldots, S_N\}$ of N subsets of $\mathcal{S}$ is called a *partition* of $\mathcal{S}$ if $\mathcal{S} = S_1 \cup \ldots \cup S_N$, $S_i \neq \emptyset$ and $S_i \cap S_j = \emptyset$ for all i, j, with $i \neq j$. The partitions $\mathcal{P} = \{\mathcal{S}\}$ and $\mathcal{P} = \{\{i\} \mid i \in \mathcal{S}\}$ are the trivial partitions. Let $\mathcal{P}_1 = \{S_1, \ldots, S_N\}$ be a partition of $\mathcal{S}$ and $\mathcal{P}_2 = \{T_1, \ldots, T_M\}$, in turn, a partition of $\mathcal{P}_1$. The *composition* $\mathcal{P}_1 \circ \mathcal{P}_2$ of the partitions $\mathcal{P}_1$ and $\mathcal{P}_2$ is a partition of $\mathcal{S}$ given by $\mathcal{P}_1 \circ \mathcal{P}_2 = \{U_1, \ldots, U_M\}$, where $U_i = \bigcup_{C \in T_i} C$.

2   Discontinuous Markov Reward Chains

In the standard theory (cf. [18,19,1]) Markov chains are assumed to be stochastically continuous. This means that when $t \to 0$, the probability of the process occupying at time t the same state as at time 0 is 1. As we include instantaneous transitions in our theory [12], this requirement must be dropped. Therefore, we work in the more general setting of Discontinuous Markov Chains [11].

A Discontinuous Markov Reward Chain is a time-homogeneous finite-state stochastic process with an associated (state) reward structure that satisfies the Markov property. It is completely determined by: (1) a stochastic row initial probability vector that gives the starting probabilities of the process for each state, (2) a transition matrix function $P(t)$ that defines the stochastic behavior of the transitions, at time $t > 0$, and (3) a state reward vector that associates a number to each state representing the gain of the process while spending time in the state. The transition matrix function gives a stochastic matrix $P(t)$ at any time $t > 0$, and has the property $P(t + s) = P(t) \cdot P(s)$ [18,19]. It has a convenient characterization independent of time [12,20], which allows for the following equivalent definition.

Definition 1. *A discontinuous Markov reward chain* P *is a quadruple* P = (σ, Π, Q, ρ) *where σ is a stochastic row initial probability vector, ρ is a state reward vector and $\Pi \in \mathbb{R}^{n \times n}$ and $Q \in \mathbb{R}^{n \times n}$ satisfy the following six conditions: (1) $\Pi \geq 0$, (2) $\Pi \cdot \mathbf{1} = \mathbf{1}$, (3) $\Pi^2 = \Pi$, (4) $\Pi Q = Q \Pi = Q$, (5) $Q \cdot \mathbf{1} = \mathbf{0}$, and (6) $Q + c\Pi \geq 0$, for some $c \geq 0$.*

The matrix function $P(t) = \Pi e^{Qt}$ is the transition matrix of a discontinuous Markov chain P = (σ, Π, Q, ρ). It is continuous at zero if and only if $\Pi = I$. In this case, Q is a standard generator matrix [12,8]. Otherwise, the matrix Q might contain negative non-diagonal entries. We note that, unlike for standard Markov Reward Chains, a meaningful graphical representation of Discontinuous Markov Reward Chains when $\Pi \neq I$ is not possible. The intuition behind the matrix Π is that $\Pi[i, j]$ denotes the probability that a process occupies two states via an instantaneous transition. Therefore, in case of no instantaneous transitions, i.e., when $\Pi = I$, we get a standard (continuous) Markov chain.

For every Discontinuous Markov Chain P = (σ, Π, Q, ρ), Π gets the following 'ergodic' form after a suitable renumbering of the states [12]:

$$\Pi = \begin{pmatrix} \Pi_1 & 0 & \dots & 0 & 0 \\ 0 & \Pi_2 & \dots & 0 & 0 \\ \vdots & \vdots & \ddots & \vdots & \vdots \\ 0 & 0 & \dots & \Pi_M & 0 \\ \overline{\Pi}_1 & \overline{\Pi}_2 & \dots & \overline{\Pi}_M & 0 \end{pmatrix} \quad L = \begin{pmatrix} \mu_1 & 0 & \dots & 0 & 0 \\ 0 & \mu_2 & \dots & 0 & 0 \\ \vdots & \vdots & \ddots & \vdots & \vdots \\ 0 & 0 & \dots & \mu_M & 0 \end{pmatrix} \quad R = \begin{pmatrix} 1 & 0 & \dots & 0 \\ 0 & 1 & \dots & 0 \\ \vdots & \vdots & \ddots & \vdots \\ 0 & 0 & \dots & 1 \\ \delta_1 & \delta_2 & \dots & \delta_M \end{pmatrix}$$

where for all $1 \leq k \leq M$, $\Pi_k = \mathbf{1} \cdot \mu_k$ and $\overline{\Pi}_k = \delta_k \cdot \mu_k$ for a row vector $\mu_k > 0$ such that $\mu_k \cdot \mathbf{1} = 1$ and a vector $\delta_k \geq 0$ such that $\sum_{k=1}^{m} \delta_k = 1$. Then the pair of matrices (L, R) depicted above forms a canonical product decomposition of Π (cf. Section 2.1 below), needed for the definition of the reduction-based method of aggregation.

The new numbering induces a partition $\mathcal{E} = \{E_1, \dots, E_M, T\}$ of the state set $\mathcal{S} = \{1, \dots, n\}$, where $E_1, \dots, E_M$ are the ergodic classes, determined by

$\Pi_1, \ldots, \Pi_M$, respectively, and T is the class of transient states, determined by any $\overline{\Pi}_i$, $1 \leq i \leq M$. The partition $\mathcal{E}$ is called the ergodic partition. For every ergodic class E_k, the vector μ_k is the vector of ergodic probabilities. If an ergodic class E_k contains exactly one state, then $\mu_k = (1)$ and the state is called regular. The vector δ_k contains the trapping probabilities from transient states to the ergodic class E_k.

We are now able to explain the behavior of a Discontinuous Markov Reward Chain $\mathsf{P} = (\sigma, \Pi, Q, \rho)$. It starts in a state with a probability given by the initial probability vector σ. In an ergodic class with multiple states the process spends a non-zero amount of time switching rapidly (infinitely many times) among the states. The probability that it is found in a specific state of the class is given by the vector of ergodic probabilities. The time the process spends in the class is exponentially distributed and determined by the matrix Q. In an ergodic class with a single state the row of Q corresponding to that state has the form of a row in a generator matrix, and $Q[i, j]$ for $i \neq j$ is interpreted as the rate from i to j. In a transient state the process spends no time (with probability one) and goes to some ergodic class, where it is trapped for some amount of time. Note that $\delta_k[i] > 0$ iff $i \in T$ can be trapped in the ergodic class E_k.

The total reward gained by the process up to time $t > 0$, notation $R(t)$, is calculated as $R(t) = \sigma P(t) \rho$. We have that the total reward remains unchanged if the reward vector ρ is replaced by $\Pi \rho$. To see this, note that $P(t) = P(t)\Pi$ (cf. [12]), so $\sigma P(t)\Pi\rho = \sigma P(t)\rho = R(t)$. Intuitively, the reward in a transient state can be replaced by the sum of the rewards of the ergodic states that it can get trapped in as the process gains no reward while 'residing' in transient states. The reward of an ergodic state is the sum of the rewards of all states inside its ergodic class weighted according to their ergodic probabilities.

2.1   Aggregation Methods

In this section we recall the definitions and the main properties of the aggregation methods for Discontinuous Markov Reward Chains [8,9,10].

Ordinary Lumping. We define ordinary lumping in terms of matrices. Every partition $\mathcal{P} = \{C_1, \ldots, C_N\}$ of $\mathcal{S} = \{1, \ldots, n\}$ can be associated with a so-called collector matrix $V \in \mathbb{R}^{n \times N}$ defined as $V[i, k] = 0$ if $i \notin C_k$, $V[i, k] = 1$ if $i \in C_k$, and vice versa. The k-th column of V has 1's for elements corresponding to states in C_k and has 0's otherwise. Note that $V \cdot \mathbf{1} = \mathbf{1}$. A distributor matrix $U \in \mathbb{R}^{N \times n}$ for $\mathcal{P}$ is defined as a matrix $U \geq 0$, such that $UV = I^N$. To satisfy these conditions, the elements of the k-th row of U, which correspond to states in the class C_k, sum up to one, whereas the other elements of the row are 0.

An ordinary lumping is a partition of the state space into classes such that the states that are lumped together have equivalent behavior for transiting to other classes and additionally they have the same reward.

Definition 2. *A partition $\mathcal{L}$ of $\{1, \ldots, n\}$ is an ordinary lumping, or lumping for short, of a Discontinuous Markov Reward Chain* $\mathsf{P} = (\sigma, \Pi, Q, \rho)$ *iff the* *following holds: (1)* $VU\Pi V = \Pi V$, *(2)* $VUQV = QV$ *and (3)* $VU\rho = \rho$, *where* V *is the collector matrix and* U *is any distributor matrix for* $\mathcal{L}$.

The lumping conditions only require that the rows of ΠV (resp. QV and ρ) that correspond to the states of the same partition class are equal. The following property [8,9,10] holds.

Proposition 1. *Let* $\mathsf{P} = (\sigma, \Pi, Q, \rho)$ *be a Discontinuous Markov Reward Chain and let* $\mathcal{L} = \{C_1, \ldots, C_N\}$ *be an ordinary lumping. Define (1)* $\overline{\sigma} = \sigma V$, *(2)* $\overline{\Pi} = U\Pi V$, *(3)* $\overline{Q} = UQV$ *and (4)* $\overline{\rho} = U\rho$, *for the collector matrix* V *of* $\mathcal{L}$ *and any distributor* U. *Then* $\overline{\mathsf{P}} = (\overline{\sigma}, \overline{\Pi}, \overline{Q}, \overline{\rho})$ *is a Discontinuous Markov Reward Chain.*
□

Definition 3. *If the conditions of Proposition 1 hold, then* $\mathsf{P} = (\sigma, \Pi, Q, \rho)$ *lumps to* $\overline{\mathsf{P}} = (\overline{\sigma}, \overline{\Pi}, \overline{Q}, \overline{\rho})$, *called the lumped Discontinuous Markov Reward Chain, with respect to* $\mathcal{L}$. *We write* $P \xrightarrow{\mathcal{L}} \overline{P}$.

It can readily be seen that neither the definition of a lumping, nor the definition of the lumped process depends on the choice of a distributor matrix U. In the continuous case when $\Pi = I$ we have $\overline{\Pi} = I$, so $\overline{Q}$ is a generator matrix and our notion of ordinary lumping coincides with the standard definition [15,21]. The total reward is preserved by ordinary lumping: The lumped process has the same reward $\overline{R}(t)$ as the one of the original process $R(t)$, i.e., $\overline{R}(t) = \sigma V U P(t) V U \rho = \sigma P(t) V U \rho = \sigma P(t) \rho = R(t)$.

Reduction. The reduction-based aggregation method masks the stochastic discontinuity of a Discontinuous Markov Reward Chain $\mathsf{P} = (\sigma, \Pi, Q, \rho)$ and transforms it into a Markov Reward Chain [17,12,9,10]. The idea of the method is to abstract away from the behavior of individual states in an ergodic class. It is based on the notion of a canonical product decomposition.

Definition 4. *Let* $\mathsf{P} = (\sigma, \Pi, Q, \rho)$ *and assume that* $\mathrm{rank}(\Pi) = M$, *i.e., that there are* M *ergodic classes. A canonical product decomposition of* Π *is a pair of matrices* (L, R) *with* $L \in \mathbb{R}^{M \times n}$ *and* $R \in \mathbb{R}^{n \times M}$ *such that* $L \geq 0$, $R \geq 0$, $\mathrm{rank}(L) = \mathrm{rank}(R) = M$, $L \cdot \mathbf{1} = \mathbf{1}$, *and* $\Pi = RL$.

A canonical product decomposition always exists and can be constructed from the ergodic form of Π (see page 22). Moreover, it can be shown that any other canonical product decomposition is permutation equivalent to this one. Since a canonical product decomposition (L, R) of Π is a full-rank decomposition, and since Π is idempotent, we also have that $LR = I^M$. Note that $R \cdot \mathbf{1} = \mathbf{1}$. Also, we have $L\Pi = LRL = L$ and $\Pi R = RLR = R$. Now we can define the reduction method.

Definition 5. *For a Discontinuous Markov Reward Chain* $\mathsf{P} = (\sigma, \Pi, Q, \rho)$, *the reduced Discontinuous Markov Reward Chain* $\overline{\mathsf{P}} = (\overline{\sigma}, I, \overline{Q}, \overline{\rho})$ *is given by* $\overline{\sigma} = \sigma R$, $\overline{Q} = LQR$ *and* $\overline{\rho} = L\rho$, *where* (L, R) *is a canonical product decomposition. We write* $\mathsf{P} \rightarrow_r \overline{\mathsf{P}}$.

The reduced process is unique up to a permutation of the states, since so is the canonical product decomposition. The states of the reduced process are given by the ergodic classes of the original process, the transient states are 'ignored'. Intuitively, the transient states are split probabilistically between the ergodic classes according to their trapping probabilities. In case a transient state is also an initial state, its initial probability is split according to its trapping probabilities. The reward is calculated as the sum of the individual rewards of the states of the ergodic class weighted by their ergodic probabilities. Like lumping, the reduction also preserves the total reward: $\bar{R}(t) = \sigma RLP(t)RL\rho = \sigma \Pi P(t)\Pi \rho = R(t)$. In case the original process has no stochastic discontinuity, i.e., $\Pi = I$, the reduced process is equal to the original.

3   Markov Reward Chains with Fast Transitions

A Markov Reward Chain with Fast Transitions is obtained by adding parameterized, so-called fast, transitions to a standard Markov reward chain. The remaining standard transitions are referred to as slow. The behavior of a Markov Reward Chain with Fast Transitions is determined by two generator matrices Q_s and Q_f, which represent the rates of the slow transitions and the speeds of the fast transitions, respectively.

Definition 6. *A Markov Reward Chain with Fast Transitions* $\mathsf{P} = (\sigma, Q_s, Q_f, \rho)$ *is a function assigning to each* $\tau > 0$, *the Markov Reward Chain*

$$\mathsf{P}_\tau = (\sigma, I, Q_s + \tau Q_f, \rho)$$

where $\sigma \in \mathbb{R}^{1 \times n}$ *is an initial probability vector,* $Q_s, Q_f \in \mathbb{R}^{n \times n}$ *are two generator matrices, and* $\rho \in \mathbb{R}^{n \times 1}$ *is the reward vector.*

By taking the limit when $\tau \to \infty$, fast transitions become instantaneous. Then, a Markov Reward Chain with Fast Transitions behaves as a Discontinuous Markov Reward Chain [12].

Definition 7. *Let* $\mathsf{P} = (\sigma, Q_s, Q_f, \rho)$ *be a Markov Reward Chain with Fast Transitions. The Discontinuous Markov Chain* $\mathsf{Q} = (\sigma, \Pi, Q, \Pi\rho)$ *is the limit of* P, *where the matrix* Π *is the so-called ergodic projection at zero of* Q_f, *that is* $\Pi = \lim_{t \to \infty} e^{Q_f t}$, *and* $Q = \Pi Q_s \Pi$. *If* Q *is the limit of* P, *we write* $\mathsf{P} \to_\infty \mathsf{Q}$.

The initial probability vector and the reward vector are not affected by the limit construction. Below we motivate the choice of using the reward vector $\Pi\rho$ instead of just ρ.

3.1   Aggregation Methods

Next, we recall the aggregation methods for Markov reward chains with fast transitions.

τ-Lumping. The notion of τ-lumping is based on ordinary lumping for Discontinuous Markov Reward Chains.

Definition 8. *A partition $\mathcal{L}$ of the state space of a Markov Reward Chain with Fast Transitions P is called a τ-lumping, if it is an ordinary lumping of its limiting Discontinuous Markov Reward Chain Q, i.e. $\mathsf{P} \to_\infty \mathsf{Q}$.*

Note that since we defined the reward of the limit by $\Pi\rho$, a τ-lumping may identify states with different rewards.

Like for ordinary lumping, we define the τ-lumped process by multiplying σ, Q_s, Q_f and ρ with a collector matrix and a distributor matrix. However, unlike for ordinary lumping, not all distributors are allowed. Following [8,9,10], we provide a class of special distributors, called τ-distributors, that yield a τ-lumped process.

Definition 9. *Let $\mathsf{P} = (\sigma, \Pi, Q, \rho)$ be a Discontinuous Markov Reward Chain. Let V be a collector matrix for this chain. A matrix W is a τ-distributor for V iff it is a distributor for V, i.e. $\Pi V W \Pi = \Pi V W$, and the entries of W for the transient states that lump only with other transient states are positive.*

An alternative, explicit definition of the τ-distributors can be found in [8,9,10]. Having defined τ-distributors, we can define a τ-lumped process.

Definition 10. *Let $\mathsf{P} = (\sigma, Q_s, Q_f, \rho)$ and let $\mathcal{L}$ be a lumping with a collector matrix V, and a corresponding τ-distributor W. The τ-lumped Markov Reward Chain with Fast Transitions $\overline{\mathsf{P}} = (\overline{\sigma}, \overline{Q}_s, \overline{Q}_f, \overline{\rho})$ is defined as $\overline{\sigma} = \sigma V$, $\overline{Q}_s = W Q_s V$, $\overline{Q}_f = W Q_f V$, $\overline{\rho} = W\rho$. We say that P τ-lumps to $\overline{\mathsf{P}}$ and write $\mathsf{P} \overset{\mathcal{L}}{\rightsquigarrow} \overline{\mathsf{P}}$.*

In general, for a lumping with collector V and distributor U, $U Q_s V$ and $U Q_f V$ are not uniquely determined, i.e., they depend on the choice of the distributor. The restriction to τ-distributors does not change this. Subsequently, the τ-lumped process depends on the choice of the τ-distributor. The motivation for restricting to τ-distributors is that all τ-lumped processes are then equivalent in the limit. This is shown in the following proposition that, in addition, gives the exact connection between lumping and τ-lumping [8].

Proposition 2. *The following diagram commutes*

$$
\begin{array}{ccc}
\mathsf{P} & \overset{\mathcal{L}}{\rightsquigarrow} & \overline{\mathsf{P}} \\
{\scriptstyle\infty}\downarrow & & \downarrow{\scriptstyle\infty} \\
\mathsf{Q} & \overset{\mathcal{L}}{\longrightarrow} & \overline{\mathsf{Q}}
\end{array}
$$

that is, if $\mathsf{P} \overset{\mathcal{L}}{\rightsquigarrow} \overline{\mathsf{P}} \to_\infty \overline{\mathsf{Q}}$ and if $\mathsf{P} \to_\infty \mathsf{Q} \overset{\mathcal{L}}{\to} \overline{\mathsf{Q}}'$, then $\overline{\mathsf{Q}} = \overline{\mathsf{Q}}'$, for P and $\overline{\mathsf{P}}$ Markov Reward Chains with Fast Transitions, and $\mathsf{Q}, \overline{\mathsf{Q}}, \overline{\mathsf{Q}}'$ the respective limiting Discontinuous Markov Reward Chains. □

Moreover, the τ-lumped processes that originate from the same Markov reward chain with fast transitions become exactly the same once all fast transitions are eliminated [9,10].

Proposition 3. *Let* P *be a Markov Reward Chain with Fast Transitions. Suppose* P $\overset{\mathcal{L}}{\leadsto}$ $\overline{\mathsf{P}}$ *and* $\overline{\mathsf{P}}$ *has no fast transitions, i.e., its speed matrix is the zero matrix. Then, whenever* P $\overset{\mathcal{L}}{\leadsto}$ $\overline{\mathsf{P}}'$ *for any (other) τ-distributor, it holds that* $\overline{\mathsf{P}} = \overline{\mathsf{P}}'$. □

τ-Reduction. We now define a reduction-based aggregation method called τ-reduction. It aggregates a Markov Reward Chain with Fast Transitions to an asymptotically equivalent Markov Reward Chain.

Definition 11. *A Markov Reward Chain with Fast Transitions* P $= (\sigma, Q_s, Q_f, \rho)$ *τ-reduces to the Markov Reward Chain* R $= (\overline{\sigma}, I, \overline{Q}, \overline{\rho})$, *given by (1)* $\overline{\sigma} = \sigma R$, *(2)* $\overline{Q} = LQ_sR$, *and (3)* $\overline{\rho} = L\rho$, *where* P $\rightarrow_\infty (\sigma, \Pi, Q, \Pi\rho)$ *and* (L, R) *is a canonical product decomposition of Π. When* P *τ-reduces to* R, *we write* P $\leadsto_r$ R.

The following simple property relates τ-reduction to reduction. It holds since $LQR = LQ_sR$ and $L\Pi\rho = L\rho$.

Proposition 4. *The following diagram commutes*

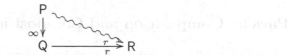

that is, if P $\leadsto_r$ R *and* P $\rightarrow_\infty$ Q $\rightarrow_r$ R', *then* R $=$ R', *for* P *a Markov Reward Chain with Fast Transitions,* Q *a Discontinuous Markov Reward Chain and* R, R' *(continuous) Markov reward chains.* □

4   Relational Properties

We investigate the relational properties of ordinary lumping for Discontinuous Markov Reward Chains and τ-lumping for Markov Reward Chains with Fast Transitions. The combination of transitivity and strong confluence ensures that iterative application of ordinary lumping yields a uniquely determined process. In the case of τ-lumping, by Proposition 2 and Proposition 3, only the limit of the final reduced process is uniquely determined, unless the final process contains no fast transitions.

There is no need to investigate the relational properties of reduction and τ-reduction, since they act in one step (no iteration is possible), in a unique way, between different types of models. Proofs of the results of this section can be found in [22].

The following result gives the transitivity of ordinary lumping. Actually, we show the transitivity of the relation $\geq$ on Discontinuous Markov Reward Chains defined by

$$\mathsf{P}_1 \geq \mathsf{P}_2 \iff (\exists \mathcal{L})\, \mathsf{P}_1 \overset{\mathcal{L}}{\rightarrow} \mathsf{P}_2.$$

Transitivity enables replacement of repeated application of ordinary lumping by a single application using an ordinary lumping that is a composition of the individual lumpings.

Theorem 1. *Let* $P \overset{\mathcal{L}}{\rightarrow} \overline{P}$ *and let* $\overline{P} \overset{\overline{\mathcal{L}}}{\rightarrow} \overline{\overline{P}}$. *Then* $P \overset{\mathcal{L} \circ \overline{\mathcal{L}}}{\rightarrow} \overline{\overline{P}}$. ☐

The above relation is clearly reflexive, since the trivial partition is always a lumping, i.e., we have $P \overset{\Delta}{\rightarrow} P$ where Δ is the trivial partition in which every class is a singleton. Transitivity of τ-lumping also holds, i.e. the relation $\geq$ defined by

$$P_1 \geq P_2 \iff (\exists \mathcal{L}) \, P_1 \overset{\mathcal{L}}{\rightsquigarrow} P_2$$

is transitive. This relation is reflexive as well, via the trivial lumping Δ.

Theorem 2. *Let* $P \overset{\mathcal{L}}{\rightsquigarrow} \overline{P}$ *and let* $\overline{P} \overset{\overline{\mathcal{L}}}{\rightsquigarrow} \overline{\overline{P}}$. *Then* $P \overset{\mathcal{L} \circ \overline{\mathcal{L}}}{\rightsquigarrow} \overline{\overline{P}}$. ☐

Lumping and τ-lumping also have the strict confluence property. In case of lumping this means that if $P \overset{\mathcal{L}_1}{\rightarrow} P_1$ and $P \overset{\mathcal{L}_2}{\rightarrow} P_2$, then there exist two partitions $\overline{\mathcal{L}}_1$ and $\overline{\mathcal{L}}_2$ such that $P_1 \overset{\mathcal{L}_1 \circ \overline{\mathcal{L}}_1}{\rightarrow} \overline{P}$ and $P_2 \overset{\mathcal{L}_2 \circ \overline{\mathcal{L}}_2}{\rightarrow} \overline{P}$. One can prove the strict confluence property by adapting the proof for Markov reward chains, from [16] for example.

5   Parallel Composition and Compositionality

In this section we define the parallel composition for each of the models, and prove the compositionality results. The definitions of parallel composition are based on Kronecker products and sums, as for standard Markov reward chains [14]. The intuition behind this is that the Kronecker sum represents interleaving whereas the Kronecker product represents synchronization. Let us first recall the definition of Kronecker product and sum.

Definition 12. *Let* $A \in \mathbb{R}^{n_1 \times n_2}$ *and* $B \in \mathbb{R}^{m_1 \times m_2}$. *The Kronecker product of* A *and* B *is a matrix* $(A \otimes B) \in \mathbb{R}^{n_1 m_1 \times n_2 m_2}$ *defined by*

$$(A \otimes B)[(i-1)m_1 + k, (j-1)m_2 + \ell] = A[i,j]B[k,\ell]$$

for $1 \leq i \leq n_1$, $1 \leq j \leq n_2$, $1 \leq k \leq m_1$ *and* $1 \leq \ell \leq m_2$.
   The Kronecker sum of two square matrices $A \in \mathbb{R}^{n \times n}$ *and* $B \in \mathbb{R}^{m \times m}$ *is a matrix* $(A \oplus B) \in \mathbb{R}^{nm \times nm}$ *defined as* $A \oplus B = A \otimes I^m + I^n \otimes B$.

We also need the notion of a Kronecker product of two partitions. Let $\mathcal{L}_1$ and $\mathcal{L}_2$ be two partitions with corresponding collector matrices V_1 and V_2, respectively. Then $\mathcal{L}_1 \otimes \mathcal{L}_2$ denotes the partition corresponding to the collector matrix $V_1 \otimes V_2$. In this section we present our results without proofs. Proof outlines are given in [22].

5.1   Composing Discontinuous Markov Reward Chains

First, we present the definition of parallel composition of Discontinuous Markov Reward Chains. The intuition is that 'rates' interleave, and the probabilities of the instantaneous transitions synchronize, i.e., are independent.

Definition 13. *Let* $P_1 = (\sigma_1, \Pi_1, Q_1, \rho_1)$ *and* $P_2 = (\sigma_2, \Pi_2, Q_2, \rho_2)$ *be two Discontinuous Markov Reward Chains. Their parallel composition is defined as:*

$$P_1 \parallel P_2 = (\sigma_1 \otimes \sigma_2, \Pi_1 \otimes \Pi_2, Q_1 \otimes \Pi_2 + \Pi_1 \otimes Q_2, \rho_1 \otimes 1^{|\rho_2|} + 1^{|\rho_1|} \otimes \rho_2).$$

The following theorem shows that the parallel composition of two Discontinuous Markov Reward Chains is well defined.

Theorem 3. *Let* P_1 *and* P_2 *be two Discontinuous Markov Reward Chains. Then* $P_1 \parallel P_2$ *is a Discontinuous Markov Reward Chain.* □

In the special case, when both Discontinuous Markov Reward Chains are continuous, their parallel composition is again a Markov Reward Chain as defined in [14]. Moreover, the following property shows that the parallel composition of two Discontinuous Markov Reward Chains has a transition matrix that is the Kronecker product of the individual transition matrices, corresponding to the intuition that the Kronecker product represents synchronization. It justifies the definition of the parallel composition.

Theorem 4. *Let* P_1 *and* P_2 *be Discontinuous Markov Reward Chains. If* $P_1(t)$ *is the transition matrix of* P_1 *and* $P_2(t)$ *is the transition matrix of* P_2, *then the transition matrix of* $P_1 \parallel P_2$ *is given by* $P_1(t) \otimes P_2(t)$. □

It is easy to see that the total reward of the parallel composition is the sum of the total rewards of the components. The following theorem shows that both lumping and reduction are compositional with respect to the parallel composition of Discontinuous Markov Reward Chains.

Theorem 5. *If* $P_1 \overset{\mathcal{L}_1}{\to} \overline{P}_1$ *and* $P_2 \overset{\mathcal{L}_2}{\to} \overline{P}_2$, *then* $P_1 \parallel P_2 \overset{\mathcal{L}_1 \otimes \mathcal{L}_2}{\to} \overline{P}_1 \parallel \overline{P}_2$. *Also, if* $P_1 \to_r \overline{P}_1$ *and* $P_2 \to_r \overline{P}_2$, *then* $P_1 \parallel P_2 \to_r \overline{P}_1 \parallel \overline{P}_2$. □

5.2 Composing Markov Reward Chains with Fast Transitions

We now present the definition of the parallel composition of Markov Reward Chains with Fast Transitions. It comprises a Kronecker sum of the generator matrices, i.e. interleaving of the rates for both slow and fast transitions.

Definition 14. *Let* $P_1 = (\sigma_1, Q_{s,1}, Q_{f,1}, \rho_1)$ *and* $P_2 = (\sigma_2, Q_{s,2}, Q_{f,2}, \rho_2)$ *be two Markov Reward Chains with Fast Transitions. Then their parallel composition is defined as:*

$$P_1 \parallel P_2 = (\sigma_1 \otimes \sigma_2, Q_{s,1} \oplus Q_{s,2}, Q_{f,1} \oplus Q_{f,2}, \rho_1 \otimes 1 + 1 \otimes \rho_2).$$

It is not difficult to see that the parallel composition of Markov Reward Chains with Fast Transitions is well defined. In Fig. 1 we present an example of parallel composition of two Markov Reward Chains with Fast Transitions: 1c) is the parallel composition of 1a) and 1b). The initial probabilities are depicted left

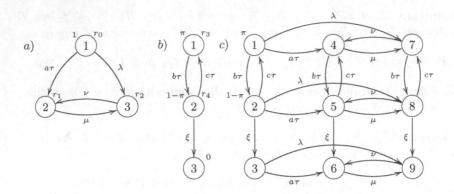

Fig. 1. Parallel composition of Markov Reward Chains with Fast Transitions

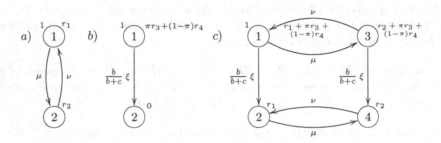

Fig. 2. Aggregated Markov Reward Chains with Fast Transitions

above each state, and the reward values right above. An exception is 1c) where for readability the rewards are omitted. They are given by the vector

$$(r_0 + r_3, r_0 + r_4, r_0, r_1 + r_3, r_1 + r_4, r_1, r_2 + r_3, r_2 + r_4, r_2).$$

Next we show that τ-lumping and τ-reduction are also compositional, with respect to the parallel composition of Markov Reward Chains with Fast Transitions.

Theorem 6. *If* $P_1 \overset{\mathcal{L}_1}{\rightsquigarrow} \overline{P}_1$ *and* $P_2 \overset{\mathcal{L}_2}{\rightsquigarrow} \overline{P}_2$, *then* $P_1 \parallel P_2 \overset{\mathcal{L}_1 \otimes \mathcal{L}_2}{\rightsquigarrow} \overline{P}_1 \parallel \overline{P}_2$. *Also, if* $P_1 \rightarrow_r \overline{P}_1$ *and* $P_2 \rightarrow_r \overline{P}_2$, *then* $P_1 \parallel P_2 \rightarrow_r \overline{P}_1 \parallel \overline{P}_2$.   □

Fig. 2 presents the aggregated versions of the Markov Reward Chains with Fast Transitions from Fig. 1. The Markov Reward Chain with Fast Transitions in 2c) is the parallel composition of the Markov Reward Chains with Fast Transitions in 2a) and 2b). Remarkably, the aggregated versions 2a), 2b) and 2c) can be obtained from 1a), 1b), 1c), respectively, by either applying τ-reduction or τ-lumping. The τ-lumpings used are $\{\{1, 2\}, \{3\}\}$ for 1a) and 1b), and $\{\{1, 2, 4, 5\}, \{3, 6\}, \{7, 8\}, \{9\}\}$ for 1c). By Theorem 6, we have that the chain in 1c), in fact, is the parallel composition of the chains in 1a) and 1b).

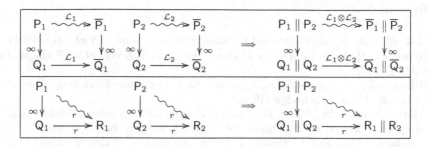

Fig. 3. Summary compositionality results

Having defined parallel composition for both models, we show how they are related: the limit of the parallel composition of two Markov Reward Chains with Fast Transitions is the parallel composition of the limits of the components (that are Discontinuous Markov Reward Chains). Hence, a continuity property of the parallel composition holds as stated in the next theorem.

Theorem 7. *Let* $P_1 \to_\infty Q_1$ *and* $P_2 \to_\infty Q_2$. *Then* $P_1 \parallel P_2 \to_\infty Q_1 \parallel Q_2$. $\qquad\square$

6 Conclusion

We considered two types of performance models: discontinuous Markov reward chains and Markov reward chains with fast transitions. The former models represent the limit behavior of the later ones. For both types of models, we presented two aggregation methods: lumping and reduction for Discontinuous Markov Reward Chains, respectively, τ-lumping and τ-reduction for Markov Reward Chains with Fast Transitions. In short, the contributions of the paper are:

- A definition of parallel composition of Discontinuous Markov Reward Chains and of Markov Reward Chains with Fast Transitions, allowing for compositional modeling.
- Identification of preorder properties of the aggregation methods for both types of models.
- Compositionality theorems for each type of models and each corresponding aggregation preorder, and continuity property of the parallel compositions.

The results on compositionality are summarized by Fig. 3. In words, the parallel composition for Markov reward chains with fast transitions and the parallel composition for discontinuous Markov reward chains preserve the diagrams from Proposition 2 and Proposition 4. Fig. 3 is justified by the Theorems 1–6, as well as by Proposition 2 and Proposition 4.

For future work we schedule the analysis of extensions of Markov reward chains with fast and silent transitions to model both probabilistic and nondeterministic behavior. Our aim is to extend the compositionality results to that setting, as well as to add action labeled transitions so that in addition to interleaving, synchronization can also be expressed.

References

1. Howard, R.A.: Semi-Markov and Decision Processes. Wiley, Chichester (1971)
2. Hermanns, H. (ed.): Interactive Markov Chains. LNCS, vol. 2428. Springer, Heidelberg (2002)
3. Hillston, J.: A Compositional Approach to Performance Modelling. Cambridge University Press, Cambridge (1996)
4. Ajmone Marsan, M., Balbo, G., Conte, G., Donatelli, S., Franceschinis, G.: Modelling with Generalized Stochastic Petri Nets. Wiley, Chichester (1995)
5. Ciardo, G., Muppala, J., Trivedi, K.S.: On the solution of GSPN reward models. Performance Evaluation 12, 237–253 (1991)
6. Wu, S.-H., Smolka, S., Stark, E.: Composition and behaviors of probabilistic I/O automata. Theoretical Computer Science 176(1–2), 1–38 (1997)
7. Plateau, B., Atif, K.: Stochastic automata network of modeling parallel systems. IEEE Transactions on Software Engineering 17(10), 1093–1108 (1991)
8. Markovski, J., Trčka, N.: Lumping Markov chains with silent steps. In: QEST'06, Riverside, pp. 221–230. IEEE Computer Society Press, Los Alamitos (2006)
9. Markovski, J., Trčka, N.: Aggregation methods for Markov reward chains with fast and silent transitions. Technical Report CS 07/08, Technische Universiteit Eindhoven (2007)
10. Trčka, N.: Silent Steps in Transition Systems and Markov Chains. PhD thesis, Eindhoven University of Technology (2007)
11. Doeblin, W.: Sur l'équation Matricielle $A(t + s) = A(t) \cdot A(s)$ et ses Applications aux Probabilités en Chaine. Bull. Sci. Math. 62, 21–32 (1938)
12. Coderch, M., Willsky, A., Sastry, S., Castanon, D.: Hierarchical aggregation of singularly perturbed finite state Markov processes. Stochastics 8, 259–289 (1983)
13. Ammar, H., Huang, Y., Liu, R.: Hierarchical models for systems reliability, maintainability, and availability. IEEE Transactions on Circuits and Systems 34(6), 629–638 (1987)
14. Buchholz, P.: Markovian process algebra: composition and equivalence. In: Proc. PAPM 94, Erlangen, Universität Erlangen-Nürnberg, pp. 11–30 (1994)
15. Kemeny, J., Snell, J.: Finite Markov chains. Springer, Heidelberg (1976)
16. Sokolova, A., de Vink, E.: On relational properties of lumpability. In: Proc. 4th PROGRESS symposium on Embedded Systems, Utrecht (2003)
17. Delebecque, F., Quadrat, J.: Optimal control of Markov chains admitting strong and weak interactions. Automatica 17, 281–296 (1981)
18. Doob, J.: Stochastic Processes. Wiley, Chichester (1953)
19. Chung, K.: Markov Chains with Stationary Probabilities. Springer, Heidelberg (1967)
20. Hille, E., Phillips, R.: Functional Analysis and Semi-Groups. AMS, Washington, DC (1957)
21. Nicola, V.: Lumping in Markov reward processes. IBM Research Report RC 14719, IBM (1989)
22. Markovski, J., Sokolova, A., Trčka, N.: de Vink, E.: Compositionality for Markov chains with fast transitions. Technical Report CS 07/17, Technische Universiteit Eindhoven (2007)

Closed Form Absorption Time Bounds*

Ana Bušić[1] and Nihal Pekergin[1,2,3]

[1] PRiSM, Université de Versailles-St-Quentin,
45, Av. des Etats-Unis, 78035 Versailles, France
[2] Laboratory Marin Mersenne, Université Paris 1, 75013 Paris, France
[3] LACL, Université Paris 12, 61, Av. Général de Gaulle, 94010 Créteil, France

Abstract. We consider a class of Markov chains known for its closed form transient and steady-state distributions. We show that some absorbing chains can be also seen as members of this class and we provide the closed form solution for their absorption time distributions. By constructing upper and lower bounding chains that belong to this particular class one can easily compute both lower and upper bounds for absorption time distribution of an arbitrary absorbing Markov chain. We provide a new algorithm for the construction of bounding chains from this class and we show a possible application of these bounds.

1 Introduction

Markov chains are widely used to model complex systems due to their simplicity to represent in an intuitive manner the studied system behavior. Various high-level formalisms such as Stochastic Petri Nets, Stochastic Automata Networks or PEPA nets have been proposed making the modeling task more efficient since one needs only to specify different components of the system, their local behaviors and their interactions. The generation of the underlying Markov chain and the computation of different performance or reliability measures of interest behavior of a can then be derived by one of many existing tools, depending on the formalism used. However, most of the resolution techniques for transient or steady-state distributions of Markov chains depend on the size of the entire state space, which is often near to the product of the number of states of each component of the system.

In order to overcome the state space explosion problem various approximation methods have been proposed which ignore or simplify the complicating aspects of the underlying models. However, only some of those methods estimate the error committed by the approximation or guarantee that the approximate value of measure of interest is smaller (resp. greater) than the exact one. Different bounding methods have been proposed for the steady-state analysis. Most of them use linear algebra arguments and resume the steady-state analysis to the solution of a linear system. The advantage of stochastic comparison techniques

---

* This work was supported by SMS, ANR-05-BLAN-009-02 and Checkbound, ANR-06-SETI-002.

K. Wolter (Ed.): EPEW 2007, LNCS 4748, pp. 33–47, 2007.

is that they use probabilistic arguments, allowing thus both steady-state and transient analysis of the system.

Stochastic orderings have been largely studied in different areas of applied probability [12]. Various stochastic orders have been proposed and the most well known is certainly the strong stochastic order defined through the comparison of expectations of all increasing rewards. Different bounding methods have been proposed by using this stochastic order. The main idea behind all these methods is to modify the transitions of the original chain in order to simplify its analysis, yet preserving the comparison of both steady-state and transient distributions. The proof of this comparison can be established by different techniques such as sample-path arguments or the stochastic monotonicity. While the first one is specific to the strong stochastic order, construction of monotone bounding chains can be used with different stochastic orders such as for instance increasing convex order allowing to compare the variability of two Markov chains. Moreover, it is possible to construct algorithmically a bounding monotone chain using both strong stochastic ordering [1] or increasing convex stochastic ordering [3]. Finally, the simplification of the model can consist in a special structure adapted to some special numerical resolution methods [10], in construction of lumpable bounding models reducing thus the size of the model [15] or in construction of the bounding models having known closed-form solutions that will be considered in this paper.

In [5,6] a class of Markov chains having closed-form solution for the steady-state distribution has been introduced by Ben Mamoun and Pekergin: class $\mathcal{C}$ chains. The same authors showed that the chains from this class have also closed-form solutions for their transient distributions [7]. A generalization of this class to a larger $\mathcal{C}^{\mathcal{G}}$ class of Markov chains has been recently proposed in [4]. This larger class allows one more degree of freedom and permits thus to obtain more precise bounds. We show in this paper that this additional degree of freedom allows also simple construction of bounding matrices that belong to this new class. Class $\mathcal{C}^{\mathcal{G}}$ structures can be imposed as the bounding matrices, in the algorithmic stochastic comparison approach [6,4]. Thus, bounds on distributions can be computed by means of closed-form solutions of class $\mathcal{C}^{\mathcal{G}}$ matrices leading to important numerical complexity reductions. For instance, in [8], class $\mathcal{C}$ bounds have been applied to perform a first step rapid model checking.

Several two-level resolution methods which consist in analyzing several smaller sub-models separately and then finding the global solution by combining sub-solutions have been proposed. In [9], the cycle time of PEPA model where each component is a PEPA sub-model is considered. Holding times of sub-models which are continuous Phase distributions are bounded by exponential random variables, providing thus a far simpler precedence PEPA model that can be then analyzed by classical numerical techniques. In reliability studies, bounding schemes have been proposed by dividing large state spaces in several macro-states. One macro-state is taken into account explicitly while the others are reduced to single states. The transition rates for these states are obtained by computing bounds on the underlying sub-models [13,11]. Class $\mathcal{C}^{\mathcal{G}}$ bounds may be useful to compute bounds of sub-models. To illustrate the applicability of this approach, we consider in this work a task graph where task execution times are given by discrete time Phase distributions. We first compute $\mathcal{C}^{\mathcal{G}}$ class bounds for task execution times and then incorporate them in the considered task graph which is the high-level model.

We present briefly in Section 2 the generalized class $\mathcal{C}$ matrices and their basic properties: closed-form solutions for transient and steady-state distributions. We show that some absorbing chains also belong to this class and we give the closed form solution for their absorption times. This class of matrices can therefore be used to compute simple lower or upper absorption time bounds. In Section 3 we provide a new algorithm for construction of bounds that belong to this class. This new algorithm presents different advantages compared to the algorithm presented in [4]. The most important is certainly its simplicity and the possibility of computing both upper and lower class $\mathcal{C}^{\mathcal{G}}$ bounds. Finally, we show in Section 4 how this new algorithm can be used to obtain rapid closed form bounds for PH distributions modeling service times in a multi-level model.

2   Class $\mathcal{C}^{\mathcal{G}}$ Matrices

The $\mathcal{C}^{\mathcal{G}}$ class of stochastic matrices has been introduced recently in [4] as the generalization of the $\mathcal{C}$ class introduced in [5,6]. We give first the definition of the $\mathcal{C}^{\mathcal{G}}$ class and the closed form solution for transient and steady-state distributions for transition matrices that belong to this class. Further details and proofs can be found in [4].

2.1   Definition and Basic Properties

Throughout this paper we will denote the vectors and the matrices with boldface letters. All the vectors are row vectors and $\boldsymbol{x}^t$ will denote column vector obtained by transposing vector $\boldsymbol{x}$. When comparing vectors or matrices $\boldsymbol{x} \leq \boldsymbol{y}$ stands for the usual component-wise comparison: $\boldsymbol{x} \leq \boldsymbol{y} \Leftrightarrow x_i \leq y_i, \forall i$.

Definition 1 (Class $\mathcal{C}^{\mathcal{G}}$). *A stochastic matrix $\boldsymbol{P}$ of size n belongs to $\mathcal{C}^{\mathcal{G}}$ if there are three vectors $\boldsymbol{v}$, $\boldsymbol{c}$ and $\boldsymbol{r}$ in $\mathbb{R}^n$ such that:*

$$\boldsymbol{P} = \boldsymbol{1}^t \boldsymbol{v} + \boldsymbol{r}^t \boldsymbol{c},$$

where $\boldsymbol{1}$ denotes the row-vector having all the components equal to 1 and vectors $\boldsymbol{v}$ and $\boldsymbol{c}$ satisfy:

- *$\boldsymbol{v}$ is a probability vector ($v_i \geq 0, \forall i$, $\boldsymbol{v1}^t = \sum_{i=1}^n v_i = 1$),*
- *$\boldsymbol{c1}^t = \sum_{i=1}^n c_i = 0$.*

For vector $\boldsymbol{r}$ such that $r_i = i - 1, \forall i$ we obtain the class $\mathcal{C}$ Markov chains defined in [5]. Thus the class $\mathcal{C}^{\mathcal{G}}$ is larger than the class $\mathcal{C}$.

Certainly one of most important properties of class $\mathcal{C}^{\mathcal{G}}$ matrices is that they have closed form solution for transient distributions:

Theorem 1 (Transient distributions). *[4, Theorem 2] Let $\{X_k,\ k \geq 0\}$ be a discrete time Markov chain with probability transition matrix P that belongs to the class $\mathcal{C}^{\mathcal{G}}$, such that $P = 1^t v + r^t c$, and let ν^k be the distribution vector of X_k. Let α, β and γ be the following constants:*

$$\alpha = cr^t, \quad \beta = vr^t \text{ and } \gamma = \nu^0 r^t.$$

Then for all $k \geq 0$,

$$\nu^k = v + a_k c, \tag{1}$$

where a_k is the constant defined as:

$$a_k = \beta \sum_{i=0}^{k-2} \alpha^i + \gamma \alpha^{k-1} = \begin{cases} \beta \frac{(1-\alpha^{k-1})}{1-\alpha} + \gamma\, \alpha^{k-1}, & \alpha \neq 1 \\ \beta\, (k-1) + \gamma, & \alpha = 1. \end{cases}$$

The following corollary gives now the closed-form form for the steady-state distribution:

Corollary 1 (Steady-state distribution). *[4, Corollary 1] Let $\{X_k,\ k \geq 0\}$ be a discrete time Markov chain with probability transition matrix $P \in \mathcal{C}^{\mathcal{G}}$ such that $P = 1^t v + r^t c$ and let $\alpha = cr^t$. If $|\alpha| < 1$, then $\{X_k,\ k \geq 0\}$ has a steady-state distribution given by:*

$$\pi = v + Rc, \tag{2}$$

where R is a constant defined as: $R = \frac{vr^t}{1-cr^t}$.

2.2   Closed Form Solution for Absorption Time Distribution

Note that one can easily construct absorbing transition matrices that belong to the class $\mathcal{C}^{\mathcal{G}}$. Indeed, take an arbitrary probability vector v and define vector c as follows:

$$c_i = -v_i, \ i < n, \ c_n = 1 - v_n.$$

Then obviously $c1^t = 0$. Then for an arbitrary vector r satisfying:

$$0 \leq r_i \leq 1, \ \forall i,$$
$$r_n = 1,$$

the matrix is clearly stochastic, thus $P \in \mathcal{C}^{\mathcal{G}}$. Furthermore, we have $P_{n,*} = (0, 0, \ldots, 0, 1)$, so state n is absorbing.

Example 1. Let $v = (0.1 \quad 0.3 \quad 0.6)$. Thus $c = (-0.1 \quad -0.3 \quad 0.4)$. By taking $r = (0.1\ 0.2\ 1)$, matrix $P = 1^t v + r^t c$ is defined as follows:

$$\begin{pmatrix} 1 \\ 1 \\ 1 \end{pmatrix} (0.1\,0.3\,0.6) + \begin{pmatrix} 0.1 \\ 0.2 \\ 1 \end{pmatrix} (-0.1\,-0.3\,0.4) = \begin{pmatrix} 0.09\,0.27\,0.64 \\ 0.08\,0.24\,0.68 \\ 0\quad 0\quad 1 \end{pmatrix}$$

Suppose now that we have an absorbing discrete time Markov chain $\{X_k, \ k \geq 0\}$ such that the unique absorbing state is the last state (state n). Denote by $\boldsymbol{P}$ the transition matrix of this chain. We show now that class $\mathcal{C}^{\mathcal{G}}$ matrices have also the closed form solution for the absorption time.

Proposition 1. *Let T denote the absorption time of an absorbing discrete time Markov chain $\{X_k, \ k \geq 0\}$ such that the unique absorbing state is the last state (state n). Denote by $\boldsymbol{t} \in \mathbb{N}^{\infty}$ the probability distribution vector of T. If the transition matrix $\boldsymbol{P} \in \mathcal{C}^{\mathcal{G}}$ ($\boldsymbol{P} = \mathbf{1}^t \boldsymbol{v} + \boldsymbol{r}^t \boldsymbol{c}$), then vector $\boldsymbol{t}$ satisfies:*

$$
\begin{aligned}
t_0 &= \nu_n^0, \\
t_1 &= v_n + \gamma c_n - \nu_n^0, \\
t_k &= \alpha^{k-2}(\beta + \gamma(\alpha - 1))c_n, \ k \geq 2,
\end{aligned}
$$

Proof. Note first that for each k, $P(T \leq k) = P(X_k = n)$. Thus $t_0 = P(T = 0) = \nu_n^0$ and

$$
t_k = P(T = k) = P(T \leq k) - P(T \leq k - 1) = \nu_n^k - \nu_n^{k-1}, \ \forall k > 0,
$$

where $\boldsymbol{\nu}^k$ denotes the distribution of X_k. From Theorem 1 we have

$$
\begin{aligned}
t_1 &= v_n + \gamma c_n - \nu_n^0, \\
t_k &= (\boldsymbol{v} + a_k \boldsymbol{c})_n - (\boldsymbol{v} + a_{k-1} \boldsymbol{c})_n = (a_k - a_{k-1})\,c_n \\
&= \beta \alpha^{k-2} + \gamma(\alpha^{k-1} - \alpha^{k-2})c_n = \alpha^{k-2}(\beta + \gamma(\alpha - 1))c_n, \ k \geq 2.
\end{aligned}
$$

$\square$

Corollary 2. *If $|\alpha| < 1$ then the mean absorption time $E[T]$ is finite and equals to:*

$$
E[T] = v_n + \left[\gamma + (\beta + \gamma(\alpha - 1))\frac{2 - \alpha}{(1 - \alpha)^2}\right] c_n.
$$

Proof. From Proposition 1 we have :

$$
E[T] = v_n + \gamma c_n + \sum_{k=2}^{\infty} k t_k = v_n + \gamma c_n + (\beta + \gamma(\alpha - 1))c_n \sum_{k=2}^{\infty} k \alpha^{k-2}
$$

$$
= v_n + \gamma c_n + (\beta + \gamma(\alpha - 1))c_n \left(2 \sum_{i=0}^{\infty} \alpha^i + \sum_{i=0}^{\infty} i \alpha^i\right)
$$

$$
= v_n + \gamma c_n + (\beta + \gamma(\alpha - 1))c_n \left(\frac{2}{1 - \alpha} + \frac{\alpha}{(1 - \alpha)^2}\right) =
$$

$$
= v_n + \left[\gamma + (\beta + \gamma(\alpha - 1))\frac{2 - \alpha}{(1 - \alpha)^2}\right] c_n.
$$

$\square$

3   Algorithmic Construction of Bounding Matrices

The closed-form solutions to compute transient distributions and absorption time distribution make class $\mathcal{C}^g$ matrices interesting to construct bounding chains. These bounds can be derived by means of stochastic comparison techniques. We first state the basic definitions and theorems of this approach and refer to [12] for further details.

3.1   Stochastic Comparison

Let denote by $\mathcal{F}_{st}$ the class of all increasing real functions on $\mathcal{E}$ and by $\mathcal{F}_{icx}$ the class of all increasing and convex real functions on $\mathcal{E}$. We denote by $\preceq_{\mathcal{F}}$ the stochastic order relation, where $\mathcal{F}$ can be replaced by st or icx to be associated respectively to the class of functions $\mathcal{F}_{st}$ or $\mathcal{F}_{icx}$.

Definition 2. *Let X and Y be two random variables taking values on a totally ordered state space $\mathcal{E}$.*

$$X \preceq_{\mathcal{F}} Y \iff Ef(X) \le Ef(Y), \quad \forall f \in \mathcal{F}$$

whenever the expectations exist.

In the sequel, we consider $\mathcal{E} = \{1, \ldots, n\}$ with the usual total order $\le$. Stochastic orders $\preceq_{st}$ and $\preceq_{icx}$ can be also defined through matrices. We give here $\boldsymbol{K}_{st}$ and $\boldsymbol{K}_{icx}$ matrices related respectively to the $\preceq_{st}$ and $\preceq_{icx}$ orders. In the sequel $\boldsymbol{K}_{\mathcal{F}}$ denotes the matrix related to the $\preceq_{\mathcal{F}}$ order, $\mathcal{F} \in \{st, icx\}$.

$$\boldsymbol{K}_{st} = \begin{pmatrix} 1\,0\,0\ldots 0 \\ 1\,1\,0\ldots 0 \\ 1\,1\,1\ldots 0 \\ \vdots\ \vdots\ \vdots\ \ddots\ \vdots \\ 1\,1\,1\ldots 1 \end{pmatrix} \qquad \boldsymbol{K}_{icx} = \begin{pmatrix} 1\ 0 & 0 & \ldots 0 \\ 2\ 1 & 0 & \ldots 0 \\ 3\ 2 & 1 & \ldots 0 \\ \vdots\ \vdots & \vdots & \ddots\ \vdots \\ n\ n-1 & n-2 & \ldots 1 \end{pmatrix}$$

Notice that for discrete random variables X and Y with probability vectors $\boldsymbol{p}$ and $\boldsymbol{q}$, the notations $\boldsymbol{p} \preceq_{\mathcal{F}} \boldsymbol{q}$ and $X \preceq_{\mathcal{F}} Y$ are used interchangeably. Moreover, we have the following characterization [12]:

Property 1. $X \preceq_{\mathcal{F}} Y$ if and only if $\boldsymbol{p}\boldsymbol{K}_{\mathcal{F}} \le \boldsymbol{q}\boldsymbol{K}_{\mathcal{F}}$.

It is shown in Theorem 5.2.11 of [12, p.186] that monotonicity and comparability of the probability transition matrices of time-homogeneous Markov chains yield sufficient conditions to compare stochastically the underlying chains. We first define the monotonicity and the comparability of stochastic matrices and then state this theorem.

Definition 3. *Let $\boldsymbol{P}$ be a stochastic matrix. $\boldsymbol{P}$ is said to be stochastically $\preceq_{\mathcal{F}}$-monotone if for any probability vectors $\boldsymbol{p}$ and $\boldsymbol{q}$,*

$$\boldsymbol{p} \le_{\mathcal{F}} \boldsymbol{q} \implies \boldsymbol{p}\boldsymbol{P} \le_{\mathcal{F}} \boldsymbol{q}\boldsymbol{P}.$$

Definition 4. *Let P and Q be two stochastic matrices. Q is said to be an upper bounding matrix of P in the sense of the $\preceq_{\mathcal{F}}$ order ($P \preceq_{\mathcal{F}} Q$) if*

$$P\,K_{\mathcal{F}} \leq Q\,K_{\mathcal{F}}.$$

Note that this is equivalent to saying that $P \preceq_{\mathcal{F}} Q$, if $P_{i,*} \preceq_{\mathcal{F}} Q_{i,*}$, $\forall i \in \{1,\ldots,n\}$, where $P_{i,*}$ denotes the ith row of matrix P.

Theorem 2. *Let P (resp. Q) be the probability transition matrix of the time-homogeneous Markov chain $\{X_k, k \geq 0\}$ (resp. $\{Y_k, k \geq 0\}$). If*

- *$X_0 \preceq_{\mathcal{F}} Y_0$,*
- *at least one of the probability transition matrices is monotone, that is, either P or Q is $\preceq_{\mathcal{F}}$-monotone,*
- *the transition matrices are comparable, that is, $P \preceq_{\mathcal{F}} Q$,*

then

$$X_k \preceq_{\mathcal{F}} Y_k \quad \forall k.$$

Let $X = \{X_k, k \geq 0\}$ and $Y = \{Y_k, k \geq 0\}$ be now two Markov chains with an absorbing state n. Then under the same conditions as in the above theorem we have also the $\preceq_{st}$-comparison of absorption times to n. We will denote by T^X (resp. by T^Y) the absorption time to n of chain X (resp. Y).

Corollary 3. *[3, Proposition 2.9] Let P and Q be the transition matrices of two Markov chains $X = \{X_k, k \geq 0\}$ and $Y = \{Y_k, k \geq 0\}$ with an absorbing state n. If $X_0 \preceq_{\mathcal{F}} Y_0$, P or Q is $\preceq_{\mathcal{F}}$-monotone, and $P \preceq_{\mathcal{F}} Q$, then*

$$T^Y \preceq_{st} T^X.$$

Note that we obtain the $\preceq_{st}$-comparison of absorption times even if the two chains are comparable only in the increasing convex ordering sense. Indeed, the above result is even more general and the ordering relation needs only to allow the comparison of the probabilities of being in state n (see [3] for further details). Note also that the absorption time is $\preceq_{st}$-larger for a smaller chain in the $\preceq_{\mathcal{F}}$-ordering sense. This might seem strange at a first sight. Intuitively, as we consider the absorption time to the last state, the larger chain goes faster to this state and its absorption time is thus smaller.

Monotonicity Properties of $\mathcal{C}^{\mathcal{G}}$ Matrices. The sufficient conditions for the monotonicity of class $\mathcal{C}^{\mathcal{G}}$ matrices are given in terms of vectors c and r.

Proposition 2. *[4, Proposition 2] A matrix $P \in \mathcal{C}^{\mathcal{G}}$, $P = 1^t v + r^t c$ such that:*

$$c K_{\mathcal{F}} \geq 0 \quad and \quad r \in \mathcal{F}$$

is $\preceq_{\mathcal{F}}$-monotone.

3.2   Algorithms for Upper and Lower Bounding Class $\mathcal{C}^{\mathcal{G}}$ Monotone Matrices

In [4] an algorithm for construction of upper bounding monotone $\mathcal{C}^{\mathcal{G}}$ matrices has been proposed for $\preceq_{st}$ and $\preceq_{icx}$-orders. The proposed algorithm takes as input an arbitrary stochastic matrix P and a non-negative vector $r \in \mathcal{F}$ ($\mathcal{F}$ denotes either st or icx), and it returns vectors c and v such that $Q = \mathbf{1}^t v + r^t c \in \mathcal{C}^{\mathcal{G}}$, $P \preceq_{\mathcal{F}} Q$ and Q is $\preceq_{\mathcal{F}}$-monotone. Some heuristics for choosing a vector r by using some information from the original matrix P have also been proposed. However, the algorithm proposed in [4] is far from being intuitive and it cannot be easily modified to compute lower bounds. Note that this is not a problem in the case of the $\preceq_{st}$ order: due to the symmetry properties of this order, lower $\preceq_{st}$-bounds can be obtained by inversing the order on the states of the chain and then computing an upper bound. In the case of class $\mathcal{C}$ or $\mathcal{C}^{\mathcal{G}}$ bounds, $\preceq_{icx}$ order provides often considerably more precise results [6,4]. Unfortunately, this order is not symmetric thus the algorithms that compute upper $\preceq_{icx}$-bounds cannot be used to derive lower bounds by inversing the order of states. The algorithm proposed in [4] is a direct generalization of algorithms proposed in [5,6] to $\mathcal{C}^{\mathcal{G}}$ class of matrices. We propose here a far more intuitive algorithm, more adapted to the $\mathcal{C}^{\mathcal{G}}$ structure. Furthermore, we propose the algorithms for both upper and lower bounds.

Let P be an arbitrary stochastic matrix. We take the first row of matrix P as vector v. In order to find a vector c, we compute first a probability vector x that is greater in the $\preceq_{\mathcal{F}}$-ordering sense than all the rows of matrix P. We will discuss this step of the algorithm more in details after presenting the general structure of the algorithm, since this step depends on the considered stochastic order. We would like to obtain a bounding matrix Q such that $Q_{1,*} = v$ and $Q_{n,*} = x$. In order to assure this, we can take $Q = \mathbf{1}^t\, v + h^t c$, where $h_1 = 0$, $h_n = 1$. Then $Q_{n,*} = v + c = x$ defines completely vector c:

$$c = x - v.$$

Notice that we have $cK_{\mathcal{F}} \geq 0$, as $v \preceq_{\mathcal{F}} x$ by the construction of vectors x and v. In order to satisfy $P \preceq_{\mathcal{F}} Q$ we need to compute a vector h such that:

$$P_{i,*} \preceq_{\mathcal{F}} v + h_i c = Q_{i,*},$$

i.e. $vK_{\mathcal{F}} + h_i cK_{\mathcal{F}} \geq P_{i,*}K_{\mathcal{F}}$. In the sequel, we will use the following notations: $w = vK_{\mathcal{F}}$, $A = PK_{\mathcal{F}}$, and $z = cK_{\mathcal{F}}$. Since $z \geq 0$, we can take:

$$h_i = \max_{j \,|\, z_j > 0} \frac{A_{i,j} - w_j}{z_j}.$$

We obtain a vector $h \leq 1$ as $z = w + y$, where $y \geq A_{i,*}$, $\forall 1 \leq i \leq n$. It remains us to satisfy the monotonicity constraints for matrix Q. If vector $h \in \mathcal{F}$, then Proposition 2 and $cK_{\mathcal{F}} \geq 0$ imply that Q is $\preceq_{\mathcal{F}}$-monotone. Unfortunately, we do not always have $h \in \mathcal{F}$. However, note that we can modify the entries of vector h as long as they stay smaller than 1. Indeed, for a vector r such that $h \leq r \leq 1$, matrix $\tilde{Q} = 1^t\,v + r^t c$ is also a stochastic matrix such that $P \preceq_{\mathcal{F}} \tilde{Q}$. Thus we need to find a vector r satisfying:

$-\; r \in \mathcal{F}$,
$-\; h \leq r \leq 1$.

The construction of such a vector for the case of strong stochastic order and increasing convex order will be discussed later. The construction of upper bounding, $\preceq_{\mathcal{F}}$-monotone, $\mathcal{C}^{\mathcal{G}}$ matrix is given in Algorithm 1. The following theorem states the properties of the output matrix obtained from this algorithm. The proof follows directly from the above discussion.

Theorem 3. *The matrix Q obtained by Algorithm 1 is a stochastic matrix that belongs to the class $\mathcal{C}^{\mathcal{G}}$. Moreover, matrix Q is $\preceq_{\mathcal{F}}$-monotone and $P \preceq_{\mathcal{F}} Q$.*

Algorithm 1. Construction of an $\preceq_{\mathcal{F}}$-monotone class $\mathcal{C}^{\mathcal{G}}$ upper bound

---

1 Set $v = P_{1,*}$ and set $w = v\,K_{\mathcal{F}}$.
2 Find a probability vector x such that $P_{i,*} \preceq_{\mathcal{F}} x$, $\forall 1 \leq i \leq n$. Set $y = x K_{\mathcal{F}}$.
3 Compute $z = y - w$ and $c = z\,K_{\mathcal{F}}^{-1}$.
4 Let $A = P\,K_{\mathcal{F}}$. Compute vector $h = (h_1, \ldots, h_n)$:

$$h_i = \max_{j\,|\,z_j > 0} \frac{A_{i,j} - w_j}{z_j}.$$

Note that we have always $h_1 = 0$.
5 Find a vector r such that $h \leq r \leq 1$ (component-wise) and $r \in \mathcal{F}$.
6 Set $Q = 1^t\,v + r^t c$.

A lower-bounding $\preceq_{\mathcal{F}}$-monotone matrix $Q \in \mathcal{C}^{\mathcal{G}}$ can be obtained by a similar algorithm. Here we preserve the last row of the original matrix and we compute a probability vector v that is smaller in the $\preceq_{\mathcal{F}}$-sense than all the rows in the original matrix P:

$$v \preceq_{\mathcal{F}} P_{i,*}.$$

In order to obtain a bounding matrix Q such that $Q_{1,*} = v$ and $Q_{n,*} = P_{n,*}$ we can take $Q = 1^t\,v + h^t c$, where $h_1 = 0$, $h_n = 1$ and $c = P_{n,*} - v$. As $v \preceq_{\mathcal{F}} P_{n,*}$, we have $cK_{\mathcal{F}} = P_{n,*} - vK_{\mathcal{F}} \geq 0$. To guarantee the comparison of matrices P and Q we compute a vector h such that:

$$Q_{i,*} = v + h_i c \preceq_{\mathcal{F}} P_{i,*},$$

i.e. $vK_{\mathcal{F}} + h_i cK_{\mathcal{F}} \leq P_{i,*}K_{\mathcal{F}}$. Let us denote by $w = vK_{\mathcal{F}}$ and $A = PK_{\mathcal{F}}$. Since $z = cK_{\mathcal{F}} \geq 0$, we can take:

$$h_i = \min_{j\,|\,z_j > 0} \frac{A_{i,j} - w_j}{z_j}.$$

Note that by the construction of vector v as a vector that is smaller than all the rows of matrix P, we clearly have: $h \geq 0$ and $h_n = 1$. If vector $h \in \mathcal{F}$, then Proposition 2 and $cK_\mathcal{F} \geq 0$ imply that matrix Q is $\preceq_\mathcal{F}$-monotone. As unfortunately this is not always the case, we need to modify this vector and, in order to preserve the comparison of matrices P and Q and the stochastic property of matrix Q, we can only decrease the entries of vector h. Thus, in order to satisfy the monotonicity constraints for matrix Q we need to compute a vector r such that:

- $r \in \mathcal{F}$,
- $0 \leq r \leq h$.

We resume the construction of a lower bounding monotone $\mathcal{C}^\mathcal{G}$ matrix in Algorithm 2 and we give its properties in the following theorem. The proof follows from the above discussion.

Theorem 4. *The matrix Q obtained by Algorithm 2 is a stochastic matrix that belongs to the class $\mathcal{C}^\mathcal{G}$. Moreover, matrix Q is $\preceq_\mathcal{F}$-monotone and $Q \preceq_\mathcal{F} P$.*

Algorithm 2. Construction of an $\preceq_\mathcal{F}$-monotone class $\mathcal{C}^\mathcal{G}$ lower bound

1 Find a probability vector v such that $v \preceq_\mathcal{F} P_{i,*}$, $\forall 1 \leq i \leq n.$, Set $w = vK_\mathcal{F}$.
2 Compute $c = P_{n,*} - v$, $z = cK_\mathcal{F}$.
3 A Let $A = P\ K_\mathcal{F}$. Compute vector $h = (h_1, \ldots, h_n)$:

$$h_i = \min_{j \mid z_j > 0} \frac{A_{i,j} - w_j}{z_j}.$$

Note that we have always $h_n = 1$.
4 Find a vector r such that $0 \leq r \leq h$ (component-wise) and $r \in \mathcal{F}$.
5 Set $Q = 1^t v + r^t c$.

Computation of an Upper or Lower Bounding Vector for All the Rows of the Original Matrix. We discuss now the construction of an upper bounding vector x (resp. a lower bounding vector v) for all the rows of the original matrix P in line 2 of Algorithm 1 (resp. line 1 of Algorithm 2) for the strong stochastic order and increasing convex order. The construction is similar for both orders, thus we will denote by $K_\mathcal{F}$ the corresponding matrix $K_\mathcal{F} = K_{st}$ (resp. $K_\mathcal{F} = K_{icx}$). Let $A = PK_\mathcal{F}$. Then the upper bounding vector x:

$$P{i,*} \preceq_\mathcal{F} x,$$

can be obtained as $x = yK_\mathcal{F}^{-1}$, where:

$$y_j = \max_{1 \leq i \leq n} A_{i,j}, \ \forall j.$$

We have clearly $P{i,*} \preceq_\mathcal{F} x$. It remains us to show that vector x is stochastic. We will show first that $\sum_{i=1}^n x_i = 1$. For the strong stochastic order this is trivial since $\sum_{i=1}^{n} x_i = y_1 = \max_{1 \le i \le n} A_{i,1} = 1$, as $A_{i,1} = 1$, $\forall i$. For the increasing convex order notice that $A_{i,1} = A_{i,2} + 1$, $\forall i$, thus $\sum_{i=1}^{n} x_i = y_1 - y_2 = 1$. Finally, we need to show that $x_i \ge 0$, $\forall i$. For the strong stochastic order we have clearly $1 = y_1 \ge y_2 \ge \ldots \ge y_n \ge 0$, thus $x_n = y_n \ge 0$ and $x_j = y_j - y_{j+1} \ge 0$, $j < n$. For the increasing convex order the proof is slightly more complex. Note that for an arbitrary vector $\boldsymbol{a}$ we have

$$(\boldsymbol{a} \boldsymbol{K_{icx}})_j = (\boldsymbol{a} \boldsymbol{K_{st}})_j + (\boldsymbol{a} \boldsymbol{K_{icx}})_{j+1}, \ j < n, \tag{3}$$

Let $\boldsymbol{z} = \boldsymbol{x} \boldsymbol{K_{st}}$. Note that we have also:

$$\boldsymbol{z} = \boldsymbol{y} \boldsymbol{K_{st}}^{-1}.$$

By using (3) it is now easy to show that vector $\boldsymbol{z}$ satisfies:

$$1 = z_1 \ge z_2 \ge \ldots \ge z_n \ge 0.$$

Therefore, $x_j \ge 0$, $\forall j$ and vector $\boldsymbol{x}$ is stochastic. Note that this vector $\boldsymbol{x}$ is the smallest upper bounding vector for all the rows of matrix $\boldsymbol{P}$.

Similarly, a lower bounding vector $\boldsymbol{v}$ can be obtained as $\boldsymbol{v} = \boldsymbol{w} \boldsymbol{K_\mathcal{F}}$ where:

$$w_j = \min_{1 \le i \le n} A_{i,j}, \ \forall j.$$

The vector $\boldsymbol{v}$ is the greatest lower bounding vector for rows of matrix $\boldsymbol{P}$. The proof that vector $\boldsymbol{v}$ is a stochastic vector is similar to the proof for the upper bounding case.

Computation of Monotone Bounding Vectors. It remains us to show how to compute the upper or lower bounding monotone vectors in line 5 of Algorithm 1 and line 4 of Algorithm 2. We consider again the strong stochastic and the increasing convex order.

Strong Stochastic Order. In the upper bound case we need to find an increasing vector $\boldsymbol{r}$ such that $\boldsymbol{h} \le \boldsymbol{r} \le \boldsymbol{1}$. Additionally, we know that $h_1 = 0$ and $h_i \le 1$, $\forall i$ by the construction of vector $\boldsymbol{h}$. Therefore vector $\boldsymbol{r}$, defined as $r_i = max_{k \le i} h_i$, $\forall i$ and computed by:

$$r_1 = h_1, \ r_i = \max\{h_i, \ r_{i-1}\}, \ i > 0,$$

satisfies clearly $\boldsymbol{h} \le \boldsymbol{r} \le \boldsymbol{1}$.

Similarly, in the case of a lower bound we have $h_n = 1$ and $\boldsymbol{h} \ge \boldsymbol{0}$ and a vector $\boldsymbol{r}$ such that $\boldsymbol{0} \le \boldsymbol{r} \le \boldsymbol{h}$ can be obtained by taking $r_i = min_{k \le i} h_i$, $\forall i$, i.e.

$$r_n = h_n, \ r_i = \min\{h_i, \ r_{i+1}\}, \ i < n.$$

Increasing Convex Order. Consider first the upper bounding case. We will suppose that vector h is increasing. Note that if this is not the case, then an increasing vector h' such that $h \leq h' \leq 1$ should be first computed as described in the strong stochastic upper bound case described above. Then we need to find a vector r such that $h' \leq r \leq 1$. For an increasing vector h, an increasing and convex vector r such that $h \leq r \leq 1$ can then be easily obtained as follows:

$$r_n = h_n, \ r_{n-1} = h_{n-1}, \ r_i = \max\{h_i, \ 2r_{i+1} - r_{i+2}\}, \ i \leq n - 2.$$

Let us now consider the lower bound computation. We need to find a vector r that is increasing and convex and that $0 \leq r \leq h$. Similarly as in the upper bounding case, we can suppose that vector h is increasing. If this is not the case, we can find an increasing vector h' such that $0 \leq h' \leq h$ as described in the lower bound computation case for the strong stochastic order. For an increasing vector h, an increasing and convex vector r such that $0 \leq r \leq h$ can be find by Algorithm 3. We illustrate this Algorithm on an example in Figure 1.

Algorithm 3. Computation of lower bounding increasing convex vector

---

Notation : We will denote by $1 < s_1 < s_2 < \ldots < s_m \leq n$ the indexes for which vector h strictly increases. Then we define $z_0 = 1$, and for i such that $1 \leq i \leq m$ we define z_i as the last index just before vector h strictly increases: $z_i = s_i - 1$, $1 \leq i \leq m$. Finally, if $z_m < n$ then we define $z_{m+1} = n$. For example for $(0.1, 0.3, 0.3, 0.5, 0.6)$ we have: $s_1 = 2, s_2 = 4, s_3 = 5$ and $z_0 = 1, z_1 = 1, z_2 = 3, z_3 = 4, z_5 = 5$.

1 $i = 0, \ r_1 = h_1$
2 while *($z_i < n$)* **do**
3 $a = \min_{j>i} \frac{h_{z_j} - h_{z_i}}{z_j - z_i}, \quad k = \arg\min_{j>i} \frac{h_{z_j} - h_{z_i}}{z_j - z_i}$
4   **for** *($u = z_i + 1$ **to** z_k)* **do** $r_u = a\,u + r_{z_i}$
5 $i = k$
6 end

Remark 1 (Complexity of Algorithms 1 and 2). The complexity of Algorithms 1 and 2 is quadratic with the size of the state space in the case of the full

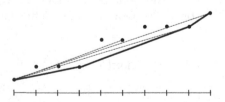

Fig. 1. Computation of the lower bounding increasing convex vector by Algorithm 3. The bounding vector is constructed per intervals, by taking the smallest slope at each step.

Table 1. Class $\mathcal{C}^{\mathcal{G}}$ bounds for mean absorption time

	exact	st-inf (new)	st-inf [4]	st-sup	icx-inf (new)	icx-inf [4]	icx-sup
A	3.3333	2.3243	2.3243	3.3333	3.2386	2.5556	3.3333
B	1.8182	1.4704	1.7544	16.6667	1.7544	1.7544	3.4379

matrix implementation. Indeed, we used a matrix notation in both algorithms to simplify the presentation. Note that for instance $(\boldsymbol{PK_{st}})_{i,j}$ can be simply obtained as $(\boldsymbol{PK_{st}})_{i,j+1} + P_{i,j}$, $j < n$ where $(\boldsymbol{PK_{st}})_{i,n} = P_{i,n}$. $\boldsymbol{PK_{icx}}$ can be easily computed using the fact that $\boldsymbol{K_{icx}} = \boldsymbol{K_{st}}^2$. In a similar way, $(\boldsymbol{AK_{\mathcal{F}}^{-1}})_{i,j}$ can be easily computed by applying the inverse transformation. For $\preceq_{st}$: $(\boldsymbol{AK_{st}}^{-1})_{i,j} = A_{i,j} - A_{i,j+1}$, $j < n$, where $(\boldsymbol{AK_{st}}^{-1})_{i,n} = A_{i,n}$.

Example 2. We illustrate here the $\mathcal{C}^{\mathcal{G}}$ absorption time bounds for mean absorption time (Corollary 2). Note however that Algorithms 1 and 2 can also be used to compute both transient and steady-state bounds. We consider a very simple example of an absorbing chain with n states, where state n is absorbing. We suppose that the initial state is 1 and for each state $i < n$ we have the following transitions:

- with probability a_i the system goes directly to the absorbing state n,
- with probability b_i the system goes to the next state $(i + 1)$,
- with probability $c_i = 1 - a_i - b_i$ the system returns to state 1.

Although the class $\mathcal{C}^{\mathcal{G}}$ bounds become interesting only for huge chains for which we cannot directly compute the absorption times using the classical numerical methods, we will consider here a small state space in order to easily compare the bounds with the exact values. In Table 1 we give the exact values and the bounds for the following parameters ($p = 0.6$, $n = 20$):

- Case A: $a_i = \frac{p}{2}$, $b_i = 1 - p$, $c_i = \frac{p}{2}$, $\forall i < n$.
- Case B: $a_i = \frac{pi}{n}$, $b_i = 1 - p$, $c_i = \frac{p(n-i)}{n}$, $\forall i < n$.

We can see from this example that it is not possible to compare the accuracy of the new upper bounds (providing lower bounds for absorption time) with those of [4]: they may be better or worse depending on the parameter values. We can see also that for this example $\preceq_{icx}$ bounds are more accurate than the $\preceq_{st}$ bounds as it is usually the case with class $\mathcal{C}$ or $\mathcal{C}^{\mathcal{G}}$ bounds.

4   Bounding PH-Distributions Modeling Service Times

We consider a task graph with n nodes representing tasks where arcs represent synchronization constraints. The task execution (service) times are defined by discrete time PHase (PH) distributions. Let d_i (resp. t_i) be the execution time (resp. the completion) time of task (node) i and $Preced(i)$ be the set of immediate predecessors of i. Since task i can start its execution once all the predecessors have completed, task i terminates its execution at time t_i :

$$t_i = d_i + max_{j \in Preced(i)} t_j$$

Without loss of generality, we assume that task 1 has no predecessor and task n has no successor. Therefore $t_1 = d_1$ and t_n is the completion time of the task graph which is the measure of interest.

The absorbing chains representing discrete PH distributions constitute the low-level formalism while the task graph formalism is the high level formalism. Let us remark here that high level formalism can be extended to any (max,+) formalism [2].

The state space size of the Markov chain to compute the completion time grows exponentially with the number of tasks even for exponential (geometric) execution times. The stochastic bounds on the execution times of acyclic task graphs have been proposed in [14]. These bounds are based on the compatibility of the $\preceq_{icx}$ order with the max and the $+$ operators. It has been proven that if $d_i^{inf} \preceq_{icx} d_i \preceq_{icx} d_i^{sup}$ $\forall i$, then the completion time of the same task graph by considering bounding execution times, provides bounds on the completion time: $t_n^{inf} \preceq_{icx} t_n \preceq_{icx} t_n^{sup}$. Thus we propose to compute class $\mathcal{C}^{\mathcal{G}} \preceq_{icx}$ bounds on d_i which can be computed by the close-form solution of absorbing time given in section 2.2.

In the high-level model, bounds are provided by considering specific distributions with the same mean for task execution times. Lower bounds are computed by deterministic random variables while upper bounds are computed by geometric random variables. We do not give the proof here but refer to [14] for bounds on task graphs. The lower bound is well-known as *folk theorem*: deterministic minimizes the randomness [2]. The upper bound is established for a family of distributions used in reliability [12]. An integer valued X is called Discrete New Better than Used (DNBU), if $[X - t | X > t] \preceq_{st} X, \forall t$; X is called DNBUE if this is satisfied for the expectations: $E[X - t | X > t] \leq E[X], \forall t$. Geometric distributions are the maximal distributions for DNBUE distributions: If X is DNBUE of mean m, then X is smaller in the $\preceq_{icx}$ sense than geometric distributed random variable of mean m ($X \preceq_{icx} Geom(m)$). In [3], it has been shown that monotone PH distributions belong to DNBU distributions. Therefore d_i^{sup} can be replaced by geometric distributions with the same means to provide upper bounds.

5   Conclusion

We have shown in this paper that the class $\mathcal{C}^{\mathcal{G}}$ matrices can be used to derive rapid bounds for absorption times. We proposed simple numerical algorithms to construct both lower and upper $\preceq_{st}$-(resp. $\preceq_{icx}$-)monotone bounds that belong to this class. To the best of our knowledge this is the first algorithm for lower $\preceq_{icx}$-monotone bound computation. For the simplicity of presentation, we consider here only discrete Markov chains. Similar results can be obtained for uniformizable continuous time Markov chains by applying the Algorithms 1 and 2 to the uniformized chain.

References

1. Abu-Amsha, O., Vincent, J.-M.: An algorithm to bound functionals of markov chains with large state space. In: 4th INFORMS Conference on Telecommunications, Boca Raton, FL (1998)
2. Baccelli, F., Cohen, G., Olsder, G.J., Quadrat, J.-P.: Synchronization and Linearity: An Algebra for Discrete Event Systems. Willey, New York (1992)
3. Ben Mamoun, M., Busic, A., Fourneau, J.M., Pekergin, N.: Increasing convex monotone markov chains: Theory, algorithm and applications. In: MAM 2006: Markov Anniversary Meeting, Raleigh, North Carolina, USA, pp. 189–210 (2006)
4. Ben Mamoun, M., Busic, A., Pekergin, N.: Generalized class C Markov chains and computation of closed-form bounding distributions. Probability in the Engineering and Informational Sciences 21(2), 235–260 (2007)
5. Ben Mamoun, M., Pekergin, N.: Computing closed-form stochastic bounds on the stationary distribution of Markov chains. In: Mathematics and Computer Science: Algorithms, Trees, Combinatorics and Probabilities, Basel, pp. 197–209. Birkhauser (2000)
6. Ben Mamoun, M., Pekergin, N.: Closed-form stochastic bounds on the stationary distribution of Markov chains. Probability in the Engineering and Informational Sciences 16(4), 403–426 (2002)
7. Ben Mamoun, M., Pekergin, N.: Computing closed-form stochastic bounds on transient distributions of Markov chains. In: SAINT-W '05: Proceedings of the 2005 Symposium on Applications and the Internet Workshops (SAINT 2005 Workshops), pp. 260–263. IEEE Computer Society Press, Washington, DC, USA (2005)
8. Ben Mamoun, M., Pekergin, N., Younès, S.: Model checking of continuous-time Markov chains by closed-form bounding distributions. In: QEST, pp. 189–198. IEEE Computer Society Press, Los Alamitos (2006)
9. Fourneau, J.-M., Kloul, L.: A precedence pepa model for performance and reliability analysis. In: Horváth, A., Telek, M. (eds.) EPEW 2006. LNCS, vol. 4054, pp. 1–15. Springer, Heidelberg (2006)
10. Fourneau, J.-M., Pekergin, N.: An algorithmic approach to stochastic bounds. In: Performance Evaluation of Complex Systems: Techniques and Tools, Performance 2002, Tutorial Lectures, pp. 64–88. Springer, London (2002)
11. Mahevas, S., Rubino, G.: Bound computation of dependability and performance measures. IEEE Trans. Comput. 50(5), 399–413 (2001)
12. Muller, A., Stoyan, D.: Comparison Methods for Stochastic Models and Risks. Wiley, New York (2002)
13. Muntz, R.R., de Souza e Silva, E., Goyal, A.: Bounding availability of repairable computer systems. IEEE Trans. on Computers 38(12), 1714–1723 (1989)
14. Pekergin, N., Vincent, J.-M.: Stochastic bounds on execution times of parallel programs. IEEE Trans. Softw. Eng. 17(10), 1005–1012 (1991)
15. Truffet, L.: Reduction technique for discrete time Markov chains on totally ordered state space using stochastic comparisons. Journal of Applied Probability 37(3), 795–806 (2000)

A Canonical Representation of Order 3 Phase Type Distributions[*]

Gábor Horváth and Miklós Telek

Department of Telecommunications
Budapest University of Technology and Economics
1521 Budapest, Hungary

Abstract. The characterization and the canonical representation of order n phase type distributions (PH(n)) is an open research problem.

This problem is solved for $n = 2$, since the equivalence of the acyclic and the general PH distributions has been proven for a long time. However, no canonical representations have been introduced for the general PH distribution class so far for $n > 2$. In this paper we summarize the related results for $n = 3$. Starting from these results we recommend a canonical representation of the PH(3) class and present a transformation procedure to obtain the canonical representation based on any (not only Markovian) vector-matrix representation of the distribution.

Using this canonical transformation method we evaluate the moment bounds of the PH(3) distribution set and present the results of our numerical investigations.

Keywords: Phase Type Distribution, Canonical Form, Moment Bounds.

1 Introduction

The Markovian structures are efficiently applied in various fields of stochastic modeling because of their computability and numerical stability. Phase type distributions are non-negative distributions with Markovian structure [10,7]. They are widely used in distribution approximation due to their computational advantages and easy integration in complex stochastic models.

The most common representation of a Phase type distribution is the definition of its initial probability vector α, and generator matrix A. This representation is known to be non-unique and non-minimal, thus there might be a vector α' and a matrix A', which define the same distribution. Furthermore, the number of parameters (non-determined elements) of this representation is $n^2 + n - 1$ when the cardinality of vector α' and square matrix A' is n (since A has n^2 elements and α has $n-1$ assuming no probability mass at zero), while the Laplace transform of PH(n) distributions – that uniquely determines the distribution – has $2n - 1$ roots and zeros.

[*] This work is partially supported by the Italian-Hungarian R&D project 9/2003 and by the OTKA K61709 grant.

K. Wolter (Ed.): EPEW 2007, LNCS 4748, pp. 48–62, 2007.
© Springer-Verlag Berlin Heidelberg 2007

To overcome these drawbacks a unique, minimal representation is required which is commonly referred to as canonical representation. A canonical representation is available for any order acyclic phase type distributions by Cumani [4], and it is also known that any PH(2) distribution can be transformed to an acyclic form [3] and this way the same canonical form is applicable of PH(2).

The canonical representation of PH(n) distributions is not known for $n \geq 4$ and we present a proposal for the canonical representation of the PH(3) class in this paper. The proposed representation has a special α vector and A matrix such that it has exactly $2n - 1 = 5$ parameters and it is proved to exist for all PH(3) distributions. We also provide a procedure for transforming any (not only Markovian) vector-matrix representation of the distribution to the canonical form. The transformation procedure is composed of explicit computational steps, whose most complex element is the evaluation of the eigenvalues of the generator matrix (finding the roots of an order 3 polynomial, for which symbolic solution is available).

Our results are very much based on the results of [5], where the unicyclic representation of PH(3) distributions is proved. Indeed, the presented canonical representation is unicyclic, but it extends the results of [5] with the careful analysis of the initial probability vector of the canonical representation, which is not taken into consideration in [5], because it aims to solve a different problem.

With the help of this transformation procedure, which fails only when the input vector-matrix pair cannot be transformed into a valid PH(3) representation, we investigate also the moments bounds of the PH(3) class. Some results on the bounds of the first 3 moments of PH(3) distributions are provided in [2], but the behaviour of the 4th and 5th moments are unknown to the best of our knowledge.

The rest of the paper is organized as follows. Section 2 gives the definition and the basic properties of PH(3) distributions. The unicyclic transformation of PH(3) distributions is summarized in Section 3 and the proposed canonical representation is presented in Section 4. Section 5 lists some applications of the canonical form and the associated transformation method and Section 6 demonstrates the behaviour of the parameters used in the transformation procedure. The paper is concluded in Section 7.

2 PH(3) Distributions

Let $\mathcal{X}$ be a continuous non-negative random variable with cumulative distribution function

$$F(t) = Pr(\mathcal{X} < t) = 1 - ve^{Ht}\mathbb{1} \,,$$

where the row vector v is referred to as the initial vector, square matrix H as the generator and $\mathbb{1}$ as the closing vector. Without loss of generality [8], we assume that the closing vector, $\mathbb{1}$, is a column vector of ones, i.e., $\mathbb{1} = [1, 1, \ldots, 1]^T$.

Since $\mathcal{X}$ is a continuous random variable, it has no probability mass at zero, i.e., $v\mathbb{1} = 1$. The density, the Laplace transform and the moments of $\mathcal{X}$ are

$$f(t) = ve^{Ht}(-H)\mathbb{1} , \tag{1}$$

$$f^*(s) = E(e^{-s\mathcal{X}}) = v(sI - H)^{-1}(-H)\mathbb{1} , \tag{2}$$

$$\mu_n = E(\mathcal{X}^n) = n!v(-H)^{-n}\mathbb{1} . \tag{3}$$

When the cardinality of vector v and of square matrix H is 3, we have the following cases:

- If $f(t) \geq 0$ and $\int_0^\infty f(t)dt = 1$, then X has an order 3 matrix exponential (ME(3)) distribution. The elements of v and H may be arbitrary real numbers.
- If v is a probability vector and H is a transient Markovian generator matrix (i.e., the generator matrix of a transient continuous-time Markov chain (CTMC)), then X has a PH(3) distribution. (The set of PH(3) distributions form a true subset of the ME(3) set.)

Vector v is a probability vector when $v_i \geq 0$, $v\mathbb{1} = 1$ and matrix H is a transient Markovian generator when $H_{ii} < 0$, $H_{ij} \geq 0$ for $i \neq j$, $H\mathbb{1} \leq 0$, $H\mathbb{1} \neq 0$. Scalars like H_{ij} denote the ijth element of matrix H.

Definition 1. *The (v, H) representation is a Markovian representation, if v is a probability vector and H is a transient Markovian generator matrix.*

In general it is not easy to check whether an $f(t)$ in (1) corresponding to a (v, H) pair is a density function. We have the following necessary conditions (those that we use in the sequel, [9]):

- the eigenvalues of H have negative real part,
- the largest eigenvalue of H is real, and
- the initial value of the density function is non-negative:

$$f(0) = -vH\mathbb{1} \geq 0 . \tag{4}$$

Definition 2. *Assuming B is a non-singular matrix such that $B\mathbb{1} = \mathbb{1}$ then the vector-matrix pair vB, $B^{-1}HB$ define a similarity transform of the vector-matrix pair v, H.*

Note that the vector-matrix pairs v, H and vB, $B^{-1}HB$ represent the same distribution, since

$$\hat{F}(t) = 1 - vBe^{B^{-1}HBt}\mathbb{1} = 1 - vBB^{-1}e^{Ht}B\mathbb{1} = 1 - ve^{Ht}\mathbb{1} = F(t) .$$

Example 1.

$$v = [0.1 \, 0.5 \, 0.4] , \quad H = \begin{bmatrix} -5 & 2 & 1 \\ 1 & -2 & 1 \\ 1 & 0 & -4 \end{bmatrix}$$

and

$$z = \begin{bmatrix} -1.1 & 2.5 & -0.4 \end{bmatrix}, \quad G = \begin{bmatrix} -11 & 10 & -1 \\ -6.6 & 6 & -1 \\ -15 & 20 & -6 \end{bmatrix}$$

represent the same distribution, since $z = vB$ and $G = B^{-1}HB$ with $B = \begin{bmatrix} 1 & 0 & 0 \\ -4 & 5 & 0 \\ 2 & 0 & -1 \end{bmatrix}$. (z, G) is a non-Markovian representation of this PH(3) distribution.

Now, we can refine the above definition of PH(3) distributions with the help of similarity transform.

Definition 3. *The random variable, $\mathcal{X}$, with density function (1), is PH(3) distributed if there is a non-singular matrix B, such that $B\mathbb{I} = \mathbb{I}$, and $(vB, B^{-1}HB)$ is a Markovian representation.*

Note that this definition implies that $f(t) \geq 0$.

One of the main goals of this paper is to decide if such similarity transform exists for a given non-Markovian vector-matrix pair, since the definition is obvious when the vector-matrix pair is Markovian.

3 Unicyclic Representation of PH(3) Distributions

The results of this paper are based on the unicyclic transformation of PH(3) distributions presented in [5]. We summarize the related results, in a bit modified way, for completeness.

Theorem 1. *[5] If (v, H) is a Markovian representation of a PH(3) distribution then it can be similarity transformed to the following unicyclic Markovian representation*

$$\pi = \begin{bmatrix} \pi_1 & \pi_2 & \pi_3 \end{bmatrix}, \quad A = \begin{bmatrix} -x_1 & 0 & x_{13} \\ x_2 & -x_2 & 0 \\ 0 & x_3 & -x_3 \end{bmatrix}, \tag{5}$$

where $x_1 \geq x_2 \geq x_3 > 0$, $0 \leq x_{13} \leq x_1$, $0 \leq \pi_1, \pi_2, \pi_3$, $\pi_1 + \pi_2 + \pi_3 = 1$ and the procedure in Figure 2 generates this unicyclic representation.

The structure of the resulting unicyclic PH distribution is depicted in Figure 1.

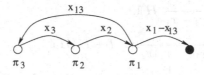

Fig. 1. The structure of the considered unicyclic PH(3) distribution

function PH(3)–to–unicyclic PH(3)
    input: v, H (Markovian)
    output: π, A (unicyclic)
begin
    $\lambda_1, \lambda_2, \lambda_3$ = decreasingly ordered eigenvalues of $-H$,
    $a_0 = \lambda_1 \lambda_2 \lambda_3$, $a_1 = \lambda_1 \lambda_2 + \lambda_1 \lambda_3 + \lambda_2 \lambda_3$, $a_2 = \lambda_1 + \lambda_2 + \lambda_3$,
    $\gamma_u = \frac{1}{3}\left(a_2 + 2\sqrt{a_2^2 - 3\,a_1}\right)$, $\gamma_0 = \frac{1}{3}\left(a_2 + \sqrt{a_2^2 - 3\,a_1}\right)$,
    $\gamma_\ell = \begin{cases} \lambda_1 \text{ if } \lambda_1 \in \text{real},\\ \gamma_0 \text{ if } \lambda_1 \in \text{complex}, \end{cases}$
    $\phi = \max\left\{-H_{1,1}, -H_{2,2}, -H_{3,3}\right\}$,
    $x_1 = \max\left\{\phi, \gamma_\ell\right\}$,
    $x_{13} = x_1 - a_0 \,/\, (x_1^2 - a_2\,x_1 + a_1)$,
    $x_2 = \frac{1}{2}\left(a_2 - x_1 + \sqrt{(a_2 - x_1)^2 - 4\left(x_1^2 - a_2\,x_1 + a_1\right)}\right)$,
    $x_3 = \frac{1}{2}\left(a_2 - x_1 - \sqrt{(a_2 - x_1)^2 - 4\left(x_1^2 - a_2\,x_1 + a_1\right)}\right)$,
    $\pi_1 = v\,H\,\mathbb{1} \,/\, (x_{13} - x_1)$,
    $\pi_2 = v\,(x_1 I + H)\,H\,\mathbb{1} \,/\, (x_{13} - x_1)\,x_2$,
    $\pi_3 = v\,(x_2 I + H)\,(x_1 I + H)\,H\,\mathbb{1} \,/\, (x_{13} - x_1)\,x_2\,x_3$,
    return $\pi = \begin{bmatrix} \pi_1 & \pi_2 & \pi_3 \end{bmatrix}$, $A = \begin{bmatrix} -x_1 & 0 & x_{13} \\ x_2 & -x_2 & 0 \\ 0 & x_3 & -x_3 \end{bmatrix}$,
end

Fig. 2. Unicyclic transformation of PH(3) distributions

The main difference between Theorem 1 ([5]) and the goal of this paper is that Theorem 1 assumes that (v, H) is Markovian, while we look for a transformation which is applicable for any non-Markovian (v, H) representation. For example the procedure of Figure 2 gives a proper unicyclic representation when it is called with the (v, H) pair of Example 1, but it gives complex results when it is called with the (z, G) representation of the same PH(3) distribution.

Let $\lambda_1, \lambda_2, \lambda_3$ denote the eigenvalues of $-H$ which are ordered such that $Re(\lambda_1) \geq Re(\lambda_2) \geq Re(\lambda_3)$ and a_0, a_1, a_2 the coefficients of the characteristic polynomial of $-H$, i.e.,

$$a_0 = \lambda_1 \lambda_2 \lambda_3, \ a_1 = \lambda_1 \lambda_2 + \lambda_1 \lambda_3 + \lambda_2 \lambda_3, \ a_2 = \lambda_1 + \lambda_2 + \lambda_3. \tag{6}$$

A simple interpretation of Theorem 1 is that the similarity transform with matrix B makes the transformed matrix to be unicyclic if B is composed by the column vectors $\{b_1, b_2, b_3\}$ where

$$
\begin{aligned}
b_1 &= \frac{1}{x_{13} - x_1}\,H\mathbb{1}, \\
b_2 &= \frac{1}{(x_{13} - x_1)x_2}\,(x_1 I + H)H\mathbb{1}, \\
b_3 &= \frac{1}{(x_{13} - x_1)x_2 x_3}\,(x_2 I + H)(x_1 I + H)H\mathbb{1},
\end{aligned}
\tag{7}
$$

and

$$x_{13} = x_1 - \frac{a_0}{x_1^2 - a_2 x_1 + a_1},$$

$$x_2 = \frac{a_2 - x_1 + \sqrt{(a_2 - x_1)^2 - 4(x_1^2 - a_2 x_1 + a_1)}}{2}, \tag{8}$$

$$x_3 = \frac{a_2 - x_1 - \sqrt{(a_2 - x_1)^2 - 4(x_1^2 - a_2 x_1 + a_1)}}{2}.$$

These expressions are obtained from the fact that the resulting generator A has the same characteristic polynomial as the original H, i.e., the parameters are obtained from the solution of the equations

$$a_0 = (x_1 - x_{13})x_2 x_3, \quad a_1 = x_1 x_2 + x_2 x_3 + x_3 x_1, \quad a_2 = x_1 + x_2 + x_3. \tag{9}$$

The transformation matrix B and the transformed unicyclic representation A depend on the choice of x_1. [5] showed the following properties of PH(3) distributions and this similarity transform.

P1) When H is a Markovian generator then

$$\gamma_u = \frac{a_2 + 2\sqrt{a_2^2 - 3a_1}}{3}, \tag{10}$$

$$\gamma_0 = \frac{a_2 + \sqrt{a_2^2 - 3a_1}}{3}, \tag{11}$$

$$\gamma_\ell = \begin{cases} \lambda_1, & \text{if } \lambda_1 \text{ is real,} \\ \gamma_0, & \text{if } \lambda_1 \text{ is complex} \end{cases} \tag{12}$$

are real and positive such that $\gamma_\ell \leq \gamma_u$.

P2) When $\gamma_\ell \leq x_1 \leq \gamma_u$ then the transformed generator matrix, $A = B^{-1}HB$ is Markovian such that $x_1 \geq x_2 \geq x_3 > 0$.

Indeed, property P2 holds also for all non-Markovian matrix H if its eigenvalues satisfies the requirements of PH(3) distributions:

- λ_3 is real and positive,
- $a_2^2 - 3a_1 \geq 0$.

Due to the fact that the similarity transform leaves the eigenvalues unchanged, this generalization of property P2 is a consequence of property P1 and Theorem 1.

We can summarize the results of [5] as follows. It defines a similarity transformation of PH(3) distributions to a unicyclic representation. This transformation depends on a parameter, x_1. [5] also defines the range of parameter x_1, (γ_ℓ, γ_u), where the transformed generator matrix is Markovian. The problem which remains open is how to set parameter x_1 such the initial vector is Markovian, i.e., is a proper probability vector.

In the procedure in Figure 2 parameter ϕ is used to ensure the positivity of the initial vector. Unfortunately that approach is not sufficient when we have a non-Markovian (v, H) representation, as it is the case with the non-Markovian representation of Example 1. The next section investigates the range of x_1 where the initial vector is Markovian.

4   Canonical Representation of PH(3) Distributions

Using the similarity matrix defined in (7) the elements of the initial vector $\pi = vB$ are:

$$\pi_1 = \frac{-vH\mathbb{1}}{x_1 - x_{13}} = \frac{d_1}{x_1 - x_{13}}, \tag{13}$$

$$\pi_2 = \frac{-v(x_1 I + H)H\mathbb{1}}{(x_1 - x_{13})x_2} = \frac{x_1 d_1 + d_2}{(x_1 - x_{13})x_2}, \tag{14}$$

$$\pi_3 = \frac{-v(x_2 I + H)(x_1 I + H)H\mathbb{1}}{(x_1 - x_{13})x_2 x_3} = \frac{x_1 x_2 d_1 + (x_1 + x_2)d_2 + d_3}{(x_1 - x_{13})x_2 x_3}, \tag{15}$$

where $d_i = -vH^i\mathbb{1}, i = 1, 2, 3$. The derivatives of the density function at 0 are closely related with these parameters since $f^{(i)}(0) = d_{i+1} = -vH^{i+1}\mathbb{1}$. Consequently, for a Markovian (v, H) pair

P3) $d_1 > 0$, or $d_1 = 0$ and $d_2 \geq 0$,

must hold for having a non-negative density around zero.

The canonical form we propose in this paper is based on the following theorem.

Theorem 2. *If (v, H) has a Markovian representation, then the similarity transform with matrix B, defined in (7), with parameter*

$$x_1 = \begin{cases} \max\{\gamma_2, \gamma_\ell\}, & \text{if } vH\mathbb{1} < 0, \\ \gamma_\ell, & \text{if } vH\mathbb{1} = 0, \end{cases} \tag{16}$$

$$\gamma_2 = -\frac{vH^2\mathbb{1}}{vH\mathbb{1}}, \tag{17}$$

provides a Markovian representation.

Proof   Due to Theorem 1 and $B\mathbb{1} = \mathbb{1}$ it is enough to prove that $\pi_1, \pi_2, \pi_3 \geq 0$ in (13), (14), (15), for some x_1 in the $[\gamma_\ell, \gamma_u]$ interval, where $x_1 - x_{13}, x_2, x_3$ are positive and $[\gamma_\ell, \gamma_u]$ is not empty.

$\pi_1 \geq 0$ follows immediately from (4), since if (v, H) has a Markovian representation, then its density is non-negative at 0.

When $vH\mathbb{1} = 0$, π_2 must be non-negative according to property P3. When $vH\mathbb{1} < 0$, we can re-write (14) as:

$$\pi_2 = \frac{-vH\mathbb{1}}{(x_1 - x_{13})x_2}(x_1 - \gamma_2). \tag{18}$$

The first term of (18) is positive and the second term is non-negative when $x_1 = \max\{\gamma_2, \gamma_\ell\}$ according to (16).

For the analysis of π_3 we re-write (15) as

$$\pi_3 = \frac{1}{(x_1 - x_{13})x_2 x_3} \underbrace{(x_1 x_2 d_1 + (x_1 + x_2)d_2 + d_3)}_{g(x_1)} \qquad (19)$$

The first term is positive again, thus it remains to prove that $g(x_1) > 0$ if x_1 is according to (16). The first derivative of $g(x_1)$ has two roots:

$$\frac{d}{dx_1} g(x_1) = 0 \quad \Leftrightarrow \quad x_1 = \frac{a_2 \pm \sqrt{a_2^2 - 3a_1}}{3}. \qquad (20)$$

The larger root equals to γ_0, hence $g(x_1)$ is a monotone function when $x_1 > \gamma_0$. In the $x_1 > \gamma_0$ region the increasing/decreasing behaviour of $g(x_1)$ is determined by the sign of the second derivative at $x_1 = \gamma_0$:

$$\frac{d^2}{dx_1^2} g(x_1)|_{x_1 = \gamma_0} = \frac{-2(a_2 d_1 + 4d_1 \sqrt{a_2^2 - 3a_1} + 3d_2)}{3\sqrt{a_2^2 - 3a_1}} \qquad (21)$$

When $d_1 = -v\boldsymbol{H}\mathbb{1} = 0$, then the second derivative is non-positive due to property P1 and P3 and when $d_1 = -v\boldsymbol{H}\mathbb{1} > 0$ we have

$$\frac{d^2}{dx_1^2} g(x_1)|_{x_1 = \gamma_0} = \frac{-2(a_2 + 4\sqrt{a_2^2 - 3a_1} - 3\gamma_2)}{3d_1\sqrt{a_2^2 - 3a_1}}$$

$$= -\underbrace{\frac{2}{3d_1\sqrt{a_2^2 - 3a_1}}}_{\geq 0} \left[3\underbrace{(\gamma_u - \gamma_2)}_{\geq 0} + \underbrace{(3\gamma_u - a_2)}_{\geq 0} \right] \leq 0, \qquad (22)$$

where the non-negativity of the first under-braced term follows from property P1, the non-negativity of the second term must hold since $(v, \boldsymbol{H})$ is Markovian and according to Theorem 1 it must have a unicyclic representation $(x_1 \leq \gamma_u)$ with a non-negative π_2 $(x_1 \geq \gamma_2)$. The non-negativity of the third under-braced term follows from $Re(\lambda_1) \leq \gamma_u$ and the fact that $Re(\lambda_1) \geq Re(\lambda_2) \geq Re(\lambda_3)$.

If the second derivative in (22) equals to 0 it means that there is only a single x_1 value, $x_1 = \gamma_u$, which results in a Markovian representation.

If the second derivative in (22) is negative then $g(x_1)$ has a local maximum at $x_1 = \gamma_0$, and it is monotone decreasing function at $x_1 > \gamma_0$. To obtain a valid generator $x_1 > \gamma_\ell$ must hold as well, and since $\gamma_\ell \geq \gamma_0$, the largest feasible π_3 value is obtained at $x_1 = \gamma_\ell$. Since $(v, \boldsymbol{H})$ has a unicyclic representation according to Theorem 1, π_3 is non-negative in this point. □

We demonstrate the numerical behaviour of π_2 and π_3 as a function of x_1 in Section 6.

4.1   The Canonical Transformation Procedure

The transformation procedure is presented in Figure 3. If the procedure exits with one of the error messages then the input does not represent a PH(3) distribution. If the procedure completes, it gives back the canonical representation of the given PH(3) distribution, which is Markovian, minimal and unique as it is discussed in the next subsection.

function Canonical–PH(3)–transformation
    input: v, H (any matrix representation)
    output: π, A (Canonical representation if v, H is a PH(3))
begin
    if $v_1 + v_2 + v_3 \neq 1$
        error "Probability mass at 0",
    $\lambda_1, \lambda_2, \lambda_3$ = decreasingly ordered eigenvalues of $-H$,
    if $\lambda_3 < 0$ **or** $\lambda_3 \in \mathbb{C}$ **or** $v H \mathbb{1} < 0$
        error "Invalid eigenvalues",
    $a_0 = \lambda_1 \lambda_2 \lambda_3$, $a_1 = \lambda_1 \lambda_2 + \lambda_1 \lambda_3 + \lambda_2 \lambda_3$, $a_2 = \lambda_1 + \lambda_2 + \lambda_3$
    if $a_2^2 - 3 a_1 < 0$
        error "Invalid characteristic polynomial",
    $\gamma_u = \frac{1}{3} \left(a_2 + 2\sqrt{a_2^2 - 3 a_1} \right),$ $\gamma_0 = \frac{1}{3} \left(a_2 + \sqrt{a_2^2 - 3 a_1} \right),$
    $\gamma_\ell = \begin{cases} \lambda_1 & \text{if } \lambda_1 \in \text{real}, \\ \gamma_0 & \text{if } \lambda_1 \in \text{complex}, \end{cases}$
    if $v H \mathbb{1} > 0$ **or** $(v H \mathbb{1} == 0$ **and** $v H^2 \mathbb{1} > 0)$
        error "Negative density around 0",
    $\gamma_2 = \begin{cases} -v H^2 \mathbb{1} / v H \mathbb{1} & \text{if } v H \mathbb{1} < 0, \\ 0 & \text{if } v H \mathbb{1} == 0, \end{cases}$
    if $\gamma_2 > \gamma_u$
        error "π_2 is negative",
    $x_1 = \max \{\gamma_2, \gamma_\ell\},$
    $x_{13} = x_1 - a_0 / (x_1^2 - a_2 x_1 + a_1),$
    $x_2 = \frac{1}{2} \left(a_2 - x_1 + \sqrt{(a_2 - x_1)^2 - 4 (x_1^2 - a_2 x_1 + a_1)} \right),$
    $x_3 = \frac{1}{2} \left(a_2 - x_1 - \sqrt{(a_2 - x_1)^2 - 4 (x_1^2 - a_2 x_1 + a_1)} \right),$
    $\pi_1 = v H \mathbb{1} / (x_{13} - x_1),$
    $\pi_2 = v (x_1 I + H) H \mathbb{1} / (x_{13} - x_1) x_2,$
    $\pi_3 = v (x_2 I + H) (x_1 I + H) H \mathbb{1} / (x_{13} - x_1) x_2 x_3,$
    if $\pi_3 < 0$
        error "π_3 is negative",
    return $\pi = \begin{bmatrix} \pi_1 & \pi_2 & \pi_3 \end{bmatrix}$, $A = \begin{bmatrix} -x_1 & 0 & x_{13} \\ x_2 & -x_2 & 0 \\ 0 & x_3 & -x_3 \end{bmatrix}$,
end

Fig. 3. Canonical transformation of PH(3) distributions

4.2   Properties of the Proposed Canonical Form

If v is an arbitrary vector and H is an arbitrary matrix of cardinality 3 such that (v, H) represents an order 3 phase type distribution, then (π, A) is a Markovian representation of this PH(3) distribution.

(π, A) is unique, in the sense that for any (v, H) representation of a PH(3) distribution the procedure provides the same (π, A) pair.

The PH(3) distributions are known to be determined by 5 parameters. E.g., the first 5 moments, or the 5 coefficients of the Laplace rational transform uniquely determines a PH(3) distribution. Although not obvious from the first sight, the presented canonical form is also determined by exactly 5 independent parameters. In the unicyclic form [5] there are 6 parameters $(x_1, x_2, x_3, x_{13}, \pi_1, \pi_2)$ and in the transformation procedure presented in this paper one of these parameters is additionally set to a special value. The following constraint decreases the number of parameters to 5:

f1) λ_1 real, $\gamma_2 < \gamma_\ell$ $\quad \rightarrow \quad$ $x_{13} = 0$,
f2) λ_1 complex, $\gamma_2 < \gamma_\ell$ $\quad \rightarrow \quad$ $x_1 = x_2$,
f3) $\gamma_\ell < \gamma_2$ $\quad \rightarrow \quad$ $\pi_2 = 0$.

Indeed, these cases represent three different forms of the canonical representation.

It is an additional nice feature of the proposed canonical form that it is compatible with the widely used canonical representation of acyclic phase type distributions [4], since when (v, H) represents an order 3 acyclic phase type distribution, then form f1 gives the Cumani's canonical representation of that distribution.

5   Practical Application of the Canonical form and the Transformation Procedure

5.1   Phase Type Fitting

The currently available PH(3) fitting methods are either restricted to the acyclic subclass of PH(3) distributions (e.g., [6]) or they are not restricted, but their performance is limited by the fact that they optimize too many parameters (e.g., [1]). The canonical representation allows to eliminate the weakness of the second type of fitting methods. Using the 3 potential forms of the canonical representation one can compose 3 fitting methods (for form f1, f2 and f3) with minimal number of parameters and the best of the 3 gives the best fit over the whole PH(3) class.

5.2   Moment Matching with PH(3)

The presented transformation procedure is also applicable for moment matching with PH(3) distributions. For a given set of $\{\mu_1, \dots \mu_5\}$ moments we can generate a PH(3) distribution, whose first five moments are the same. This moments fitting procedure is composed by the following 2 steps.

- The first step is to compute a vector and matrix pair, v, H, for which $i! v(-H)^{-i} \mathbb{1} = \mu_i, i = 1, \ldots, 5$. The procedure of Appie van de Liefvoort in [12] produces such v, H pair with a proper transformation of the closing vector[1].
- Starting from v, H the canonical PH(3) transformation procedure generates the Markovian representation of the PH(3) distribution, whose first 5 moments are $\{\mu_1, \ldots \mu_5\}$.

Example 2. For example, when the first 5 moments are $\{1.85111, 5.45136, 22.2838, 118.094, 774.513\}$ the procedure of [12] gives

$$v = \begin{bmatrix} 1/3 & 1/3 & 1/3 \end{bmatrix}, \quad H = \begin{bmatrix} -2.92628 & 44.7789 & -40.8522 \\ -0.398989 & -3.56926 & 3.0189 \\ -0.267678 & 2.9026 & -3.68557 \end{bmatrix},$$

and the canonical transformation procedure gives

$$\pi = \begin{bmatrix} 0.0865519 & 0.124609 & 0.788839 \end{bmatrix}, \quad A = \begin{bmatrix} -4.20997 & 0 & 0.360255 \\ 4.20997 & -4.20997 & 0 \\ 0 & 1.76118 & -1.76118 \end{bmatrix}.$$

5.3   Moments Bounds of the PH(3) Class

The presented transformation procedure is also applicable for evaluating the borders of the PH(3) distribution class. Indeed the above described moment fitting procedure terminates properly only when $\{\mu_1, \ldots \mu_5\}$ are the moments of a PH(3) distribution and the moment matching method aborts with some error if there is no PH(3) distribution whose moments are $\{\mu_1, \ldots \mu_5\}$.

To demonstrate the moment bounds of the PH(3) distribution set we first introduce the normalized moments $n_i = \frac{\mu_i}{\mu_1 \mu_{i-1}}$. The normalized moments are time unit independent "normalized" quantities, which carry the structural information of the moments apart of a time unit dependent scaling factor. n_2 is closely associated with the squared coefficient of variation, c_v^2. $n_2 = c_v^2 + 1$. The second and third normalized moments of APH(n) distributions are studied in [2,11].

Example 3. We study the fourth and fifth normalized moments of PH(3) distributions with two pairs of second and third normalized moments.

The first point, $n_2 = 1.6$ and $n_3 = 2.3$, is taken in the $n_2 < 2$ range, where the coefficient of variation is less than 1, while the second point, $n_2 = 2.018$ and $n_3 = 3.036$, is taken in the $n_2 > 2$ range. The feasible range of normalized moment n_4 and n_5 are depicted in Figure 4 and 5, respectively. It is interesting to see that the fifth normalized moment, n_5, is both upper and lower bounded as well in the first case, while it is only lower bounded in the second case.

---

[1] In [12] the initial and the closing vector are $\{1, 0, 0, \ldots, 0\}$. In our case the closing vector is $\{1, 1, \ldots, 1\}$, hence a similarity transformation is required.

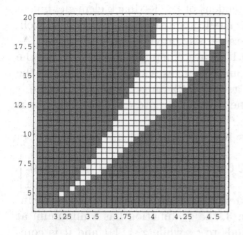
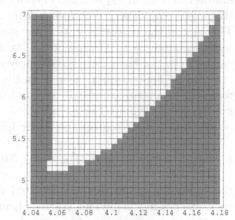

Fig. 4. Legal n_4, n_5 normalized moments of PH(3) distributions when $n_2 = 1.6$ and $n_3 = 2.3$

Fig. 5. Legal n_4, n_5 normalized moments of PH(3) distributions when $n_2 = 2.018$ and $n_3 = 3.036$

The presented canonical transformation procedure gives a tool for the numerical investigation of the moments bounds, but the detailed qualitative investigation of these moments bounds is out of the scope of this paper.

6   Numerical Examples

6.1   Dependence of Bounding Quantities on the Matrix Elements

We demonstrate the dependence of the bounding quantities of the canonical representation, $\gamma_0, \gamma_\ell, \gamma_2, \gamma_u$, on the elements of the PH representation through some numerical examples.

We study the dependence of the bounding quantities on the initial distribution using the following representation, $v = \begin{bmatrix} x & 0.8-x & 0.2 \end{bmatrix}$ and $H = \begin{bmatrix} -3 & 0 & 2.5 \\ 2 & -2 & 0 \\ 0 & 1 & -1 \end{bmatrix}$.

The result is presented in Figure 6. In this case all quantities which are associated with the Markovian representation of the generator matrix (the coefficients of the characteristic polynomial, a_0, a_1, a_2, the eigenvalues, $\lambda_1, \lambda_2, \lambda_3$ and the associated bounding quantities, $\gamma_0 = 2.57735, \gamma_\ell = 2.57735, \gamma_u = 3.1547$) remain constant and only γ_2 changes which is associated with the Markovian representation of the initial vector. The x_1 value of the canonical representation is determined by γ_ℓ if $x < 0.660434$ and it is determined by γ_2 for larger x values.

The dependence on the feedback element, x_{13}, is investigated using $v = \begin{bmatrix} 0.62 & 0.246 & 0.134 \end{bmatrix}$ and $H = \begin{bmatrix} -3 & 0 & x \\ 2 & -2 & 0 \\ 0 & 1 & -1 \end{bmatrix}$. The curves in Figure 7 indicates another behaviour. $\gamma_2 = 2.20645$ is independent of the feedback element, but in this case some other, generator matrix related quantities, are constant as well. The a_1 and the a_2 coefficients of the characteristic polynomial are constant. As a consequence $\gamma_0 = 2.57735$ and $\gamma_u = 3.1547$ are independent on x_1. Only the a_0 coefficient of the characteristic polynomial changes with x, which makes the eigenvalues depend on x as well. In the $x \in \{0, 0.2\}$ range the λ_1 eigenvalue is real and it determines the x_1 value of the canonical representation. When x is greater γ_0 determines the x_1 value.

The most complicated behaviour has been obtained when the intensity of a transition is changing. For $v = \begin{bmatrix} 0.62 \ 0.246 \ 0.134 \end{bmatrix}$ and $\boldsymbol{H} = \begin{bmatrix} -3 & 0 & 1 \\ x & -x & 0 \\ 0 & 1 & -1 \end{bmatrix}$ the bounding quantities are depicted in Figure 8. In this case γ_2 has a linearly decreasing behaviour starting from 3, the γ_u function has a minimum at $x = 1$, the λ_1 eigenvalue is real and equals to γ_ℓ while $x < 1.1$ and it is complex and $\gamma_\ell = \gamma_0$ when $x > 1.1$. γ_0 is an increasing function of x starting from 2.21525. The x_1 value equals to γ_2 when $x < 2.01$ and it equals to γ_0 for larger x.

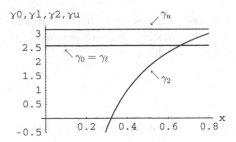

Fig. 6. Dependence of bounding quantities on the initial vector

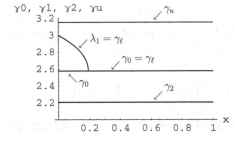

Fig. 7. Dependence of bounding quantities on the feedback element

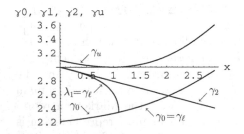

Fig. 8. Dependence of bounding quantities on a transition rate

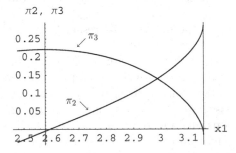

Fig. 9. The function of $\pi_2 \ \pi_3$ as a function of x_1

6.2 Dependence of the Unicyclic Representation on x_1

In the majority of the cases γ_ℓ and/or γ_u allows a Markovian representation. The case when $v = \begin{bmatrix} 0.72\ 0.146\ 0.134 \end{bmatrix}$ and $H = \begin{bmatrix} -3 & 0 & 2.025 \\ 2 & -2 & 0 \\ 0 & 1 & -1 \end{bmatrix}$, is different, since in this case $\gamma_2 = 2.59444 > \gamma_\ell = \gamma_0 = 2.57735$ and $\gamma_u = 3.1547 > \gamma_z = 3.15186$, i.e., none of γ_ℓ and γ_u results in a Markovian representation. The behaviours of π_2 and π_3 are depicted in Figure 9. The y axis is set to $\gamma_\ell = \gamma_0$ and the grid line to γ_u. It is also visible that π_3 has a maximum at γ_0.

7 Conclusion

In a number of practical applications it is very efficient using the canonical representation of PH distributions that have as few parameters as possible. The problem of canonical representation of high order PH distributions is still open, but in this paper we presented a canonical representation for order 3 PH distributions. This canonical representation uses the unicyclic structure of He and Zhang and additionally ensures that the initial vector is positive.

We demonstrated potential applications of the canonical form and the associated transformation method through the analysis of the moments bounds of the PH(3) class.

Acknowledgement

The authors thank the effort of Laura Fábián whose numerical investigations led to the basic idea of this paper.

References

1. Asmussen, S., Nerman, O.: Fitting Phase-type distributions via the EM algorithm. In: Proceedings: Symposium i Advent Statistik, Copenhagen, pp. 335–346 (1991)
2. Bobbio, A., Horváth, A., Telek, M.: Matching three moments with minimal acyclic phase-type distributions. Stochastic Models 21(2-3), 303–323 (2005)
3. Cox, D.R.: A use of complex probabilities in the theory of stochastic processes. Proc. Cambridge Phil. Soc. 51, 313–319 (1955)
4. Cumani, A.: On the canonical representation of homogeneous Markov processes modelling failure-time distributions. Microelectronics and Reliability 22, 583–602 (1982)
5. Qi-Ming, H., Hanqin, Z.: A note on unicyclic representation of ph-distributions. Stochastic Models 21, 465–483 (2005)
6. Horváth, A., Telek, M.: PhFit: A general purpose phase type fitting tool. In: Field, T., Harrison, P.G., Bradley, J., Harder, U. (eds.) TOOLS 2002. LNCS, vol. 2324, pp. 82–91. Springer, Heidelberg (2002)
7. Latouche, G., Ramaswami, V.: Introduction to Matrix-Analytic Methods in Stochastic Modeling. Series on statistics and applied probability. ASA-SIAM (1999)

8. Lipsky, L.: Queueing Theory: A linear algebraic approach. MacMillan, New York (1992)
9. Mocanu, S., Commault, C.: Sparse representations of phase-type distributions. Commun. Stat., Stochastic Models 15(4), 759–778 (1999)
10. Neuts, M.: Matrix-Geometric Solutions in Stochastic Models. John Hopkins University Press, Baltimore, MD, USA (1981)
11. Osogami, T., Harchol-Balter, M.: A closed form solution for mapping general distributions to minimal ph distributions. In: Kemper, P., Sanders, W.H. (eds.) TOOLS 2003. LNCS, vol. 2794, pp. 200–217. Springer, Heidelberg (2003)
12. van de Liefvoort, A.: The moment problem for continuous distributions. Technical report, University of Missouri, WP-CM-1990-02, Kansas City (1990)

SPAMR: Extending PAMR with Stochastic Time[*]

Natalia López, Manuel Núñez, and Ismael Rodríguez

Dept. Sistemas Informáticos y Computación
Universidad Complutense de Madrid, E-28040 Madrid. Spain
{natalia,mn,isrodrig}@sip.ucm.es

Abstract. In this paper we introduce time information in PAMR (Process Algebra for the Management of Resources). PAMR is a process algebra that simplifies the task of specifying processes whose behavior strongly depend on the resources that they have. One of the drawbacks of PAMR is that there is not an appropriate notion of time. In this paper we will consider that the duration of actions is controlled by a random variable. These random variables will take values, according to some probability distribution functions, that may depend, in particular, on the available resources. We present two examples showing the main features of our stochastic version of PAMR.

1 Introduction

The process algebra PAMR [18], as well as its adaptions/extensions [20,21], represents a formalism to specify systems where resources play a fundamental role. The main advantage of PAMR consists in the separation between the *behavior* of processes (specified in a usual process algebra) and the management of the *resources* that a process can make use of. By doing so, specifications get clearer as many details can be encoded in the resources part. Let us show the main advantages by using a simple example. Let us consider the classical five dining philosophers example. If we try to specify this problem in a CCS-like language, we have to consider that forks are usual processes. Besides, the philosophers must also include some actions indicating *communication* with the forks. In PAMR we may separate between *real* processes (the philosophers) and available resources (the forks). In our case, a philosopher is simply defined as

$$\text{philosopher}_i ::= \text{think} \,;\, \text{eat} \,;\, \text{philosopher}_i$$

We consider that the philosopher i needs no resources to think. Besides, he needs forks i and $(i \bmod 5) + 1$ to perform the action eat.

Another interesting feature of PAMR allows processes to exchange resources among them. By doing so, processes will improve their performances. For example, consider a system where two processes are running. One of them is making intensive use of RAM while the other one is mainly sending packets through a

---

[*] Research partially supported by the Spanish MEC project WEST/FAST TIN2006-15578-C02-01 and the Marie Curie RTN *TAROT* (MRTN-CT-2003-505121).

K. Wolter (Ed.): EPEW 2007, LNCS 4748, pp. 63–79, 2007.

LAN. So, the first process should have a big amount of memory (and a limited access to the local bus) while the situation should be the opposite for the other process. Besides, let us suppose that this situation may change as time passes (for example, the first process may eventually become an I/O-bound process). In order to model such a situation, we could consider a centralizer allocating the available resources to processes. Nevertheless, in PAMR no centralizer is needed. Processes will exchange resources according both to some predefined policy and to some information about their preferences towards resources. So, an exchange is allowed if it is profitable with respect to the chosen policy, for example, if some processes improve and no one deteriorates. This first policy is equivalent to consider that processes are the real owners of resources. Another possibility is that exchanges are allowed only if the whole system improves. The results of this policy are similar to consider a centralizer who looks for an improvement of the global behavior of the system.

Even though PAMR has been already applied to different fields (from concurrent systems to a variant of e-commerce [20] or to the specification of autonomous agents [21,17]) we think that there is (at least) an aspect that could be more satisfactorily covered: The modeling of time. In PAMR, a primitive notion of time could be introduced by using the *necessity function*. In short, each process has a function $n : \text{Act} \times \mathbb{R}_+^n \longrightarrow \mathbb{R}_+ \cup \{\infty\}$. A value $n(a, \bar{x}) = \infty$ indicates that the amount of resources owned by the process (that is, $\bar{x}$) is not enough to perform the action a. If $n(a, \bar{x}) = r \in \mathbb{R}_+$, the value r could be considered as the *time* that the process needs to perform a, given the resources $\bar{x}$. In fact, this approach was somehow implemented in [19]. However, it presents some problems. First, in PAMR there is no notion of concurrent passing of time. In other words, if we have a parallel composition of several processes, the passage of time in one of the processes could not be reflected in the other ones. Second, this notion of time would be completely deterministic, that is, for any n, a, and $\bar{x}$ the *time* that the process needs to perform a is fixed. It seems more interesting to consider a *stochastic* approach where the necessity function returns a random variable. So, we may consider that $n(a, \bar{x}) = \xi$ indicates that, if the process may use the resources $\bar{x}$, then it will perform the action a before time t with probability equal to $F_\xi(t)$, where F_ξ is the probability distribution function associated with ξ. For example, we could have that ξ is uniformly distributed over the interval $[0, \frac{1}{\sum x_i}]$.

In order to include our notion of time, we profit from the study in the field of *stochastic process algebras* (e.g. [8,1,11,3,10]). Even though most of the models that were originally proposed were restricted to only use exponential distributions, there are already several proposals for stochastic models with general distributions (e.g. [9,13,5,15,4,14,6,7]). The restriction to *Markovian* models simplifies several of the problems that appear when considering general distributions. In particular, some quantities of interest, like reachability probabilities or steady-state probabilities, can be efficiently calculated by using well known methods on Markov chains. Besides, the (operational) definition of the language is usually simpler than the one for languages allowing general distributions.

Nevertheless, this restriction does not allow to properly specify systems where time distributions are not exponential. Moreover, the main weakness of non-exponential models, that is the analysis of properties, can be (partially) overcome by restricting the class of distributions. A good candidate are phase-type distributions, where the analysis of performance measures can be efficiently done in some general cases. There are other proposals dealing with these limitations in a different way. For example, [12,22] show how model checking can be extended to semi-Markov Chains while [15] presents a framework for translating specifications with general distributions into a functional language where simulations can be performed.

In order to cope with the usual problem of general distributions in the scope of parallel compositions, actions are split into two events: *start* and *termination*. A similar mechanism is used in [5,15]. Nevertheless, in those approaches stochastic and action transitions are separated (already in the syntax on the corresponding languages). In our case, transitions must contain both information about the action and the associated random variable. Besides, processes engaged in the execution of an action (that is, they have performed a start event but they did not perform the corresponding termination event) will have some trading limitations. For example, they will not be able to trade resources that they need to perform the corresponding action. These two facts complicate the operational rules for the definition of systems.

The rest of the paper is structured as follows. In Section 2 we present our language, that we call SPAMR and its operational semantics. In Section 3 we present two examples showing the main features of SPAMR. Finally, in Section 4 we present our conclusions and some lines for future work.

2   The Language SPAMR

In this section we present the syntax and operational semantics of our language. In SPAMR, as well as in PAMR, systems are defined in two steps. First, we introduce the notion of process. A *process* consists of a behavior (expressed in a LOTOS-like language) together with some information about resources (the amounts that it owns, how they are consumed/produced after performing actions, etc). A *system* is defined as the parallel composition of several processes. These processes may perform exchanges of resources so that they improve with respect to a given policy. Once no more exchanges can be made, indicating that a (somehow) good distribution of resources has been reached, processes may perform actions (possibly by synchronizing with other processes). Next we introduce some preliminary notations.

Definition 1. We consider $\mathbb{R}_+ = \{x \in \mathbb{R} \mid x \geq 0\}$. For any $r \in \mathbb{R}_+$, we have that $\mathtt{trunc}(r)$ denotes the natural number resulting from discarding the decimal part of the real r.

We will usually denote *vectors* in $\mathbb{R}^n$ (for $n \geq 2$) by $\overline{x}, \overline{y}, \ldots$ Given $\overline{x} \in \mathbb{R}^n$, x_i denotes its *i-th* component. Let $\overline{x}, \overline{y} \in \mathbb{R}^n$. We define the addition of $\overline{x}$ and $\overline{y}$

as the vector $\overline{x} + \overline{y} = (x_1 + y_1, \ldots, x_n + y_n)$. We write $\overline{x} \leq \overline{y}$ if we have $x_i \leq y_i$ for all $1 \leq i \leq n$.

Let A be a set and $n, m \geq 1$. We denote by $A^{n \times m}$ the *matrices* of dimension $n \times m$ of elements of A (we use calligraphic letters $\mathcal{E}, \mathcal{E}_1 \ldots$ to range over $A^{n \times m}$). $\qquad \square$

Stochastic information is introduced by means of *random variables*. We will consider that the sample space (that is, the domain of random variables) is the set of real numbers $\mathbb{R}$ and that random variables take positive values only in $\mathbb{R}^+$, that is, given a random variable ξ we have $F_\xi(t) = 0$ for all $t < 0$. The reason for this restriction is that random variables will always be associated with time distributions.

Definition 2. We denote by $\mathcal{V}$ the set of random variables. We will extend this set with a special symbol $\xi_\infty \notin \mathcal{V}$. It will be used to represent the case when an action cannot be performed (because the process does not own enough resources). We consider $\mathcal{V}_* = \mathcal{V} \cup \{\xi_\infty\}$ ($\xi, \psi, \ldots$ to range over $\mathcal{V}_*$).

Let ξ be a random variable. Its *probability distribution function*, denoted by F_ξ, is the function $F_\xi : \mathbb{R} \to [0, 1]$ such that $F_\xi(x) = \mathrm{P}(\xi \leq x)$, where $\mathrm{P}(\xi \leq x)$ is the probability that ξ assumes values less than or equal to x.

We consider a *distinguished* random variable. By *unit* we denote a random variable such that $F_{unit}(x) = 1$ for all $x \geq 0$, that is, *unit* is distributed as the Dirac distribution in 0.

Let ξ_1 and ξ_2 be independent random variables with probability distribution functions F_{ξ_1} and F_{ξ_2}, respectively. We define the *combined addition* of ξ_1 and ξ_2, denoted by $\xi_1 \oplus \xi_2$, as the random variable with probability distribution function defined as $F_{\xi_1 \oplus \xi_2}(x) = F_{\xi_1}(x) + F_{\xi_2}(x) - F_{\xi_1}(x) \cdot F_{\xi_2}(x)$. This operator can be generalized to an arbitrary (finite) number of random variables. Let $\Psi = \{\xi_i\}_{i \in I}$ be a non-empty finite set of independent random variables. We define the *combined addition* of the variables in Ψ, denoted by $\oplus \Psi$, as the random variable with probability distribution function defined, for any $x \in \mathbb{R}$, as $F_{\oplus \Psi}(x) = \sum_{\emptyset \subset \Phi \subseteq \Psi} (-1)^{(|\Phi|+1)} F_{\otimes \Phi}(x)$ where $F_{\otimes \Psi}(x) = \prod_{i \in I} F_{\xi_i}(x)$. Note that for singleton sets of random variables, $\Psi = \{\xi\}$, we have $\oplus \Psi = \xi$. We consider, for convenience, $F_{\oplus \emptyset}(x) = 0$ for all $x \in \mathbb{R}$.

Let ξ and ϕ be two random variables. We say that ξ and ϕ are *identically distributed*, denoted by $\xi \asymp \phi$, if for any $t \geq 0$, we have that $F_\xi(t) = F_\phi(t)$. $\quad \square$

The operator $\oplus$ can be used when random variables are combined. Let us note that this operator does not correspond with the usual definition of addition of random variables (we will denote that addition of random variables by $+$). Actually, it is easy to show that $F_{\oplus \Psi}$ computes the probability distribution function associated with the random variable $\min(\Psi)$. Finally, let us remark that if we consider the addition of random variables, for all random variable ξ we have that $\xi + unit = \xi$.

Example 1. Let us show some examples of random variables and the probability distribution functions governing their behavior. Let us consider the following probability distribution functions:

$$F_1(x) = \begin{cases} 0 & \text{if } x \leq 0 \\ \frac{x}{3} & \text{if } 0 < x < 3 \\ 1 & \text{if } x \geq 3 \end{cases}$$

$$F_2(x) = \begin{cases} 0 & \text{if } x < 4 \\ 1 & \text{if } x \geq 4 \end{cases}$$

$$F_3(x) = \begin{cases} 1 - e^{-3 \cdot x} & \text{if } x \geq 0 \\ 0 & \text{if } x < 0 \end{cases}$$

If a random variable ξ_1 has as associated probability distribution function F_1 then we say that ξ_1 is uniformly distributed in the interval $[0, 3]$. Uniform distributions allow us to keep compatibility with time intervals in (non-stochastic) timed models in the sense that the same *weight* is assigned to all the times in the interval. If ξ_2 has as associated probability distribution function F_2 then we say that ξ_2 follows a Dirac distribution in 4. The idea is that the corresponding delay will be equal to 4 time units. Dirac distributions allow us to simulate deterministic delays appearing in timed models. If ξ_3 has as associated probability distribution function F_3 then we say that ξ_3 is exponentially distributed with parameter 3. □

One of the components of a process will be given by its *behavior*. These behaviors will be specified in a LOTOS-like processes algebra, but any other similar formalism could be used. We consider a fixed set of visible actions Act ($a, b, \ldots$ to range over Act). We assume the existence of a special action $\tau \notin$ Act which represents the internal behavior of a process. We also consider the set of internal actions Act_τ such that $\tau \in \text{Act}_\tau$, $\text{Act}_\tau \cap \text{Act} = \emptyset$, and there exists a bijection $f : \text{Act} \longrightarrow (\text{Act}_\tau - \{\tau\})$ such that for all $a \in \text{Act}$, we will denote $f(a)$ by τ_a. We denote by ACT the set of actions, that is, $\text{ACT} = \text{Act} \cup \text{Act}_\tau$ ($\alpha, \alpha', \ldots$ to range over ACT). Let us note that we do not consider a unique internal action, even though an *external* observer will not be able to distinguish them. The difference among them comes from the fact that they will need different resources to be performed. So, if a process needs a set of resources $\overline{x}$ to perform a visible action a, and this action is *hidden*, the resulting action, that is τ_a, needs the same amount of resources $\overline{x}$ to be performed. Sets of internal actions appear in other models for concurrent processes (for example, for I/O automata [16]). Finally, we consider a set of process variables Id.

Definition 3. The set of *basic processes*, denoted by $\mathcal{B}$, is given by the following BNF-expression $B ::= \text{stop} \mid X \mid \alpha \, ; B \mid B + B \mid B \parallel_A B \mid \text{hide } A \text{ in } B \mid X := B$, where $\alpha \in \text{ACT}$, $A \subseteq \text{Act}$, and $X \in Id$. □

The term stop defines the process that performs no actions. The process $\alpha \, ; B$ performs the action α and, after that, it behaves like B. Choice is represented by

$$(\text{Pre}) \frac{}{\alpha;B \xrightarrow{\alpha} B} \qquad (\text{Rec}) \frac{B\{X:=B/X\} \xrightarrow{\alpha} B'}{X:=B \xrightarrow{\alpha} B'}$$

$$(\text{Cho1}) \frac{B_1 \xrightarrow{\alpha} B_1'}{B_1+B_2 \xrightarrow{\alpha} B_1'} \qquad (\text{Cho2}) \frac{B_2 \xrightarrow{\alpha} B_2'}{B_1+B_2 \xrightarrow{\alpha} B_2'}$$

$$(\text{Par1}) \frac{B_1 \xrightarrow{\alpha} B_1' \wedge \alpha \notin A}{B_1 \|_A B_2 \xrightarrow{\alpha} B_1' \|_A B_2} \qquad (\text{Par2}) \frac{B_2 \xrightarrow{\alpha} B_2' \wedge \alpha \notin A}{B_1 \|_A B_2 \xrightarrow{\alpha} B_1 \|_A B_2'}$$

$$(\text{Par3}) \frac{B_1 \xrightarrow{a} B_1' \wedge B_2 \xrightarrow{a} B_2' \wedge a \in A}{B_1 \|_A B_2 \xrightarrow{a} B_1' \|_A B_2'}$$

$$(\text{Hid1}) \frac{B_1 \xrightarrow{\alpha} B_1' \wedge \alpha \notin A}{\textbf{hide } A \textbf{ in } B_1 \xrightarrow{\alpha} \textbf{hide } A \textbf{ in } B_1'}$$

$$(\text{Hid2}) \frac{B_1 \xrightarrow{a} B_1' \wedge a \in A}{\textbf{hide } A \textbf{ in } B_1 \xrightarrow{\tau_a} \textbf{hide } A \textbf{ in } B_1'}$$

Fig. 1. Operational Semantics for the Base Language

$B+B'$, and the process will behave either like B or like B'. The expression $B \|_A B'$ represents the parallel composition of B and B' (with synchronization set A). The term **hide** A **in** B will perform any action that B performs if the action is not in A; an action $a \in A$ will be hidden, becoming τ_a. The term $X := B$ represents a (possibly) recursive definition of a process. In Figure 1 the operational semantics for behaviors is presented. The rules are quite standard. Let us remind that $B\{B'/X\}$ represents the replacement of the free occurrences of the variable X in B by the term B'. Let us also remark that, in rule (Hid2), the result of hiding a visible action a is not τ but τ_a. Let us also note that the parallel operator works in an interleaving way. Concurrent execution of actions (by several processes) is considered only in the scope of a system. The following definition is given to compute the actions that a basic process may immediately perform.

Definition 4. Let $B \in \mathcal{B}$. We define its *set of immediate actions*, denoted by $\texttt{Imm}(B)$, as $\texttt{Imm}(B) = \{\alpha \in \texttt{ACT} \mid \exists\, B' \in \mathcal{B} : B \xrightarrow{\alpha} B'\}$. $\qquad\Box$

As we have already commented, a process consists of its basic behavior (previously defined), a set of assigned resources, and some information relating both resources and behavior.

Definition 5. Let us consider that there exists a number $m > 0$ of different resources. A *process* is a tuple $P = (B, \overline{x}, u, n, c)$, where $B \in \mathcal{B}$ (the *basic process* defining its behavior), $\overline{x} = (x_1, \ldots x_m) \in \mathbb{R}_+^m$ (the *amounts* of resources), $u : \mathcal{P}(\texttt{ACT}) \times \mathbb{R}_+^m \longrightarrow \mathbb{R}$ (the *utility* function), $n : \texttt{ACT} \times \mathbb{R}_+^m \longrightarrow V_*$ (the *necessity* function), and $c : \texttt{ACT} \times \mathbb{R}_+^m \longrightarrow \mathbb{R}^m$ (the *consumption* of resources function). We denote by $\mathcal{P}$ the set of processes.

Given a process P_i, we will usually consider $P_i = (B_i, \overline{x}_i, u_i, n_i, c_i)$, that is, indices will denote the process to which $B, \overline{x}, \ldots$ are related. $\qquad\Box$

Next we briefly explain the components of a process. If $P = (B, \overline{x}, u, n, c)$ is a process then $\overline{x}$ indicates that P owns x_i units of the i-th resource. The *utility* function u contains *preferences* between *baskets* of resources. This function is applied to the set of actions that B can immediately perform and to a set of resources. It returns a real value. If we have that $u(A, \overline{x}) < u(A, \overline{y})$ then P would prefer the basket $\overline{y}$ to the basket $\overline{x}$, considering that $A = \text{Imm}(B)$. Given the fact that the utility function is only applied to sets of immediate actions, we suppose $u(\emptyset, \overline{x}) = 0$. That is, a *deadlocked* process does not need any resource, so they will be shared with the rest of the processes. The utility function plays a fundamental role in the exchange of resources as it allows to decide whether a new basket would improve the situation of the process.

The *necessity* function n relates the resources and the speed of execution of actions. Thus, if $n(\alpha, \overline{x}) = \xi \neq \xi_\infty$ then the action α will be performed by P, that owns the resources $\overline{x}$, following the probability distribution function F_ξ. In other words, α will be performed before time t with probability $F_\xi(t)$. If $n(\alpha, \overline{x}) = \xi_\infty$ then we have that the owned resources are not enough to perform α. It is important to note that, usually, random variables will depend on the resources the process owns. Finally, we assume $n(a, \overline{x}) = n(\tau_a, \overline{x})$.

The *consumption* of resources function indicates the consumed/produced resources after performing an action. That is, $c(\alpha, \overline{x}) = \overline{y}$ means that, after performing α, the set of resources of the process varies from $\overline{x}$ to $\overline{y}$. A necessary condition for a process to perform an action α is $c(\alpha, \overline{x}) \geq \overline{0}$. We do not allow *debts*, even transient ones, because they could generate inconsistencies. For example, such debts could produce that two processes simultaneously use a printer.

Systems will perform transitions according to the possible transitions of processes. These transitions are defined by the following operational rule:

$$\frac{B \xrightarrow{\alpha} B' \land n(\alpha, \overline{x}) = \xi \in \mathcal{V} \land c(\alpha, \overline{x}) \geq \overline{0}}{P \xrightarrow{(\alpha, \xi)} P'}$$

where $P = (B, \overline{x}, u, n, c)$ and $P' = (B', c(\alpha, \overline{x}), u, n, c)$. Intuitively, a process may perform an action if its corresponding behavior can, it has enough resources to perform it, and this performance does not produce any debts.

A system will be the parallel composition of several processes. We allow m among n synchronization. Let us consider the compositions of the processes $P_1, \ldots, P_n$. Each process has a synchronization set A_i. The process P_i is allowed to asynchronously perform any action in $\text{ACT} - A_i$; if P_i is able to perform an action $a \in A_i$ then P_i has to synchronize with the rest of processes P_j such that $a \in A_j$. In order to deal with the usual semantic problems of general distributions in the scope of a parallel operator, we have chosen an approach inspired in [5,15]. That is, actions are split into *start* (belonging to the set $\text{ACT}^+ = \{\alpha^+ \mid \alpha \in \text{ACT}\}$) and *termination* (belonging to the set $\text{ACT}^- = \{\alpha^- \mid \alpha \in \text{ACT}\}$). So, labels appearing in the forthcoming operational semantics for systems may contain elements from $\text{ACT}^+ \cup \text{ACT}^-$.

$$\frac{\texttt{valid}(S,\mathcal{E}) \;\wedge\; \texttt{allowed}(S,\mathcal{E})}{S \overset{\mathcal{E}}{\leadsto}\;_{M}\|_n^{A_i} P_i' \quad \left[\forall\, 1 \le i \le n:\; P_i' = (B_i, \overline{x_i} - \textstyle\sum_j \mathcal{E}_{ij} + \sum_j \mathcal{E}_{ji}, u_i, n_i, c_i)\right]}$$

$$\frac{S \not\leadsto \;\wedge\; P_j \xrightarrow{(\alpha,\xi)} P_j' \;\wedge\; \alpha \notin A_j \;\wedge\; j \notin \mathrm{Ind}(M)}{S \xrightarrow{(\alpha^+,\xi)\{j\}}\;_{M_1}\|_n^{A_i} P_i'' \quad \left[\forall\, 1 \le i \le n,\; P_i'' = \begin{cases} P_j' \text{ if } i = j \\ P_i \text{ if } i \ne j \end{cases}\right]}$$

$$\frac{S \not\leadsto \;\wedge\; S \not\!\xrightarrow{\texttt{Act}^+} \;\wedge\; (j,\alpha,\xi,\bar{x}) \in M \;\wedge\; \alpha \notin A_j}{S \xrightarrow{(\alpha^-,\xi)\{j\}}\;_{M_2}\|_n^{A_i} P_i}$$

$$\frac{S \not\leadsto \;\wedge\; P_j \xrightarrow{(a,\xi)} P_j' \;\wedge\; a \in A_j \;\wedge\; \forall\, k \in B(a):\, (k \notin \mathrm{Ind}(M) \;\wedge\; \exists\, P_k':\; P_k \xrightarrow{(a,\xi_k)} P_k')}{S \xrightarrow{(a^+,\psi)B(a)}\;_{M_3}\|_n^{A_i} P_i'' \quad \left[\forall\, 1 \le i \le n,\; P_i'' = \begin{cases} P_i' \text{ if } a \in A_i \\ P_i \text{ if } a \notin A_i \end{cases}\right]}$$

$$\frac{S \not\leadsto \;\wedge\; S \not\!\xrightarrow{\texttt{Act}^+} \;\wedge\; (j,a,\psi,\bar{x}) \in M \;\wedge\; a \in A_j \;\wedge\; \forall\, k \in B(a):\, (\exists\, \overline{x_k}:\, (k,a,\psi,\overline{x_k}) \in M)}{S \xrightarrow{(a^-,\psi)B(a)}\;_{M_4}\|_n^{A_i} P_i}$$

where

$S = \;_{M}\|_n^{A_i} P_i,\; P_i = (B_i, \overline{x_i}, u_i, n_i, c_i)$ $\qquad \mathrm{Ind}(M) = \{j \mid \exists\, \alpha, \xi, \bar{x}:\, (j,\alpha,\xi,\bar{x}) \in M\}$

$M_1 = M \cup \{(j,\alpha,\xi,\texttt{Blocked}(P_j,\alpha))\}$ $\qquad M_2 = M - \{(j,\alpha,\xi,\bar{x})\}$

$B(a) = \{k \mid 1 \le k \le n \;\wedge\; a \in A_k\}$ $\qquad \psi = \max\{n_k(a,\overline{x_k}) \mid k \in B(a)\}$

$M_3 = M \cup \{(k,a,\psi,\texttt{Blocked}(P_k,a)) \mid k \in B(a)\}$ $\quad M_4 = M - \{(k,a,\psi,\overline{x_k}) \mid k \in B(a)\}$

Fig. 2. Operational Semantics for Systems

Definition 6. Let $A_1,\ldots A_n \subseteq \texttt{Act}$. A *system* S is a parallel composition of n processes $P_1,\ldots P_n$ synchronizing, respectively, in the set A_i. We denote the system S by $_{M}\|_n^{A_i} P_i$, where $M \subseteq \{1,\ldots,n\} \times \texttt{ACT} \times \mathcal{V} \times \mathbb{R}^m$. We denote the set of systems by $\mathcal{S}$. $\qquad\qquad\square$

The set M will store information about which processes are performing actions, that is, they started an action but they did not finish it. Any element $(i,\alpha,\xi,\bar{y}) \in M$ represents that the i-th process is currently performing α, with respect to the random variable ξ, and it is using the resources given by $\bar{y}$. We will always assume that M is initially empty. In Figure 2 we present the operational semantics for systems. The first rule indicates a exchange of resources. The predicate $\texttt{valid}(S,\mathcal{E})$ controls that processes are not giving resources that they do not own or that they are currently using/producing/consuming. The predicate $\texttt{allowed}(S,\mathcal{E})$ detects whether the exchange is correct with respect to the chosen policy. We will formally define these two predicates later. As a consequence of the exchange, P_i gives to P_j the quantities of resources indicated by $\mathcal{E}_{ij}$, while P_i receives from P_j the quantities given by $\mathcal{E}_{ji}$. We will denote by $\leadsto^*$ the reflexive and transitive closure of $\leadsto$. Once we have a situation where no exchange can be performed (that is, $S \not\rightarrow$) the processes will perform *usual* transitions. Let us remark that $S \not\rightarrow$ indicates that the resources have been (somehow) well distributed. The second rule indicates that a process may start the performance of a non-synchronizing action if it is not currently performing another action (i.e. $j \notin \text{Ind}(M)$). In this case, we need to include information about this performance in the set M (see the definition of M_1 at the bottom of Figure 2). In particular, we need to indicate which resources will be *blocked* while performing that action (we will formally introduce this concept after this explanation). The fourth rule is similar but considering synchronizing actions. Let us remark that processes may perform the same action at different speeds (in particular, depending on the resources that they own). We take the slowest, that is, we consider a random variable distributed as the maximum of the corresponding random variables (see the definition of ψ at the bottom of Figure 2). The remaining rules deal with termination of actions. The third rule says that if a process P_j may terminate an action (that is, a tuple with index j belongs to M) and no other process may start an action immediately (i.e. $S \not\xrightarrow{\text{Act}^+}$) then the system can terminate this action. Let us note that $S \not\xrightarrow{\text{Act}^+}$ holds iff $\text{Ind}(M) \cup \{j \mid P_j \not\rightarrow\} = \{1, \ldots, n\}$. In this case, the corresponding tuple is removed from M. A similar situation appears in the last rule.

Next we define the remaining predicates. If a process is performing an action then there will be resources that it cannot exchange. These resources are those created/consumed during the performance of the action and the ones that the process is using (those adding utility for that particular action). So, these resources will be *blocked* for possible exchanges.

Definition 7. Let $P = (B, \overline{x}, u, n, c)$ be a process. We say that P *depends* on the resource j to perform an action $\alpha \in \text{ACT}$, denoted by $\text{Depends}(P, j, \alpha)$, if there exist $\overline{x'}, \overline{x''} \leq \overline{x}$ such that $\overline{x''} = (x'_1, x'_2, \ldots, x'_j + \epsilon, \ldots, x'_m)$, for some $\epsilon > 0$, and $u(\{\alpha\}, \overline{x'}) < u(\{\alpha\}, \overline{x''})$.

The tuple of *blocked* resources for P while performing and action $\alpha \in \text{ACT}$, denoted by $\text{Blocked}(P, \alpha)$, is defined as $c(\alpha, \overline{x}) - \overline{x} + \overline{y}$, where for all $1 \leq j \leq m$ we have $y_j = x_j$ if $\text{Depends}(P, j, \alpha)$ and $y_j = 0$ otherwise. $\qquad\square$

Let us note that P will perform exchanges by taking into account that it will own (after performing α) the resources given by $c(\alpha, \overline{x})$. This is so because the operational rule for processes *updates* the set of owned resources. However, the net creation/consumption of resources, that is $c(\alpha, \overline{x}) - \overline{x}$, cannot be used in these exchanges. In addition, the resources that the process is using for performing α are also excluded. All these resources are *liberated* when the action is finished (by removing the corresponding information from M). Let us also remark that a process may receive (after future exchanges, before completing the performance of α) new quantities of the blocked resources. Nevertheless, these resources will neither improve the performance of the action being performed nor will be added to the set of blocked resources.

The `valid(S, E)` predicate controls that a exchange is possible. It holds if the processes do not give resources that they do not own and the diagonal of the matrix is filled with $\bar{0}$. In addition, blocked resources (that is, those included in the set M) cannot be exchanged.

Definition 8. Let $S = {}_M\|_n^{A_i} P_i$ be a system, where for all $1 \le i \le n$ we have $P_i = (B_i, \overline{x_i}, u_i, n_i, c_i)$. We say that $\mathcal{E} \in (\mathbb{R}_+^m)^{n*n}$ is a *valid exchange matrix for S*, denoted by `valid(S, E)`, if for all $1 \le i \le n$ we have $\mathcal{E}_{ii} = \bar{0}$, and $\sum_j \mathcal{E}_{ij} \le \overline{x_i} - \overline{x}$ if there exists $\alpha, \xi : (i, \alpha, \xi, \overline{x}) \in M$, and $\sum_j \mathcal{E}_{ij} \le \overline{x_i}$ otherwise. □

The `allowed(S, E)` predicate detects whether an exchange conforms the chosen policy. In [18] two different policies were introduced, but others could be defined.[1] In this paper we will only consider the *preserving utility policy*. Under this assumption, exchanges are allowed only if, after the exchange, at least one process improves and no process gets worse. Intuitively, processes are the owners of the resources and they will not give them up if they do not receive a *compensation*.

Definition 9. For all $1 \le i \le n$ let $P_i = (B_i, \overline{x_i}, u_i, n_i, c_i)$, let $S = {}_M\|_n^{A_i} P_i$ be a system, and $\mathcal{E} \in (\mathbb{R}_+^m)^{n \times n}$ be such that `valid(S, E)`. The `allowed(S, E)` predicate holds if for all $1 \le i \le n$ we have $u_i(\text{Imm}(B_i), \overline{x_i}) \le u_i(\text{Imm}(B_i), \overline{x_i} - \sum_j \mathcal{E}_{ij} + \sum_j \mathcal{E}_{ji})$ and there exists $1 \le k \le n$ such that we have $u_k(\text{Imm}(B_k), \overline{x_k}) < u_k(\text{Imm}(B_k), \overline{x_k} - \sum_j \mathcal{E}_{kj} + \sum_j \mathcal{E}_{jk})$. □

3   Examples

In this section we will show how SPAMR can be used to specify and analyze concurrent systems where both resources and actions taking time to be performed play an important role. First, we present a classic and simple example: The readers/writers problem. Next, we give a more elaborated example where three researchers share some hardware in a laboratory.

During the rest of the section we assume that an undefined value of the utility, necessity, or consumption functions is set to an arbitrary value. Actually, these cases will not be possible because they will correspond to an action (or a set of actions for the utility function) not reachable by the corresponding processes. For the sake of simplicity in the presentation, we will use probability distribution functions instead of random variables. We will consider that $U(t_1, t_2)$ denotes a random variable uniformly distributed on the interval $[t_1, t_2]$; $E(\lambda)$ denotes a random variable exponentially distributed with parameter λ; $\delta(t)$ denotes a Dirac distribution in t. Let us remember that a Dirac distribution models deterministic time, that is, $\delta(t)$ indicates a delay of t time units.

---

[1] The choice of a *good* policy is not a trivial task. Actually, it is impossible to choose a *perfect* policy because this problem is related with the social welfare aggregator problem. Arrow's *impossibility theorem* [2] shows that there does not exist such an aggregator fulfilling a certain set of *desirable* properties.

3.1   The Readers and Writers Problem

We suppose n readers and m writers which may access a file. Any number of readers may simultaneously read from the file, but when a writer holds access to the file, neither readers nor other writers are allowed to access it. The behaviors for readers and writers are given by:

$$Reader := read \; ; \; other\_tasks \; ; \; Reader$$
$$Writer := write \; ; \; other\_tasks \; ; \; Writer$$

We consider that there is only one resource, the *access* to the file, and that there are n units of it. We initially assign a unit of the resource to each reader. For any process, its utility function is defined as:

$$u(\{read\}, \bar{x}) = \begin{cases} K_1 \text{ if } \texttt{trunc}(x) \geq 1 \\ 0 \quad \text{otherwise} \end{cases}$$

$$u(\{write\}, \bar{x}) = \begin{cases} K_2 \text{ if } x = n \\ 0 \quad \text{otherwise} \end{cases}$$

$$u(\{other\_tasks\}, \bar{x}) = K_3$$

where $K_1, K_2 > 0$, and $K_3 \geq 0$. Let us comment on the way the access of a writer forbids the access of any reader or any other writer. For a writer to access the file, it must own all the *access* resources of the system. Also note that if a reader desires to read, it needs at least one unit of the resource; additional units do not increase utility. Regarding necessity functions, they can be defined as follows:

$$n(read, \bar{x}) = \begin{cases} U(K_4, K_5) \text{ if } \texttt{trunc}(x) \geq 1 \\ \xi_\infty \quad\quad\quad \text{otherwise} \end{cases}$$

$$n(write, \bar{x}) = \begin{cases} U(K_6, K_7) \text{ if } x = n \\ \xi_\infty \quad\quad\quad \text{otherwise} \end{cases}$$

$$n(other\_tasks, \bar{x}) = E(K_8)$$

where $0 \leq K_4 < K_5, 0 \leq K_6 < K_7$, and $K_8 > 0$. Note that resources are neither consumed nor created. So, $c(\alpha, \bar{x}) = \bar{x}$. Finally, the system is:

$$Readers\_Writers = {}_0\|_{n+m}^{A_i} \, P_i$$

where, for all $1 \leq i \leq n$ we have $P_i = (Reader, 1, u, n, c)$, and for all $1 \leq i \leq m$ we have $P_{n+i} = (Writer, 0, u, n, c)$. Besides, for all $1 \leq i \leq n + m$ we have $A_i = \emptyset$. The following result shows that this system cannot get deadlocked. Let us remark that the definition of the utility functions plays an important role in this absence of deadlocks. The proof follows from the fact that if a local equilibrium is reached then there exists (at least) a process such that either it is willing to perform *other tasks* (no resources are needed to perform this action) or it has utility greater than zero. Let us remark that no process gets utility by

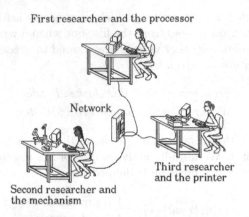

First researcher and the processor

Network

Second researcher and
the mechanism

Third researcher
and the printer

Fig. 3. Three Researchers in a Laboratory

having less number of accesses that the ones it needs. In both cases, this process
will be able to perform its corresponding action.

Lemma 1. (*Absence of Deadlocks for Readers_Writers*). Let us consider a system S such that

$$Readers\_Writers \rightsquigarrow^* S_1 \xrightarrow{(\alpha_1,\xi_1)B_1} S_1' \rightsquigarrow^* S_2 \cdots \xrightarrow{(\alpha_k,\xi_k)B_k} S_n' \rightsquigarrow^* S$$

where for all $1 \leq i \leq k$ we have $\alpha_i \in \mathsf{ACT}^- \cup \mathsf{ACT}^+$ and $B_i \subseteq \{1,\ldots,n+m\}$. If S is not a local equilibrium then there exist $S', \mathcal{E}$ such that $S \xrightarrow{\mathcal{E}} S'$; otherwise, there exist S', α, ξ, B such that $S \xrightarrow{(\alpha,\xi)B} S'$.   □

3.2   The Three Researchers

We present a more complex example that shows most of the characteristics
of the language. We consider the situation depicted in Figure 3. We have a
laboratory where three (female) researchers, that we call R_1, R_2, and R_3, are
making some experiments. Each researcher is placed in front of a computer. One
of the computers has a very powerful *processor* that allows to make complex
computations. The second computer has a *mechanism* that allows to make some
experiments to confirm the analysis given by the previous computations. Finally,
the third computer has a *printer*. Each researcher can access *directly* the resource
(processor, mechanism or printer) placed in her computer; the other resources
are accessed remotely. So, in this example we have four resources: processor,
mechanism, printer and network.

The behavior of a researcher is defined as follows. First, she thinks and discusses with the other researchers via electronic chat until an idea comes out.

$$Researcher_i := brain\_storming \; ; \; Computing_i$$

Afterwards, she tries to access the first computer. If she is R_1 and she has enough *quantity* of the processor, she will be able to perform the computations on her computer. Afterwards, she will analyze the results. If the results confirm her hypothesis, she will try to perform an experiment; otherwise, she will start to think on another idea. The process is similar for the second and third researchers. The only difference is that they must send her data through the channel, then the computations will be done, and then they will receive the results through the channel.

$$Computing_1 := comp_1 \; ; \; analize\_comp_1 \; ; \; \begin{pmatrix} good \; ; \; Experimenting_1 \\ + \\ bad \; ; \; Researcher_1 \end{pmatrix}$$

$$\begin{aligned} Computing_i &:= send\_data\_comp_i \; ; \; comp_i; \\ {\scriptstyle [i \in \{2,3\}]} & \quad\; rec\_data\_comp_i \; ; \; analize\_comp_i \; ; \end{aligned} \begin{pmatrix} good \; ; \; Experimenting_i \\ + \\ bad \; ; \; Researcher_i \end{pmatrix}$$

In the case of the experimenting process, R_2 does not need the channel to perform the experiment, while the other two researchers need it. Nevertheless, this fact will not be reflected in the specification of the behaviors, but in the utility and necessity functions: They will not depend on the amount of the channel that the second researcher has, while they will for the other two researchers. After performing the experiment, if the results confirm their hypothesis then they will print; otherwise, they will discard the idea.

$$\begin{aligned} Experimenting_i &:= experiment_i \; ; \; analyze\_exp_i \; ; \; \begin{pmatrix} good \; ; \; Printing_i \\ + \\ bad \; ; \; Researcher_i \end{pmatrix} \\ {\scriptstyle [i \in \{1,2,3\}]} & \end{aligned}$$

Finally, R_3 will print the results, and will start to think on another idea. The other two researchers need to send the data to the printer through the channel. Note that in this case the printer will not send back any results.

$$Printing_3 := print_3 \; ; \; Researcher_3$$

$$\begin{aligned} Printing_i &:= send\_data\_print_i \; ; \; print_i \; ; \; Researcher_i \\ {\scriptstyle [i \in \{2,3\}]} & \end{aligned}$$

Next we define the rest of the components of the processes. We suppose that each researcher initially owns her local resource, and that they have the same amount of broad-band. Without losing generality, we consider that both the total amount of processor and of broadband are equal to 1. That is, $\overline{x_1} = (1,0,0,\frac{1}{3})$, $\overline{x_2} = (0,1,0,\frac{1}{3})$, $\overline{x_3} = (0,0,1,\frac{1}{3})$. Regarding utility functions we have:

$$u_i(\{brain\_storming\}, \bar{z}) = \begin{cases} z_4 \text{ if } z_4 < \frac{1}{3} \\ \frac{1}{3} \text{ otherwise} \end{cases}$$
$[i \in \{1,2,3\}]$
$$u_i(\{comp_i\}, \bar{z}) = C_i \cdot z_1$$
$[i \in \{1,2,3\}]$
$$u_2(\{experiment_2\}, \bar{z}) = E_2 \cdot \mathtt{trunc}(z_2)$$
$$u_i(\{experiment_i\}, \bar{z}) = E_i \cdot \mathtt{trunc}(z_2) \cdot z_4^2$$
$[i \in \{1,3\}]$
$$u_i(\{print_i\}, \bar{z}) = P_i \cdot \mathtt{trunc}(z_3)$$
$[i \in \{1,2,3\}]$
$$u_1(\{send\_data\_print_1\}, \bar{z}) = z_4$$
$$u_2(\{c\}, \bar{z}) = z_4$$
$[c \in \{send\_data\_comp_2, rec\_data\_comp_2, send\_data\_print_2\}]$
$$u_3(\{c\}, \bar{z}) = z_4$$
$[c \in \{send\_data\_comp_3, rec\_data\_comp_3,\}]$
$$u_i(A_i, \bar{z}) = 0$$
$[i \in \{1,2,3\} \wedge A_i \in \{\{good, bad\}, \{analize\_comp_i\}\}]$

Let us comment on the previous definitions. If the researchers are willing to perform a brainstorm, then they will need the broadband to use the chat application. Due to the three researchers are committed to chat together, a limit in the utility of the broadband must be imposed to avoid any researcher to keep the whole resource. After a new idea comes out, each researcher will be willing to perform a computation. In this case, their utility depends only on the amount of (time) processor that they own. The additional constant (i.e. $C_i > 0$) measures the *propensity* of the researcher i to make computations. A similar situation appears for the case of printing. On the contrary, the utility when trying to perform an experiment does not depend only on the *amount* of the mechanism; in the case of R_1 and R_3, it will also depend on the amount of broadband that they own because they are supposed to interact with the mechanism. Let us note that in these last two cases, researchers get no utility if they do not exclusively own the mechanism or the printer, respectively (this is indicated by using the *truncate* function). In the case of the processor and the network, a fraction of the whole amount reports utility greater than zero. If the researchers try to send data, their utilities depend only on the amount of broadband that they have. Finally, no resources are needed to perform the rest of the actions. In this case, the utility is given by a constant.

The execution time will sometimes depend only on the amount of resources (e.g. $comp_i$) and sometimes will also depend on a constant indicating the skills of the researcher (e.g. $experiment_i$).

$$n_i(comp_i, \bar{z}) = \begin{cases} E(C \cdot z_1) \text{ if } z_1 > 0 \\ \xi_\infty \quad\quad \text{otherwise} \end{cases}$$
$[i \in \{1,2,3\}]$

$$n_2(experiment_2, \bar{z}) = \begin{cases} E(E_2) \text{ if } \mathtt{trunc}(z_2) \geq 1 \\ \xi_\infty \quad \text{otherwise} \end{cases}$$

$$n_i(experiment_i, \bar{z}) = \begin{cases} E(E_i \cdot z_4^2) \text{ if } \mathtt{trunc}(z_2) \geq 1 \wedge z_4 > 0 \\ \xi_\infty \quad\quad \text{otherwise} \end{cases}$$
$[i \in \{1,3\}]$

$$n_i(print_i, \bar{z}) = \begin{cases} U(P_1, P_2) \text{ if } \mathtt{trunc}(z_3) \geq 1 \\ \xi_\infty \quad\quad \text{otherwise} \end{cases}$$
$[i \in \{1,2,3\}]$

$$n_1(c, \bar{z}) = \xi$$
$[c \in \{send\_data\_print_1\}]$

$$n_2(c, \bar{z}) = \xi$$
$[c \in \{send\_data\_comp_2, rec\_data\_comp_2, send\_data\_print_2\}]$

$$n_3(c, \bar{z}) = \xi$$
$[c \in \{send\_data\_comp_3, rec\_data\_comp_3\}]$

$$n_i(good, \bar{z}) = n_i(bad, \bar{z}) = \delta(BG)$$
$[i \in \{1,2,3\}]$

$$n_i(brain\_storming, \bar{z}) = \begin{cases} E(T_i \cdot z_4) \text{ if } z_4 > 0 \\ \xi_\infty \quad\quad \text{otherwise} \end{cases}$$
$[i \in \{1,2,3\}]$

$$n_i(analize\_comp_i, \bar{z}) = E(AC_i)$$
$[i \in \{1,2,3\}]$

$$n_i(analyze\_exp_i, \bar{z}) = E(AE_i)$$
$[i \in \{1,2,3\}]$

where

$$\xi = \begin{cases} U(\frac{K_1}{z_4}, \frac{K_2}{z_4}) \text{ if } z_4 > 0 \\ \xi_\infty \quad\quad\quad \text{otherwise} \end{cases}$$

Let us note that the delay associated with choosing whether a result is *good* or *bad* is deterministic as the (random) time for the analysis is consumed by the previous actions ($analize\_comp_i$ and $analyze\_exp_i$). In this system, resources are neither created nor consumed. So, $c_i(\alpha, \bar{z}) = \bar{z}$. The laboratory is defined as:

$$Laboratory = {}_\emptyset\|_3^{A_i} P_i$$

where for all $1 \leq i \leq 3$ we have $P_i = (B_i, \overline{x_i}, u_i, n_i, c_i)$ and $A_i = \{brain\_storming\}$.

The proof of deadlock-freedom is a little bit more involved in this case because there are more possibilities. Nevertheless, the technique is exactly the same as in Lemma 1. First, let us remark that all the resources where the `truncate` function is applied have one full unit of them. After reaching a local equilibrium S, if all the processes have zero utility then we get a contradiction; otherwise, because of the relation between utility and necessity functions, a process will be able to perform one of its immediate actions.

Lemma 2. (*Absence of Deadlocks for Laboratory*). Let us consider a system S such that

$$Laboratory \leadsto^* S_1 \xrightarrow{(\alpha_1, \xi_1)B_1} S_1' \leadsto^* S_2 \cdots \xrightarrow{(\alpha_n, \xi_n)B_n} S_n' \leadsto^* S$$

where for all $1 \le i \le n$ we have $\alpha_i \in \text{ACT}^- \cup \text{ACT}^+$ and $B_i \subseteq \{1,2,3\}$. If S is not a local equilibrium then there exist $S', \mathcal{E}$ such that $S \xrightarrow{\mathcal{E}} S'$; otherwise, there exist S', α, ξ, B such that $S \xrightarrow{(\alpha, \xi)B} S'$. ☐

Besides, it is guaranteed that the system is starvation-free. This is so because the three researchers are forced to synchronize when brainstorming, so that their progress can help their partners when looking for new ideas. This fact disallows a researcher to advance forever in her research while the other ones are stopped.

4   Conclusions and Future Work

In this paper we have introduced an stochastic version of **PAMR** where random variables have been associated with the performance of actions. We have defined an operational semantics for the new language. Since we do not restrict the probability distribution functions associated with random variables, we need to use complex technicalities to define this semantics. In order to show the usefulness of our language, we have given two examples showing most of its features.

As future work we plan to define semantic frameworks for our language. We have already developed a notion of (strong) bisimulation and two trace-based semantics. The difference between the alternative trace semantics comes from the point of observation: Whether we check only *visible* events or also *internal* ones. In addition, we plan to consider a testing semantics for our language in the line of [13] and a stochastic weak bisimulation following [14].

References

1. Marsan, M.A., Bianco, A., Ciminiera, L., Sisto, R., Valenzano, A.: A LOTOS extension for the performance analysis of distributed systems. IEEE/ACM Transactions on Networking 2(2), 151–165 (1994)
2. Arrow, K.J.: Social Choice and Individual Values, 2nd edn. Wiley, Chichester (1963)
3. Bernardo, M., Gorrieri, R.: A tutorial on EMPA: A theory of concurrent processes with nondeterminism, priorities, probabilities and time. Theoretical Computer Science 202(1-2), 1–54 (1998)
4. Bravetti, M., D'Argenio, P.R.: Tutte le algebre insieme: Concepts, discussions and relations of stochastic process algebras with general distributions. In: Baier, C., Haverkort, B., Hermanns, H., Katoen, J.-P., Siegle, M. (eds.) Validation of Stochastic Systems. LNCS, vol. 2925, pp. 44–88. Springer, Heidelberg (2004)
5. Bravetti, M., Gorrieri, R.: The theory of interactive generalized semi-Markov processes. Theoretical Computer Science 282(1), 5–32 (2002)

6. D'Argenio, P.R., Katoen, J.-P.: A theory of stochastic systems part I: Stochastic automata. Information and Computation 203(1), 1–38 (2005)
7. D'Argenio, P.R., Katoen, J.-P.: A theory of stochastic systems part II: Process algebra. Information and Computation 203(1), 39–74 (2005)
8. Götz, N., Herzog, U., Rettelbach, M.: Multiprocessor and distributed system design: The integration of functional specification and performance analysis using stochastic process algebras. In: Donatiello, L., Nelson, R. (eds.) SIGMETRICS 1993 and Performance 1993. LNCS, vol. 729, pp. 121–146. Springer, Heidelberg (1993)
9. Harrison, P.G., Strulo, B.: SPADES – a process algebra for discrete event simulation. Journal of Logic Computation 10(1), 3–42 (2000)
10. Hermanns, H., Herzog, U., Katoen, J.-P.: Process algebra for performance evaluation. Theoretical Computer Science 274(1-2), 43–87 (2002)
11. Hillston, J.: A Compositional Approach to Performance Modelling. Cambridge University Press, Cambridge (1996)
12. Infante López, G.G., Hermanns, H., Katoen, J.-P.: Beyond memoryless distributions: Model checking semi-Markov chains. In: de Luca, L., Gilmore, S.T. (eds.) PROBMIV 2001, PAPM-PROBMIV 2001, and PAPM 2001. LNCS, vol. 2165, pp. 57–70. Springer, Heidelberg (2001)
13. López, N., Núñez, M.: A testing theory for generally distributed stochastic processes. In: Larsen, K.G., Nielsen, M. (eds.) CONCUR 2001. LNCS, vol. 2154, pp. 321–335. Springer, Heidelberg (2001)
14. López, N., Núñez, M.: Weak stochastic bisimulation for non-markovian processes. In: Van Hung, D., Wirsing, M. (eds.) ICTAC 2005. LNCS, vol. 3722, pp. 454–468. Springer, Heidelberg (2005)
15. López, N., Núñez, M., Rubio, F.: An integrated framework for the analysis of asynchronous communicating stochastic processes. Formal Aspects of Computing 16(3), 238–262 (2004)
16. Lynch, N.A., Tuttle, M.R.: Hierarchical correctness proofs for distributed algorithms. In: 6th ACM Symp. on Principles of Distributed Computing, PODC'87, pp. 137–151. ACM Press, New York (1987)
17. Merayo, M.G., Núñez, M., Rodríguez, I.: Formal specification of multi-agent systems by using EUSMs. In: FSEN'07. 2nd IPM Int. Symposium on Fundamentals of Software Engineering. LNCS (to appear, 2007)
18. Núñez, M., Rodríguez, I.: PAMR: A process algebra for the management of resources in concurrent systems. In: FORTE'01. 21st IFIP WG 6.1 Int. Conf. on Formal Techniques for Networked and Distributed Systems, pp. 169–185. Kluwer Academic Publishers, Dordrecht (2001)
19. Núñez, M., Rodríguez, I.: Encoding PAMR into (timed) EFSMs. In: Peled, D.A., Vardi, M.Y. (eds.) FORTE 2002. LNCS, vol. 2529, pp. 1–16. Springer, Heidelberg (2002)
20. Núñez, M., Rodríguez, I., Rubio, F.: Formal specification of multi-agent e-barter systems. Science of Computer Programming 57(2), 187–216 (2005)
21. Núñez, M., Rodríguez, I., Rubio, F.: Specification and testing of autonomous agents in e-commerce systems. Software Testing, Verification and Reliability 15(4), 211–233 (2005)
22. Sen, K., Viswanathan, M., Agha, G.: On statistical model checking of stochastic games. In: Etessami, K., Rajamani, S.K. (eds.) CAV 2005. LNCS, vol. 3576, pp. 266–280. Springer, Heidelberg (2005)

Faster SPDL Model Checking Through Property-Driven State Space Generation

Matthias Kuntz and Boudewijn R. Haverkort

University of Twente,
Faculty for Electrical Engineering, Mathematics and Computer Science

Abstract. In this paper we describe how both, memory and time requirements for stochastic model checking of SPDL (stochastic propositional dynamic logic) formulae can significantly be reduced. SPDL is the stochastic extension of the multi-modal program logic PDL. SPDL provides means to specify path-based properties with or without timing restrictions. Paths can be characterised by so-called programs, essentially regular expressions, where the executability can be made dependent on the validity of test formulae. For model-checking SPDL path formulae it is necessary to build a product transition system (PTS) between the system model and the program automaton belonging to the path formula that is to be verified. In many cases, this PTS can be drastically reduced during the model checking procedure, as the program restricts the number of potentially satisfying paths. Therefore, we propose an approach that directly generates the reduced PTS from a given SPA specification and an SPDL path formula. The feasibility of this approach is shown through a selection of case studies, which show enormous state space reductions, at no increase in generation time.

1 Introduction

It is extremely important to develop techniques that allow the construction and analysis of distributed computer and communication systems. These systems must work correctly and meet high performance and dependability requirements. Using stochastic model checking it is possible to perform a combined analysis of both qualitative (correctness) and quantitative (performance and dependability) aspects of a system model. Models that incorporate both qualitative and quantitative aspects of system behaviour can be modelled by various high-level formalisms, such as stochastic process algebras [12,11], stochastic Petri nets [1], stochastic activity networks [17] (SANs), etc.

In order to do model checking of stochastic systems, over the last years a number of stochastic extensions of the logic CTL [8] have been devised. The most notable extension is the logic CSL [4] (continuous stochastic logic). More recently, in [14,3], action-based extensions of CSL were introduced. These logics allow for the specification of desired system behaviour by means of action sequences. This makes them very well suited for modelling formalisms in which the actual system

K. Wolter (Ed.): EPEW 2007, LNCS 4748, pp. 80–96, 2007.
© Springer-Verlag Berlin Heidelberg 2007

behaviour is specified as a sequence of actions or transitions, as is the case for SPAs, SPNs and SANs.

The applicability of stochastic model checking is limited by the complexity, i.e., the size of system models that are to be verified. At the heart of stochastic model checking lies the solution process of huge sparse sets of linear (differential) equations. This limits the size of systems that are practically analysable to some 10^8 states.

To overcome these limitations we can think of several approaches. One standard approach is the use of some notion of Markovian bisimulation. This approach has the following drawbacks. Computing the bisimulation quotient of a system is computationally expensive, and before reduction takes place the entire system has to be generated. Furthermore, depending on the system, the reduction in size may not be very large, and finally, due to reasons that are related to numerical analysis, the verification of the reduced system may be slower than that of the original system (cf. [13]).

We propose a different approach, which reduces the system size in many cases already during the state space generation, by exploiting the SPDL path formula that is to be verified.

Related Work. For stochastic model checking we are not aware of any approach that generates the state space in a way which depends on the formula that is to be verified. For CSL model checking, in [4] an approach is described that makes states absorbing that do not functionally satisfy a given until-formula, but this state space reduction is performed only after the state space was generated. Following this proposal, in [14] model checking algorithms for SPDL path formulae were implemented. For CSL model checking this was done in [13]. For CTL model checking in [2] an approach is reported, where for interacting finite state machines equivalence relations are computed, depending on the CTL formula that is to be verified.

The paper is further organised as follows. In Section 2 we briefly introduce the syntax and semantics of SPDL; we will explain in an informal style the traditional approach to the model checking of SPDL path formulae. In Section 3 we then describe the stochastic process algebra $\mathcal{YAMPA}$, on which our property-driven state space generation approach relies. Section 4 is devoted to a denotational, symbolic property-driven semantics of $\mathcal{YAMPA}$. In Section 5 we will show the feasibility of our approach via some experimental results. Finally, Section 6 concludes the paper with a short summary and some pointers to future work.

2   SPDL - Syntax, Semantics and Model Checking

The logic SPDL is the stochastic extension of the logic PDL [9], a multi-modal program logic. PDL enriches the standard modal operator $\diamond$ ("possibly") with so-called programs, which are essentially regular expressions and tests (cf. Def. 1). In PDL, the formula $< \rho > \Phi$ means, that it is possible to execute program

ρ and end in a state that satisfies Φ. SPDL adds the following extensions to PDL: The operator $< \rho >$ is replaced by the time-bounded path operator $[\rho]^I$, a probability operator $\mathcal{P}_{\bowtie p}$ to reason about the transient system behaviour, and a steady state operator $\mathcal{S}_{\bowtie p}$ to reason about system behaviour, once stationarity has been reached. In what follows, we discuss the syntax, semantics, and a model checking procedure for SPDL.

2.1 Syntax of SPDL

Definition 1 (Syntax of SPDL). *Let p be a probability value in $[0,1]$, $q \in$ AP an atomic proposition, where AP is the set of atomic propositions, and $\bowtie \in \{\leq , <, \geq, >\}$ a comparison operator. The state formulae Φ of SPDL are defined as:*

$$\Phi := q \,|\, \Phi \vee \Phi \,|\, \neg\Phi \,|\, \mathcal{P}_{\bowtie p}(\phi) \,|\, \mathcal{S}_{\bowtie p}(\Phi) \,|\, (\Phi)$$

Path formulae are defined as:

$$\phi := \Phi[\rho]^I \Phi,$$

where I is the closed interval $[t, t']$, Φ is assumed not to possess sub-formulae containing the steady state operator $\mathcal{S}_{\bowtie p}$.[1] Programs ρ are described by the grammar given in Def. 2.

Definition 2 (Programs). *Let Act be a set of actions, which are also called atomic programs, and TEST be a set of SPDL state formulae, again not containing the steady state operator $\mathcal{S}_{\bowtie p}$. A program ρ is defined by the following grammar:*

$$\rho := \epsilon \,|\, \Phi? ; a \,|\, \rho ; \rho \,|\, \rho \cup \rho \,|\, \rho^* \,|\, \Phi? ; \rho \,|\, (\rho)$$

where $\epsilon \notin$ Act is the empty program, $a \in$ Act and $\Phi \in$ TEST.

Sequence (;), choice ($\cup$), and Kleene-star ($*$) have their usual meaning as known from the theory of regular expressions. The operator $\Phi?$ is the so-called test operator. Informally speaking, it tests whether Φ holds in the current state of the model. If this is the case, then execute program ρ, otherwise ρ is not executable. Following language theory, we can derive words from a program ρ (here also called program instances) according to the rules of regular expressions. The set of all these program instances is called a language.

Example 1. Throughout this paper, we use the example of a fault-tolerant packet collector, which has the following repeating behaviour. Arrivals can either be error-free (upper transition *arr*, rate λ) or erroneous (lower transition *error*, rate μ). If a data packet contains an error, this error can be correctable (*co*) non-correctable (*nco*). In case of a correctable error, the error is corrected (transition *co*) and more data packets can be received. If the error is non-correctable, the data packet has to be retransmitted (transition *rt*). In Fig. 1, the SLTS $\mathcal{M}$ for the packet collector is shown, where we assume that the number n of data

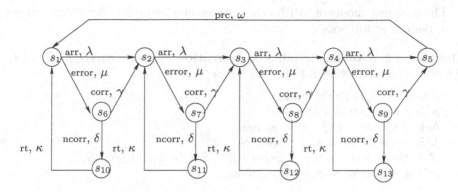

Fig. 1. Fault tolerant packet collector for $n = 4$ packets

packets that are to be processed is equal to four. The system has the following state labels:

$$L(s_5) = \{\text{full}\}, \quad L(s_6) = \ldots = L(s_9) = \{\text{error}\},$$
$$L(s_{10}) = \ldots = L(s_{13}) = \{\text{waitrt}\}, \quad L(s_{14}) = \ldots = L(s_{17}) = \{\text{waitcor}\}$$

The set of actions is given as follows:

$$\text{Act} := \{arr, error, rt, corr, ncorr, prc\}$$

Using SPDL, we can easily express the following properties:

- $\Phi_1 := \mathcal{P}_{\bowtie p}((\neg\text{full})[arr^*]^{[0,t]}(\text{full}))$: Is the probability to receive N data packets without error within t time units greater or less than p?
- $\Phi_2 := \mathcal{P}_{\bowtie p}(\neg\text{full}[arr; \text{TEST1}?; error; rt; arr^* \cup arr^*]^{[0,t]}\text{full})$: Is the probability to receive N data packets without error or with at most one non-correctable error within t time units greater or less than p, given that this non-correctable error appears in the first data packet? The test formula TEST1 defines those states, in which it holds that 1 packet has arrived.
- $\Phi_3 := \mathcal{P}_{\bowtie p}(\text{true}[arr^*; \text{TEST2}?; arr; corr]^{[0,t]}\text{full})$: Is the probability that the buffer is full after at most t time units and that the Nth packet contains a correctable error, given that all preceeding packets were error free, within the probability bounds given by $\bowtie p$? The test formula TEST2 describes those states, in which it holds that $N - 1$ packets have arrived.

2.2   Semantics of SPDL

We will now show, both the model over which SPDL formulae are interpreted and the semantics of SPDL formulae.[2]

---

[1] Mixing formulae that express transient behaviour ($\mathcal{P}_{\bowtie p}$) with formulae expressing steady state behaviour ($\mathcal{S}_{\bowtie p}$) is considered less meaningful.

[2] The stochastic process algebra from Sections 3 and 4 and SPDL share the same semantic model.

The semantic model of SPDL is a so-called stochastic labelled transition system, defined as follows.

Definition 3 (Stochastic labelled transition system (SLTS)). *An SLTS $\mathcal{M}$ is a six-tuple $(s, S, \mathsf{Act}, L, R, \mathsf{AP})$, where*

- *s is the unique initial state,*
- *S is a finite set of states,*
- *Act is a finite set of action names,*
- *L is the state labelling function: $S \to 2^{AP}$,*
- *R is the state transition relation : $R \subseteq S \times (\mathsf{Act} \times \mathbb{R}_{>0}) \times S$,*
- *AP is the set of atomic propositions.*

Definition 4 (Semantics of SPDL)

- *The semantics of propositional logic formulae $\neg\Phi$ and $\Phi \vee \Psi$ is defined the usual way.*
- *$\mathcal{S}_{\bowtie p}(\Phi)$ asserts that the steady state probability of the Φ-states, i.e., the probability to reside in a Φ-state once the system has reached stationarity satisfies the probability bounds as given by $\bowtie p$.*
- *$\mathcal{P}_{\bowtie p}(\phi)$ asserts that the probability measure of all paths that satisfy ϕ lies within the bounds as imposed by $\bowtie p$.*
- *$\Phi[\rho]^I \Psi$ asserts that a path that satisfies this formula reaches a Ψ-state within at least t time units, but after at most t' time units. All preceeding states must satisfy Φ. Alternatively, a $\Phi \wedge \Psi$-state can be reached before the passage of t time units, but not left before at least t time units have passed. Additionally, the action sequence on the path to the Ψ-state must correspond to the action sequence of a word from the language induced by program ρ. All test formulae that are part of ρ must be satisfied by corresponding states of the path.*

2.3   Model Checking SPDL

The overall model checking algorithm of SPDL is similar to that of CTL, in the sense that it starts with the verification of atomic properties and then proceeds with the checking of ever more complex sub-formulae until the overall formula has been checked.

Model Checking SPDL

- Propositional formulae $\neg\Phi$ and $\Phi \vee \Psi$ are checked as in the CTL case.
- Steady state formulae $\mathcal{S}_{\bowtie p}(\Phi)$ can be checked as for CSL [4].
- Model checking formulae with a leading $\mathcal{P}_{\bowtie p}$ operator is more involved. We assume, we want to check whether in an SLTS $\mathcal{M}$ a state s satisfies $\mathcal{P}_{\bowtie p}(\phi)$, with $\phi = \Phi[\rho]^I \Psi$. The basic idea is to reduce the model checking problem of SPDL to one of CSL, which consists of deciding whether a continuous time Markov chain (CTMC) $\mathcal{M}^\times$ (to be constructed) and a state $s^\times$ in $\mathcal{M}^\times$ satisfies the CSL formula $\mathcal{P}_{\bowtie p}(\mathsf{F}^I \mathsf{succ})$. A path satisfies $\mathsf{F}^I \mathsf{succ}$, if within time

interval I a state is reached that satisfies the atomic property succ. To reach this goal, we proceed as follows:

1. From the program ρ we derive a deterministic program automaton A_ρ, which is a variant of deterministic finite automata.[3]
2. Using the given SLTS $\mathcal{M}$ and the program automaton A_ρ we build a product Markov chain. $\mathcal{M}^\times$. The state space of $\mathcal{M}^\times$ is the product of $\mathcal{M}$ and A_ρ, i.e., its states are of the form (s_i, z_i), where s_i is a state of $\mathcal{M}$ and z_i a state of A_ρ. Additionally, $\mathcal{M}^\times$ possesses one new, absorbing state: the state $FAIL$.

   In $\mathcal{M}^\times$ a transition $(s_i, z_i) \xrightarrow{\lambda} (s_j, z_j)$ is kept, where λ is the rate of the transition from s_i to s_j, iff the following two constraints are satisfied:

   - (s_i, z_i) must satisfy Φ, this is the case iff s_i satisfies Φ.
   - Both s_i and z_i must be capable to perform the same action, and if the current action is associated with a test, then s_i must also satisfy this test.

   If one of these two constraints is violated, we have to introduce a transition $(s_i, z_i) \xrightarrow{\lambda} FAIL$ and delete transition $(s_i, z_i) \xrightarrow{\lambda} (s_j, z_j)$.
3. Finally, to compute the probability measure of the paths that satisfy ϕ we proceed as follows. All states (s_j, z_j) of $\mathcal{M}^\times$ for which s_j is a Ψ-state and z_j is an accepting state of A_ρ are replaced by the newly introduced absorbing success state $SUCC$, labelled with the special, newly introduced atomic state formula succ, thereby redirecting all incoming transitions from the old states to the new $SUCC$ state.
4. At this point, it is possible to check, whether $\mathcal{P}_{\bowtie p}(\Phi[\rho]^{[t,t']}\Psi)$ is functionally satisfiable: If in $\mathcal{M}^\times$ a path to a succ state exists, then $\mathcal{P}_{\bowtie p}(\Phi[\rho]^{[t,t']}\Psi)$ can be satisfied at least on the functional level.
5. On $\mathcal{M}^\times$ (which was transformed as described in step 3) we can compute the probability measure of all paths satisfying the CSL formula $\mathcal{P}_{\bowtie p}(\mathsf{F}^{[t,t']}\mathsf{succ})$, which is equal to the probability measure of the paths satisfying the original formula $\mathcal{P}_{\bowtie p}(\Phi[\rho]^{[t,t']}\Psi)$ in the original model $\mathcal{M}$.

3   Stochastic Process Algebras

In the past 15 years, a number of stochastic process algebras have been devised, such as PEPA [12] and TIPP [11]. Here, we use the stochastic process algebra $\mathcal{YAMPA}$ (yet another Markovian process algebra), that is used in the tool CASPA [16], which we use for our empirical studies. Instead of giving a formal account of $\mathcal{YAMPA}$, we will introduce its most important operators by means of a small example.

---

[3] For the derivation of A_ρ from program ρ we refer to [14] for a thorough discussion of this issue. As such this issue does not play a crucial role in understanding this paper.

```
(1)    int max = 15000;
(2)    System := Arr(0)|[error, corr,ncorr]| Errorhandler
(3)    Arr(i [max]) := [i=0] -> (arr, lambda);Arr(i+1) +
(4)                                    (error, mu);((corr, 1);Arr(i+1) + (ncorr,1);(rt,kappa);Arr(0))
(5)                    [i<max, i > 0] -> (arr, lambda);Arr(i+1) + (error, mu);((corr, 1);Arr(i+1) +
(6)                                    (ncorr,1);(rt,kappa);Arr(i-1))
(7)                    [i=max] -> (prc, omega);Arr(0)
(8)    Errorhandler := (error, 1);((corr, gamma);Errorhandler + (ncorr, delta);Errorhandler)
```

Fig. 2. Example $\mathcal{YAMPA}$ specification

Example 2. In fig. 2 we list the $\mathcal{YAMPA}$ specification of the fault tolerant packet collector of example 1. In line (1) we can specify the maximum number of packets that must arrive, before processing starts. We see in this specification some "syntactic sugar" that eases the concise specification of complex systems, e.g., guarded choice in line (3). In lines (2) and (3) we find that process Arr is parameterised with parameter i, that can take the maximum value max. This parameter records the number of packets that arrived. In line (2) we see that Arr is initialised with i = 0, i.e., zero packets arrived in the beginning.

The overall system consists of the processes Arr and Errorhandler that are composed in parallel and that have to synchronise over the actions error, corr, ncorr, i.e., these actions must be performed by both processes at the same time. For all other actions, the processes can evolve independently. (arr, lambda);Arr(i+1) (line (3)) is an example of prefix: After an exponentially distributed delay time, which is governed by rate lambda, action arr can be taken. In line (4) we find an example of choice: This process can either behave as (arr, lambda);Arr(i+1) or (error, mu);((corr, 1);Arr(i+1) + (ncorr,1);(rt,kappa);Arr(0)). In line (3) to (7) we see examples of guarded choice: Depending on the actual value of i different branches of the specification in lines (3) to (7) can be taken. In line (3), this branch of the specification can only be taken, if the value of parameter i is equal to zero. Process Arr(i [max]) possesses cyclic (recursive) behaviour, as, after arr it can again behave as Arr.

4   A Property-Driven Symbolic Semantics for $\mathcal{YAMPA}$

In this section we introduce the new property-driven semantics for $\mathcal{YAMPA}$. In Sec. 4.1 we will give the general idea of this semantics. Sec. 4.2 introduces multi-terminal binary decision diagrams (MTBDDs) as data structure to represent SLTSs. In Sec. 4.3 the semantics rules is introduced by means of a small example, and in Sec 4.4 their formal definition is given.

4.1   General Idea

In Section 2.3 we have presented a straight-forward model checking procedure for SPDL path formulae. The size of the product CTMC, before it is reduced is the product of the sizes of the original model $\mathcal{M}$ and the program automaton A_ρ. During the model checking procedure, many states are merged into the states

$FAIL$ resp. $SUCC$. This means, we needlessly generate a state space that is much larger than actually required, which is both a waste of memory space and time.

To overcome this weakness in the usual model checking procedure we propose an approach that generates only those states that are actually needed to verify the property at hand. In order to reach this goal, we introduce a property-driven semantics for the stochastic process algebra $\mathcal{YAMPA}$, that uses the path formula that is to be verified to direct the state space generation process. This new semantics cuts off state space generation as soon as it becomes clear a path is either not satisfying, i.e., it leads to a $FAIL$ state, or satisfying, i.e., leads to a $SUCC$ state. This significantly reduces the number of states and transitions that are generated.

We will use the symbolic semantics of [15] as a basis for our new SPA semantics. Like in [15], the property-driven semantics maps the SPA specification directly to the MTBDD representation of its underlying SLTS. The semantics proceeds in a compositional manner, according to the syntactic structure of the process term at hand. Additionally to [15], the new semantics takes, as already said, during generation of the SLTS the SPDL property that is to be verified into account. We chose MTBDDs as data structures for the SLTS representation as it was shown convincingly [18] that MTBDDs allow a compact representation of even huge state spaces.

4.2   Multi-terminal Binary Decision Diagrams Encode SLTSs

MTBDDs [10] are an extension of BDDs [6] for the graph-based representation of pseudo-Boolean functions, i.e., functions of type $\mathbb{B}^n \mapsto \mathbb{R}$. Informally spoken, MTBDDs are collapsed binary decision trees, i.e., each non-terminal nodes has exactly two outgoing edges.

They are collapsed in the sense that structural properties of the binary trees are used to reduce the size of the graph.

MTBDDs are very well suited for the representation of the semantic model of SPAs. We will demonstrate that by means of a small example.

Example 3. Consider Fig. 1 from Example 1. To represent this SLTS as an MTBDD we have to find ways to represent its "ingredients" in an appropriate way. That means we have to find representations for: the actions, the states, and the transition relation. All these can be encoded binarily resp. by means of pseudo-Boolean functions:

- Actions: The system has six actions: $arr, error, corr, ncorr, rt$, and prc, therefore, we need three variables a_1, a_2, a_3 to encode them:

$$Enc_{Act}(arr) = \neg a_3 \wedge \neg a_2 \wedge \neg a_1 = 000,$$
$$Enc_{Act}(error) = 001 \quad Enc_{Act}(corr) = 010 \quad Enc_{Act}(ncorr) = 011$$
$$Enc_{Act}(rt) = 100 \quad Enc_{Act}(prc) = 101$$

- States: The system has 13 states, i.e., we need 4 Boolean variables z_1 to z_4 to encode them:

$$Enc_s(s_1) = \neg z_4 \wedge \neg z_3 \wedge \neg z_2 \wedge \neg z_1 = 0000,$$
$$Enc_s(s_1) = 0001 \quad \cdots \quad Enc_s(s_{13}) = 1011$$

- Transition relation: A single transition $s \xrightarrow{a,\lambda} s'$ can be encoded as pseudo-Boolean function: $TR(s,a,\lambda,s')$. $TR(s,a,\lambda,s')$ is the conjunction of the binary variables that encode the source state s, target state s' and action a. For source and target states we need two disjoint sets of Boolean variables, respectively denoted z_i and t_i. The pseudo-Boolean function obtained so, has as function value rate λ. Transition relation R is than the disjunction over all possible $TR(s,a,\lambda,s')$. For example $TR(s_1,arr,\lambda,s_2)$ can be encoded as follows:

$$TR(s_1, arr, \lambda, s_2) =$$
$$\underbrace{\neg z_4 \wedge \neg z_3 \wedge \neg z_2 \wedge \neg z_1}_{s_1} \wedge \underbrace{\neg a_3 \wedge \neg a_2 \wedge \neg a_1}_{arr} \wedge \underbrace{\neg t_4 \wedge \neg t_3 \wedge \neg t_2 \wedge t_1}_{s_2}$$

In terms of MTBDDs, the variables that encode states and actions are the non-terminal nodes and the transition rates are the values of the leaf nodes. In Fig. 3 we show the MTBDD representation of two transitions of the SLTS: $s_1 \xrightarrow{arr,\lambda} s_2$ and $s_1 \xrightarrow{error,\mu} s_6$. Note, that we put the action variables on top of the MTBDD, as this yields smaller MTBDDs.[4]

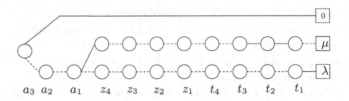

Fig. 3. MTBDD encoding transitions $TR(s_1, arr, \lambda, s_2)$ and $TR(s_1, error, \mu, s_6)$

4.3   Property-Driven Symbolic Semantics - Introduction and Example

Here, we present the general idea behind our semantics and introduce in greater detail the semantic rules for the operators of $\mathcal{YAMPA}$. Due to limited space we will not give the formal description of semantic rules for all operators. Generally, we want to encode the transitions of a given process algebraic description P by an MTBDD. The symbolic representation $[\![P]\!]$ is built from P's parse tree and the transition relation of the deterministic program automaton $\mathcal{A}_\rho$ that is

---

[4]   In practice further optimisations are possible, but not important here.

attached to the path formula we want to verify. The parse tree is traversed in a depth-first manner, thereby constructing $[P]$ inductively from smaller portions of the overall specification. Finally, we obtain the MTBDD representation of P's transitional behaviour, taking the restrictions imposed by the path formula at hand into account.

Definition 5. *The symbolic representation $[P]$ of a process algebra term P consists of the following parts:*

- *The MTBDD $B(P)$, encoding the transition relation,*
- *a list of encodings of process variables X, that appear in P, denoted $Encs(X)$,*
- *the encoding of the initial state of P, denoted $Encs(s_P^{DS})$,*
- *the transition relation δ_{A_ρ} for A_ρ,*
- *the current state of A_ρ.*

Before we list the formal rules for the property-driven semantics, we will give another example.

Example 4. We want to generate the SLTS for the specification from Example 2, with max = 2. and SPDL formula $\Phi_1 := \mathcal{P}_{\bowtie p}((\neg \mathsf{full})[arr^*]^{[0,t]}(\mathsf{full}))$ from Example 1. We assume, that the actions and their encodings are globally known, i.e., we know the number of Boolean variables required for their encoding, which is three (like in Example 3). As we derive the MTBDD representation of the SLTS directly from the given specification we do not know in advance the size of the state space and therefore the number of Boolean variables to encode the states and the transition relation. Therefore, we take in the beginning as small a number as possible, and extend the number of variables, if required. The initial state of the specification Arr(0) | [error, corr,ncorr] | Errorhandler can be encoded by one Boolean variable $Encs(s_1) = \neg z_1 = 0$. Given Φ_1, we check if $\neg \mathsf{full}$ is satisfied, which is the case, then we check whether a transition labelled with arr is possible, which is the case, i.e., we add $Encs(s_2) = z_1 = 1$. As for s_2 the condition full is not satisfied, $s_2 \neq SUCC$. The MTBDD encodes at this point the transition relation R consisting of $TR(s_0, arr, \lambda, s_1)$. In s_1 a second transition, labelled by *error* is possible, we see from Φ_1 that *err* does not belong to the actions that yield a satisfying path, i.e., we have to introduce a transition to the failure state $FAIL$, which has no encoding up to now. To do so, we have to extend the number of Boolean variables that encode states, i.e., the states s_1 and s_2 are re-encoded:

$$Encs(s_1) = \neg z_2 \land z_1 = 00 \quad Encs(s_2) = \neg z_2 \land z_1 = 01$$
$$Encs(FAIL) = z_2 \land \neg z_1 = 10$$

Now, we can introduce a new transition encoding: $TR(s_1, error, \mu, FAIL)$. The overall transition relation R is now the disjunction of $TR(s_0, arr, \lambda, s_1)$ and $TR(s_1, error, \mu, FAIL)$

The state s_2 corresponds to Arr(1) | [error, corr,ncorr] | Errorhandler, i.e., $\neg \mathsf{full}$ is satisfied, and again arr and $error$ transitions are possible, due to the

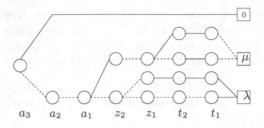

$$a_3 \quad a_2 \quad a_1 \quad z_2 \quad z_1 \quad t_2 \quad t_1$$

Fig. 4. MTBDD representation of the fault-tolerant packet collector's SLTS for max $=$ 2 and Φ_1

(1) **if** not first appearance of X within present seq. component **then**
(2)   **skip** /* do nothing */
(3) **if** no free encodings available **then** /* need to extend the set of possible encodings */
(4)   Extend the number of Boolean variables
(5) Extend all existing encodings
(6) $B(X) := 0$ /*In case of stop: $B(\text{stop}) := ...$

Fig. 5. Algorithm for process variable X and stop

restrictions imposed by the path formula, *error* leads to the $FAIL$ state, i.e., we introduce a new transition: $TR(s_2, error, \mu, FAIL)$. For *arr* we add a new transition from s_2 to s_3, as s_3 satisfies full, $s_3 = SUCC$, and $TR(s_2, arr, \lambda, SUCC)$, where $Encs(s_3) = 11$. In Fig. 4 we find the MTBDD encoding the transition relation of this SLTS.

4.4   Property-Driven Symbolic Semantics - Formal Definition

Process Variables. A process variable X specifies a reference state within a surrounding recX operator. Therefore, process variables are encoded in a similar fashion as states. Within each sequential component[5] process variables having the same name get the same encoding. Upon first appearance of a process variable X, the MTBDD associated with X is the 0-MTBDD (cf. Fig. 5). The stop process is a special case of a process variable (a process constant).

Prefix $P := (a, \lambda); Q$. For a given formula $\Psi := \mathcal{P}_{\bowtie p}(\Phi_1[\rho]^I \Phi_2)$, we want to generate the symbolic representation of P, $[\![P]\!]$. To construct $B(P)$ we have to distinguish the following cases:

1. If the current state s_P^{DS} satisfies Φ_1 and in A_ρ's current state z an a-labelled transition to a state z' is possible, s_P^{DS} satisfies the test formula Ξ, possibly attached to A_ρ's a-transition, then, we can introduce a transition from s_P^{DS} to the encoding of Q's initial state.

---

[5] A sequential component is a process term which does not include the parallel composition operator.

Case 1:

(1) **if** $((s_P^{DS} \models \Phi_1) \wedge (z \xrightarrow{a}_{A_\rho} z' \wedge s_P^{DS} \models \Xi))$

(2) $B(P) := TR(s_P^{DS}, a, \lambda, s_Q^{DS})$

Case 2:

(3) **if** $((s_P^{DS} \models \Phi_1) \wedge (s_Q^{DS} \models \Phi_2) \wedge (z \xrightarrow{a}_{A_\rho} z' \wedge s_P^{DS} \models \Xi))$

(4) $B(P) := TR(s_P^{DS}, a, \lambda, SUCC)$

Case 3:

(5) **if** $((s_P^{DS} \models \Phi_1) \wedge (z \not\xrightarrow{a}_{A_\rho} z' \wedge s_P^{DS} \models \Xi))$

(6) $B(P) := TR(s_P^{DS}, a, \lambda, FAIL)$

Fig. 6. Algorithm for prefix $P := (a, \lambda); Q$

2. If, additionally to case 1, the target state of A_ρ is an accepting state and s_Q^{DS} satisfies Φ_2, then a transition from the encoding of s_P^{DS} to the encoding of state $SUCC$[6] is introduced.
3. If the state s_P^{DS} satisfies Φ_1, but no transition labelling in A_ρ's current state matches a, then we have to introduce a transition from the encoding of P to the encoding of the error state $FAIL$.
4. If state s_P^{DS} does not satisfy Φ_1, then we have to introduce a transition from the encoding of P to the encoding of the error state $FAIL$.
5. If state s_P^{DS} does not satisfy the test formula, attached to A_ρ's a transition, then we have to introduce a transition from the encoding of P to the encoding of the error state $FAIL$.

In Fig. 6 we give the formal description of the prefix algorithm.[7] We only give the first, second, and third case from above, the remaining cases can be treated similarly.

Choice $P := Q + R$. Here, we can assume that $[\![Q]\!]$ and $[\![R]\!]$ are already available. To derive $[\![P]\!]$ from $[\![Q]\!]$ and $[\![R]\!]$ we have to proceed as follows: A new initial state is introduced for $Q + R$. All transitions emanating from the initial states of the subprocesses Q and R have to be copied, as they may also take place in the initial state of the overall process.

Recursion $P = \mathrm{rec}X : Q$. When constructing $[\![P]\!] = [\![\mathrm{rec}X : Q]\!]$ from $[\![Q]\!]$ we can distinguish the following cases:

1. X does not appear (unbound) in Q: In this case we simply identify the symbolic representation of $\mathrm{rec}X : Q$ with that of Q.
2. X appears in Q and s_Q^{DS} satisfies Φ_2 and the current state in A_ρ is an accepting state, then the process variable X is identified/replaced by the process constant $SUCC$.

---

[6] $SUCC$ can be handled like stop.

[7] In this and the following algorithm we omit details on choosing fresh Boolean variables and possibly extending encodings.

Case 1:

(1) **if** $(a \notin L \wedge (s_Q^{DS} \models \Phi_1) \wedge (z \xrightarrow{a}_{A_\rho} z' \wedge s_Q^{DS} \models \Xi))$

/*with Ξ being a test formula attached to the current transition of A_ρ. */

(2) $B(Q') := TR(Enc_S(Q) \circ Enc_S(R), a, \lambda, Enc_S(Q') \circ Enc_S(R))$

(3) $B(P) := B(P) + B(Q')$

Case 2:

(4) **if** $(a \notin L \wedge (s_Q^{DS} \models \Phi_1) \wedge (z \xrightarrow{a}_{A_\rho} z' \wedge s_Q^{DS} \models \Xi))$

(5) $B(Q') := TR(Enc_S(Q) \circ Enc_S(R), a, \lambda, FAIL)$

(6) $B(P) := B(P) + B(Q')$

Case 3:

(7) **if** $(a \in L \wedge (s_Q^{DS} \models \Phi_1) \wedge (z \xrightarrow{a}_{A_\rho} z' \wedge s_Q^{DS} \models \Xi) \wedge (s_R^{DS} \models \Phi_1) \wedge (s_R^{DS} \models \Xi))$

(8) $B(Q') := TR(Enc_S(Q) \circ Enc_S(R), a, \lambda, Enc_S(Q') \circ Enc_S(R'))$

(9) $B(P) := B(P) + B(Q')$

Case 4:

(10) **if** $(a \in L \wedge (s_Q^{DS} \models \Phi_1) \wedge (s_{Q'}^{DS} \models \Phi_2) \wedge (z \xrightarrow{a}_{A_\rho} z' \wedge s_Q^{DS} \models \Xi) \wedge (s_R^{DS} \models \Phi_1) \wedge (s_{R'}^{DS} \models \Phi_2) \wedge (s_R^{DS} \models \Xi))$

(11) $B(Q') := TR(Enc_S(Q) \circ Enc_S(R), a, \lambda, SUCC)$

(12) $B(P) := B(P) + B(Q')$

Fig. 7. Algorithm for parallel composition $P := Q|[L]|R$

3. X appears in Q and either s_Q^{DS} does not satisfy Φ_2 or the current state in A_ρ is not an accepting state: In this case the process variable X is identified with the encoding of the initial state of Q.

Parallel Composition $P := Q|[L]|R$. To derive $[\![P]\!]$ from P and $\Phi = \mathcal{P}_{\bowtie p}(\Phi_1[\rho]^I \Phi_2)$, we must not assume that $[\![Q]\!]$ resp. $[\![R]\!]$ are already available. Instead, we have to derive $[\![P]\!]$ from Q and R step by step, by respecting the same conditions as for the prefix operator, i.e., depending on the current state of s_P^{DS} of P, and z of A_ρ, we add transitions either to a "regular" successor of s_P^{DS} or to $FAIL$, resp. $SUCC$.

In Fig. 7 the algorithm for the derivation of $[\![P]\!]$ from Q and R for a single transition is given. We list only a few of the possible cases. This procedure has to be repeated, until all potential transitions that are possible are generated. This can be done using standard depth- or breadth-first search applied to P's parse tree.

5   Empirical Results

For our case studies we have employed the symbolic stochastic model checker CASPA. All results have been computed on a standard PC with Pentium IV 3.2 GHz processor, 1 GB RAM, running the operating system SuSe Linux 10.0.

5.1   Fault-Tolerant Packet Collector

Let us consider the system from Example 1. We will check the SPDL path formulae presented there. In Table 1 we find the model sizes for these formulae. In columns three to five, we list the maximum size of the product CTMC that is generated for model checking SPDL without property-driven state space generation, which is the product of the size of the automaton and the system model.

In columns six to eight we list the state space sizes as they are generated when using the property-driven approach proposed in this paper, and on which model checking is actually carried out. We see, that we can avoid the generation of many states, thereby reducing the memory requirements for SPDL model checking. We see in Table 2 that for both formulae the property-driven state space generation also requires less time than the traditional approach.

Table 1. State space sizes for Φ_1 to Φ_3 (Packet collector)

max	State space size	Not Property-driven			Property-driven		
		Φ_1	Φ_2	Φ_3	Φ_1	Φ_2	Φ_3
5,000	15,001	15,001	60,004	45,003	5,002	20,003	10,003
15,000	45,001	45,001	180,004	135,003	15,002	60,003	30,003
30,000	90,001	90,001	360,004	270,003	30,002	120,003	60,003
50,000	150,001	150,001	600,004	450,003	50,002	200,003	100,003

5.2 Kanban System

The Kanban manufacturing system was first described as a stochastic Petri net in [7]. We consider a Kanban system with four cells, a single type of Kanban cards and the possibility that some workpieces may need to be reworked. We will check the following properties:

- Φ_1: Is the requirement, that within t time units exactly three reworks are required in station 1 satisfied with a probability that is at most p?
- Φ_2 :: Is the probability that a single job needs at most t time units to go through all 4 stations greater than p percent?
- Φ_3: Is the probability to reach station 4, within t time units, given in station 1 are no reworks required and in stations 2 and 3 in total exactly 2 reworks are necessary within $\bowtie p$?

From Table 3 we observe that for the formulae Φ_1 to Φ_3 the state space of the product CTMC is dramatically smaller than that of the original system, which stems from the fact that for all three formulae only very specific paths in the system are of interest. We can observe that for Φ_2 the size of the product CTMC is independent of the number of Kanban cards, which is not surprising, as we consider a specific card that goes through the system. In the second column we find the size of the original state space, in columns three to five we show the maximum size of the state space for the traditional approach, and in columns six through eight we list the final state space on which model checking actual is performed. We see in Table 4 for all three formulae that property-driven state space generation requires less time than the traditional approach. This is not surprising, as billions of states and even more important, billions of transitions of the original model do not to be explored in the property-driven approach.

Table 2. State space generation times for Φ_1 to Φ_3 (Packet collector)

max	Not Property-driven			Property-driven		
	Φ_1	Φ_2	Φ_3	Φ_1	Φ_2	Φ_3
5,000	2.9 sec.	3.3 sec.	3.1 sec.	2.0 sec.	2.8 sec.	2.9 sec.
15,000	10.00 sec.	10.8 sec.	11.2 sec.	6.9 sec.	9.0 sec.	9.0 sec.
30,000	21.4 sec.	22.7 sec.	22.5 sec.	17.8 sec.	18.9 sec.	19.6 sec.
50,000	37.9 sec.	45.3 sec.	44.4 sec.	33.6 sec.	40.4 sec.	32.8 sec.

Table 3. State space sizes for Φ_1 and Φ_2 (Kanban)

n	State space size	Not Property-driven			Property-driven		
		Φ_1	Φ_2	Φ_3	Φ_1	Φ_2	Φ_3
5	2,546,432	22,917,888	33,103,616	43,289,344	83	13	159
8	133,865,325	1,204,787,925	1,740,249,225	2275710525	189	13	240
10	1,005,927,208	9,053,344,872	13,077,053,704	17,100,762,536	276	13	294
12	5,519,907,575	49,679,168,175	71,758,798,475	93,838,428,775	364	13	348
15	46,998,779,904	-	-	-	496	13	411

Table 4. State space generation times for Φ_1 and Φ_2 (Kanban)

n	Not Property-driven			Property-driven		
	Φ_1	Φ_2	Φ_3	Φ_1	Φ_2	Φ_3
5	0.8 sec.	0.7 sec.	0.7 sec.	0.1 sec.	0.1 sec.	0.1 sec.
8	4.7 sec.	4.2 sec.	4.5 sec.	0.2 sec.	0.2 sec.	0.2 sec.
10	11.4 sec.	10.8 sec.	11.0 sec.	0.5 sec.	0.5 sec.	0.5 sec.
12	21.7 sec.	21.5 sec.	22.1 sec.	0.8 sec.	0.7 sec.	0.7 sec.
15	-	-	-	1.6 sec.	1.5 sec.	1.5 sec.

5.3   Fault-Tolerant Multiprocessor System

This example is based on [17]. The original model consists of N computers each of which has the following components: Memory modules, CPUs, I/O ports, and error handlers. Each of these computer components consists of several subcomponents, that can fail, leading to the failure of one computer. The overall system is operational if at least one computer is operational.

We have generated the CTMC for three different configurations: C1 is the configuration consisting of two computers with three memory modules each; C1 has about 750,000 reachable states. C2 consists of 3 computers, with one memory module each. C3 comprises 3 computers and 3 memory modules each.

We will check the following formula Φ_1: Does the probability that computer failures and subsequently a system failure is only due to memory failures lie within the bounds as given by $\bowtie p$, given that the maximum time to reach a system failure state is at most t?

Table 5. State space generation times for Φ_1 (fault-tolerant multi-processor)

Conf	State space size	Not Property-driven	Property-driven
		Φ_1	Φ_1
C1	753,664	2,260,992	53,306
C2	123,760	371,280	1,475
C3	381,681,664	1,145,044,992	6,554,329

In Table 5 we show the model sizes for the above formulae. In column three, we list the maximum size of the product CTMC that is generated for model checking SPDL without property-driven state space generation, which is the product of the size of the automaton and the system model. In column 4 we give the model size, when applying the property-driven state space generator. We do not list the model generation times here, which are below 0.1 sec. for all configurations, in both the property-driven and the non-property-driven case.

6   Conclusions

In this paper we have introduced a property-driven symbolic semantics for the stochastic process algebra $\mathcal{YAMPA}$. We have shown its usage of a property-driven semantics for model checking probabilistic SPDL path formulae reduces both time and memory requirements. These savings can be considerable, as shown for the Kanban system, where an overhead of several billion states could be avoided. The numerical algorithms for stochastic model checking have a time complexity at least linear in state space size, so that an enormous overall time gain can be expected.

Generally, when doing numerical analysis of CTMCs with a huge state space some caution is required. As reported in [5], the accuracy of the numerical analysis depends on many factors, e.g. state space ordering, the actual iterative solution method, etc. But it must be stressed, that this is a problem that applies to all approaches that rely on numerical analysis. In fact, the probability masses on both the model, generated using property-driven state space generation, and the model using the "traditional" approach are identical. The experiments we conducted, on both the reduced and non-reduced model did not yield any differences.

In the future we plan to combine this property-driven semantics with some notion of bisimulation reduction in order to obtain further state-space reductions and to investigate the possibilities to transfer the results from [2] to the stochastic case.

References

1. Marsan, M.A., Balbo, G., Conte, G.: A Class of Generalized Stochastic Petri Nets for the Performance Evaluation of Multiprocessor Systems. ACM Transactions on Computer Systems 2(2), 93–122 (1984)
2. Aziz, A., Shiple, T., Singhal, V., Brayton, R., Sangiovanni-Vincentelli, A.: Formula-Dependent Equivalence for Compositional CTL Model Checking. Form. Methods Syst. Des. 21(2), 193–224 (2002)

3. Baier, C., Cloth, L., Haverkort, B.R., Kuntz, M., Siegle, M.: Model Checking Markov Chains with Actions and State Labels. IEEE Transactions on Software Engineering 33(4), 209–224 (2007)
4. Baier, C., Haverkort, B., Hermanns, H., Katoen, J.P.: Model-Checking Algorithms for Continuous-Time Markov Chains. IEEE Trans. Software Eng. 29(7), 1–18 (2003)
5. Bell, A.: Distributed Evaluation of Stochastic Petri Nets. PhD thesis, RWTH Aachen, Fakultät für Mathematik, Informatik und Naturwissenschaften (2003)
6. Bryant, R.E.: Graph-based Algorithms for Boolean Function Manipulation. IEEE Transactions on Computers C-35(8), 677–691 (1986)
7. Ciardo, G., Tilgner, M.: On the use of Kronecker operators for the solution of generalized stochastic Petri nets. Technical Report 96-35, ICASE (1996)
8. Clarke, E.M., Emerson, E.A., Sistla, A.: Automatic verification of finite state concurrent systems using temporal logic specifications: A practical approach. In: 10th ACM Annual Symp. on Principles of Programming Languages, pp. 117–126. ACM Press, New York (1983)
9. Fischer, M., Ladner, R.: Propositional dynamic logic of regular programs. J. Comput. System Sci. 18, 194–211 (1979)
10. Fujita, M., McGeer, P., Yang, J.C.-Y.: Multi-terminal Binary Decision Diagrams: An efficient data structure for matrix representation. Formal Methods in System Design 10(2/3), 149–169 (1997)
11. Hermanns, H., Herzog, U., Katoen, J.-P.: Process Algebra for Performance Evaluation. Theoretical Computer Science 274(1-2), 43–87 (2002)
12. Hillston, J.: A Compositional Approach to Performance Modelling. Cambridge University Press, Cambridge (1996)
13. Katoen, J.-P., Kemna, T., Zapreev, I., Jansen, D.: Bisimulation minimisation mostly speeds up probabilistic model checking. In: TACAS 2007. LNCS, vol. 4424, pp. 76–92. Springer, Heidelberg (2007)
14. Kuntz, M.: Symbolic Semantics and Verification of Stochastic Process Algebras. PhD thesis, Universität Erlangen-Nürnberg, Institut für Informatik 7 (2006)
15. Kuntz, M., Siegle, M.: Deriving symbolic representations from stochastic process algebras. In: Hermanns, H., Segala, R. (eds.) PROBMIV 2002, PAPM-PROBMIV 2002, and PAPM 2002. LNCS, vol. 2399, pp. 188–206. Springer, Heidelberg (2002)
16. Kuntz, M., Siegle, M., Werner, E.: CASPA - A Tool for Symbolic Performance and Dependability Evaluation. In: Núñez, M., Maamar, Z., Pelayo, F.L., Pousttchi, K., Rubio, F. (eds.) FORTE 2004. LNCS, vol. 3236, p. 293. Springer, Heidelberg (2004)
17. Sanders, W.H., Malhis, L.M.: Dependability Evaluation Using Composed SAN-Based Reward Models. Journal of Parallel and Distributed Computing 15(3), 238–254 (1992)
18. Siegle, M.: Advances in model representation. In: de Alfaro, L., Gilmore, S. (eds.) PROBMIV 2001, PAPM-PROBMIV 2001, and PAPM 2001. LNCS, vol. 2165, pp. 1–22. Springer, Heidelberg (2001)

Testing Finite State Machines Presenting Stochastic Time and Timeouts*

Mercedes G. Merayo, Manuel Núñez, and Ismael Rodríguez

Dept. Sistemas Informáticos y Programación
Universidad Complutense de Madrid, 28040 Madrid, Spain
mgmerayo@fdi.ucm.es,{mn,isrodrig}@sip.ucm.es

Abstract. In this paper we define a formal framework to test implementations that can be represented by the class of finite state machines introduced in [10]. First, we introduce an appropriate notion of test. Next, we provide an algorithm to derive test suites from specifications such that the constructed test suites are sound and complete with respect to two of the conformance relations introduced in [10]. In fact, the current paper together with [10] constitute a complete formal theory to specify and test the class of systems covered by the before mentioned stochastic finite state machines.

1 Introduction

The scale and heterogeneity of current systems make impossible for developers to have an overall view of them. Thus, it is difficult to foresee those errors that are either critical or more probable. In this line, *formal testing techniques* [8,14,3,15] allow to test the correctness of a system with respect to a specification. Formal testing originally targeted the functional behavior of systems, such as determining whether the tested system can, on the one hand, perform certain actions and, on the other hand, does not perform some non-expected ones. While the relevant aspects of some systems only concern *what* they do, in some other systems it is equally relevant *how* they do what they do. Thus, after the initial consolidation stage, formal testing techniques started also to deal with *non-functional* properties. In fact, there are already several proposals for timed testing (e.g. [9,4,16,5,11,12,7,6,2,13]). In these papers, with the only exception of [12], time is considered to be *deterministic*, that is, time requirements follow the form "after/before t time units..." In fact, in most of the cases time is introduced by means of clocks following [1]. Even though the inclusion of time allows to give a more precise description of the system to be implemented, there are frequent situations that cannot be accurately described by using this notion of deterministic time. For example, we may desire to specify a system where a message is expected to be received with probability $\frac{1}{2}$ in the interval $(0, 1]$, with probability $\frac{1}{4}$ in $(1, 2]$, and so on.

---

* Research partially supported by the Spanish MEC project WEST/FAST (TIN2006-15578-C02-01) and the Marie Curie project TAROT (MRTN-CT-2003-505121).

K. Wolter (Ed.): EPEW 2007, LNCS 4748, pp. 97–111, 2007.
© Springer-Verlag Berlin Heidelberg 2007

In order to use a formal technique, we need that the systems under study can be expressed in terms of a formal language. A suitable representation of the temporal behavior is critical for constructing useful models of real-time systems. A language to represent these systems should enable the definition of temporal conditions that may direct the system behavior, as well as the time consumed by the execution of tasks. In this line, the time consumed during the execution of a system falls into one of the following categories:

(a) The system consumes time while it performs its operations. This time may depend on the values of certain parameters of the system, such as the available resources.
(b) The time passes while the system waits for a reaction from the environment. In particular, the system can change its internal state if an interaction is not received before a certain amount of time.

A language focussing on temporal issues should allow the specifier to define how the system behavior is affected by both kinds of temporal aspects. Even though there exists a myriad of timed extensions of classical frameworks, most of them specialize only in one of the previous variants: Time is either associated with actions or associated with delays/timeouts. In this paper we use the formalism introduced in [10] that allows to specify in a natural way both time aspects. In our framework, timeouts are specified by using fix amounts of time. In contrast, the duration of actions will be given by *random variables*. That is, we will have expressions such as "with probability p the action o will be performed before t units of time". We will consider a suitable extension of finite state machines where (stochastic) time information will be included. Intuitively, we will consider that the time consumed between the input is applied and the output is received is given by a random variable ξ. An appropriate notation for stochastic transitions could be $s \xrightarrow{i/o}_\xi s'$, meaning that "if the machine is in state s and receives an input i then it will produce the output o before time t with probability $P(\xi \leq t)$ and it will change its state to s'". The definition of conformance testing relations is more difficult than usually. In particular, even in the absence of non-determinism, the same sequence of actions may take different time values to be performed in different runs of the system. While the definition of the new language is not difficult, mixing these temporal requirements strongly complicates the posterior theoretical analysis.

As we have already indicated, this paper represents a continuation of the work initiated in [10]. In that paper we proposed several *stochastic-temporal conformance relations*: An implementation is correct with respect to a specification if it does not show any behavior that is forbidden by the specification, where both the functional behavior and the temporal behavior are considered (and, implicitly, how they affect each other). In this paper we introduce a notion of test and how to test implementations that can be represented by using our notion of finite state machine. In addition, we provide an algorithm that derives test suites from specifications. The main result of our paper indicates that these test suites have the same distinguishing power as the two most interesting conformance relations presented in [10] in the sense that an implementation successfully passes a test suite iff it is conforming to the specification.

The rest of the paper is structured as follows. In the next two sections we remind our notion of stochastic finite state machine and the two most interesting implementation relations introduced in [10]. In Section 4 we formally define a notion of test, as well as the application of tests to implementations and two notions of successfully passing a test suite. In Section 5 we present an algorithm to derive test suites and show that the derived test suites appropriately capture the relations introduced in Section 3. Finally, in Section 6 we present our conclusions.

2   SFSM: A Stochastic Extension of the FSM Model

In this section we introduce our notion of finite state machines with stochastic time. We use random variables to model the (stochastic) time output actions take to be executed. Thus, we need to introduce some basic concepts on random variables. We will consider that the sample space, that is, the domain of random variables, is a set of numeric time values Time. Since this is a *generic* time domain, the specifier can choose whether the system will use a discrete/continuous time domain. We simply assume that $0 \in$ Time. Regarding passing of time, we will also consider that machines can evolve by raising *timeouts*. Intuitively, if after a given time, depending on the current state, we do not receive any input action then the machine will change its current state.

During the rest of the paper we will use the following notation. Tuples of elements $(e_1, e_2 \ldots, e_n)$ will be denoted by $\bar{e}$. $\hat{a}$ denotes an interval of elements $[a_1, a_2)$, with $a_1, a_2 \in$ Time and $a_1 < a_2$. We will use the projection function π_i such that given a tuple $\bar{t} = (t_1, \ldots, t_n)$, for all $1 \leq i \leq n$ we have $\pi_i(t) = t_i$. Let $\bar{t} = (t_1, \ldots, t_n)$ and $\bar{t}' = (t'_1, \ldots, t'_n)$. We denote by $\sum \bar{t}$ the addition of all the elements belonging to the tuple $\bar{t}$, that is, $\sum_{j=1}^{n} t_j$. The number of elements of the tuple will be represented by $|\bar{t}|$. Finally, if $\bar{t} = (t_1 \ldots t_n)$, $\bar{p} = (\hat{t_1} \ldots \hat{t_n})$ and for all $1 \leq j \leq n$ we have $t_j \in \hat{t_j}$, we write $\bar{t} \in \bar{p}$.

Definition 1. We denote by $\mathcal{V}$ the set of random variables ($\xi, \psi, \ldots$ range over $\mathcal{V}$). Let ξ be a random variable. We define its *probability distribution function* as the function $F_\xi :$ Time $\longrightarrow [0, 1]$ such that $F_\xi(x) = P(\xi \leq x)$, where $P(\xi \leq x)$ is the probability that ξ assumes values less than or equal to x.

Given two random variables ξ and ψ we consider that $\xi + \psi$ denotes a random variable distributed as the addition of the two random variables ξ and ψ.

We will use the delimiters $\{$ and $\}$ to denote multisets. Given a set E, we denote by $\wp(E)$ the multisets of elements belonging to E. Given the multiset H over E, for all $r \in E$ we have that $H(r)$ denotes the *multiplicity* of r in H. Given two multisets H_1 and H_2 over E, $H_1 \uplus H_2$ denotes the union of H_1 and H_2, and it is formally defined as $(H_1 \uplus H_2)(r) = H_1(r) + H_2(r)$ for all $r \in E$.

We will call *sample* to any multiset of elements belonging to Time. Let ξ be a random variable and J be a sample. We denote by $\gamma(\xi, J)$ the *confidence* of ξ on J. $\qquad\square$

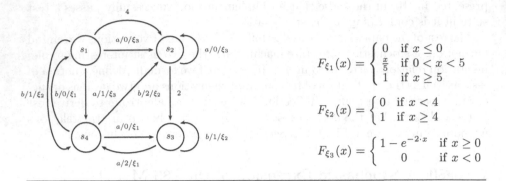

$$F_{\xi_1}(x) = \begin{cases} 0 & \text{if } x \leq 0 \\ \frac{x}{5} & \text{if } 0 < x < 5 \\ 1 & \text{if } x \geq 5 \end{cases}$$

$$F_{\xi_2}(x) = \begin{cases} 0 & \text{if } x < 4 \\ 1 & \text{if } x \geq 4 \end{cases}$$

$$F_{\xi_3}(x) = \begin{cases} 1 - e^{-2 \cdot x} & \text{if } x \geq 0 \\ 0 & \text{if } x < 0 \end{cases}$$

Fig. 1. Example of Stochastic Finite State Machine

In our setting, samples will be associated with the time values that implementations take to perform sequences of actions. We have that $\gamma(\xi, J)$ takes values in the interval $[0, 1]$. Intuitively, bigger values of $\gamma(\xi, J)$ indicate that the observed sample J is more likely to be produced by the random variable ξ. That is, this function decides how *similar* the probability distribution function generated by J and the one corresponding to the random variable ξ are.

In the appendix of [10] we show one of the possibilities to formally define the notion of confidence by means of a hypothesis contrast.

Definition 2. A *Stochastic Finite State Machine*, in short SFSM, is a tuple $M = (S, I, O, \delta, TO, s_{in})$ where S is the set of states, with $s_{in} \in S$ being the *initial state*, I and O denote the sets of input and output actions, respectively, δ is the set of transitions, and $TO : S \longrightarrow S \times (\text{Time} \cup \{\infty\})$ is the *timeout function*. Each transition belonging to δ is a tuple (s, i, o, ξ, s') where $s, s' \in S$ are the initial and final states, $i \in I$ and $o \in O$ are the input and output actions, and $\xi \in \mathcal{V}$ is the random variable defining the time associated with the transition.

Let $M = (S, I, O, \delta, TO, s_{in})$ be a SFSM. We say that M is *input-enabled* if for all state $s \in S$ and input $i \in I$ there exist s', o, ξ, such that $(s, i, o, \xi, s') \in \delta$. We say that M is *deterministically observable* if for all s, i, o there do not exist two different transitions $(s, i, o, \xi_1, s_1), (s, i, o, \xi_2, s_2) \in \delta$.   □

Intuitively, a transition (s, i, o, ξ, s') indicates that if the machine is in state s and receives the input i then the machine emits the output o before time t with probability $F_\xi(t)$ and the machine changes its current state to s'.

For each state $s \in S$, the application of the timeout function $TO(s)$ returns a pair (s', t) indicating the time that the machine can remain at the state s waiting for an input action and the state to which the machine evolves if no input is received on time. We indicate the absence of a timeout in a given state by setting the corresponding time value to ∞. In addition, we assume that $TO(s) = (s', t)$ implies $s \neq s'$, that is, timeouts always produce a change of the state. In fact, let us note that a definition such as $TO(s) = (s, t)$ is equivalent to set the timeout for the state s to infinite.

Example 1. Let us consider the machine depicted in Figure 1 in which the initial state is s_1. Each transition has an associated random variable. In the following we explain how these random variables are distributed. We consider that ξ_1 is *uniformly distributed* in the interval $[0, 5]$. Uniform distributions assign equal probability to all the times in the interval. The random variable ξ_2 follows a Dirac distribution in 4. The idea is that the corresponding delay will be equal to 4 time units. Finally, ξ_3 is *exponentially* distributed with parameter 2. Let us consider the transition $(s_4, (b, 0, \xi_1), s_1)$. Intuitively, if the machine is in state s_4 and it receives the input b then it will produce the output 0 after a time given by ξ_1. For example, we know that this time will be less than 1 time unit with probability $\frac{1}{5}$, it will be less than 3 time units with probability $\frac{3}{5}$, and so on. Finally, once 5 time units have passed we know that the output 0 has been performed (that is, we have probability 1). Regarding the timeout function we have $TO(s_1) = (s_2, 4)$. In this case, if the machine is in state s_1 and no input is received before 4 units of time then the state is changed to s_2.

Definition 3. Let $M = (S, I, O, \delta, TO, s_{in})$ be a SFSM. We say that a tuple $(s_0, s, i/o, \hat{t}, \xi)$ is a *step* for the state s_0 of M if there exist k states $s_1, \ldots, s_k \in S$, with $k \geq 0$, such that $\hat{t} = \left[\sum_{j=0}^{k-1} \pi_2(TO(s_j)), \sum_{j=0}^{k} \pi_2(TO(s_j)) \right)$ and there exists a transition $(s_k, i, o, \xi, s) \in \delta$.

We say that $(\hat{t}_1/i_1/\xi_1/o_1, \ldots, \hat{t}_r/i_r/\xi_r/o_r)$ is a *stochastic evolution* of M if there exist r steps of M $(s_{in}, s_1, i_1/o_1, \hat{t}_1, \xi_1), \ldots, (s_{r-1}, s_r, i_r/o_r, \hat{t}_r, \xi_r)$ for the states $s_{in} \ldots s_{r-1}$, respectively. We denote by $\texttt{SEvol}(M)$ the set of stochastic evolutions of M. In addition, we say that $(\hat{t}_1/i_1/o_1, \ldots, \hat{t}_r/i_r/o_r)$ is a *functional evolution* of M. We denote by $\texttt{FEvol}(M)$ the set of functional evolutions of M. We will use the shortenings $(\sigma, \bar{p})$ and $(\sigma, \bar{p}, \bar{\xi})$ to denote a functional and a stochastic evolution, respectively, where $\sigma = (i_1/o_1 \ldots i_r/o_r)$, $\bar{p} = (\hat{t}_1 \ldots \hat{t}_r)$ and $\bar{\xi} = (\xi_1 \ldots \xi_r)$. □

Intuitively, a step is a sequence of transitions that contains an action transition preceded by zero or more timeouts. The interval $\hat{t}$ indicates the time values where the transition could be performed. In particular, if the sequence of timeouts is empty then we have the interval $\hat{t} = [0, TO(s_0))$. An evolution is a sequence of inputs/outputs corresponding to the transitions of a chain of steps, where the first one begins with the initial state of the machine. In addition, stochastic evolutions also include time information which inform us about possible timeouts (indicated by the intervals $\hat{t}_j$) and random variables associated to the execution of each output after receiving each input in each step of the evolution. In the following definition we introduce the concept of *instanced evolution*. Intuitively, instanced evolutions are constructed from evolutions by instantiating to a concrete value each timeout, given by an interval, of the evolution.

Definition 4. Let $M = (S, I, O, \delta, TO, s_{in})$ be a SFSM and let us consider a *stochastic evolution* $e = (\hat{t}_1/i_1/\xi_1/o_1, \ldots, \hat{t}_r/i_r/\xi_r/o_r)$. We say that the tuple

$(t_1/i_1/\xi_1/o_1, \ldots, t_r/i_r/\xi_r/o_r)$ is an *instanced stochastic evolution of e* if for all $1 \leq j \leq r$ we have $t_j \in \hat{t}_j$. Besides, we say that the tuple $(t_1/i_1/o_1, \ldots, t_r/i_r/o_r)$ is an *instanced functional evolution* of e.

We denote by $\texttt{InsSEvol}(M)$ the set of instanced stochastic evolutions of M and by $\texttt{InsFEvol}(M)$ the set of instanced functional evolutions of M.   □

Example 2. Let us consider the SFSM depicted in Figure 1. Next, we give some of the *steps* that the machine can generate. For example, $(s_1, s_2, a/0, [0, 4), \xi_3)$ represents the transition from the state s_1 to the state s_2 when no timeouts precede it. The input a can be accepted before 4 time units pass (this is indicated by the interval $[0, 4)$). In addition, the output 0 takes t time units to be performed with probability $F_{\xi_3}(t)$. The second one, $(s_2, s_3, b/1, [2, \infty), \xi_2)$, is built from the timeout transition associated to the state s_2 and the transition outgoing the state s_3 to the state s_3. This step represents that if after 2 time units no input is received, the timeout transition associated with the state s_2 will be triggered and the state will change to s_3. After this, the machine can accept the input b. So, during the time interval $[2, \infty)$, if the machine receives an input b it will emit an output 1 and the machine remains at state s_3.

Now, we present an example of a stochastic evolution built from these steps and assuming that s_1 is the initial state: $([0, 4)/a/\xi_3/0, [2, \infty)/b/\xi_2/1)$.   □

3   Implementation Relations

In this section we remind two of the implementation relations introduced in [10]. First, we give an implementation relation to deal with functional aspects. It follows the pattern borrowed from $\texttt{conf}_{nt}$ [11]: An implementation I *conforms* to a specification S if for all possible evolution of S the outputs that the implementation I may perform after a given input are a subset of those for the specification. In addition we require that the implementation always complies with the timeouts established by the specification. Besides the non-stochastic conformance of the implementation, we require other additional conditions, related to stochastic time, to hold.

We consider that specifications and implementations are given by means of SFSMs. We will consider that both of them are deterministically observable. Besides, we assume that input actions are always enabled in any state of the implementation, that is, implementations are input-enabled according to Definition 2. This is a usual condition to assure that the implementation will react (somehow) to any input appearing in the specification. First, we introduce the implementation relation $\texttt{conf}_f$, where only functional aspects of the system (i.e., which outputs are allowed/forbidden and how timeouts are defined) are considered while the performance of the system (i.e., how fast outputs are executed) is ignored. Let us note that the time spent by a system waiting for the environment to react has the capability of affecting the set of available outputs of the system. This is because this time may trigger a change of the state. So, a relation focusing on functional aspects must explicitly take into account the maximal time the system may stay in each state. This time is given by the *timeout* of each state.

Definition 5. Let S and I be SFSMs. We say that I *functionally conforms* to S, denoted by $I \operatorname{conf}_f S$, if for each functional evolution $e \in \text{FEvol}(S)$, with $e = (\hat{t}_1/i_1/o_1, \dots, \hat{t}_r/i_r/o_r)$ and $r \geq 1$, we have that for all $t_1 \in \hat{t}_1, \dots, t_r \in \hat{t}_r$ and o'_r, $e' = (t_1/i_1/o_1, \dots, t_r/i_r/o'_r) \in \text{InsFEvol}(I)$ implies $e' \in \text{InsFEvol}(S)$.
$\square$

Intuitively, the idea underlying the definition of the functional conformance relation $I \operatorname{conf}_f S$ is that the implementation I does not *invent* anything for those sequences of inputs that are *specified* in the specification S. Let us note that if the specification has also the property of input-enabled then we may remove the condition "for each functional evolution $e \in \text{FEvol}(S)$, with $e = (\hat{t}_{t1}/i_1/o_1, \dots, \hat{t}_{tr}/i_r/o_r)$ and $r \geq 1$".

In addition to requiring this notion of *functional* conformance, we have to ask for some conditions on delays. A first approach would be to require that the random variables associated with evolutions of the implementation are identically distributed as the ones corresponding to the specification. However, the fact that we assume a black-box testing framework disallows us to check whether these random variables are indeed identically distributed. Thus, we have to give more *realistic* implementation relations based on finite sets of observations. Next, we present two implementation relations that are less *accurate* but that are *checkable*. These relations take into account the observations that we may get from the implementation. We will collect a sample of time values and we will *compare* this sample with the random variables appearing in the specification. By comparison we mean that we will apply a contrast to decide, with a certain confidence, whether the sample could be generated by the corresponding random variable.

Definition 6. Let I be a SFSM. We say that $(\sigma, \bar{t}, \bar{t}')$, with $\sigma = i_1/o_1, \dots, i_n/o_n$, $\bar{t} = (t_1 \dots t_n)$, and $\bar{t}' = (t'_1 \dots t'_n)$, is an *observed time execution* of I, or simply *time execution*, if the observation of I shows that for all $1 \leq j \leq n$ we have that the time elapsed between the acceptance of the input i_j and the observation of the output o_j is t'_j units of time, being the input i_j accepted t_j units of time after the last output was observed.

Let $\Phi = \{(\sigma_1, \bar{t}_1), \dots, (\sigma_m, \bar{t}_m)\}$ and let $H = \{(\sigma'_1, \bar{t}_{d1}, \bar{t}_{o1}), \dots, (\sigma'_n, \bar{t}_{dn}, \bar{t}_{on})\}$ be a multiset of timed executions. We say that $\text{Sampling}^k_{(H,\Phi)} : \Phi \longrightarrow \wp(\text{Time})$ is a k-*sampling application* of H for Φ if $\text{Sampling}^k_{(H,\Phi)}(\sigma, \bar{t}) = \{\pi_k(\bar{t}_o) \mid (\sigma, \bar{t}, \bar{t}_o) \in H \wedge |\sigma| \geq k\}$, for all $(\sigma, \bar{t}) \in \Phi$. We say that $\text{Sampling}_{(H,\Phi)} : \Phi \longrightarrow \wp(\text{Time})$ is a *sampling application* of H for Φ if $\text{Sampling}_{(H,\Phi)}(\sigma, \bar{t})) = \{\sum \bar{t}_o \mid (\sigma, \bar{t}, \bar{t}_o) \in H\}$, for all $(\sigma, \bar{t}) \in \Phi$.
$\square$

Regarding the definition of k-sampling applications, we just associate with each subtrace of length k the observed time of each transition of the execution at length k. In the definition of sampling applications, we assign to each trace the total observed time corresponding to the whole execution.

Definition 7. Let I and S be SFSMs, H be a multiset of timed executions of I, $0 \leq \alpha \leq 1$, $\Phi = \{(\sigma, \bar{t}) \mid \exists \bar{t}_o : (\sigma, \bar{t}, \bar{t}_o) \in H\} \cap \text{InsFEvol}(S)$, and let us consider $\text{Sampling}_{(H,\Phi)}$ and $\text{Sampling}^k_{(H,\Phi)}$, for all $1 \leq k \leq max\{|\sigma| \mid (\sigma, \bar{t}) \in \Phi\}$.

We say that I $(\alpha, H)-$*weak stochastically conforms* to S, and we denote it by $I \text{ confs}_w^{(\alpha,H)} S$, if $I \text{ conf}_f S$ and for all $(\sigma, \bar{t}) \in \Phi$ we have

$$(\sigma, \bar{t}, \bar{\xi}) \in \text{InsSEvol}(S) \Longrightarrow \gamma \left(\sum \bar{\xi}, \text{Sampling}_{(H,\Phi)}(\sigma, \bar{t}) \right) > \alpha$$

We say that I $(\alpha, H)-$*strong stochastically conforms* to S, and we denote it by $I \text{ confs}_s^{(\alpha,H)} S$, if $I \text{ conf}_f S$ and for all $(\sigma, \bar{t}) \in \Phi$ we have

$$(\sigma, \bar{t}, \bar{\xi}) \in \text{InsSEvol}(S) \Longrightarrow \forall \, 1 \leq j \leq |\sigma| : \gamma(\pi_j(\bar{\xi}), \text{Sampling}_{(H,\Phi)}^j(\sigma, \bar{t})) > \alpha$$

$\square$

The idea underlying the new relations is that the implementation must conform to the specification in the usual way (that is, $I \text{ conf}_f S$). Besides, for all observation of the implementation that can be performed by the specification, the observed execution time values *fit* the random variable indicated by the specification. This notion of *fitting* is given by the function γ that it is formally defined in the appendix of [10]. While the *weak* notion only compares the total time, the *strong* notion checks that the time values are appropiate for each performed output.

4   Tests Cases for Stochastic Systems

We consider that tests represent sequences of inputs applied to an IUT. Once an output is received, the tester checks whether it belongs to the set of expected ones or not. In the latter case, a fail signal is produced. In the former case, either a pass signal is emitted (indicating successful termination) or the testing process continues by applying another input. If we are testing an implementation with input and output sets I and O, respectively, tests are deterministic acyclic I/O labelled transition systems (i.e. trees) with a strict alternation between an input action and the set of output actions. After an output action we may find either a leaf or another input action. Leaves can be labelled either by *pass* or by *fail*. In addition to check the functional behavior of the IUT, test have also to detect whether wrong timed behaviors appear. Thus, tests have to include capabilities to deal with the two ways of specifying time. On the one hand, we will include *random variables*. The idea is that we will record the time that the implementation takes to arrive to the leaves of the test labelled with *pass*. We will collect a sample of times for each test execution and we will *compare* this sample with the random variable associated to the leaf reached in the test. By comparison we mean that we will apply a contrast to decide, with a certain confidence, whether the sample could be generated by the corresponding random variable. On the second hand, tests will include *delays* before offering input actions. The idea is that delays in tests will induce timeouts in IUTs. Thus, we may indirectly check whether the timeouts imposed by the specification are reflected in the IUT by offering input actions after a specific delay.

Definition 8. A *test case* is a tuple $T = (S, I, O, \lambda, s_0, S_I, S_O, S_F, S_P, \zeta, D)$ where S is the set of states, I and O, with $I \cap O = \emptyset$ are the sets of input and output actions, respectively, $\lambda \subseteq S \times I \cup O \times S$ is the transition relation, $s_0 \in S$ is the initial state, and the sets $S_I, S_O, S_F, S_P \subseteq S$ are a partition of S. The transition relation and the sets of states fulfill the following conditions:

- S_I is the set of *input* states. We have that $s_0 \in S_I$. For all input state $s \in S_I$ there exists a unique outgoing transition $(s, a, s') \in \lambda$. For this transition we have that $a \in I$ and $s' \in S_O$.
- S_O is the set of *output* states. For all output state $s \in S_O$ we have that for all $o \in O$ there exists a unique state s' such that $(s, o, s') \in \lambda$. In this case, $s' \notin S_O$. Moreover, there do not exist $i \in I, s' \in S$ such that $(s, i, s') \in \lambda$.
- S_F and S_P are the sets of *fail* and *pass* states, respectively. We say that these states are *terminal*. Thus, for all state $s \in S_F \cup S_P$ we have that there do not exist $a \in I \cup O$ and $s' \in S$ such that $(s, a, s') \in \lambda$.

Finally, we have two timed functions. $\zeta : S_P \longrightarrow \bigcup_{j=1}^{\infty} \mathcal{V}^j$ is a function associating random variables, to compare with the time that the implementation took to perform the outputs, with passing states. $D : S_I \longrightarrow \texttt{Time}$ is a function associating delays with input states.

We say that a test case T is *valid* if the graph induced by T is a tree with root at the initial state s_0. We say that a set of tests $\mathcal{T}_{st} = \{T_1, \ldots, T_n\}$ is a *test suite*.

Let $\sigma = i_1/o_1, \ldots, i_r/o_r$. We write $T \overset{\sigma}{\Longrightarrow} s^T$ if $s^T \in S_F \cup S_P$ and there exist states $s_{12}, s_{21}, s_{22}, \ldots s_{r1}, s_{r2} \in S$ such that $\{(s_0, i_1, s_{12}), (s_{r2}, o_r, s^T)\} \subseteq \lambda$, for all $2 \leq j \leq r$ we have $(s_{j1}, i_j, s_{j2}) \in \lambda$, and for all $1 \leq j \leq r - 1$ we have $(s_{j2}, o_j, s_{(j+1)1}) \in \lambda$.

Let T be a valid test, $\sigma = i_1/o_1, \ldots, i_r/o_r$, s^T be a state of T, and $\bar{t} = (t_1, \ldots, t_r) \in \texttt{Time}^r$. We write $T \overset{\sigma}{\Longrightarrow}_{\bar{t}} s^T$ if $T \overset{\sigma}{\Longrightarrow} s^T$, $t_1 = D(s_0)$, and for all $1 < j \leq r$ we have $t_j = D(s_{j1})$. $\qquad\square$

Let us remark that $T \overset{\sigma}{\Longrightarrow} s^T$, and its variant $T \overset{\sigma}{\Longrightarrow}_{\bar{t}} s^T$, imply that s^T is a terminal state. Next we define the application of a test suite to an implementation. We say that the test suite $\mathcal{T}_{st}$ is *passed* if for all test the terminal states reached by the composition of implementation and test are *pass* states. Besides, we give different timing conditions in a similar way to what we did for implementation relations.

Definition 9. Let I be SFSM and $T = (S_t, I, O, \delta_T, s_0, S_I, S_O, S_F, S_P, \zeta, D)$ be a valid test, $\sigma = i_1/o_1, \ldots, i_r/o_r$, s^T be a state of T, $\bar{t} = (t_1, \ldots, t_r)$, and $\bar{t}_o = (t_{o1}, \ldots, t_{or})$. We write $I \,\|\, T \overset{\sigma}{\Longrightarrow}_{\bar{t}} s^T$ if $T \overset{\sigma}{\Longrightarrow}_{\bar{t}} s^T$ and $(\sigma, \bar{t}) \in \texttt{InsFEvol}(I)$. We write $I \,\|\, T \overset{\sigma}{\Longrightarrow}_{\bar{t}, \bar{t}_o} s^T$ if $I \,\|\, T \overset{\sigma}{\Longrightarrow}_{\bar{t}} s^T$ and $(\sigma, \bar{t}, \bar{t}_o)$ is a observed timed execution of I. In this case we say that $(\sigma, \bar{t}, \bar{t}_o)$ is a *test execution* of I and T.

We say that I *passes* the test suite $\mathcal{T}_{st}$, denoted by $\texttt{pass}(I, \mathcal{T}_{st})$, if for all test $T \in \mathcal{T}_{st}$ there do not exist $(\sigma, \bar{t}) \in \texttt{InsFEvol}(I)$, $s^T \in S$ such that $I \,\|\, T \overset{\sigma}{\Longrightarrow}_{\bar{t}} s^T$ and $s^T \in S_F$. $\qquad\square$

Let us remark that since we are assuming that implementations are input-enabled, the testing process will conclude only when the test reaches either a fail or a pass state.

In addition to this notion of passing tests, we will have different time conditions. We apply the time conditions to the set of *observed timed executions*, not to stochastic evolutions of the implementations, due to the fact that stochastic evolutions do not have a single time value that we can directly compare with the time stamp attached to the pass state. In fact, we need a set of test executions associated to each evolution to evaluate if they match the distribution function associated to the random variable indicated by the corresponding state of the test. In order to increase the degree of reliability, we will not take the classical approach where passing a test suite is defined according only to the results for each test. In our approach, we will put together all the observations, for each test, so that we have more samples for each evolution. In particular, some observations will be used several times. In other words, an observation from a given test may be used to check the validity of another test sharing the same observed sequence.

Definition 10. Let I be a SFSM and $\mathcal{T}_{st} = \{T_1, \ldots, T_n\}$ be a test suite. Let $H_1, \ldots, H_n$ be multisets of test executions of I and $T_1, \ldots, T_n$, respectively. Let $H = \biguplus_{i=1}^{n} H_i$, $\Phi = \{(\sigma, \bar{t}) \mid \exists \bar{t}_o : (\sigma, \bar{t}, \bar{t}_o) \in H\}$, $0 \leq \alpha \leq 1$ and let us consider $\text{Sampling}_{(H,\Phi)}$ and $\text{Sampling}^k_{(H,\Phi)}$, for all $1 \leq k \leq max\{|\sigma| \mid (\sigma, \bar{t}) \in \Phi\}$.

Let $e = (\sigma, \bar{t}) \in \Phi$. We define the set $\text{Test}(e, \mathcal{T}_{st}) = \{T \mid T \in \mathcal{T}_{st} \land I \parallel T \overset{\sigma}{\Longrightarrow}_{\bar{t}} s^T\}$.

We say that the implementation I *weakly* $(\alpha, H)-passes$ the test suite $\mathcal{T}_{st}$ if $\text{pass}(I, \mathcal{T}_{st})$ and for all $e = (\sigma, \bar{t}) \in \Phi$ we have that for all $T \in \text{Test}(e, \mathcal{T}_{st})$ such that $I \parallel T \overset{\sigma}{\Longrightarrow}_{\bar{t}} s^T$ it holds $\gamma(\sum \zeta(s^T), \text{Sampling}_{(H,\Phi)}(\sigma, \bar{t})) > \alpha$.

We say that the implementation I *strongly* $(\alpha, H)-passes$ the test suite $\mathcal{T}_{st}$ if $\text{pass}(I, \mathcal{T}_{st})$ and for all $e = (\sigma, \bar{t}) \in \Phi$ we have that for all $T \in \text{Test}(e, \mathcal{T}_{st})$ such that $I \parallel T \overset{\sigma}{\Longrightarrow}_{\bar{t}} s^T$ it holds $\forall 1 \leq j \leq |\sigma| : \gamma(\pi_j(\zeta(s^T)), \text{Sampling}^j_{(H,\Phi)}(\sigma, \bar{t})) > \alpha$. $\square$

Let us note that an observed timed execution does not return the random variable associated with performing the evolution (that is, the addition of all the random variables corresponding to each transition of the implementation) but the time that it took to perform the evolution. Intuitively, an implementation passes a test if there does not exist an evolution leading to a fail state. Once we know that the functional behavior of the implementation is correct with respect to the test, we need to check time conditions. The set H corresponds to the observations of the (several) applications of the tests belonging to the test suite $\mathcal{T}_{st}$ to I. Thus, we have to decide whether, for each evolution e, the observed time values (that is, $\text{Sampling}_{(H,\Phi)}(e)$) *match* the definition of the random variables appearing in the successful state of the tests corresponding to the execution of that evolution (that is, $\zeta(s^T)$). As we commented previously, we assume a function γ, formally defined in the appendix of [10], that can perform this hypothesis contrast.

5   Test Derivation: Soundness and Completeness

In this section we present an algorithm to derive test cases from specifications and we show that the derived test suites are sound and complete with respect to the two implementation relations presented in Section 3. As usual, the idea underlying our algorithm consists in traversing the specification in order to get all the possible traces in an appropriate way. First, we introduce some additional notation.

Definition 11. Let $M = (S, I, O, \delta, TO, s_{in})$ be a SFSM. We consider the following sets:

$$\text{out}(s, i) = \{o \mid \exists \, s', \xi : (s, i, o, s', \xi) \in \delta\}$$

$$\text{afterTO}(s, t) = \begin{cases} s & \text{if } \pi_2(TO(s)) > t \\ \text{afterTO}(\pi_1(TO(s)), t - \pi_2(TO(s))) & \text{otherwise} \end{cases}$$

$$\text{after}(s, i, o, \bar{\xi}) = \begin{cases} (s', \bar{\xi}') & \text{if } \exists \, \xi : (s, i, o, s', \xi) \in \delta \\ \text{error} & \text{otherwise} \end{cases}$$

where if $\bar{\xi} = (\xi_1, \ldots, \xi_n)$ then $\bar{\xi}' = (\xi_1, \ldots, \xi_n, \xi)$ □

The function $\text{out}(s, i)$ computes the set of output actions associated with those transitions that can be executed from s after receiving the input i. The next function, $\text{afterTO}(s, t)$ returns the state that would be reached by the system if we start in the state s and t time units elapsed without receiving an input. The last function, $\text{after}(s, i, o, \bar{\xi})$, computes the state reached from a state s after receiving the input i, producing the output o, supposing that $\bar{\xi}$ denotes the random variables associated to the transitions previously performed. In addition, it returns the new tuple of random variables associated to the transitions performed since the system started its performance. Let us also remark that due to the assumption that SFSMs are observable we have that $\text{after}(s, i, o, \bar{\xi})$ is uniquely determined. Besides, we will apply this function only when the side condition holds, that is, we will never receive **error** as result of applying **after**.

The algorithm to derive tests from a specification is given in Figure 2. It is a non-deterministic algorithm that returns a single test. By considering the possible available choices in the algorithm we extract a full test suite from the specification (this set will be infinite in general). For a given specification M, we denote this set of tests by $\text{tests}(M)$. Next we explain how the algorithm works. A set of *pending situations* S_{aux} keeps those triplets denoting the possible states and the tuple of random variables that could appear in a state of the test whose definition, that is, its outgoing transitions, has not been completed yet. A triplet $(s^M, \bar{\xi}, s^T) \in S_{aux}$ indicates that we did not complete the state s^T of the test, the tuple of random variables $\bar{\xi}$ associated to the transitions of the specification that have been traversed from the initial state, and the current state in the transversal of the specification is s^M.

Input: A specification $M = (S, I, O, \delta, TO, Tr, s_{in})$.
Output: A test case $T = (S', I, O \cup \{\texttt{null}\}, \lambda, s_0, S_I, S_O, S_F, S_P, \zeta, D)$.

Initialization:

- $S' := \{s_0\}, \delta := S_I := S_O := S_F := S_P := \zeta := D := \emptyset.$
- $S_{aux} := \{(s_{in}, null, s_0)\}.$

Inductive Cases: Choose one of the following two options until $S_{aux} = \emptyset.$

1. If $(s^M, \bar{\xi}, s^T) \in S_{aux}$ then perform the following steps:
   (a) $S_{aux} := S_{aux} - \{(s^M, \bar{\xi}, s^T)\}.$
   (b) $S_P := S_P \cup \{s^T\}; \zeta(s^T) := \bar{\xi}.$
2. If $S_{aux} = \{(s^M, \bar{\xi}, s^T)\}$ and $\exists\, t_d \in \texttt{Time}, i \in I$ such that
   $\texttt{out}(\texttt{afterTO}(s^M, t_d), i) \neq \emptyset$ then perform:
   (a) Choose $t_d \in \texttt{Time}$ and $i \in I$ fulfilling the previous conditions.
   (b) $s^M = \texttt{afterTO}(s^M, t_d); S_{aux} := \emptyset.$
   (c) Consider a fresh state $s' \notin S'$ and let $S' := S' \cup \{s'\}.$
   (d) $S_I := S_I \cup \{s^T\}; S_O := S_O \cup \{s'\}; \lambda := \lambda \cup \{(s^T, i, s')\}.$
   (e) $D(s^T) := t_d.$
   (f) For all $o \notin \texttt{out}(s^M, i)$ do {null is in this case}
       − Consider a fresh state $s'' \notin S'$ and let $S' := S' \cup \{s''\}.$
       − $S_F := S_F \cup \{s''\}; \lambda := \lambda \cup \{(s', o, s'')\}.$
   (g) For all $o \in \texttt{out}(s^M, i)$ do
       − Consider a fresh state $s'' \notin S'$ and let $S' := S' \cup \{s''\}.$
       − $\lambda := \lambda \cup \{(s', o, s'')\}.$
       − $(s_1^M, \bar{\xi}') := \texttt{after}(s^M, i, o, \bar{\xi}).$
       − $S_{aux} := S_{aux} \cup \{(s_1^M, \bar{\xi}', s'')\}.$

Fig. 2. Derivation of test cases from a specification

Let us consider the steps of the algorithm. The set S_{aux} initially contains a tuple with the initial states (of both the specification and the test) and the initial tuple of random variables (that is, empty tuple of random variables). For each tuple belonging to S_{aux} we may choose one possibility between two choices. It is important to remark that the second choice can be taken only when the set S_{aux} becomes singleton. So, our derived tests correspond to valid tests as given in Definition 8. The first possibility simply indicates that the state of the test becomes a passing state. The second possibility takes an input and generates a transition in the test labelled by this input. At this step, we choose a delay for the next input state. We select a time value and replace the states of the pending situation by the situation that can be reached if we apply as delay for accepting a new input, the time value selected. This is because, during the delay, the timeout transition associated to the state s_M can be triggered, so a change of state will be prompted by this fact. That fact allow us to consider sequences of

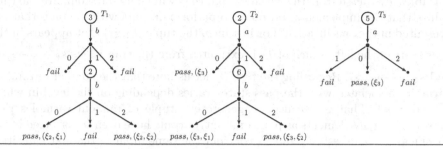

Fig. 3. Examples of Tests

timeout transitions, that is, traces where those transitions are triggered because no input action is received by the system.

Then, the whole sets of outputs is considered. If the output is not expected by the implementation (step 2.(f) of the algorithm) then a transition leading to a failing state is created. This could be simulated by a single branch in the test, labelled by **else**, leading to a failing state (in the algorithm we suppose that *all* the possible outputs appear in the test). For the expected outputs (step 2.(g) of the algorithm) we create a transition with the corresponding output action and add the appropriate tuple to the set S_{aux}.

Finally, let us remark that finite test cases are constructed simply by considering a step where the second inductive case is not applied. Finally, let us comment on the *finiteness* of our algorithm. If we do not impose any restriction on the implementation (e.g., a bound on the number of states) we cannot determine some important information such as the maximal length of the traces that the implementation can perform. In other words, we would need a *coverage criterium* to generate a finite test suite. Since we do not assume, by default, any criteria, all we can do is to say that this is the, in general, infinite test suite that would allow to prove completeness. Obviously, one can impose restrictions such as "generate n tests" or "generate all the tests with m inputs" and *completeness* will be obtained up to that coverage criterium.

Example 3. In Figure 3 we present some examples of test cases. These tests are derived from the specification presented in Figure 1. In the test T_1 we consider a delay of 3 time units in the step 2.(a) of the algorithm as well as the input b. A transition labelled by this input is generated in the test. Next, all outputs are considered. Due to the fact that the specification only accepts the output 1, two transitions leading to a fail state are created for the outputs 0 and 2 respectively (step 2.(f) of the algorithm). Moreover, we create a transition for the output 1 (step 2.(g) of the algorithm). After this, we select again the input b and establish a delay of 2 time units for this input. The corresponding transitions are created in the test. Finally, we apply the step 1 of the algorithm in order to conclude the generation of this test. The pass states contain some random variables, extracted from the specification, that will be used to compare the time values that the implementation takes to perform outputs with the ones that are presented in the specification. For instance, the tuple (ξ_2, ξ_1) that appears in the pass state of the left branch of T_1 is extracted from the transitions $s_1 \xrightarrow{b/1}_{\xi_2} s_4$ and $s_4 \xrightarrow{b/0}_{\xi_1} s_1$. Regarding the test T_2, let us note that the number of random variables associated with the pass states varies depending on the level in which it is derived. That is because we generate a tuple of random variables that presents so many elements as pairs of input/outputs have been transversed in the specification. The tests T_2 and T_3 consider the same input in the first transition a. The difference lies in the delays we consider for each of them, 2 and 5 time units, respectively. This fact makes that for the test T_2 the output 1 is accepted. However, in the test T_3 it leads to a fail state, because in this case the timeout associated to the initial state should be triggered after 4 time units and the machine would change its state to s_2, where the output 1 is not accepted for the input a. $\quad\Box$

Finally, we present the result that relates, for a specification S and an implementation I, implementation relations and application of test suites.

Theorem 1. Let S, I be SFSMs. Let H be a multiset of test executions of I, $0 \le \alpha \le 1$, and $\Phi = \{(\sigma, \bar{t}) \mid \exists \bar{t}_o : (\sigma, \bar{t}, \bar{t}_o) \in H\} \cap \texttt{InsFEvol}(S)$. We have that:

- $I \ \texttt{confs}_w^{(\alpha, H)} \ S$ iff I weakly $(\alpha, H)-passes$ $\texttt{tests}(S)$.
- $I \ \texttt{confs}_s^{(\alpha, H)} \ S$ iff I strongly $(\alpha, H)-passes$ $\texttt{tests}(S)$.

$\quad\Box$

6   Concluding Remarks

This paper concludes the work initiated in [10]. There, we presented a new notion of finite state machine to specify, in an easy way, both the passing of time due to timeouts and the time due to the performance of actions. In addition, we presented several implementation relations based on the notion of conformance. These relations shared a common pattern: The implementation must conform to the specification regarding functional aspects. In this paper we introduce a notion of test, how to apply a test suite to an implementation, and what is the meaning of successfully passing a test suite. Even though implementation relations and passing of test suites are, apparently, unrelated concepts, we provide a link between them: We give an algorithm to derive test suites from specifications in such a way that a test suite is successfully passed iff the implementation conforms to the specification. This result, usually known as *soundness* and *completeness*, allows a user that in order to check the correctness of an implementation, it is the same to consider an implementation relation or to apply a derived test suite.

References

1. Alur, R., Dill, D.: A theory of timed automata. Theoretical Computer Science 126, 183–235 (1994)
2. Brandán, L., Brinksma, E.: Testing real-time multi input-output systems. In: Lau, K.-K., Banach, R. (eds.) ICFEM 2005. LNCS, vol. 3785, pp. 264–279. Springer, Heidelberg (2005)
3. Brinksma, E., Tretmans, J.: Testing transition systems: An annotated bibliography. In: Cassez, F., Jard, C., Rozoy, B., Dermot, M. (eds.) MOVEP 2000. LNCS, vol. 2067, pp. 187–195. Springer, Heidelberg (2001)
4. Clarke, D., Lee, I.: Automatic generation of tests for timing constraints from requirements. In: 3rd Workshop on Object-Oriented Real-Time Dependable Systems, WORDS'97, pp. 199–206. IEEE Computer Society Press, Los Alamitos (1997)
5. En-Nouaary, A., Dssouli, R., Khendek, F.: Timed Wp-method: Testing real time systems. IEEE Transactions on Software Engineering 28(11), 1024–1039 (2002)
6. Krichen, M., Tripakis, S.: An expressive and implementable formal framework for testing real-time systems. In: Khendek, F., Dssouli, R. (eds.) TestCom 2005. LNCS, vol. 3502, pp. 209–225. Springer, Heidelberg (2005)
7. Larsen, K.G., Mikucionis, M., Nielsen, B.: Online testing of real-time systems using Uppaal. In: Grabowski, J., Nielsen, B. (eds.) FATES 2004. LNCS, vol. 3395, pp. 79–94. Springer, Heidelberg (2005)
8. Lee, D., Yannakakis, M.: Principles and methods of testing finite state machines: A survey. Proceedings of the IEEE 84(8), 1090–1123 (1996)
9. Mandrioli, D., Morasca, S., Morzenti, A.: Generating test cases for real time systems from logic specifications. ACM Transactions on Computer Systems 13(4), 356–398 (1995)
10. Merayo, M.G., Núñez, M., Rodríguez, I.: Implementation relations for stochastic finite state machines. In: Horváth, A., Telek, M. (eds.) EPEW 2006. LNCS, vol. 4054, pp. 123–137. Springer, Heidelberg (2006)
11. Núñez, M., Rodríguez, I.: Encoding PAMR into (timed) EFSMs. In: Peled, D.A., Vardi, M.Y. (eds.) FORTE 2002. LNCS, vol. 2529, pp. 1–16. Springer, Heidelberg (2002)
12. Núñez, M., Rodríguez, I.: Towards testing stochastic timed systems. In: König, H., Heiner, M., Wolisz, A. (eds.) FORTE 2003. LNCS, vol. 2767, pp. 335–350. Springer, Heidelberg (2003)
13. Núñez, M., Rodríguez, I.: Conformance testing relations for timed systems. In: Grieskamp, W., Weise, C. (eds.) FATES 2005. LNCS, vol. 3997, pp. 103–117. Springer, Heidelberg (2006)
14. Petrenko, A.: Fault model-driven test derivation from finite state models: Annotated bibliography. In: Cassez, F., Jard, C., Rozoy, B., Dermot, M. (eds.) MOVEP 2000. LNCS, vol. 2067, pp. 196–205. Springer, Heidelberg (2001)
15. Rodríguez, I., Merayo, M.G., Núñez, M.: HOTL: Hypotheses and observations testing logic. In: Journal of Logic and Algebraic Programming (2007), http://dx.doi.org/10.1016/j.jlap.2007.03.002
16. Springintveld, J., Vaandrager, F., D'Argenio, P.R.: Testing timed automata. Theoretical Computer Science, 254(1-2):225–257, 2001. Previously appeared as Technical Report CTIT-97-17, University of Twente (1997)

Evaluation of P2P Search Algorithms for Discovering Trust Paths

Emerson Ribeiro de Mello[1,*], Aad van Moorsel[2,**], and Joni da Silva Fraga[1]

[1] Department of Automation and Systems
Federal University of Santa Catarina
Florianópolis, SC - Brazil
emerson@das.ufsc.br,fraga@das.ufsc.br
[2] School of Computing Science
Newcastle University
Newcastle upon Tyne, UK
aad.vanmoorsel@newcastle.ac.uk

Abstract. Distributed security models based on a 'web of trust' eliminate single points of failure and alleviate performance bottlenecks. However, such distributed approaches rely on the ability to find trust paths
between participants, which introduces performance overhead. It is therefore of importance to develop trust path discovery algorithms that minimize such overhead. Since peer-to-peer (P2P) networks share various
characteristics with the web of trust, P2P search algorithms can potentially be exploited to find trust paths. In this paper we systematically
evaluate the application of P2P search algorithms to the trust path discovery problem. We consider the number of iterations required (as expressed by the TTL parameter) as well as the messaging overhead, for
discovery of single as well as multiple trust paths. Since trust path discovery does not allow for resource replication (usual in P2P applications), we
observe that trust path discovery is very sensitive to parameter choices
in selective forwarding algorithms (such as K-walker), but is relatively
fast when the underlying network topology is scale-free.

Keywords: Peer-to-Peer, Web of Trust, Trust Paths.

1 Introduction

The effectiveness and efficiency of any commercial interaction depends strongly
on the level of trust that exists between involved parties. Trust determines if
parties are willing to depend on each other, even if negative consequences are

---

* Supported by CNPq. This work was conducted while the first author was in the
  School of Computing Science at Newcastle University, UK. This work has been
  developed within the scope of the "Security Infrastructure for Service Oriented Distributed Applications" project (CNPq 550114/2005-0).
** Supported in part by EPSRC grant EP/C009797/1 "Dynamic Operating Policies
  for Commercial Hosting Environments" and EU Network of Excellence grant 026764
  "Resilience for Survivability in IST".

K. Wolter (Ed.): EPEW 2007, LNCS 4748, pp. 112–124, 2007.

possible [1], and without it, commercial transactions will be inefficient because of doubts about payments, ability to deliver a service, etc. Trust establishment in real life is usually a complex and subjective process, and in electronic commerce, trust establishment arguably becomes even more challenging [1]. The absence of human interaction and the frequency and speed with which new electronic commerce interactions can be established contribute to this challenge.

Several automated trust solutions have been proposed in the literature and some are in common use, such as, X.509 [2], PGP [3] and SPKI/SDSI [4,5]. These solutions provide ways of determining and assuring that information is being exchanged with a trusted source. Of particular interest in large scale deployment of trust solutions is the notion of a *web of trust*. In a web of trust each party has the ability to express their trust in entities and communicate this to other parties (by signing messages). By association, these other parties may decide to trust the entities as well. Web of trust solutions are in contrast to the traditional model that relies on the trust in central entities, namely the Certification Authorities (CA).

The literature discusses trust relation creation and management extensively [6,7,8,9], and the PGP and SPKI/SDSI standard proposals discuss the concept of trust paths as well. Recently, various authors have proposed algorithms for discovering trust paths [10,11,12] to fill the void left by the standards (which purposely do not specify how trust paths should be discovered), but no experimental or simulation results have been presented to study the effectiveness and performance of the algorithms.

Trust path discovery is equivalent to finding paths in graphs (we make this precise in Section 2). To be of practical value, a trust path discovery algorithm must take into account that participants are only aware of their direct neighbours. This immediately suggests that P2P search algorithms may be applicable to this domain, as also realized in [10,11,12]. After all, in P2P networks each node keeps track of a partial index with a subset of all nodes of the network. In this paper we therefore evaluate how existing P2P algorithms perform when applied to the trust path discovery problem.

There exist important differences between traditional P2P applications and the web of trust. In particular, in a typical P2P application (such as file sharing), files will be replicated across peers, thus allowing for tremendous scaling. In the web of trust, however, a trust relationship will be present only in the two nodes that compose the trust relationship. Replication is possible in some settings (as we will explain in Section 2), but will be far less prevalent and straightforward than in traditional P2P applications. As a consequence, our simulation results will show that an underlying scale-free network topology performs relatively well for the trust path discovery problem compared to resource discovery in traditional P2P applications (as reported in [13,14,15]). Furthermore, we will see that the performance of the search algorithms is extremely sensitive to parameter choices in modified flooding algorithms that limit the amount of forwarding (such as selective querying and K-walker).

2   Trust Path Discovery Problem

In abstract terms, the web of trust can be seen as a graph, where the nodes are participants and the arcs denote trust (an arc from A to B denotes that A trusts B). In terms of PGP, one can restate this as nodes being keys and arcs being signatures that signify trust, e.g., [16]. Arcs can be uni-directional or bi-directional, since the trust relationship could be one-way or two-way. For instance, in the X.509 model the users trust in the Certificate Authorities but the inverse is not true. Thus, in this case we have a one-way trust relationship. In PGP and SPKI model each principal can be the issuer or the subject of a trust relationship, amounting to a two-way trust relationship. Such two-way relations can be implemented through various mechanisms, for example through exchange of two signed certificates. In this paper we assume the PGP and SPKI model, in which trust relations are bi-directional, i.e., the underlying graph is undirected.

In a web of trust, if there is no trust relation between two parties A and C, they can still trust each other if there exists at least one path between A and C in the graph (we will call A the origin, and C the target in what follows). That is, we exploit the fact that trust can be said to be transitive [17,18]: if A trusts B, and B trusts C, then A trusts C. The trust path discovery problem then is to find at least one trust path between two given principals. Discovering such a path is complicated because each node has only knowledge about its own trust relations. This suggests, however, that unstructured P2P search algorithms are natural candidates to solve the trust path discovery problem.

2.1   P2P Networks

There are two categories of decentralized P2P networks: *unstructured*, such as Gnutella [19], and *structured*, such as those based on a distributed hash table [20,21]. We will discuss trust path discovery only for unstructured approach, since we found that the mapping of a web of trust on a structured P2P network does not seem to provide any benefits for discovering trust paths. In traditional P2P networks, one would search for 'resources'. When searching trust paths the 'resources' a node contains are the trust relationships it knows about. In the default setting, each node only knows about its own trust relationships, and thus in the underlying P2P network each node is connected to the nodes it trusts. Discovering a trust path between A and B then is identical to A querying for a resource that is only present at B.

To find resources (such as files) in unstructured P2P networks, each query is propagated through the network by *flooding*. For instance, in the original version of Gnutella [19] a node receiving or generating a query forwards it to a fixed number of neighbours (typically four). These neighbours forward it to their neighbours, and so on until the message time to live (TTL) threshold (typically seven) has been exceeded. Flooding can directly be applied to the problem of discovering trust paths. If existing, trust paths will be discovered using exhaustive flooding.

Flooding has an obvious disadvantage, namely that many query messages may be needed to find a resource. When establishing trust paths, this problem is magnified by the fact that there is no replication of resources (i.e., trust relationships) across multiple nodes. Several variations and modifications of straightforward flooding have been proposed for traditional P2P networks. Depth-first search was used in [13,14,22], and breadth-first search with incrementing message time to live values was proposed and analysed in [15,23,24]. In the Kazaa network [25] the concept of super-nodes (or ultra-peers) was introduced to create a hierarchical structure in the network, where queries are propagated on a super-nodes overlay that acts like shortcuts between distant principals. An improvement important for the problem of trust path discovery is that of caching 'hits'. In these solutions a "queryHit" message is created when a desired trust path is found, and this message is propagated in the reverse path. Subsequent queries then can immediately use the cached result. This approach is very beneficial for discovering trust paths, and we will evaluate it below.

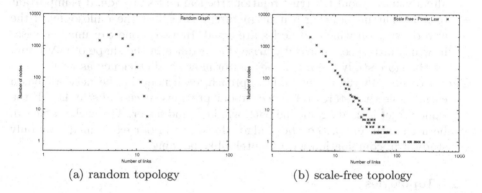

(a) random topology   (b) scale-free topology

Fig. 1. Distribution of trust relations ('links') per node in different network topologies

3   Experiment Setup

3.1   Trust Path Discovery Algorithms

We will compare the following trust path discovery algorithms, which all are variations of flooding in unstructured P2P networks. For the evaluation of these approaches in the context of file sharing and similar applications, we refer to, e.g., [13,14,15,22,23].

K-walker. In K-walker every node propagates the query to K randomly selected neighbour nodes, resulting in a variation of breadth-first search.

Selective querying. Selective querying works like K-walker, but a query will be propagated through the K *best* nodes according to some specific criterion, for instance, location, bandwidth, number of neighbours, results in previous queries, etc. In trust path discovery, it seems logical to select nodes with the most neighbours, since this implies these nodes contain more trust relationships.

Expanding ring. The expanding ring approach repeatedly increments the message time to live (TTL) until the trust path is found. Initially the search starts with a small value of TTL (expressed in terms of the number of hops) and if the search does not succeed the TTL value will be increased and the same query will be sent. This process repeats itself until some pre-defined maximum value for TTL is reached. The reasoning behind the expanding ring approach is that it avoids the problem that if a resource is found but TTL has not been reached, unnecessary messages continue to be forwarded.

Ultra-peers. The ultra-peer approach introduces a hierarchy between nodes. When a leaf node joins the network it associates itself with one or more ultra-peers (super-nodes). In the context of trust paths, each ultra-peer stores information about trust relationships of its leaf nodes. The search started by a leaf node will be propagated only in the ultra-peer layer, since these nodes already know about the trust relations the leaf nodes provide. It is important to note that introducing a node hierarchy is against the philosophy of the web of trust, in which all nodes are equal. However, one can imagine cases in which ultra-peers naturally arise (for instance in the shape of CAs), and we therefore study the ultra-peer performance and efficiency as well.

Cache table. In the cache table approach, each node in the network has a cache table that stores references about previous successful searches. If the same target is used again, the path will be found faster. The cache table can be used with any of the above algorithms, but in our experiments we only study it in combination with Gnutella-like flooding.

3.2 Topologies

The topology of a P2P network heavily influences the effectiveness of various algorithms. The topology is determined by the number of neighbours each node knows about (the degree of a node), and in our study we consider two classes of topologies: the random graph and the scale free or power law graph [26].

There exist different variations of random graphs and various approaches to generating random graphs. We use one of the standard approaches provided by Peersim (see below), namely one that generates for each node a fixed number d of edges, and then connects these edges with d randomly selected neighbouring nodes. Since our simulations use undirected graphs, this results in an average degree of $2d$ for each node. Figure 1(a) shows (using logarithmic scale) the number of nodes with a certain degree, where the average degree for a node is 4. In the simulation, we generated random graphs with up to 20,000 nodes, and average degree 4.

Scale free graphs follow the power law distribution where many nodes have few connections and few nodes have many connections. This kind of distribution represents the small world concept [27] observed in several different areas, including in the web of trust [28] and traditional P2P file-sharing applications [29].

We use the Barabasi-Albert approach [26] to generate scale free graphs (using the implementation provided in Peersim, see below). Again, we set the average degree to 4. An example of the degree of nodes in the resulting graph is given in Figure 1(b).

Peersim - A P2P Simulator. We used the P2P network simulator Peersim [30] to carry out the discrete-event simulations. Peersim is implemented in Java; it generates networks according to several possible topology classes (including random and scale-free topologies) and has a discrete-event simulator. The simulation execution scales very well when using Peersim's 'cycle-based' approach, which ignores certain transport layer elements and concurrency, as recommended in [31]. Peersim also provide a way to create independent replicas of experiments based on a pseudo random generator, which we used to gain confidence in our simulation results. Using Peersim's Java API, various P2P algorithms can be very quickly implemented and evaluated. The simulation runs for which we present results in the next section typically lasted on the order of (tens of) seconds.

4   Results

There are a number of metrics one may want to consider when establishing the quality of a trust path discovery algorithm. In this section, we will first discuss the cost of establishing a single trust path, and then multiple trust paths. (The latter may be important because the existence of multiple trust paths may increase the trust level the origin associates with the target.) The cost we consider is the number of messages passed over the network to find the trust path(s). We will also analyse the sensitivity of the results with respect to the TTL value, which is a critical parameter that needs to be set in all algorithms. Moreover, in absence of a notion of time in our simulation, the minimum required TTL may also be used as an indicator of the time it will take to find the trust paths. As we mentioned above, the simulation is based on graphs with 20,000 nodes for both the random and scale free graph topology, with average node degree 4. We ran simulations with three different distances from the (arbitrary chosen) origin node: closest (that is, two hops), average and farthest node from the origin node. For the random topology, the distances were as follows: average is 7 hops and farthest is 10 hops; for the scale free topology: average is 4 hops and farthest is 6 hops. In our simulations, for all algorithms, TTL was incremented from 2 until 7, and sometimes increased higher to observe specific phenomena. For the algorithms selective querying and K-walker we chose three different values for the number of neighbours to which the query will be propagated: 10%, 50% and 70%. In the ultra-peers algorithm the number of super-nodes in the network was chosen randomly, selecting the most connected nodes. The amount of nodes selected to be ultra peers was chose by the integer part of the square root of network size.

Table 1. Number of trust paths found for random graph topology for different TTL values. Target is 7 hops away. The last three lines indicate required TTL value to find at least one path but even with big TTL values "Selective 10%" did not find any path.

TTL	Gnutella		K-walker			Selective			Ultra-peers
	original	cacheTable	10%	50%	70%	10%	50%	70%	
5	0	0	0	0	0	0	0	0	0
6	2	2	0	0	2	0	0	1	2
7	3	3	0	0	2	0	0	1	3
10							first hit		
11				first hit					
32			first hit						

Discovery of the first trust path. Table 1 and Table 2 show the number of trust paths found, for different values of TTL, for the random and scale-free topology, respectively. The graphs in Figure 2 and Figure 3 show the number of messages propagated through the network for each algorithm, for different values of TTL. We can see in Figure 2 and Figure 3 that both the network topology and the specific algorithm have an important influence on the number of messages propagated. In scale free networks some nodes have a high number of neighbours, resulting in more messages in the network when flooding techniques are used. Moreover, these messages can be redundant, because they forward a query to a node that earlier received that same query (see [14] for an in-depth discussion). However, Table 1 and Table 2 demonstrate the benefit of this higher number of messages in the scale-free topology: the trust path is found within only a few hops for all algorithms. More precisely, the trust path is found in the minimum number of hops (TTL=3 for a target 4 hops away), except for K-walker with 10% forwarding. In the random graph, trust paths are not always found for low values of TTL. The minimum possible value of the TTL is 6 for a target at the average distance of 7 hops, but algorithms that do not forward to a high number of neighbours require higher TTL values. Table 1 shows this number in the three last rows: to find the first trust path K-walker with 50% requires a TTL value of 11, and K-walker wit 10% needs TTL value 32. Moreover, selective forwarding with 10% never reaches the target, as indicated in Table 1.

If one is interested in the number of messages used to find the first trust path, one combines the above-mentioned figures and tables. For the scale free topology, the Selective and K-walker algorithms with only 10% forwarding work best, using only 178 and 425 messages, respectively. For comparison, the original flooding (Gnutella) method would generate close to 4000 messages before it finds the first path. For the random graph, Selective and K-walker still outperform flooding, but only if the forwarding is at a high level (70%). To illustrate this, flooding uses about 2700 message to find the first trust path, and K-walker with 10% and 50% require as many or more: 2200 and 9000, respectively (the latter numbers are not visible in Figure 2 because they require higher values of TTL than displayed there). However, K-walker with 70% and Selective with 50 and 70% require less

Table 2. Number of trust paths found for scale free topology for different TTL values. Target is 4 hops away.

TTL	Gnutella		K-walker			Selective			Ultra-peers
	original	cache	10%	50%	70%	10%	50%	70%	
2	0	0	0	0	0	0	0	0	1
3	1	2	0	1	1	1	1	1	3
4	4	19	0	3	2	1	2	3	7
5	4	95	0	3	3	1	2	3	9
6	5	138	1	4	4	1	3	3	10
7	5	180	1	5	5	1	3	3	11

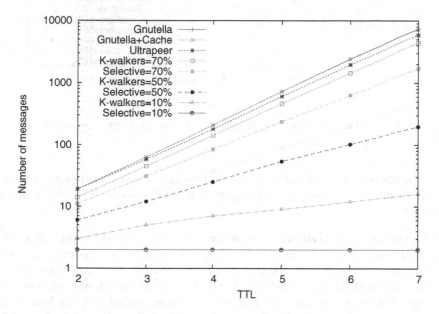

Fig. 2. Number of messages under different TTL values: Random graph topology – Distance = 7 hops

than 1000 messages. In other words, we notice extreme sensitivity to the chosen amount of forwarding in the K-walker as well as Selective querying algorithm.

If we compare the above findings with for instance [14], where networks of similar size were simulated, we note that the main difference is the lack of replication of the target in our setting. Hence, the conclusion drawn in [14] that scale-free topologies should be avoided does not necessarily hold for discovering trust paths. We find that the amount of messages needed to find the first trust path is similar for both topologies, and is very sensitive to specific parameter choices such as the K value in K-walker. However, trust paths can be found for low values of TTL in scale-free topologies–this indicates that the time it

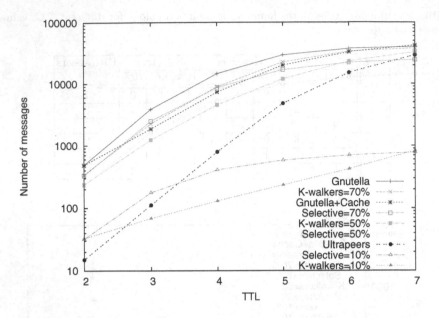

Fig. 3. Number of messages under different TTL values: Scale free topology – Distance = 4 hops

takes to discover a trust path will be less for the scale-free topology, and this also indicates that the expanding ring approach will work well for the scale-free topology.

Performance of individual algorithms. The distributed flooding algorithm (labelled 'Gnutella' in figures and tables) is known to be expensive in terms of the amount of messages used, and certainly for the scale-free topology our results confirm this insight. Instead, it is better to limit the number of forwarded messages using selective or K-walker with values as low as 10% (as long as the topology is scale-free). Flooding with caching ('Gnutella + Cache') did not differ much from Gnutella, except in terms of the number of paths found, a result we discuss in more detail below. We obtained the results for the caching algorithm as follows. We conducted several consecutives searches using the same origin and target nodes. The values obtained with the first search were cached. In the second search each node that has the trust path to the target in its cache will reply with this answer. The same query was repeated until every neighbour of the source node obtained cached results. In our test environment we needed four consecutive queries, at which moment we obtained the results presented in the tables and figures.

As we mentioned above, selective querying or K-walker algorithms are natural alternatives for flooding, typically outperforming it. However, selective querying proves a more stable solution, in that K-walker can lead to very poor and hard to predict results in terms of the number of messages needed. To find one trust

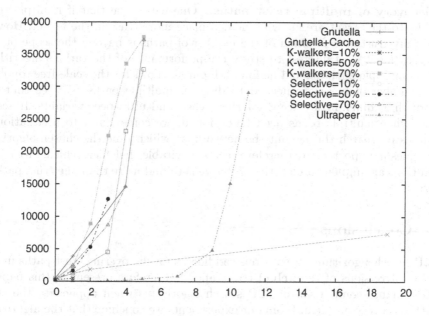

Fig. 4. Number of messages for different number of discovered trust paths: Scale-free graph topology – Distance = 4 hops

path with $K = 50\%$ in the random graph topology leads to a worst case scenario (9000 messages, quadruple the number needed by Gnutella). In our simulation, selective querying forwards to the nodes with the higher number of neighbours (as opposed to the randomly selected neighbours in K-walker), and that pays off in the random graph topology as well.

The ultra-peers algorithm in the random graph topology uses an amount of message very similar to the Gnutella protocol. However, in scale free graphs this algorithm got superior results, with trust paths found in as little as 15 messages. The reason for this is that we select the nodes with the highest number of neighbours as ultra peers, a fact that hardly helps if the topology is random, but works very well in the scale-free case.

In a practical implementation one needs a mechanism to increase the TTL value using expanding rings (or use one of the more advanced suggestions in [14]). The results for expanding ring are the sum of the results for individual TTL values. Therefore, it is important that an algorithm finds the trust path for a low value of TTL. In that respect, the results for the scale-free topology compare favourably to those for the random topology. So, even though selective forwarding to 50% of the neighbours in the random topology, with TTL equal to 32 may require as little as 200 messages, following the expanding ring approach the search would have to be repeated for increasing TTL values, thus proving costly after all. The scale-free topology, on the other hand, requires only few iterations in the expanding ring approach because the TTL needed is low.

Discovery of multiple trust paths. One can argue that if multiple trust paths to the target are known, one can place more trust in the target. How to quantify trust as a function of the number of paths is beyond the scope of this paper, but it is of interest to study the performance of the various algorithms when multiple paths should be found. Figure 4 shows for the scale-free topology the number of messages needed to discover multiple paths. We see that the algorithms differ little except for the cached and ultra-peer variants. It seems that when multiple paths need to be found, we come closer to a situation of exhaustive search throughout the network, at which time the chosen algorithm becomes unimportant. It therefore seems inevitable that hierarchical or caching solutions are implemented if the objective is to find more than one trust path to targets.

5   Conclusions

P2P search algorithms are obvious candidates for discovering trust paths in distributed versions of the web of trust, and we therefore present in this paper a performance comparison of P2P search algorithms when applied to the trust path discovery problem. From our experiments we conclude that the algorithms perform relatively well for a scale-free network topology, especially when compared to traditional file sharing applications, and we argued that the reason for this is that replication of resources has no counterpart in trust path discovery. We also saw that in trust path discovery the performance of restrictive forwarding algorithms such as K-walker can be extremely sensitive to the value of K, the amount of nodes to which a query is forwarded. Furthermore, we obtained results that indicate that when one is interested in discovering multiple trust paths, most algorithms become prohibitively expensive and instead ultra-peer or caching alternatives need to be explored.

References

1. Patil, V., Shyamasundar, R.: Trust management for e-transactions. Sadhana 30(2-3), 141–158 (2005)
2. Housley, R., Polk, W., Ford, W., Solo, D.: Internet X. 509 Public Key Infrastructure Certificate and Certificate Revocation List (CRL) Profile. IETF RFC 3280 (April 2002)
3. Zimmerman, P.: PGP User's Guide. Massachusetts Institute of Technology (May 1994)
4. Ellison, C.M., Frantz, B., Lampson, B., Rivest, R., Thomas, B.M., Ylonen, T.: SPKI Certificate Theory. Internet Engineering Task Force RFC 2693 (September 1999)
5. Rivest, R.L., Lampson, B.: SDSI – A simple distributed security infrastructure. In: Koblitz, N. (ed.) CRYPTO 1996. LNCS, vol. 1109, Springer, Heidelberg (1996)
6. Jøsang, A., Keser, C., Dimitrakos, T.: Can we manage trust? In: Herrmann, P., Issarny, V., Shiu, S.C.K. (eds.) iTrust 2005. LNCS, vol. 3477, pp. 93–107. Springer, Heidelberg (2005)

7. Skogsrud, H., Benatallah, B., Casati, F.: Model-driven trust negotiation for web services. In: IEEE Internet Computing, pp. 45–52. IEEE Computer Society Press, Los Alamitos (2003)
8. Spantzel, A.B., Squicciarini, A.C., Bertino, E.: Integrating federated identity management and trust negotiation. Technical Report 2005-46, CERIAS – Purdue University (2005)
9. Winslett, M., Yu, T., Seamons, K.E., Hess, A., Jacobson, J., Jarvis, R., Smith, B., Yu, L.: Negotiating trust on the web. In: IEEE Internet Computing. 6(6), pp. 30–37. IEEE Computer Society Press, Los Alamitos (2002)
10. Atif, Y.: Building trust in E-commerce. IEEE Internet Computing 6(1), 18–24 (2002)
11. de Mello, E.R., da Silva Fraga, J., Santin, A.O.: O uso do spki/sdsi em redes p2p. In: I Workshop sobre Redes Peer-to-Peer (WP2P'05), Fortaleza, CE - Brasil, XXIII Simpósio Brasileiro de Redes de Computadores (SBRC'05) (2005)
12. Santin, A.O., da Silva Fraga, J., Siqueira, F., de Mello, E.R.: Federation web: A scheme to compound authorization chains on large-scale distributed systems. In: 22nd Symposium on Reliable Distributed Systems (SRDS'03), Florence - Italy (2003)
13. Gkantsidis, C., Mihail, M., Saberi, A.: Random walks in peer-to-peer networks. In: INFOCOM (2004)
14. Lv, Q., Cao, P., Cohen, E., Li, K., Shenker, S.: Search and replication in unstructured peer-to-peer networks. In: Proceedings of the 16th international conference on Supercomputing, pp. 84–95 (2002)
15. Zhuang, Z., Liu, Y., Xiao, L., Ni, L.M.: Hybrid periodical flooding in unstructured peer-to-peer networks. In: ICPP, pp. 171–178. IEEE Computer Society Press, Los Alamitos (2003)
16. Penning, H.P.: Analysis of the strong set in the pgp web of trust (2006), http://www.cs.uu.nl/people/henkp/henkp/pgp/pathfinder/plot/
17. Burrows, M., Abadi, M., Needham, R.: A logic of authentication. ACM Trans. on Computer Sys. 8(1), 18 (1990)
18. Jøsang, A., Pope, S.: Semantic Constraints for Trust Transitivity. In: Research and Practice in Information Technology, vol. 43, ACS, Newcastle, Australia (2005)
19. Gnutella: The Gnutella Protocol Specification v0.4. Clip2 (2001)
20. Rowstron, A., Druschel, P.: Pastry: scalable, decentraized object location and routing for large-scale peer-to-peer systems. In: Proceedings of the 18th IFIP/ACM International Conference on Distributed Systems Platforms (Middleware), November 2001 (2001)
21. Stoica, I., Morris, R., Liben-Nowell, D., Karger, D.R., Kaashoek, M.F., Dabek, F., Balakrishnan, H.: Chord: a scalable peer-to-peer lookup protocol for internet applications. IEEE/ACM Trans. Netw 11(1), 17–32 (2003)
22. Chawathe, Y., Ratnasamy, S., Breslau, L., Lanham, N., Shenker, S.: Making gnutella-like P2P systems scalable. In: Proceedings of the ACM SIGCOMM 2003 Conference on Applications, Technologies, Architectures, and Protocols for Computer Communication, pp. 407–418. ACM Press, New York (2003)
23. Jiang, H., Jin, S.: Exploiting dynamic querying like flooding techniques in unstructured peer-to-peer networks. In: ICNP, pp. 122–131. IEEE Computer Society Press, Los Alamitos (2005)
24. Yang, B., Garcia-Molina, H.: Improving search in peer-to-peer networks. In: ICDCS, pp. 5–14 (2002)
25. Kazaa media desktop (2001), http://www.kazaa.com

26. Albert, R., Barabási, A.L: Statistical mechanics of complex networks. Reviews of Modern Physics 74, 47 (2002)
27. Milgram, S.: The small world problem. Psychology Today 1, 61 (1967)
28. Capkun, S., Buttyan, L., Hubaux, J.P.: Small worlds in security systems: an analysis of the PGP certificate graph. In: Proceedings of the 2002 New Security Paradigms Workshop, September 2002, pp. 28–35 (2002)
29. Gnumap project (2002), http://home.comcast.net/~gregory.bray
30. Peersim p2p simulator (2004), http://peersim.sourceforge.net
31. Jesi, G.P.: Peersim howto: Build a new protocol for the peersim 1.0 simulator (December 2005)

Building Online Performance Models of Grid Middleware with Fine-Grained Load-Balancing: A Globus Toolkit Case Study

Ramon Nou[1], Samuel Kounev[2], and Jordi Torres[1]

[1] Barcelona Supercomputing Center (BSC), Technical University of Catalonia (UPC)
Barcelona Spain
{rnou,torres}@ac.upc.edu
[2] University of Cambridge Computer Laboratory, Cambridge, CB3 0FD UK
skounev@acm.org

Abstract. As Grid computing increasingly enters the commercial domain, performance and Quality of Service (QoS) issues are becoming a major concern. To guarantee that QoS requirements are continuously satisfied, the Grid middleware must be capable of predicting the application performance on the fly when deciding how to distribute the workload among the available resources. One way to achieve this is by using online performance models that get generated and analyzed on the fly. In this paper, we present a novel case study with the Globus Toolkit in which we show how performance models can be generated dynamically and used to provide online performance prediction capabilities. We have augmented the Grid middleware with an online performance prediction component that can be called at any time during operation to predict the Grid performance for a given resource allocation and load-balancing strategy. We evaluate the quality of our performance prediction mechanism and present some experimental results that demonstrate its effectiveness and practicality. The framework we propose can be used to design intelligent QoS-aware resource allocation and admission control mechanisms.

1 Introduction

Having established itself as a major computing paradigm for advanced science and engineering, Grid computing is now promising to become the future computing paradigm for enterprise computing and distributed system integration [1,2]. By enabling flexible, secure and coordinated sharing of resources and services among dynamic collections of disparate organizations and parties, Grid computing provides a number of advantages to businesses, for example faster response to changing business needs, better utilization and service level performance, and lower IT operating costs [2]. However, as Grid computing increasingly enters the commercial domain, performance and QoS (Quality of Service) aspects, such as customer observed response times and throughput, are becoming a major concern. The inherent complexity, heterogeneity and dynamics of Grid computing environments pose some challenges in managing their capacity to ensure that QoS requirements are continuously met.

K. Wolter (Ed.): EPEW 2007, LNCS 4748, pp. 125–140, 2007.

Enterprise grids are typically composed of heterogeneous components deployed in disjoint administrative domains, in highly distributed and dynamic environments. The resource allocation and job scheduling mechanisms used at the global and local level play a critical role for the performance and availability of Grid applications [3]. To prevent resource congestion and unavailability, it is essential that admission control mechanisms are employed by local resource managers. Furthermore, to achieve maximum performance, the Grid middleware must be smart enough to schedule tasks in such a way that the workload is load-balanced among the available resources and they are all roughly equally utilized. However, in order to guarantee that QoS requirements are satisfied, the Grid middleware must be capable of predicting the application performance when deciding how to distribute the workload among the available resources. Prediction capabilities are prerequisite to implementing intelligent QoS-aware resource allocation and admission control mechanisms.

Performance prediction in the context of traditional enterprise systems is typically done by means of performance models that capture the major aspects of system behavior under load [4]. Numerous performance prediction and capacity planning techniques for conventional distributed systems, most of them based on analytic or simulation models, have been developed and used in the industry. However, these techniques generally assume that the system is static and that dedicated resources are used. To address the need for performance prediction in Grid environments, new techniques are needed that use performance models generated on the fly to reflect changes in the environment. The term *online performance models* was recently coined for this type of models [5]. The *online* use of performance models defers from their traditional use in capacity planning in that configurations and workloads are analyzed that reflect the real system over relatively short periods of time. Since performance analysis is carried out on the fly, it is essential that the process of generating and analyzing the models is completely automated.

In this paper, we present a case study with the Globus Toolkit [6], the world's leading open-source framework for building Grid infrastructures. We have augmented the Grid middleware with an online performance prediction component that can be called at any time during operation to predict the Grid performance for a given resource allocation and load-balancing strategy. The case study shows how performance models can be generated dynamically and used to provide online performance prediction capabilities. We employ hierarchical queueing Petri net models that are dynamically composed to reflect the system configuration and workload. Queueing Petri nets make it possible to accurately model the behavior of our resource allocation and load balancing mechanism which combines hardware and software aspects of system behavior. Moreover, queueing Petri nets have been shown to lend themselves very well to modeling distributed component-based systems [7] which are commonly used as building blocks of Grid infrastructures [8]. We have evaluated the quality of our online performance prediction mechanism and present some results that demonstrate its effectiveness and practicality. The framework presented in this paper can be used as a basis to implement intelligent mechanisms for QoS-aware resource allocation, load-balancing and admission control. Finally, although our approach is targeted at Grid computing environments, it is not in any way limited to such environments and can be readily applied in the context of more general Service-Oriented Architectures (SOA).

The paper is structured as follows. We start by introducing the Globus Toolkit and discussing some of our previous work related to the paper in Section 2. Section 3 presents our approach to online performance prediction. In Section 4, we present our case study and the experimental evaluation of our performance prediction mechanism. Finally, in Section 5 we present some concluding remarks and discuss our future work.

2 The Globus Toolkit

The Globus Toolkit (GT) is a community-based, open-architecture, open-source set of services and software libraries that support Grids and Grid applications [6]. The toolkit addresses issues of security, information discovery, resource management, data management, communication, fault detection, and portability. Globus Toolkit mechanisms are in use at hundreds of sites and by dozens of major Grid projects worldwide.

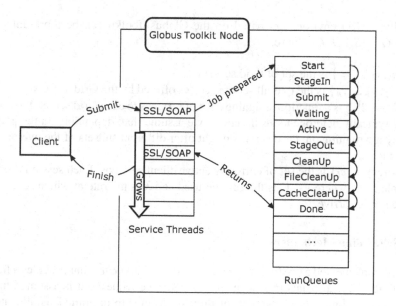

Fig. 1. Job Workflow in Globus Toolkit 4

Unfortunately, despite its popularity and success, the current implementation of the Globus Toolkit (GT4) exhibits very poor performance and reliability when the Grid middleware is overloaded. In our previous work [9,10], we have studied the behavior of Globus under heavy load and proposed enhancing the Grid middleware with a self-management layer to improve its performance and reliability under load [11]. In this paper, we show how the Grid middleware can be further enhanced with online performance prediction capabilities that are required in order to implement intelligent QoS control mechanisms. We plan to use the online performance prediction framework proposed in this paper to extend our self-management layer with some more sophisticated QoS-aware resource allocation and admission control mechanisms.

We now take a brief look at the internal flow of control in Globus when processing jobs. Figure 1 shows the workflow of a job executed by Globus. When a client submits a job to a Globus server (using the *globusrun-ws* interface in its non-batch working mode), the job is picked by a ServiceThread which performs an SSL handshake. After the handshake, the SOAP request is parsed preparing the job for execution. The job is then started and proceeds through several stages as shown in Figure 1. At each stage the job is placed in a RunQueue and processed by a pool of threads. The most important stage is when the job is executed at the OS level. This is done by a separate OS process forked by Globus. After the job execution finishes, it goes through several clean up stages (RunQueues) and finally a ServiceThread generates the SOAP response and sends it back to the client.

3   Modeling Approach

Formally, a Grid environment based on the Globus Toolkit can be represented as a 4-tuple $G = (S, V, F, C)$ where:

$S = \{s_1, s_2, ..., s_m\}$ is the set of Grid servers,

$V = \{v_1, v_2, ..., v_n\}$ is the overall set of services offered by the Grid servers,

$F \in [S \longrightarrow 2^V]^1$ is a function assigning a set of services to each Grid server. Since Grids are typically heterogeneous in nature, we assume that, depending on the platform they are running on, Grid servers might offer different subsets of the overall set of services,

$C = \{c_1, c_2, ..., c_l\}$ is the set of currently active client sessions. Each session $c \in C$ is a tuple (v, λ) where $v \in V$ is the service used and λ is the rate at which requests for the service arrive.

3.1   Scheduling Mechanism

We have implemented a configurable *service request dispatcher* that provides a flexible scheduling and load-balancing mechanism for service requests. It is assumed that for each client session, a given number of threads (from 0 to unlimited) is allocated on each Grid server offering the respective service. Incoming service requests are then load-balanced across the servers according to thread availability. Threads serve to limit the concurrent requests executed on each server, so that different scheduling strategies can be enforced.

A scheduling strategy can be represented by a function $T \in [C \times S \longrightarrow \mathbb{N}_0 \cup \{\infty\}]$ which will be referred to as *thread allocation function*. The service request dispatcher queues incoming service requests (as part of a client session) and schedules them for service at the Grid servers as threads become available. Note that threads are used here

---

[1] 2^V denotes the set of all possible subsets of V, i.e. the power set.

as a *logical* entity to enforce the desired concurrency level on each server. Thread management is done entirely by the service request dispatcher and there is no need for Grid servers to know anything about the client sessions and how many threads are allocated to each of them. While the service request dispatcher might use a separate physical thread for each logical thread allocated to a session, this is not required by the architecture and there are many ways to avoid doing this in the interest of performance. For maximum scalability, multiple service request dispatchers can be instantiated and they can be distributed across multiple machines if needed.

Service request dispatchers completely decouple the Grid clients from the Grid servers which provides some important advantages that are especially relevant to commercial Grid environments. First of all, the decoupling enables us to introduce *fine-grained* load-balancing at the service request level, as opposed to the session level. Second, service request dispatchers make it possible to load-balance requests across heterogeneous server resources without relying on any platform-specific scheduling or load-balancing mechanisms. Finally, since clients do not interact with the servers directly, it is possible to adjust the resource allocation and load-balancing strategies dynamically.

3.2   Online Performance Prediction

In order to enhance the Grid middleware with online performance prediction capabilities, we have developed an *online performance prediction component* that can be called at any time during operation to predict the Grid performance for a given scheduling strategy represented by a thread allocation function T. Performance prediction is carried out by means of an online performance model generated and analyzed on the fly. The online performance prediction component can be used to find an optimal scheduling strategy that satisfies the client SLAs under given resource utilization constraints. Based on this, intelligent QoS-aware admission control mechanisms can be developed. For example, when a client sends a request to start a new session, the scheduler can reject the request if it is not able to find a scheduling strategy that satisfies the client SLAs. The design of intelligent mechanisms for QoS control is outside the scope of this paper. In the following, we focus on the performance prediction component and evaluate its effectiveness in the context of a real-life Globus deployment.

The performance prediction component is made of two subcomponents - *model generator* and *model solver*. The model generator automatically constructs a performance model based on the active client sessions and the available Grid servers. The model solver is used to analyze the model either analytically or through simulation. Different types of performance models can be used to implement the performance prediction component. In this paper, we use Queueing Petri Nets (QPNs) which provide greater modeling power and expressiveness than conventional modeling formalisms like queueing networks, extended queueing networks and generalized stochastic Petri nets [12,13,14]. In [7], it was shown that QPN models lend themselves very well to modeling distributed component-based systems and provide a number of important benefits such as improved modeling accuracy and representativeness. The expressiveness that QPNs models offer makes it possible to model the logical threads used in our scheduling mechanism accurately. Depending on the size of QPN models, different

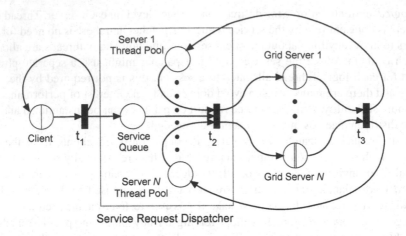

Fig. 2. High-level QPN model of the Grid environment

methods can be used for their analysis, from product-form analytical solution methods [15] to highly optimized simulation techniques [16].

Figure 2 shows a hierarchical QPN model of a set of Grid servers accessed through our service request dispatcher. The Grid servers are modeled with nested QPNs represented as subnet places. The *Client* place contains a $G/G/\infty/IS$ queue which models the arrival of service requests sent by clients. Service requests are modeled using tokens of different colors, each color representing a client session. For each active session, there is always one token in the Client place. When the token leaves the Client queue, transition t_1 fires moving the token to place *Service Queue* (representing the arrival of a service request) and depositing a new copy of it in the Client queue. This new token represents the next service request which is delayed in the Client queue for the request interarrival time. An arbitrary request interarrival time distribution can be used. For each Grid server, the service request dispatcher has a *Server Thread Pool* place containing tokens representing the logical threads on this server allocated to the different sessions (using colors to distinguish between them). An arriving service request is queued at place Service Queue and waits until a thread for its session becomes available. When this happens, the request is sent to the subnet place representing the respective Grid server. After the request is processed, the logical service thread is returned back to the thread pool from where it was taken. By encapsulating the internal details of Grid servers in separate nested QPNs, we decouple them from the high-level performance model. Different servers can be modeled at different level of detail depending on the complexity of the services they offer.

At each point in time, the online performance prediction component keeps track of the active client sessions and the currently available Grid servers. It is assumed that when servers are added to the Grid, for every server a performance model is provided in the form of a nested QPN that captures the server capacity and its internal behavior when processing service requests. When invoked, the performance prediction component uses the models of the Grid servers to dynamically construct an up-to-date model of the Grid environment that reflects the current workload (in terms of active client sessions) and the currently available server resources. The model is constructed by integrating the Grid server models into the high-level QPN model discussed above. The model generation and analysis is completely automated and happens on the fly.

4 Case Study

In this section, we present our case study of a deployment of GT4 which we have enhanced with online performance prediction functionality as described in the previous section. We evaluate the quality of our performance prediction mechanism and present some experimental results that demonstrate its effectiveness. Our testing environment depicted in Figure 3 consists of two heterogeneous Grid servers, the first one 2-way Pentium Xeon at 2.4 GHz with 2 GB of memory and the second one 4-way Pentium Xeon at 1.4 GHz with 4 GB of memory. Both servers run Globus Toolkit 4.0.3 (with the latest patches) on a Sun 1.5.0_06 JVM. The Grid clients are emulated on a separate machine with identical hardware as the first Grid server. The machines communicate over a Gigabit network.

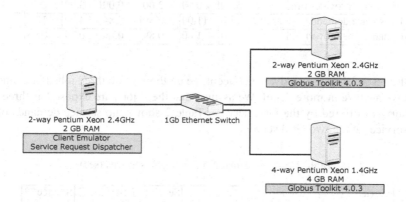

Fig. 3. High-level view of our testing environment

4.1 Workload Characterization

As a basis for our experiments, we use several sample jobs each executing some business logic requiring a given amount of CPU time. Some of the jobs include calls to external (third-party) service providers that are not part of the Grid environment. In order to build performance models of the two Grid servers, we must first characterize their workload in terms of the service demands of the jobs they execute.

There are several approaches to determining the CPU service demands. The most reliable method is to use a Globus profiler to measure the CPU service times directly. We can use the BSC Monitoring Framework (BSC-MF) [9] developed at the Barcelona Supercomputing Center in conjunction with the Paraver performance analysis tool [17]. Another approach which does not require profiling Globus is to estimate the service times based on measured CPU utilization and job throughput data. This approach is very general and does not require any profiling tools. For each job type, an experiment is run injecting jobs of the respective type. Based on the utilization law [18], we can then compute the average job service demand D as the ratio of the measured CPU utilization U to the job throughput X. In certain cases, techniques can be employed that help to estimate the service demands without the need to do any measurements on the system [19]. Such techniques are based on analyzing the business logic that jobs execute at the source code level.

Table 1 shows the service demands of the sample jobs we analyzed. For each job type, the internal job processing CPU time is shown, the time waited for external service providers, the measured total job CPU service demand and the job management overhead introduced by Globus. The overhead is consistently around 1 second across the seven job types.

Table 1. Estimated job service demands and Globus processing overhead (sec)

Job	A	B	C	D	E	F	G
Internal job processing CPU time	20.00	10.00	6.00	5.00	4.00	1.00	0.50
External service provider time	5.00	0.00	2.00	0.00	3.00	0.20	0.00
Job CPU service demand	21.00	11.00	6.89	5.84	4.79	1.93	1.54
Globus management overhead	1.00	1.00	0.89	0.84	0.79	0.93	1.04

In the rest of the case study, we concentrate on the middle three jobs (C, D and E), which we analyze in more detail. We assume that these jobs are exposed as three separate *services* offered by the Grid servers. Table 2 shows the service demands of the three services at the two Grid servers.

Table 2. Service demands of workload services (sec)

Service	Service 1 (Job C)	Service 2 (Job E)	Service 3 (Job D)
CPU service demand on the 2-way server	6.89	4.79	5.84
CPU service demand on the 4-way server	7.72	5.68	6.49
External service provider time	2.00	3.00	0.00

4.2   Grid Server Models

We assume that when Grid servers join the Grid they first register with the online performance prediction component responsible for the local environment. Each server provides a performance model in the form of a nested QPN that captures its internal behavior when processing service requests. When invoked, the performance prediction component dynamically constructs an up-to-date model of the Grid environment by integrating the Grid server models into the high-level model presented in Section 3.2 (see Figure 2). The two servers used in our case study were each modeled using a nested QPN as shown in Figure 4. Service requests arriving at a Grid server circulate between queueing place *Server CPUs* and queueing place *Service Providers*, which model the time spent using the server CPUs and the time spent waiting for external service providers, respectively. Place *Server CPUs* contains a $G/M/m/PS$ queue where m is the number of CPUs, whereas place *Service Providers* contains a $G/M/\infty/IS$ queue. The service times of service requests at these queues are set according to the measured service demands shown on Table 2. For simplicity, we assume that the service times at the server CPUs, the request interarrival times and the times spent waiting for external service providers are all exponentially distributed. In the general case this is not required. The firing weights of transition t_2 are set in such a way that place *Service Providers* is visited one time for Services 1 and 2 and it is not visited for Service 3. The model solver component of the performance prediction component was implemented using SimQPN - our highly optimized simulation engine for QPNs [16].

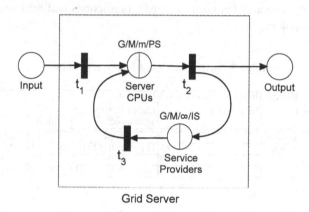

Fig. 4. Grid server QPN model

Before the Grid server models can be used for performance prediction they must be validated. This is normally done by comparing the model predictions against measurements on the real system. Our initial attempts to validate the model revealed that predictions were accurate in scenarios with no limitation on the number of concurrently scheduled requests and much less accurate in scenarios with limited number of threads allocated to client sessions (see Section 3.1). Table 3 shows four of the scenarios we considered. Given that for some scenarios the error was higher than 15%, the models could not pass our initial validation attempt. To investigate the problem, we analyzed the internal behavior of Globus when processing service requests. Figure 5 shows the stages and the CPU usage during the processing of a request for Service 3 (job D) in isolation. This view was obtained from a trace generated by BSC-MF [9] and processed using Paraver [17]. The black zones show periods when a CPU was used and the zones in between, marked with red horizontal lines, correspond to periods during which all CPUs were idle (in total about 1 sec). The idle CPU periods were occurring during job state transitions. Note that the service was executed in single user mode and therefore the idle CPU periods were not being caused by contention for software or hardware resources, neither were they being caused by I/O, since the disk utilization was negligible. Taking these "hidden internal delays" introduced by Globus into account helped us to understand why the model predictions were much less accurate in the case with limited concurrency. Indeed in this case, given that there are limited threads available and client requests have to wait at the service request dispatcher to obtain a thread, a difference of 1 sec in the time spent by jobs on the server obviously would have a much bigger impact on the overall response time than in the case with unlimited threads. Monitoring Globus under load with multiple concurrent requests revealed that the idle CPU periods during service execution were pretty much constant and were not affected much by the workload intensity or transaction mix. Having concluded this, we decided to calibrate our models by introducing an additional 1 sec delay during service execution. For simplicity, we added this delay to the time waited in place *Service Providers*. After this calibration, the discrepancy between the model predictions and measurements on the real system disappeared.

Table 3. Model predictions before calibration

Services	No of threads allocated	Request interarrival time (sec)	Request response time (sec) measured	predicted	Error (%)
2	unlimited	4	11.43	10.47±0.033	8.3%
1—3	unlimited	8 / 8	13.66 / 12.91	12.21±0.019 / 11.17±0.031	11% / 13%
3	5	2.5	10.93	8.14±0.030	25%
1—3	2/2	8 / 8	18.15 / 9.79	15.58±0.23 / 7.8±0.05	14.1% / **20.3%**

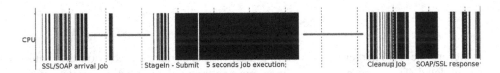

Fig. 5. Paraver view of a job execution inside Globus

An alternative approach to model the Grid environment is to use a general purpose simulation system such as OMNeT++ [20] which is based on message-passing. We have used OMNeT++ successfully to model a Tomcat Web server [21] with software admission control. Figure 6 compares the precision of interval estimates provided by SimQPN and OMNeT++ when simulating a model of our Grid environment described above with several concurrent client sessions. The precision is measured in terms of the maximum width of 95% confidence intervals for job response times. For run times below 1 second, SimQPN provided slightly wider confidence intervals than OMNeT++, however, there was hardly any difference for run times greater than 1 second. At the same time, while OMNeT++ results were limited to job response times, SimQPN results were more comprehensive and included estimates of job throughputs, server utilization,

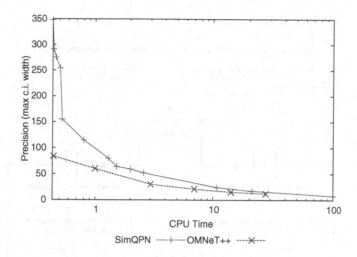

Fig. 6. Precision of interval estimates provided by SimQPN and OMNeT++ for a given simulation run time (sec)

queue lengths, etc. Moreover, QPN models have the advantage that they are much easier to build and, as discussed in Section 3.2, they can be hierarchically composed which facilitates the dynamic model construction. The hierarchical composition is essential since it introduces a clear separation of the high-level system model from the individual Grid server models. The latter can be developed independantly without knowing in which environment they will be used.

4.3 Experimental Results

We now evaluate the quality of our online performance prediction mechanism in the context of the scenario described above. We have developed a client emulator framework that emulates client sessions sending requests to the Grid environment. The user can configure the target session mix specifying for each session the service used and the time between successive service requests (the interarrival time). Client requests are received by the service request dispatcher and forwarded to the Grid servers according to the configured scheduling strategy as described in Section 3.1. Figure 7 illustrates the flow of control when processing service requests.

Whenever the online performance prediction component is invoked, it uses the QPN models of the Grid servers to dynamically construct a QPN model of the Grid environment that reflects the current workload in terms of active client sessions and the selected scheduling strategy. The generated model is then analyzed by means of simulation using SimQPN. The method of non-overlapping batch means was used with a batch size of 300 and the simulation was configured to run sequentially until the half-widths of 95% confidence intervals for response times dropped below half a second.

We used the online performance prediction component to predict the Grid performance under a number of different workload and configuration scenarios varying the

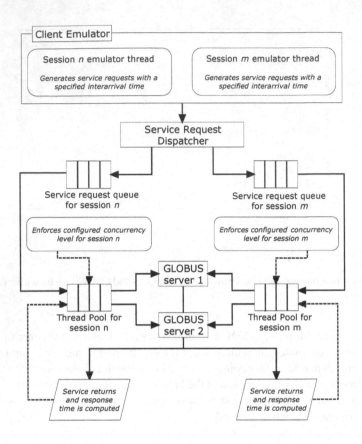

Fig. 7. Flow of control when processing service requests

session mix, the scheduling strategy and the number of servers available. Table 4 presents the results from an experiment in which the workload evolved through five different stages each one with different session mix and duration between 1200 and 3600 seconds. In the beginning of each stage, the scheduling strategy was modified dynamically and the online performance prediction component was called to predict the system performance on the fly. The average time needed to predict the system performance (including model generation and analysis) was 6.12 seconds, the maximum was 12 seconds. Performance predictions were recorded and were later compared against the actual performance measured during the run. The experiment was repeated multiple times and exhibited negligible variation in the measured performance metrics. Table 4 shows the results from comparing the model predictions against the measurements on the system. 95% confidence intervals for response times are provided. The mean modeling error was only 7.9% (with standard deviation 6.08) and it did not exceed 22.5% across all scenarios. We conducted a similar experiment for a number of different workload and configuration scenarios. The results from the analysis were of similar accuracy

Table 4. Comparison of model predictions against measurements on the real system

Services	No of threads allocated		Request interarrival time (sec)	Request response time (sec)		Error (sec)	Avg. CPU utilization	
	server 1	server 2		measured	predicted		measured	predicted
1	3	2	12.5	13.86	13.23±0.591	+0.63	0.66	0.65
1	5	3	13	14.57	13.41±0.622	+1.16		
2	2	4	11	11.36	10.63±0.432	+0.73		
2	1	2	12	11.07	10.49±0.452	+0.58		
2	5	4	15	12.49	10.99±0.453	+1.5		
3	1	5	13	9.37	8.36±0.331	+1.01		
3	1	2	16	9.41	8.53±0.363	+0.88		
3	4	4	16	10.17	9.79±0.520	+0.38		
1	1	10	12.5	11.61	11.13±0.597	+0.48	0.56	0.58
1	4	7	15	11.95	12.57±0.736	-0.62		
2	8	6	15	12.20	10.45±0.567	+1.75		
2	4	6	9	10.67	10.45±0.466	+0.22		
2	3	8	15.5	10.59	10.39±0.542	+0.2		
3	7	3	16	10.90	8.93±0.577	+1.97		
3	10	2	12	11.67	9.01±0.508	+2.66		
1	5	2	12.5	13.81	13.81±0.669	+0	0.64	0.66
1	2	1	13	13.76	14.19±0.750	-0.43		
2	1	4	11	10.4	10.2±0.532	+0.2		
2	1	5	12	10.3	10.18±0.507	+0.12		
2	4	1	15	13.45	11.80±0.479	+1.65		
3	1	1	13	9.61	9.7±0.504	-0.09		
3	3	2	16	10.9	9.82±0.627	+1.08		
3	2	2	16	9.51	9.57±0.617	-0.06		
1	1	1	14.5	12.36	14.28±0.443	-1.92	0.61	0.63
1	3	2	17	13.40	13.2±0.393	+0.2		
1	5	3	18	15.51	13.2±0.438	+2.31		
2	5	1	15	13.19	11.5±0.336	+1.69		
2	4	3	25	11.88	11.16±0.405	+0.72		
2	1	3	15	10.29	10.13±0.302	+0.16		
2	5	2	25.5	13.3	11.11±0.412	+2.19		
3	4	4	16	9.48	9.66±0.317	-0.18		
3	1	4	16	8.25	8.38±0.234	-0.13		
3	3	3	25	8.65	9.56±0.340	-0.91		
1	4	2	18.5	13.35	14.77±0.623	-1.42	0.64	0.65
1	4	5	15	12.05	14.56±0.618	-2.51		
1	4	4	16	12.58	14.50±0.673	-1.91		
2	1	2	15	10.67	10.78±0.460	-0.11		
2	5	1	17	11.86	12.59±0.534	-0.73		
2	2	2	19	11.09	11.51±0.492	-0.42		
2	4	2	15.5	11.53	11.99±0.528	-0.46		
3	2	5	16	9.42	10.1±0.475	-0.68		
3	1	4	19	8.98	9.14±0.413	-0.16		
3	3	5	23	8.92	10.57±0.535	-1.65		

as the ones presented here and demonstrated the effectiveness of our performance prediction mechanism. The computational overhead of the online performance prediction component was measured to be less than 60 sec for scenarios with up to 40 Grid servers and 80 concurrent sessions.

5   Conclusions and Future Work

In this paper, we presented a novel case study with the Globus Toolkit, the world's leading open-source framework for building Grid infrastructures, in which we showed how performance models can be generated dynamically and used to provide online performance prediction capabilities. We have augmented the Grid middleware with an online performance prediction component that can be called at any time during operation to predict the Grid performance for a given resource allocation and load-balancing strategy. The quality of our performance prediction mechanism has been evaluated under a number of different workload and configuration scenarios varying the session mix, the scheduling strategy and the number of servers available. We presented some experimental results that demonstrated the effectiveness, practicality and performance of our approach. The modeling error of predicted response times was only 7.9% on average (with standard deviation of 6.08) and it did not exceed 22.5% across all considered scenarios. The framework we propose provides a basis for designing intelligent QoS-aware resource allocation and admission control mechanisms.

Our performance prediction mechanism is based on hierarchical queueing Petri net models that are dynamically composed to reflect the system configuration and workload. Using queueing Petri nets we could accurately model the resource allocation and load balancing mechanism which combines hardware and software aspects of system behavior. Moreover, queueing Petri nets provide great flexibility in choosing the level of detail and accuracy at which system components are modeled. To the best of our knowledge, this is the first application of queueing Petri nets as online performance models.

The area considered in this paper has many different facets that will be subject of future work. We are currently working on extending the Globus Toolkit with online QoS control functionality. Based on the online performance prediction mechanism proposed in this paper, we are building a framework for QoS-aware resource allocation and admission control. The framework includes an intelligent QoS broker component that negotiates QoS goals and SLAs with Grid clients before making a commitment. Taken collectively these enhancements will not only provide sophisticated QoS control capabilities but can also be exploited to make the Grid middleware self-configurable and adaptable to changes in the system environment and workload. Another aspect we intend to investigate is how our framework can be extended to take into account the costs associated with using the Grid resources when negotiating QoS targets.

Acknowledgments

This work was supported by the Spanish Ministry of Science and Technology, the European Union under contract TIN2004-07739-C02-01, and the German Research Foundation under grant KO 3445/1-1. We acknowledge the support of our colleague Ferran Julià from the Technical University of Catalonia in resolving many technical issues.

References

1. Foster, I., Kesselman, C., Nick, J.M., Tuecke, S.: Grid Services for Distributed System Integration. Computer 35(6), 37–46 (2002)
2. OGF: Open Grid Forum, http://www.ogf.org
3. Menascé, D., Casalicchio, E.: A Framework for Resource Allocation in Grid Computing. In: Proceedings of the The IEEE Computer Society's 12th Annual International Symposium on Modeling, Analysis, and Simulation of Computer and Telecommunications Systems, IEEE Computer Society Press, Los Alamitos (2004)
4. Menascé, D.A., Almeida, V.A.F., Dowdy, L.W.: Performance by Design. Prentice-Hall, Englewood Cliffs (2004)
5. Menascé, D., Bennani, M., Ruan, H.: On the Use of Online Analytic Performance Models in Self-Managing and Self-Organizing Computer Systems. In: Babaoğlu, Ö., Jelasity, M., Montresor, A., Fetzer, C., Leonardi, S., van Moorsel, A.P.A., van Steen, M. (eds.) SELF-STAR 2004. LNCS, vol. 3460, Springer, Heidelberg (2005)
6. Foster, I.T.: Globus Toolkit Version 4: Software for Service-Oriented Systems. In: Proceedings of the 2005 IFIP International Conference on Network and Parallel Computing, pp. 2–13 (2005)
7. Kounev, S.: Performance Modeling and Evaluation of Distributed Component-Based Systems using Queueing Petri Nets. IEEE Transactions on Software Engineering 32(7), 486–502 (2006)
8. Foster, I., Kesselman, C.: The Grid 2: Blueprint for a New Computing Infrastructure. Morgan Kaufmann, San Francisco (2003)
9. Nou, R., Julia, F., Carrera, D., Hogan, K., Caubet, J., Labarta, J., Torres, J.: Monitoring and analysis framework for grid middleware. In: PDP, pp. 129–133. IEEE Computer Society, Los Alamitos (2007)
10. Nou, R., Juliá, F., Torres, J.: Should the grid middleware look to self-managing capabilities? In: The 8th International Symposium on Autonomous Decentralized Systems (ISADS 2007), Sedona, Arizona (2007)
11. Nou, R., Juliá, F., Torres, J.: The need for self-managed access nodes in grid environments. In: 4th IEEE Workshop on Engineering of Autonomic and Autonomous Systems (EASe 2007), IEEE Computer Society Press, Los Alamitos (2007)
12. Bause, F.: "QN + PN = QPN" - Combining Queueing Networks and Petri Nets. Technical report no.461, Department of CS, University of Dortmund, Germany (1993)
13. Bause, F., Buchholz, P., Kemper, P.: Integrating Software and Hardware Performance Models Using Hierarchical Queueing Petri Nets. In: Proc. of the 9. ITG / GI - Fachtagung Messung, Modellierung und Bewertung von Rechen- und Kommunikationssystemen (1997)
14. Kounev, S., Buchmann, A.: Performance modelling of distributed e-business applications using queuing petri nets. In: Proc. of the 2003 IEEE International Symposium on Performance Analysis of Systems and Software (ISPASS'03), mar 2003, IEEE Computer Society Press, Los Alamitos (2003)
15. Bause, F., Buchholz, P.: Queueing Petri Nets with Product Form Solution. Performance Evaluation 32(4), 265–299 (1998)
16. Kounev, S., Buchmann, A.: SimQPN - a tool and methodology for analyzing queueing Petri net models by means of simulation. Performance Evaluation 63(4-5), 364–394 (2006)
17. Jost, G., Jin, H., Labarta, J., Gimenez, J., Caubet, J.: Performance analysis of multilevel parallel applications on shared memory architectures. International Parallel and Distributed Processing Symposium (IPDPS), Nice, France (2003)

18. Denning, P.J., Buzen, J.P.: The Operational Analysis of Queueing Network Models. ACM Computing Surveys 10(3), 225–261 (1978)
19. Menascé, D., Gomaa, H.: A Method for Desigh and Performance Modeling of Client/Server Systems. IEEE Transactions on Software Engineering 26(11) (2000)
20. Varga, A.: The OMNeT++ discrete event simulation system. In: European Simulation Multiconference (ESM'2001) (June 2001)
21. Nou, R., Guitart, J., Torres, J.: Simulating and modeling secure web applications. In: Alexandrov, V.N., van Albada, G.D., Sloot, P.M.A., Dongarra, J.J. (eds.) ICCS 2006. LNCS, vol. 3991, pp. 84–91. Springer, Heidelberg (2006)

Performance Measuring Framework for Grid Market Middleware

Felix Freitag[1], Pablo Chacin[1], Isaac Chao[1], Rene Brunner[1], Leandro Navarro[1],
and Oscar Ardaiz[2]

[1] Computer Architecture Department, Polytechnic University of Catalonia, Spain
{felix,pchacin,ichao,rbrunner,leandro}@ac.upc.edu
[2] Department of Mathematics and Informatics, Public University of Navarra, Spain
oscar.ardaiz@unavarra.es

Abstract. Current implementations of Grid infrastructures provide frameworks which aim at achieve on-demand computing. In such a scenario, contribution and use of resources will be governed by business models. The challenge is to provide multi-level performance information which enables the participation of the different actors in such a system. In this paper we describe the performance measuring framework developed for Grid Market Middleware, a middleware which supports economic-model based selection of service-oriented Grid applications. This middleware is a distributed infrastructure, which we have implemented for providing a market of services and resources to be assigned to Grid applications. The objectives of the performance measuring framework is first to assess the behaviour of the middleware and the used economic models in a deployed system, and secondly allow the provision of metrics for the components of the middleware itself. We describe the design of the performance measuring framework, its implementation and show its capability and usefulness for our objectives by experiments.

Keywords: Multi-layer Performance Measurement, e-service Platforms, Grid Middleware Architecture.

1 Introduction

In an on-demand scenario of service-oriented Grid applications, these applications will need service and resource providers to participate in a distributed software infrastructure. Clients will issue requests for Grid applications. The applications will be built on the fly din terms of complex services executing a sequence of basic services. Request for basic services are given to service providers and are executed on contracted resources.

There is a need for platforms that support such an on-demand infrastructures, where complex e-services can be assigned and executed. The resources need to be dynamically obtained to satisfy the requirement of changing application requirements. There is a need for technical openness and clear interfaces to the application level. At the same time, there is a need for performance data that allows the participants making an economic evaluation of their participation.

K. Wolter (Ed.): EPEW 2007, LNCS 4748, pp. 141–153, 2007.
© Springer-Verlag Berlin Heidelberg 2007

In this paper we describe the performance measuring framework implemented in the Grid Market Middleware (GMM) [6] aiming at two objectives: 1) To obtain multi-level performance data from the deployed system, and 2) to show that the data obtained is useful for obtaining information about the system behaviour and its economic models used. The context in which we are interested to make our evaluation is that of the deployed middleware.

We have developed the Grid Market Middleware to support economic model based selection of service-oriented Grid applications. This middleware is a distributed infrastructure, which provides a market of services and resources to be assigned to Grid applications. The implemented market structure applies decentralized economic models based on bargaining [3]. The Grid Market Middleware offers an agent-based framework for dynamic location and management of Grid services based on economic criteria. It provides mechanisms to locate and manage the registered resources, services and applications, locate other trading agents, engage agents in negotiations, learn and adapt to changing conditions. Furthermore, the middleware offers a set of generic negotiation mechanism, on which specialized strategies and policies can be dynamically plugged in.

The presented performance measuring infrastructure for this middleware makes the following contribution: 1) Its functionality is shown by achieving the goal of detecting interesting behavior, such as load balancing. 2) It is a prototype that implements an approach to obtain multi-level performance data provided by the different layers of a distributed system, including application, middleware and base platform.

The remaining sections of this paper are organized as follows. Section 2 presents the Grid Market Middleware and the performance measuring goals. In section 3 we describe the design of the implemented performance measuring framework. Section 4 shows experimental results obtained with the implemented performance measuring infrastructure on the deployed middleware. Section 5 describes performance measurement frameworks of related domains. Finally, section 6 presents our conclusions.

2   Grid Market Middleware

2.1   Application Interaction with Grid Market Middleware

Grid Market Middleware as a software infrastructure, on which this performance measuring framework targets, contains an application level and the middleware. Figure 1 illustrates the interaction of the components on the application level with the middleware. When a client issues a request, an application component determines which Grid services are required to fulfill it. These Grid services represent both software services (e.g. a mathematical algorithm) and computational resources. The application service translates these requirements into a WS-Agreement format [16], which is submitted to the Grid Market Middleware.

Once a request is received by the middleware, it searches among the available service providers. When a suitable service provider is found, agents within the middleware negotiate the application requirements. These agents act in behalf of the

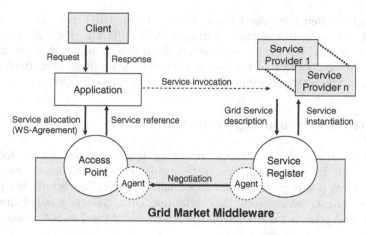

Fig. 1. Interaction between application and middleware

service providers as sellers and from the application perspective as buyers. Once an agreement is reached between the trading agents, a Grid service instance is created and a reference is returned to the application, which invokes it.

The middleware is designed in a layered architecture with the five layers shown in figure 2. The *application layer* is for the domain specific end user application. The applications interact with the Grid Market Middleware in order to obtain the Grid services required. The Grid Market Middleware itself consists of three layers. Within the Market Middleware, the *economics algorithms* layer implements the high level economic behavior like negotiation and agent strategies. The *economics framework* layer isolates these economic algorithms from the lower level technical details. The *P2P Agent* layer provides decentralized resource discovery and network topology maintenance. The *base platform* supports the application providing the hosting environment for the Grid services. A detailed description of the middleware architecture can be found in [1].

2.2 Middleware Implementation

The implementation of the middleware builds on the use of different middleware toolkits, namely the DIET agent platform [2], JXTA [10] and the WSRF/OGSA

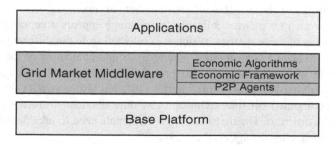

Fig. 2. Layered middleware architecture

implementation offered by the Globus Toolkit 4 [5]. DIET provides a modular, lightweight and scalable execution platform, JXTA offers a rich P2P networking environment and GT4 provides full support for resource management in different scenarios. The components of the middleware architecture have been implemented and an application, which uses this middleware, has been adapted [9].

3 Performance Measuring Framework

The development of the performance measuring framework follows the following approach. We define the goals and the metrics which should be obtained. We identify the measurement points given the developed middleware infrastructure. We proceed with the instrumentation and local data collection. Then, collecting and obtaining the data at a central point is the next step. The evaluation of the data is the final step of the process.

3.1 Goals of the Performance Measuring Framework

The framework should be able to provide a large number of diverse metrics: The measurement should allow obtaining metrics both from the application, the middleware, and the physical level (base platform). In addition, there is a need for both technical and economic metrics. The economic metrics should be calculated from the technical metrics obtained by the framework and should assist the decision makers residing in the users (or applications). The framework should allow by means of mainly technical parameters evaluating the infrastructure itself.

The instrumentation of the middleware and application needs to be done at different levels. User agent related data is obtained at the application level. Technical parameters concerning the middleware performance will need to be instrumented at the corresponding levels of the middleware architecture. Finally, the monitoring of the physical resources is done by accessing the base platform.

The component of the metrics framework at the node level should locally gather the metrics obtained from the components working at the same node but at different layers of the infrastructure. The metrics collection should be done centrally, aiming to allow evaluating the prototype at this stage. Nevertheless, it is noted that the software infrastructure should run in a distributed manner on physically different devices and at a later stage with a potentially large number of nodes. For the prototype evaluation, however, although it is distributed, the number of nodes is small, such that a centralized approach for metrics collection at this stage appears acceptable.

The evaluation of these metrics, which are collected from the different nodes of the middleware, is done at a central point. The analysis and evaluation of the middleware is done off-line with external tools that provide the needed mathematical functions. Especially the higher-level economic metrics [15], see also appendix for the metrics pyramid, are computed off-line taking the raw data obtained from the performance measuring infrastructure. The metrics, which the agents need to take decisions, should be processed on-line by the agents themselves.

3.2 Metrics Definition

We assign metrics to the layers of the software infrastructure. Beginning with the application layer (see also figure 1), there are a number of parameters to be measured in the client (which represents the end user) and the application. The client and the application perceive technical parameters, like the *service provision rate*, the *ratio between the number of requests and accepts*, and the *service provision time*, the *duration for obtaining an accept*. The client as end user will need to transform these technical parameters into economic ones, consider the benefits and the efforts, in order to determine the utility obtained by participating in this infrastructure. The application will calculate economic parameters from the technical data, if a business model for this component is defined.

Related to different levels of the middleware there are the following technical parameters: The *discovery time* refers to the time the middleware needs to find other agents to negotiate with. The *negotiation time* indicates the duration of the negotiation process. The negotiation process takes place in both the service and the resource market. Each negotiation consists of several messages according to the bargaining strategy. The *message size* is a parameter, which allows better describing the communication cost. The *number of messages* is another parameter concerning this cost. Load balancing is a metrics that should assess the efficiency of the resource assignment obtained with the Grid Market Middleware.

Concerning the base platform, the *resource usage* is measured. Initially, we focus on cpu usage.

In Table 1 some of the metrics classified into layers are summarized.

Table 1. Summary of metrics in different layers

Layer	Metrics
Application layer	*service provision rate* *ratio between the number of requests and accepts* *duration for obtaining an accept*
Middleware layer	*discovery time* *negotiation time* *message size* *number of messages*
Base Platform layer	*resource usage*

3.3 Instrumentation and Local Data Collector

In our approach, we took the design decision that data from one node should be locally collected. This way, we obtain at each node an event trace, which includes the metrics from the different middleware layers. Provision of these metrics is through agents (figure 3). The event trace contains the time stamps of the events, the metrics itself and a number of attributes like the agent number, transaction number, and others, in order to allow a detailed analysis of the behavior. The local data collector manages this data structure. In terms of implementation, a circular structure is used such that its size is controlled.

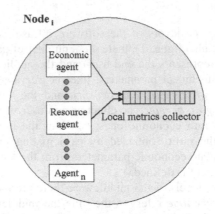

Fig. 3. Local metrics collector

Access to this data structure is given in two ways. One hand, the data can be written to a file (log file), and on the other hand the local data collector can send it regularly to a global metrics collector located on a particular node.

3.4 Global Metrics Collector

The data obtained at the different nodes is send to the global metrics collector, which resides on a particular node of the system. Data is send terms of a push mode: local data collectors initiate the sending to the global collector according to a configured behavior. The global metrics collector then processes and organizes the data into a format suitable for external packages. For our purpose we use Matlab for the evaluation of the data. We note that for larger scale usage beyond the current experimental environment, the automation of the clock synchronization between the nodes and the global metrics collector needs to be addressed.

4 Experimental Results

Given the developed prototype and the implemented measurement infrastructure, we have carried out a number of experiments. These experiments aim to assure that the components work correctly, that multi-level performance data can effectively be obtained, and that this data is actually useful for the evaluation of the behaviour of the middleware.

4.1 Setup of the Experiments

The particular goal of the experiment setting is to allow making an initial assessment on the load balancing behavior of the GMM by means of the implemented performance measuring framework.

The middleware uses as economic agents an implementation of the ZIP (Zero Intelligence Plus) agents [13]. Clients initiate negotiations with a price lower than the available budget. If they are not able to buy at that price, they increase their bids until either they win or reach the budget limit.

Services start selling the resources at a price, which is influenced by the node's utilization. Then, the pricing model is combined with the demand. If a service agent sells its resources, it will increase the price to test to what extend the market is willing to pay. When it no longer sells, it will lower the price until it becomes competitive again or it reaches a minimum price defined by the current utilization of the resource.

We have deployed the Grid Market Middleware in a Linux server farm. Each server has 2 Xeon processors and 2GB of memory. The machines in the server farm are connected by an internal Ethernet network at 100Mbps.

Three basic services (BS) are deployed on three servers (BS-74 on node 74, BS-75 on node 75, BS-79 on node 79, respectively), and two complex services (CS) are launched on two other servers (CS-72 on node 72, CS-73 on node 73, respectively). On each machine with a BS we also deploy a web service representing the application, which performs a CPU intensive calculation. These web services are exposed in a Tomcat server. Access to execute these web services is what is negotiated between complex services (buyer) and basic services (seller).

We run an artificial background load on two of the nodes (node 79, node 75) configured for 50% and 100% CPU usage to simulate background activity. This is chosen since in such a setting the behaviour of the agents should lead to load balancing of the web service executions.

The experiments consist in launching 2 clients (represented by complex services CS-72 and CS-73) concurrently as clients. Each client performs 50 requests in intervals of 15 seconds. Whenever a client wins a bid with a service, it invokes the web service in the selected node. The data obtained from the experiment with the performance measuring infrastructure has been the following:

1. *allocation*: an entry by each successful negotiation with a basic service, reported by the complex service
2. *price*: a periodic report of the price of the basic services
3. *utilization*: a periodic report of the CPU utilization given by the resource agents
4. *negotiation.time*: time needed to negotiate with a basic service, reported by the complex service (transaction-based)
5. *execution.time*: time needed to actually execute the service, reported by the somplex service (transaction-based)

We mention that the data used is mixed in nature in the sense that some metrics are collected periodically (*price*ψand *utilization*), others are recorded after each successful transaction (*execution.time*, *negotiation.time*ψand *allocation*).

4.2 Experimental Results

Figure 4 shows the load (% cpu usage) on the three nodes (74, 75, 76). A background load of 50% and 100% in nodes 79 and 75, respectively, can be observed. The up-going spikes which can be seen in the load of node 79 and node 74 correspond to the execution of the negotiated web services on these nodes.

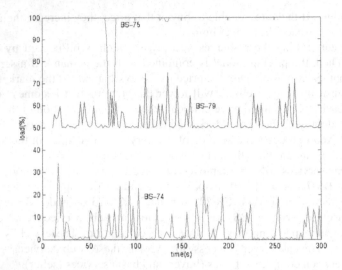

Fig. 4. Load on nodes 74, 75, and 79. Node 79 and node 75 are with 50% and 100% background load, respectively

Figure 5 shows a zoom on the price of the basic services. It can be observed that the price calculation of the agents takes into account the success of past negotiations, where the price rise is made after a successful sale. The configured buyer price is 100 money units.

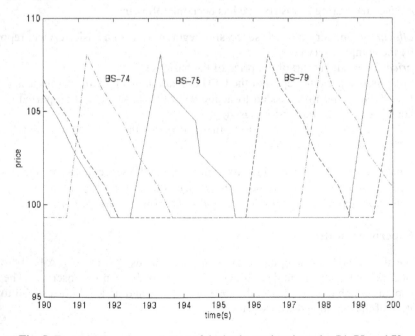

Fig. 5. Zoom on the price evolution of the basic services in nodes 74, 75, and 79

The next figure 6 is to assess the expected load balancing behavior, which we should obtain with this setting. It can be seen that effectively the BS-74, which runs on the least loaded node, makes most of the sales. And the BS-75, which runs on the node with the highest background load, makes less sells than the other two basic services. We can see that the performance measuring framework achieves one of our goals which was revealing such behavior.

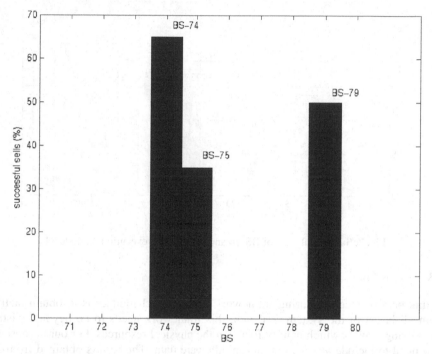

Fig. 6. Percentage of sales of the three basic services. BS-74 which resides on the least loaded node, makes most of the sells.

Finally, in figure 7 we observe two metrics together: the successful sales by BS-74 and the execution of the sold service when invoked by the clients (the web service is executed on the same node 74). Successful sales by the BS-74 are indicted with a star symbol and are normalized here to the value 30 for easier visualization. It can be seen that on each successful sale an execution of the web service follows. It can be seen that the duration of the execution is approximately 4 seconds.

The experimental results demonstrate the two contributions we want to emphasize: First, the measurement framework achieves obtaining multi-level performance data of the distributed application. The data shown in the experiment is taken from the three main levels of the architecture: The time of the web service execution is measured at the application level. The evolution of prices is taken at the economics algorithm layer of the middleware. Finally, the load at each node is taken from the base platform layer. Secondly, the obtained data is useful for the analysis of the middleware and application (the setting was deliberately chosen to force load balancing behavior). We have seen that with the obtained data the expected behavior can effectively be observed.

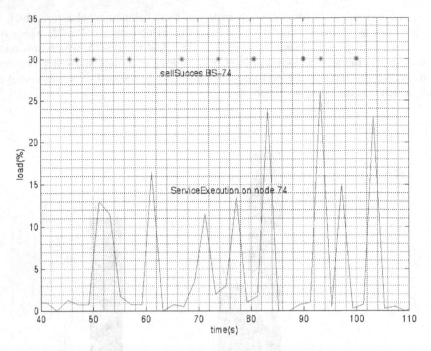

Fig. 7. Successful sells of BS-74 and web service execution on node 74

4.3 Discussion

In this performance measuring framework one of the challenges is to obtain metrics from all layers of the system. As such, this framework needs to go beyond existing monitoring toolkits which mainly focus on the physical resources. For our purpose we also need to include application and middleware data. The results obtained from the implemented measuring framework experimental show that this has been achieved.

Another challenge relates to the usage of the metrics by the middleware (agents) itself, such that there will be different destinations for some of these metrics. In this sense, there is the central metrics collection point, to which (currently for evaluation purpose) most of the data is sent and where the data is a posteriori analyzed and evaluated. On the other hand, there are the participants (the applications) as destination of metrics, since they need application layer metrics in order to take decisions and evaluate their performance. This second challenge, to route data to particular groups, has not been implemented yet in our framework. Our view on this is to apply publish/subscribe mechanisms in order to assign metrics to groups.

Anther issue, which has already become important when we measured particular agent strategies, is the scalability of the performance evaluation framework towards the quantity of the measured data, since large amounts of data are already obtained. This scalability problem affects the number of parameters which can be monitored, and may require in the future additional solutions such as shown in [4] to tackle the size of the traces obtained.

5 Related Work

Related work can be found in multi-agent systems (MAS), high-performance computing and generic monitoring toolkits. Here we describe system from these three domains which also target on the performance evaluation of distributed systems.

In [7] the performance measuring system built into the Cougaar agent architecture is described. Cougaar belongs to distributed multi-agent systems (MAS). Like the GMM, it has been implemented 100% in Java. For performance measurement of Cougaar the authors decided to develop a custom-made performance measuring system which has been built into the system architecture. Cougaar also considers multiple data categories which are accessed via channels. The need for flexibility with respect to where to carry out the data processing, the access by semantics to categories, and dynamic plug-ins for changing needs has been taken into account in Cougaar. Similar to this approach, we have also decided to develop our own performance measuring framework directly fitting to our measurement needs, instead of adapting an exiting toolkit.

There are a number of measurement toolkits mainly with origin in high-performance computing, such as DiPerF [14] and NetLogger [7]. DiPerF aims to provide automatic performance measurement of networked services. It particularly targets on deployed services (such as a particular Grid service) and has been used in real testbeds such as PlanetLab [12]. DiPerF offers besides a set of preconfigured oncs the possibility to include user specific metrics. NetLogger is oriented to anomaly detection and is presented as a service which can be activated for Grid applications. Its main purpose is monitoring and addressing the instrumentation level in running Grid processes, as part of a Grid monitoring system. Compared to our purpose, these toolkits focus on the executed application. In our case, however, we are particularly interested in measuring what happens before execution, i.e. within the middleware and the economic models used for allocating services and resources, before finally the application (service) becomes executed.

Ganglia [11] is a fairly generic measurement toolkit. It is devised to be a scalable distributed monitoring system for high performance computing systems such as clusters and Grids. It is deployed in PlanetLab [12] and has also been used with Globus [5]. The Ganglia implementation consists of the gmond deamon, which runs on every node of the system. This deamon interacts with a client in a listen/announce protocol, such that it responds to a client request by returning an XML representation of the monitored data. The metrics which gmond handles are of two types: built-in metrics and user-defined. The built-in metrics relate to the physical resources of the node. User-defined metrics could include application specific data. Due to this second possibility, Ganglia has been a candidate considered for being used with the GMM. Ganglia, however, relates machines with physical IP addresses, while some of the components we measure in the GMM cannot be identified this way, they are addressed, for instance, by identifiers from an overlay network.

6 Conclusions

Platforms, which support the execution of complex services, are needed in order to make real an on-demand scenario. In order to attract a large user and industrial community, these platforms need to have the capability to give performance feedback to users and providers.

Our performance measuring framework goes beyond the monitoring of physical resources and includes middleware and application layer metrics. These multi-level metrics are necessary, since the technical metrics from all those layers can finally be interpreted in economic terms. Such an economic evaluation of the participation in the system is needed for operating with business models.

We have shown that the implementation of such a multi-level performance measuring framework is feasible. We have applied the measuring framework to obtain performance data form several layers of the deployed middleware. We have also shown that this data is useful for observing the behavior of the system. As example for this we have shown how the balancing capacity of the system can be confirmed.

Acknowledgments. This work was supported in part by the European Union under Contract CATNETS EU IST-FP6-003769 and in part by the Ministry of Education and Science of Spain under Contract TIN2006-5614-C03-01.

References

1. 1. Ardaiz, P., Chacin, I., Chao, F., Freitag, L.: Navarro: An Architecture for Incorporating Decentralized Economic Models in Application Layer Networks. International Journal on Multiagent and Grid Systems. Special Issue on Smart Grid Technologies 1(4), 287–295 (2005)
2. Diet Agents Platform (February 2007), http://diet-agents.sourceforge.net/
3. Eymann, T., Reinicke, M., Freitag, F., Navarro, L., Ardaiz, O., Artigas, P.: A hayekian self-organizing approach to service allocation in computing systems. Advanced Engineering Informatics 19(3), 223–233 (2005)
4. Freitag, F., Caubet, J., Labarta, J.: On the Scalablitiy of Tracing Mechanisms, Euro-Par, Paderborn, Germany (August 2002)
5. Globus Toolkit (February 2007), http://www.globus.org/
6. Grid Market Middleware (GMM). http://recerca.ac.upc.edu/gmm/
7. Gunter, D., Tierney, B.: NetLogger: A Toolkit for Distributed System Performance Tuning and Debugging. Integrated Network Management, 97–100 (2003)
8. Helsinger, A., Lazarus, R., Wright, W., Zinky, J.: Tools and techniques for performance measurement of large distributed multiagent systems. In: Second International Joint conference on Autonomous agents and multiagent systems (AAMAS), Melbourne, Australia, pp. 843–850 (2003)
9. Joita, L., Rana, O.F., Chacin, P., Chao, I., Freitag, F., Navarro, L., Ardaiz, O.: Application Deployment on Catallactic Grid Middleware. IEEE Distributed Systems Onlin 7(12) (2006) art. no. 0612-oz001
10. Project JXTA (February 2007) http://www.jxta.org/

11. Massie, M.L., Chun, B.N., Culler, D.E.: The Ganglia Distributed Monitoring System: Design, Implementation, and Experience. Parallel Comput-ing 30(7) (July 2004)
12. PlanetLab. http://www.planet-lab.org/
13. Preist, C., van Tol, M.: Adaptive agents in a persistent shout double auction. In: Proceedings of the First international Conference on Information and Computation Economies (IEC), Charleston, South Carolina, United States (1998)
14. Raicu, I., Dumitrescu, C., Ripeanu, M., Foste, I.: The Design, Performance, and Use of DiPerF: An automated DIstributed PERformance evaluation Framework. Journal of Grid Computing 4(3) (September 2006)
15. Reinicke, M., Streitberger, W., Eymann, T., Catalano, M., Giulioni, G.: Economic Evaluation Framework of Resource Allocation Methods in Service-Oriented Architectures. In: Proceedings of the 8th Conference on E-Commerce Technology (CEC06), San Francisco (2006)
16. Web Services Agreement Specification (WS-Agreement) (2005/2009), http:// www.gridforum.org/ Public_Comment_Docs/Documents/ Oct-2005/WS-AgreementSpecificationDraft050920.pdf

Appendix: Metrics Pyramid [15]

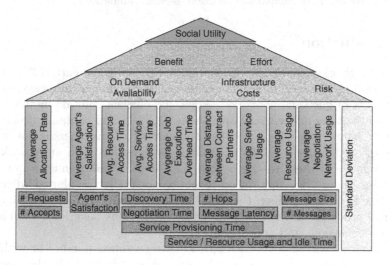

A Fixed-Point Algorithm for Closed Queueing Networks

Ramin Sadre, Boudewijn R. Haverkort, and Patrick Reinelt

University of Twente
Dept. Electrical Engineering, Mathematics and Computer Science
P.O. Box 217, 7500 AE Enschede, The Netherlands
r.sadre@cs.utwente.nl, brh@cs.utwente.nl

Abstract. In this paper we propose a new efficient iterative scheme for solving closed queueing networks with phase-type service time distributions. The method is especially efficient and accurate in case of large numbers of nodes and large customer populations. We present the method, put it in perspective, and validate it through a large number of test scenarios. In most cases, the method provides accuracies within 5% relative error (in comparison to discrete-event simulation).

1 Introduction

Queueing networks (QNs) have been used widely since the early 1970's for the analysis of performance problems in computer and communication systems. For many classes of queueing networks elegant and efficient solution methods exist.

In case the QNs under study are open ("OQNs") and contain queueing stations with infinite capacity, i.e., when the number of customers is not *a priori* restricted, product-form results exist, such as those for Jackson networks [17]. A disadvantage of these results is that they are only valid under a number of restrictions: the service times need to be exponentially distributed when combined with FCFS scheduling, the stations have unbounded buffer capacity, and all arrival processes are Poissonian. These restrictions have led researchers to search for extensions and approximations.

Queueing network models with either finite customer number or with finite buffers, and, hence, with customer losses, can be analyzed via the numerical solution of the underlying CTMC. However, this method is sensitive to the well-known phenomenon called state-space explosion. One way to handle this problem for open queueing networks is a *decomposition approach*. It has been motivated by the approximate solution method of large open queueing networks with infinite-buffer stations and FCFS scheduling, as proposed by Kühn [19] and later extended by Whitt [31,32]. The decomposition is done at queueing station level, i.e., the queueing stations are analyzed as separate models. These methods have been extended and refined lately in the context of the tool FiFiQueues. During the analysis, traffic descriptors are "exchanged between the stations", thus representing the streams of jobs flowing between them. We will elaborate on this in Section 2.

K. Wolter (Ed.): EPEW 2007, LNCS 4748, pp. 154–170, 2007.
© Springer-Verlag Berlin Heidelberg 2007

In case the QNs under study are closed ("CQNs"), i.e., when a finite fixed population of customers is present in the network, and when some other restrictions apply, Gordon and Newell first described a product-form for closed queueing networks [12], which was later extended by Baskett *et al.* to the now well-known class of BCMP networks [2]. Buzen developed an elegant solution strategy to compute the normalizing constant [8], and later, using the arrival theorem, Reiser and Lavenberg developed the now-widely used mean-value analysis approach [24]. Various extensions to these algorithms and model class have been developed, cf. textbooks like [10]. Apart from a number of modeling restrictions, such as negative exponential service times in combination with FCFS scheduling, all of the developed algorithms suffer from increasing (above linear) complexity when the number of stations, the number of customers, or the number of model classes (or routing chains) grow.

It is for the above reasons, that we have sought to come up with an alternative method for analyzing large closed queueing networks. Although little work has been reported on this so far, we found some of our inspiration in the fixed-point approach developed by Bolch *et al.* [6] (as also described in [16, Chapter 11.5]). Our approach consists of elevating the fixed-point algorithms that have been developed and successfully applied for open queueing networks to closed queueing networks. In doing so, we have encountered a number of problems, that we, however, have been able to deal with, after having experimented with the new method. In comparison to other approaches, our work is more generally applicable, and also less costly than previously reported approaches. We will discuss related work in a separate section.

The rest of this paper is structured in the following way. Section 2 is devoted to a fixed-point method for open queueing networks, as this approach forms the basis of our new method for closed queueing networks, that is described in Section 3. After that, we report experimental results on a variety of networks in Section 4. Section 5 presents directly related work, whereas Section 6 concludes the paper.

2   Fixed-Point Analysis of OQNs

Fixed-point iteration methods have been employed successfully to evaluate large open queueing networks with non-Poissonian arrivals and non-exponential service time distributions, with or without job losses (bounded buffers). The idea has been to compute, iteratively, the traffic arriving at each queueing station in such a queueing network, such that individual queueing stations can, in essence, be analyzed in isolation [13, 14, 15, 30]. The main algorithm is outlined in Figure 1. The traffic from station i to station j in the queueing network is described by a traffic descriptor $desc_{i,j}$. Note that we do, at this point, not make the form of this traffic descriptor explicit; in practice, it will contain such quantities as the traffic rate and, possibly, the variance. The external traffic arriving at a station j is denoted as $desc_{ext,j}$. In each step, a new set of traffic descriptors $desc^{(l)} = \{desc_{i,j}^{(l)} | i,j\}$ is computed. The algorithm stops when the

```
1 initialize all traffic descriptors desc_{i,j}^{(0)}:
2    set desc_{i,j}^{(0)} to the null value if i ≠ ext
3    set desc_{i,j}^{(0)} to the specified value if i = ext
4 l := 0
5 do
6    l := l + 1
7    analyze each queueing station i
8    and compute desc_{i,j}^{(l)} for all nodes j
9 while dist(desc^{(l)}, desc^{(l-1)}) > ε
```

Fig. 1. Decomposition-based analysis procedure for open queueing networks

distance $dist(desc^{(l-1)}, desc^{(l)})$ $(l \geq 1)$ between two successive sets of descriptors is smaller or equal than a given threshold ε. Descriptors set to the *null* value in line 2 are ignored in line 7; the *null* value indicates that only information about the external arriving traffic (line 3) is available when the algorithm starts. In general, it is not known whether a fixed point is unique or can/will be found. However, in our experiments with the FiFiQueues network analyzer the algorithm always terminated; furthermore, in [25] the existence of a fixed-point is proven.

The approach as described above, was developed in the mid 1990's [13, 14, 15, 30], essentially as an extension of Whitt's QNA approach [31] by replacing the core of his analysis: the analysis of the queueing stations themselves (the "service operation"). Unlike QNA, this new approach (called QNAUT) does not use the descriptor of the arrival traffic directly to compute the departure traffic descriptor, but assumes that the arrival traffic descriptor can be used to construct a phase-type (PH) renewal process which approximates the "real" underlying arrival process. This allows for the inclusion of finite-buffer queueing stations as well as for the analysis of the queueing stations by matrix-geometric and general Markovian techniques, instead of the approximations used originally in QNA.

Around the turn of the century, we extended the QNAUT-approach, in that we removed a few approximate steps and enhanced the model class [26, 28, 27]. This approach, as well as the analysis tool developed from it, is named *FiFiQueues* (*Fi*xpoint-based analysis of networks with *Fi*nite *Queues*). In FiFiQueues an open queueing network model is specified by the following parameters:

1. The number of queueing stations n.
2. The description of each queueing station. The queueing stations can have finite or infinite capacity and are analyzed as PH|PH|1(|K) queues. The service processes can be arbitrary phase-type renewal processes. A PH|PH|1(|K) queue is analyzed by means of the CTMC underlying the corresponding Quasi-Birth-and-Death process.
3. A routing matrix $\mathbf{R} = (r_{i,j})$ of size $n \times n$ for the Markovian routing where $r_{i,j}$ specifies the routing probability from station i to station j.
4. The descriptors of the external arrival traffic for each station.

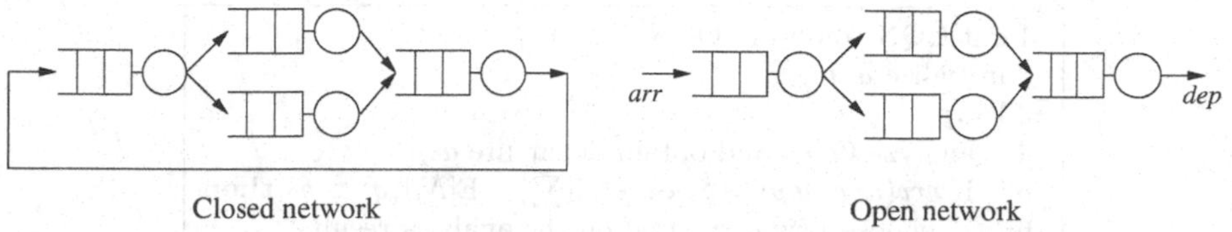

Closed network   Open network

Fig. 2. CQN and the corresponding cut OQN

As in QNA, the external arrival processes as well as the inter-node traffic streams are described by the first and second moment of the inter-arrival times. The traffic descriptor $\langle \lambda, c_a^2 \rangle$ contains the arrival rate λ and the squared coefficient of variation c_a^2 of the inter-arrival time distribution. In order to obtain the arrival process for a PH|PH|1(|K) station, a PH renewal process has to be fitted to the arrival traffic descriptor $\langle \lambda, c_a^2 \rangle$. Traffic descriptors with $c_a^2 \leq 1$ are mapped to modified Erlang-distributions. In case $c_a^2 > 1$, a hyper-exponential distribution with two phases and so-called balanced means is used. In the following sections, we use the same fitting procedure for the service processes, too, i.e., we specify a service process by the service rate μ and the squared coefficient of variation c_s^2 of the service time distribution.

Finally, FiFiQueues comprises two post-processing steps that are performed after the fixed-point iteration. They allow for the computation of additional performance measures and yield (i) node-specific results, e.g., the mean queue length $E[N_i]$ for each station i, and (ii) network-wide results, e.g., the total network throughput.

3   Fixed-Point Analysis of CQNs

We first describe in general terms an iterative approach for CQNs in Section 3.1. Before we make this approach more specific, we discuss the issue of bottleneck identification and its impact on performance measures in CQNs in Section 3.2. We then proceed with our actual algorithm in Section 3.3 and discuss complexity issues in Section 3.4.

3.1   General Procedure

The decomposition approach for OQNs cannot be directly applied to CQNs because the bounded number of customers in a closed system prevents an intuitive decomposition. Hence, we transform a CQN into an OQN by cutting one of its connections. This is shown for an example network in Figure 2. For this OQN we have to find an external arrival traffic descriptor arr such that

1. the external arrival descriptor arr is equal to the (resulting) descriptor dep of the traffic that leaves the network;
2. the number of jobs in the network is equal to the fixed population q of the CQN.

```
 1 cut CQN to obtain OQN
 2 initialize arr
 3 loop
 4    analyze OQN and obtain departure dep
 5    if err(arr, dep) > δ₁ or err'(∑ⁿᵢ₌₁ E[Nᵢ], q) > δ₂ then
 6       choose new arr based on the analysis results
 7    else
 8       stop iteration
 9    endif
10 endloop
```

Fig. 3. Iterative procedure to solve CQNs

We aim to find arr by applying the iteration procedure shown in Figure 3 to the CQN. The functions err and err' are appropriate error functions and δ_1 resp. δ_2 the corresponding error bounds. To implement this procedure we have to address three issues:

1. the location of the cut in order to obtain an open network (line 1);
2. the analysis of the open queueing network (line 4);
3. the computation of a new arrival descriptor inside the iteration (line 6).

These issues are discussed in detail in Section 3.3 but we can already make the following observations:

- (Back) blocking at the queues is not allowed if we the analyze the open queueing network by a decomposition-based method. This would require that information about free queueing capacities is exchanged between queues, which is not supported by the decomposition approach for OQN in which individual stations are analyzed in isolation. Hence, we will assume in the following that all queues have infinite capacity.
- Although the sketched procedure looks very simple, its implementation is critical for complex network classes and traffic descriptors. It is yet unknown whether the iteration procedure always terminates and whether more than one correct solution exist for a given CQN. However, in our experiments (see below) it always terminated with satisfying results.
- The stopping condition $err'(\sum_{i=1}^{n} E[N_i], q) \leq \delta_2$ provides only an approximation to the original condition that the number of jobs in the CQN is q. Indeed, variations in the number of customers present due to the stochastic nature of the arrival and service processes causes the number of jobs in the OQN to vary around q, which is clearly not the case in a true closed QN.

3.2   Characteristics of the Bottleneck

Before we present the implementation of the analysis procedure for CQNs in detail in Section 3.3, we discuss some important characteristics of the so-called

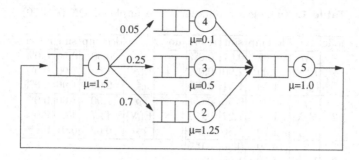

Fig. 4. Example Gordon-Newell QN

bottleneck in a CQN. We will use results from bottleneck analysis in the further development of our algorithm.

The (relative) throughput of the queueing stations in a CQN is limited by the bottleneck which can be determined by solving the (first-order) traffic equations [16]:

$$V_j = \sum_{i=1}^{n} V_i r_{i,j} = V_1 r_{1,j} + \sum_{i=2}^{n} V_i r_{i,j} = r_{1,j} + \sum_{i=2}^{n} V_i r_{i,j}, \quad \text{with} \quad V_1 = 1,$$

where the so-called visit ratios $V_j = X_j/X_1$ express the throughput of station j relative to node 1. The ratio $D_i = V_i/\mu_i$, for each station i, is the so-called service demand (per passage) at station i; the bottleneck is the node i with the highest value of D_i.

The bottleneck does not only influence the throughput of the queueing stations but also their queue length distribution. We illustrate this with the CQN shown in Figure 4. It is a Gordon-Newell queueing network (GNQN), i.e., all stations are of M|M|1-type. The figure shows the routing probabilities and the service rates of each node. A quick computation reveals that $D_1 = \frac{2}{3}$, $D_2 = \frac{14}{25}$, $D_3 = \frac{1}{2}$, $D_4 = \frac{1}{2}$ and $D_5 = 1$. Clearly, station 5 is the bottleneck. Given a large population, we can expect a large number of customers to reside in station 5, always, so that its utilization will approach 100%. A (discrete-event) simulation of the network with population $q = 50$ yields for each station the utilization ρ (note that $\rho_i = D_i/D_5 = D_i$), the mean $E[N]$ and the squared coefficient of variation c_N^2 of the queue length distribution. The results (with relative 95%-confidence intervals smaller than 3%) are shown in the column titled "sim" of Table 1. The fact that station 5 is a rather distinct bottleneck, leads to a very deterministic queue length distribution for that station (its c_N^2 is very close to 0), i.e., almost all of the time, almost all jobs are waiting in the bottleneck queue.

3.3   CQN Analysis with FiFiQueues

We now describe how the general iteration scheme for CQNs can be "implemented" using FiFiQueues (see Section 2) as analysis method for the generated

Table 1. Numerical results for the example GNQN ($q = 50$)

node		decomp	sim	relerr	node		decomp	sim	relerr
	ρ	0.67	0.67	0.0%		ρ	0.50	0.50	0.0%
1	$E[N]$	2.00	2.00	0.0%	4	$E[N]$	1.00	1.00	0.0%
	c_N^2	1.50	1.51	-0.7%		c_N^2	2.00	1.96	2.0%
	ρ	0.56	0.56	0.0%		ρ	1.00	1.00	0.0%
2	$E[N]$	1.27	1.27	0.0%	5	$E[N]$	44.7	44.7	0.0%
	c_N^2	1.79	1.80	0.6%		c_N^2	0.02	0.01	100%
	ρ	0.50	0.50	0.0%					
3	$E[N]$	1.00	1.00	0.0%					
	c_N^2	2.00	2.03	-1.5%					

```
 1 Determine bottleneck node b of closed network
 2 Cut connection to b and obtain open network
 3 Limit capacity of b to q
 4 λ_arr,low := 0 ; λ_arr,high := h
 5 c²_dep := 1
 6 do
 7     λ_arr := ½ · (λ_arr,high + λ_arr,low) ; c²_arr := c²_dep
 8     call FiFiQueues to obtain dept. descriptor (λ_dep, c²_dep)
 9     if Σⁿ_{i=1} E[N_i] > q or network is unstable then
10         λ_arr,high := λ_arr
11     else
12         λ_arr,low := λ_arr
13     endif
14 while err(λ_arr,low, λ_arr,high) > δ_1 or err'(Σⁿ_{i=1} E[N_i], q) > δ_2
```

Fig. 5. Analysis procedure for CQNs based on FiFiQueues

OQNs. We have called the resulting analysis method *FiFiQueues Non-Blocking Closed (FiFiQueues-NBC)* [23]. Its model class is the model class of the original FiFiQueues adapted to CQNs, that is, without external arrivals and departures.

The analysis procedure for CQNs using FiFiQueues is shown in Figure 5. The outer iteration uses an interval splitting technique to determine an appropriate value λ_{arr}. The algorithm is based on two assumptions.

First, we assume that the number of jobs in the network q can be reached by an interval splitting method for the arrival rate λ_{arr}. The argument is similar to the one used in the functional approximation approach for closed BCMP networks, cf. [6]. The initial value h in line 4 has to be set to an appropriate large value (a too large initial value only slows down the convergence — overloaded networks are avoided by the test in line 9). Note that we do not need to test λ_{arr} and λ_{dep} for equality since this is always fulfilled in networks without losses.

The second assumption concerns the squared coefficient of variation c^2. We have observed in the past that large queueing networks tend to "emboss" a network specific value for c^2 to the traffic stream. This means that the c^2 value of a traffic stream seems to depend only on the service processes and not on the c^2 value of the external arrival streams, whenever the traffic passes through a sufficiently large number of queueing stations, provided that the utilization of the queueing stations is reasonably high. This is the reason why we have chosen an arbitrary initial value for c_{dep}^2 in line 5 and simply assign c_{dep}^2 to c_{arr}^2 in line 7.

The lines 1–3 of the algorithm are due to our observations in Section 3.2 concerning the bottleneck. In order to approach the situation in which there is a deterministic queue length distribution at the bottleneck station, we proceed the following way. We cut the CQN directly in front of the bottleneck (lines 1–2) and transform the bottleneck station into a queueing station with finite capacity q (line 3). When the bottleneck station experiences a high load and, hence, most of the jobs are waiting in the queue of the bottleneck node, this finite capacity limits the maximum number of jobs in the network and leads to a more deterministic queue length distribution at the bottleneck. Our experiments have shown that we can select an arbitrary connection to the bottleneck for the cut if more than one connection exists. Similarly, if more than one bottleneck exists, an arbitrary one is selected as finite capacity station.

Note that the initial value h of $\lambda_{arr,high}$ (line 4) must be sufficiently high in order to obtain a load of 100% at the bottleneck station. If the bottleneck has only one incoming edge, h must be at least twice the service rate of the bottleneck due to the factor of $\frac{1}{2}$ in line 7. Our experiments suggest to use a slightly larger factor of 2.5 in order to compensate for the losses at the bottleneck station.

The numerical results for the Gordon-Newell queueing network shown in Figure 4 with $q = 50$ are displayed in the column labeled "decomp" in Table 1. The right column titled "relerr" gives the error between the decomposition approach and the simulation, relative to the latter. Note that the large relative error of node 5's c_N^2 is caused by the fact that the absolute numbers themselves are very small. The other relative errors are within the 95%-confidence intervals of the simulation.

3.4 Complexity

The proposed iterative CQN algorithm consists of two iterations of which the step count is usually not known in advance. The inner iteration is part of the FiFiQueues algorithm for OQNs. In each inner iteration all queueing stations are analyzed. Note that only the bottleneck station is modeled as a finite queueing station (of size q) and, hence, the time complexity of its analysis depends on the population q. Concerning the outer iteration, we have observed that there is no direct dependency on the population q (see Section 4.3 for a detailed example). Our experiments have shown that even for complex networks with large populations, the required number of inner and outer iterations usually stays below 15, resp. 30.

In addition to the iterations, the algorithm has to identify the bottleneck of the network. The solution of the system of traffic equations has a time complexity of $O(n^3)$ if a direct solution method like Gaussian elimination is employed, but

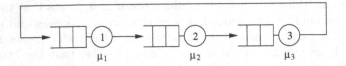

Fig. 6. Cyclic three-queue CQN

Table 2. Results for cyclic three-queue CQN for different rates μ_i and $q = 20$

One distinct bottleneck: $\mu_1 = \mu_3 = 1, \mu_2 = 0.5$				One bottleneck: $\mu_1 = 1, \mu_2 = 2, \mu_3 = 1.1$			
node		decomp	sim	relerr	node	decomp	sim	relerr
1	ρ	0.5	0.5	0.0%	1	ρ	0.95	0.95	0.0%
	$E[N]$	1.5	1.55	-3.2%		$E[N]$	11.90	11.17	6.5%
2	ρ	1.0	1.0	0.0%	2	ρ	0.48	0.47	2.1%
	$E[N]$	17.0	17.0	0.0%		$E[N]$	1.34	1.32	1.5%
3	ρ	0.5	0.5	0.0%	3	ρ	0.84	0.86	-2.3%
	$E[N]$	1.5	1.49	0.7%		$E[N]$	7.76	7.51	3.3%

Three bottlenecks: $\mu_1 = \mu_2 = \mu_3 = 1$				Two bottlenecks: $\mu_1 = \mu_3 = 1, \mu_2 = 2$			
node		decomp	sim	relerr	node	decomp	sim	relerr
1	ρ	0.81	0.85	-4.7%	1	ρ	0.88	0.91	-3.3%
	$E[N]$	5.98	6.64	-9.9%		$E[N]$	8.25	9.36	-11.9%
2	ρ	0.86	0.85	1.2%	2	ρ	0.44	0.45	-2.2%
	$E[N]$	7.45	6.66	11.9%		$E[N]$	1.12	1.22	-8.2%
3	ρ	0.83	0.85	-2.4%	3	ρ	0.93	0.91	-1.1%
	$E[N]$	6.57	6.69	-1.8%		$E[N]$	10.63	9.42	12.8%

reduces to $O(c \cdot n)$ in practice when sparse storage and an iterative solver such as Gauss-Seidel are used (where c is the average number of outgoing connections per station).

4 Validation

In this section we examine the performance of the new decomposition-based method for CQNs, using four typical examples: a cyclic CQN (Section 4.1), two CQNs with merging and splitting of traffic streams (Section 4.2) and a more general complex CQN (Section 4.3).

4.1 A Cyclic Three-Queue CQN

The first model is a simple CQN that consists of three queues in series as shown in Figure 6. All service times are hyper-exponentially distributed with $c_{service}^2 = 2$.

Table 3. Results for cyclic three-queue CQN for various population sizes

node		$q = 5$ decomp	sim	relerr	node		$q = 10$ decomp	sim	relerr
1	ρ	0.41	0.44	-6.8%	1	ρ	0.48	0.49	-2.0%
	$E[N]$	0.84	0.93	-9.7%		$E[N]$	1.28	1.35	-5.2%
2	ρ	0.89	0.89	0.0%	2	ρ	0.97	0.97	0.0%
	$E[N]$	3.27	3.14	4.1%		$E[N]$	7.42	7.34	1.1%
3	ρ	0.43	0.44	-2.3%	3	ρ	0.48	0.49	-2.0%
	$E[N]$	0.89	0.92	-3.3%		$E[N]$	1.30	1.31	-0.8%

node		$q = 30$ decomp	sim	relerr	node		$q = 60$ decomp	sim	relerr
1	ρ	0.5	0.5	0.0%	1	ρ	0.5	0.5	0.0%
	$E[N]$	1.50	1.57	-4.5%		$E[N]$	1.50	1.57	-4.5%
2	ρ	1.0	1.0	0.0%	2	ρ	1.0	1.0	0.0%
	$E[N]$	27.0	26.9	0.4%		$E[N]$	57.0	56.9	0.2%
3	ρ	0.5	0.5	0.0%	3	ρ	0.5	0.5	0.0%
	$E[N]$	1.50	1.50	0.0%		$E[N]$	1.51	1.50	0.7%

This network does not require any traffic merging or splitting, so that the cor-responding open network can be analyzed by FiFiQueues almost without any error.

Table 2 gives the results of the decomposition method in comparison to sim-ulation for three different service rates. The population size was set to 20. The last column gives the relative errors. All relative 95%-confidence intervals of the simulation were below 1%.

Table 2 shows that the algorithm does best when one distinct bottleneck is present in the network, i.e., in case $\mu_1 = \mu_3, \mu_2 = 0.5$. Then our "trick" with the finite queue provides very good results. Even when two stations have similar service rates ($\mu_1 = 1, \mu_2 = 2, \mu_3 = 1.1$), still good results are obtained. The errors are, however, slightly larger in cases where more than one bottleneck exist. Since the algorithm can select only one node as bottleneck it is not able to distribute the jobs evenly over all nodes in case all service rates are equal ($\mu_1 = \mu_2 = \mu_3 = 1$). The worst (but still okay!) results are obtained when the network consists of two bottlenecks and one fast service station ($\mu_1 = \mu_3 = 1, \mu_2 = 2$); again, the algorithm can select only one node as bottleneck which results in different average queue lengths for node 1 and node 3 whereas the simulation indicates that both queue lengths should be equal.

The next experiment uses the same queueing network but this time $\mu_2 = 0.5$, $\mu_1 = \mu_3 = 1$, and the population is varied between 5 and 60. The results are shown in Table 3. As can be seen, the relative errors are larger for small popula-tion sizes. Similar results have been obtained for other CQNs. The explanation for this behavior is that the small number of jobs in the CQN causes correlations between the queue lengths. This fact contradicts with FiFiQueues' assumptions about the network, hence, slightly worse results are obtained.

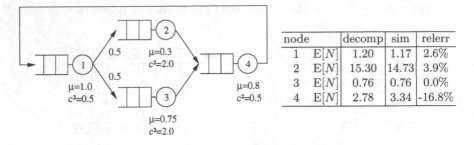

node		decomp	sim	relerr
1	E[N]	1.20	1.17	2.6%
2	E[N]	15.30	14.73	3.9%
3	E[N]	0.76	0.76	0.0%
4	E[N]	2.78	3.34	-16.8%

Fig. 7. CQN 1 with merging and splitting

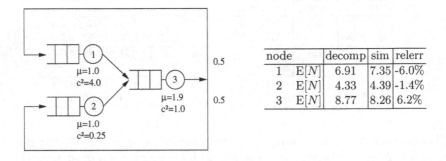

node		decomp	sim	relerr
1	E[N]	6.91	7.35	-6.0%
2	E[N]	4.33	4.39	-1.4%
3	E[N]	8.77	8.26	6.2%

Fig. 8. CQN 2 with merging and splitting

4.2   CQNs with Merging and Splitting

With these two CQNs we specifically evaluate how well our new algorithm handles queueing network topologies in which traffic streams are merged and split. The two networks and the obtained results for $q = 20$ are shown in Figure 7 (CQN 1), respectively Figure 8 (CQN 2). Table 4 shows the results for CQN 2 when the negative-exponential service time distribution of node 3 has been replaced by a hyper-exponential distribution with $c^2 = 10$.

These examples illustrate that the algorithm for CQNs can only be as good as the underlying method for the open networks. Although q is not very small here, the errors are larger than in the case of three queues in series (see previous section) because FiFiQueues employs approximations to perform the traffic merging and splitting. Still, we judge these results very good.

Table 4. Results for CQN 2 with $c^2 = 10$ at the third node

node		decomp	sim	relerr
1	E[N]	6.03	6.62	-8.9%
2	E[N]	5.08	5.39	-5.8%
3	E[N]	8.89	7.99	11.3%

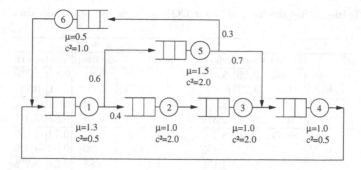

Fig. 9. A larger CQN

4.3 A Larger CQN

We finally consider a larger and more complex CQN, as shown in Figure 9. The evaluation results for populations q between 5 and 60 can be found in Table 5. As observed before, the relative errors are largest for the smallest populations.

In general, it is worth to emphasize the fact that our new algorithm provides the best results for large populations. These are exactly the most interesting cases, as for these cases the overall underlying continuous-time Markov chain (CTMC) would be the largest as well. The number of states NoS of a CTMC underlying a Gordon-Newell network is given by $NoS = \binom{n+q-1}{n-1}$, where n is the number of queueing stations and q is the population size [16]. For networks with phase-type service time distributions, the number of states for large q is approximately given by $NoS \approx \binom{n+q-1}{n-1} \cdot \prod_{i=1}^{n} m_i$, where m_i is the number of phases of the service time distribution of station i. Hence, the underlying CTMC of the CQN of Figure 9 with $n = 6$ and $q = 30$ would comprise approximately $2 \cdot 10^8$ states, whereas the largest CTMC constructed by FiFiQueues during the analysis of the same network has around 240 states only.

We finally comment on the convergence behavior of our new algorithm. For that purpose, Figure 10 shows for $q = 30$ how the algorithm modifies the arrival rate for the open network in each (outer) iteration step in order to reach the preset number of jobs. The interval splitting algorithm first lowers the arrival rate to a fourth of the initial value, then the arrival rate is slowly increased (until iteration 6). In this example the stopping criterion is met after 17 steps, however, we see that a good approximation is already reached after about 10 steps. The "dip" in the curves can easily be explained. The algorithms starts with a value for $\lambda \approx 1.22$, which clearly is too high. This value is then averaged with a value 0, leading to the second value of approximately 0.62. Again this value is too large, leading to the third value slightly above 0.3 (note: the left Y-axis starts at 0.3). Then the value for the arrival rate regains itself to a value around 0.55. The clear dip, hence, is an artifact of the interval splitting method;

Table 5. Results for the larger CQN for various population sizes

node		$q = 5$ decomp	sim	relerr	node		$q = 10$ decomp	sim	relerr
1	ρ	0.65	0.69	-5.8%	1	ρ	0.82	0.85	-3.5%
	$E[N]$	1.28	1.27	0.8%		$E[N]$	2.69	2.71	-0.7%
2	ρ	0.34	0.36	-5.6%	2	ρ	0.42	0.44	-4.5%
	$E[N]$	0.54	0.57	-5.3%		$E[N]$	0.84	0.87	-3.4%
3	ρ	0.33	0.36	-8.3%	3	ρ	0.42	0.44	-4.5%
	$E[N]$	0.56	0.59	-5.1%		$E[N]$	0.90	0.94	-4.2%
4	ρ	0.71	0.74	-4.1%	4	ρ	0.88	0.91	-3.2%
	$E[N]$	1.65	1.57	5.1%		$E[N]$	4.14	3.98	4.0%
5	ρ	0.34	0.36	-5.6%	5	ρ	0.43	0.44	-2.3%
	$E[N]$	0.54	0.56	-3.6%		$E[N]$	0.82	0.85	-3.5%
6	ρ	0.30	0.33	-9.1%	6	ρ	0.38	0.40	-5.0%
	$E[N]$	0.43	0.45	-4.4%		$E[N]$	0.62	0.65	-4.6%

node		$q = 30$ decomp	sim	relerr	node		$q = 60$ decomp	sim	relerr
1	ρ	0.93	0.93	0.0%	1	ρ	0.94	0.94	0.0%
	$E[N]$	6.87	7.11	-3.4%		$E[N]$	8.47	8.32	1.8%
2	ρ	0.48	0.49	-2.0%	2	ρ	0.49	0.49	0.0%
	$E[N]$	1.07	1.10	-2.7%		$E[N]$	1.10	1.10	0.0%
3	ρ	0.48	0.49	-2.0%	3	ρ	0.49	0.49	0.0%
	$E[N]$	1.18	1.21	-2.5%		$E[N]$	1.22	1.23	-0.8%
4	ρ	0.99	1.00	-1.0%	4	ρ	1.00	1.00	0.0%
	$E[N]$	19.10	18.76	-1.8%		$E[N]$	47.36	47.48	-0.3%
5	ρ	0.48	0.47	-2.1%	5	ρ	0.49	0.49	0.0%
	$E[N]$	1.04	1.05	-1.0%		$E[N]$	1.07	1.07	0.0%
6	ρ	0.43	0.44	-2.3%	6	ρ	0.44	0.44	0.0%
	$E[N]$	0.77	0.77	0.0%		$E[N]$	0.79	0.79	0.0%

a more advanced method could probably avoid it. In total, our implementation takes three seconds to analyze the network for $q = 30$.

Finally, Figure 11 shows the number of jobs as function of the iteration step count, for four different populations. No direct dependency between the population and the number of required iterations can be observed. We again see a clear dip in the curves, for which the explanation as above holds as well.

5   Related Work

Over the last decades, several other proposals to solve general closed queueing networks have been proposed. We discuss these below and indicate how these methods differ from ours.

Of course, the simplest way to approximate the type of CQN we address is by just ignoring the second moment and do as if the service times follow

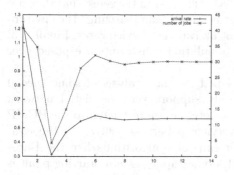 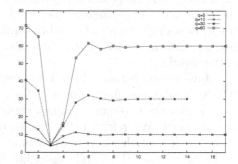

Fig. 10. Arrival rate (left Y-axis) and number of jobs (right Y-axis) in the CQN as function of the step number ($q = 30$)

Fig. 11. Number of jobs in the CQN as function of the step number, for four different populations

a negative exponential distribution. Although good results have been reported for the overall network throughput with this approach (cf. [7, Chapter 10.1.4], esp. in case of squared coefficients of variation below 1 and large populations), in general, one cannot say that this approach yields good results for per-queue performance measures.

Kouvatsos and Xenios [18] have proposed a method for the analysis of arbitrary queueing networks with multiple servers and repetitive-service blocking using the Maximum Entropy Method (MEM). The idea of MEM is to find the solution of the model that maximizes the entropy of the system under the condition that only the information given by the model specification is used. The analyzed network may be open or closed and consists of n finite multiple-server queues of type GE|GE|m|K'; K where jobs can only leave the queue if the number of jobs in the queueing station is larger than K'. The complexity of the method is quite high. The solution algorithm consists of two stages that use iterative procedures. Stage 1 has a time order of about $O(c_1 \cdot n^6)$ in case all queues may block, i.e., their queueing capacity is smaller than the population size q. The complexity of stage 2 is $O(c_2 \cdot n^2 q^2)$, where c_1 and c_2 are the numbers of iterations in the successive stages.

The method put forward by Marie [20] also describes an approximation procedure for closed queueing networks with FCFS service stations and service time distributions described via the first two moments. In the original paper, only two small-scale examples have been presented. It appears that "Marie's method" is especially suitable for small models, with multiple-server stations, a class our method does not aim at. Instead, we aim at larger models with single-sever nodes.

Dallery *et al.* report on a number of variations and extensions of Marie's method. In particular, [11] presents an alternative way ("operational analysis") to derive a number of well-known results, among others, Marie's method. [5] addresses a multiclass extension of Marie's work, however, the use of non-exponential services is not specifically addressed. [4] unifies the method of Marie and another decomposition/aggregation-based method in the sense that they are both variants of the same (higher-level) principle of "summarizing" the environment of a single server via load-dependent arrival and service rates. Finally, [3] extends Marie's work in the sense that population constraints are posed over subnetworks.

Many other methods have been developed for the analysis of some special CQNs containing finite queues. They only support very restricted network topologies, like two-queue tandem networks, etc., or are restricted to the BCMP model class. We refer to [22] for an overview paper, as well as to the citations in [1]. Furthermore, approximate mean-value algorithms like the Bard-Schweizer [29] or the SCAT algorithm [21] do not apply, as our starting point is *not* a product-form queueing network. The decomposition methods proposed for stochastic Petri nets, e.g. [9], do not apply here, as they rely on the solution of non-structured sub-CTMCs, and do refer to a completely different model class.

6   Summary and Conclusions

In this paper we have proposed a new and efficient decomposition-based method for the analysis of closed queueing networks. It is especially attractive because it is based on existing analysis methods for open queueing networks. A variety of evaluations, based on an implementation in the context of FiFiQueues, shows that the method is able to provide accurate results for a broad class of CQNs. Additionally, the method is very fast even for larger networks with large populations. However, the experiments have also shown that the method is less accurate when the CQN contains more than one bottleneck, which can be the case, for example, in load-balanced systems.

Naturally, our new method for CQN can only be as good as the method employed for the analysis of the employed underlying OQNs. Although we are quite satisfied with the performance of FiFiQueues for OQNs, improvements can still be made, e.g., one could think of using more sophisticated traffic descriptors like MAPs (Markovian arrival processes) than the two-moments descriptors of FiFiQueues. More research has to be done in this area, but it is to be expected that this requires a much more complex procedure for the estimation of the traffic descriptor than the one employed here; some recent research results in this field can be found in [25].

References

1. Balbo, G., Serazzi, G.: Asymtotic analysis of multiclass closed queueing networks: Multiple bottlenecks. Performance Evaluation 30, 52–115 (1997)
2. Baskett, F., Chandy, K.M., Muntz, R.R., Palacios, F.: Open, closed, and mixed networks of queues with different classes of customers. Journal of the ACM 22(2), 248–260 (1975)
3. Baynat, B., Dallery, Y.: Approximate techniques for general closed queueing networks with subnetworks having population constraints. European Journal on Operations research 69, 250–264 (1993)

4. Baynat, B., Dallery, Y.: A unified view of product-form approximation techniques for general closed queueing networks. Performance Evaluation 18(3), 205–224 (1993)
5. Baynat, B., Dallery, Y.: A product-form approximation method for general closed queueing networks with several classes of customers. Performance Evaluation 24(3), 165–188 (1996)
6. Bolch, G., Fleischmann, G., Schreppel, R.: Ein funktionales Konzept zur Analyse von Warteschlangennetzen und Optimierung von Leistungsgrößen. In: Messung, Modellierung und Bewertung von Rechensystemen (MMB), Proceedings, vol. 154, pp. 327–342. Springer, Heidelberg (1987)
7. Bolch, G., Greiner, S., de Meer, H., Trivedi, K.S.: Queueing Networks and Markov Chains. John Wiley & Sons, Chichester (1998)
8. Buzen, J.P.: Computational algorithms for closed queueing networks with exponential servers. Communications of the ACM 16(9), 527–531 (1973)
9. Ciardo, G., Trivedi, K.S.: A decomposition approach for stochastic reward net models. Performance Evaluation 18(3), 37–59 (1993)
10. Conway, A.E., Georganas, N.D.: Queueing Networks: Exact Computational Algorithms. MIT Press, Cambridge (1989)
11. Dallery, Y., Cao, X.-R.: Operational analysis of stochastic closed queueing networks. Performance Evaluation 14(1), 43–61 (1992)
12. Gordon, W.J., Newell, G.J.: Closed queueing systems with exponential servers. Operations Research 15, 254–265 (1967)
13. Haverkort, B.R.: Approximate analysis of networks of PH|PH|1|K queues: Theory & tool support. In: Beilner, H., Bause, F. (eds.) MMB 1995 and TOOLS 1995. LNCS, vol. 977, pp. 239–253. Springer, Heidelberg (1995)
14. Haverkort, B.R.: QNAUT: Approximately analyzing networks of PH|PH|1|K queues. In: Proceedings of the 1996 International Computer Performance and Dependability Symposium, p. 57 (1996)
15. Haverkort, B.R.: Approximate analysis of networks of PH|PH|1|K queues with customer losses: Test results. Annals of Operations Research 79, 271–291 (1998)
16. Haverkort, B.R.: Performance of Computer Communication Systems—A Model-Based Approach. John Wiley & Sons, Chichester (1998)
17. Jackson, J.R.: Networks of waiting lines. Operations Research 5, 518–521 (1957)
18. Kouvatsos, D.D., Xenios, N.P.: MEM for arbitrary queueing networks with multiple general servers and repetitive-service blocking. Performance Evaluation 10, 169–195 (1989)
19. Kühn, P.J.: Approximate analysis of general queueing networks by decomposition. IEEE Transactions on Communications 27(1), 113–126 (1979)
20. Marie, R.A.: An approximate analytical mathod for general queueing networks. IEEE Transactions on Software Engineering 5(5), 530–538 (1979)
21. Neuse, D., Chandy, K.M.: SCAT: A heuristic algorithm for queueing network models of computing systems. ACM Performance Evaluation Review 10(3), 59–79 (1981)
22. Onvural, R.O.: Survey of closed queueing networks with blocking. ACM Computing Surveys 22(2), 83–121 (1990)
23. Reinelt, P.: Erweiterung des fixpunktbasierten Analyseverfahrens von FiFiQueues auf geschlossene Warteschlangennetze. Diploma thesis, Distributed Systems group, RWTH Aachen (2001)
24. Reiser, M., Lavenberg, S.S.: Mean value analysis of closed multichain queueing networks. Journal of the ACM 22(4), 313–322 (1980)

25. Sadre, R.: Decomposition-Based Analysis of Queueing Networks. PhD thesis, University of Twente (2006)
26. Sadre, R., Haverkort, B.R.: FiFiQueues: fixed-point analysis of queueing networks with finite-buffer stations. In: MMB (Kurzvorträge), vol. 99-16, pp. 77–80. Universität Trier (1999)
27. Sadre, R., Haverkort, B.R., Ost, A.: An efficient and accurate decomposition method for open finite- and infinite-buffer queueing networks. In: Stewart, W., Plateau, B. (eds.) Proc. 3rd Int. Workshop on Numerical Solution of Markov Chains, pp. 1–20. Zaragosa University Press (1999)
28. Sadre, R., Haverkort, B.R.: FiFiQueues: fixed-point analysis of queueing networks with finite-buffer stations. In: Haverkort, B., Bohnenkamp, H.C., Smith, C.U. (eds.) TOOLS 2000. LNCS, vol. 1786, pp. 324–327. Springer, Heidelberg (2000)
29. Schweitzer, P.: Approximate analysis of multichain closed queueing networks. In: Proceedings of the International Conference on Stochastic Control and Optimization (1979)
30. Weerstra, A.J.: Using matrix-geometric methods to enhance the QNA method for solving large queueing networks. Diploma thesis, Department of Computer Science, University of Twente (1994)
31. Whitt, W.: The Queueing Network Analyzer. The Bell System Technical Journal 62(9), 2779–2815 (1983)
32. Whitt, W.: Performance of The Queueing Network Analyzer. The Bell System Technical Journal 62(9), 2817–2843 (1983)

A Framework for Automated Generation of Architectural Feedback from Software Performance Analysis*

Vittorio Cortellessa and Laurento Frittella

Dipartimento di Informatica
Università dell'Aquila
Via Vetoio, 1, Coppito (AQ), 67010 Italy
cortelle@di.univaq.it,
laurento.frittella@gmail.com

Abstract. A rather complex task in the performance analysis of software architectures has always been the interpretation of the analysis results and the generation of feedback that may help developers to improve their architecture with alternative "better performing" solutions. This is due, on one side, to the fact that performance analysis results may be rather complex to interpret (e.g., they are often collections of different indices) and, on the other side, to the problem of coupling the "right" architectural alternatives to results, that are the alternatives that allow to improve the performance by resolving critical issues in the architecture. In this paper we propose a framework to interpret the performance analysis results and to propose alternatives to developers that improve their architectural designs. The interpretation of results is based on the ability to automatically recognize performance anti-patterns in the software architecture. The whole process of result interpretation and generation of architectural alternatives is supported by a tool based on the Layered Queueing Network notation.

Keywords: Software Performance, Layered Queueing Networks, Architectural feedback, Performance indices.

1 Introduction

The validation of software performance often finds obstacles to be accepted as a daily practice in the software development processes for many reasons. One of the major drawback is the lack of automated support. The performance validation activity can be summarized in four main steps: generation of a performance model from a software model, performance model analysis, interpretation of analysis results, generation of feedback on the software model.

Among the above steps, the analysis of a performance model (e.g. a Petri Net) is the one that has been studied since more time and for which well assessed techniques exist [6]. In the last few years many efforts have been devoted to introduce automation in the

---

* This work has been partially supported by the PLASTIC project: Providing Lightweight and Adaptable Service Technology for pervasive Information and Communication. EC - 6th Framework Programme. http://www.ist-plastic.org

K. Wolter (Ed.): EPEW 2007, LNCS 4748, pp. 171–185, 2007.

first step, that is the performance model generation. Several methodologies and tools have been introduced to transform a software model (e.g., a set of UML diagrams) into a performance model (e.g. a Queueing Network) [1].

However, in order to close the 4-steps loop described above, automation shall be introduced in the last few steps that represent the reverse path from the performance model to the software model. What obviously software developers expect from performance analysis is not a repository of values and curves that represent different indices (such as throughput, utilization, etc.) at different level of granularity, and that are very hard to decipher even by performance experts. They would expect to receive an interpretation of these results in terms of directives, suggestions, architectural alternatives that can drive their development process towards a software product able to meet the performance requirements.

With the support of automated tool their decision about the software architecture (and later decisions) could be driven even by performance issues that, instead, are often discovered at the end of the process when changes are much more expensive to be made.

Goal of this paper is to introduce a process that can drive the performance result interpretation and the generation of architectural feedback. The rationale of our process founds on three main considerations: (i) performance analysis is a hierarchical task that, in order to produce feedback, often must investigate tiny details of the system architecture; for this reason, each iteration of our process lays on a zooming approach that, from system-level performance indices, drives down to resource/component-level indices; (ii) only a structured and integrated knowledge may lead to produce significant feedback; for this reason, the core data used in our process have been organized in matrices that are shared by the interpretation and the generation phases; (iii) for a hierarchical investigation, it plays a crucial role the capability to recognize architectural patterns that may adversely affect the system performance; for this reason, we have classified and solved a set of patterns that can be recognized with simple pattern matching techniques.

Few related works can be found in literature that deal with the interpretation of performance results and the generation of architectural feedback. Most of them are based on monitoring techniques and therefore are conceived to only applied after software deployment for tuning its performance. We are instead interested to model-based approaches that can be applied all along the software lifecycle to support development decisions.

In [13] the PASA (Performance Analysis of Software Architecture) approach has been introduced that aims at achieving good performance results through a deep understanding of the architectural features. This is the approach that better define the concept of antipattern that will be widely used in our approach. However, this approach is based on the interactions between software architects and performance experts, therefore its level of automation is quite poor.

A simulation based approach has been introduced in [9], where the model simulation produces data on the system states that, once processed, can offer useful suggestions about the maximum performance achievable with the current system configuration.

The Arcade tool, introduced in [2], is also based on a simulation model. Heuristic algorithms, in presence of detected system bottlenecks, are able to provide alternative solutions that practically remove the bottlenecks. The heuristics are based on architectural metrics that help to compare different solutions.

A quite interesting work has been introduced in [4], where "bad smells" are defined as structures that suggest possible problems in the system in terms of functional and non-functional aspects. Refactoring operations are suggested in presence of "bad smells". Rules for refactoring are formally defined.

The paper is organized as follows: in Section 2 we illustrate our approach along with the structures and the entities that represent its core; in Section 3 we step-by-step apply our approach to a case study, and finally in Section 4 we provide conclusive remarks and future work.

2   Automated Generation of Feedback

In this section we illustrate our approach for the interpretation of performance results and the automated generation of architectural alternatives. The approach goes through two fundamental phases:

- an *identification* phase (or interpretation phase), where the analysis of the performance results brings to identify particular scenarios that affect performance;
- a *construction* phase (or generation phase), where several architectural alternatives are constructed, basing on the information collected in the previous phase.

Even though these two phases are conceptually separate, and they are executed in sequence, in Section 2.3 we show how they need to share common knowledge on the system structure and its performance.

2.1   Software Performance Granularity: System, Subsystem, Resource

Software performance analysis can be conducted at different granularity levels. Indices like throughput, response time and utilization can be obtained from the performance analysis at the system level down to the single resource level.

A system can be logically split into several parts, and a detailed performance analysis restricted to the most critical partes can be conducted to better identify the adversary issues in a specific system's area as soon as possible. Software architectures are by definition made of subsystems and components, therefore this "zooming" approach to the performance analysis finely applies to them.

In order to define a structural approach to the analysis of performance results, we have identified three granularity levels at which a software architecture can be analyzed, that are: System level, Subsystem level, Resource level.

System level - This is the highest abstraction level for conducting a performance analysis experiment; only global indices can be obtained by a system level analysis of the architecture, such as end-to-end response time (i.e. from the input to the output), system throughput, etc.

Subsystem level - This is an intermediate abstraction level where the system's components and their interactions can be analyzed. In our approach this level does not have a fixed granularity, because any assembly of basic elements can be considered as a subsystem. We leave this definition as general as possible, so that the approach can be applied to multiple definitions of subsystems.

Zooming into architectural details (i.e. subsystem mechanism) can be driven by different strategy that aim at splitting the system following different criteria. Since our goal is to support the validation of a certain architecture vs a performance requirement, we devise two criteria for architecture splitting that depend on the type of performance requirement imposed on the system, as follows:

- *flat requirement*, i.e. one or more performance requirement are imposed on the whole system, no matter what is the service that the system will execute. An example of such requirement can be "The web server must be able to show a web page on the client side within 8 seconds from the request". In fact, this requirement must hold on the whole system, as it does not detail on the type of pages to show. To investigate such requirement, the system can be partitioned in subsystems that are clusters of components heavily coupled to perform a certain task. In this case the subsystems can be considered as *path-crossing* vs the path followed through the whole software architecture to satisfy a certain service request. In the remainder of the paper, the subsystems obtained with this type of splitting will belong to the *type1* category.
- *service oriented requirement*, i.e. one or more performance requirement are imposed on a specific system service. An example of such requirement can be "The web server must be able to show the catalog web page on the client side within 8 seconds from the request". This requirement holds only on a specific system service, that is a catalog request. To investigate such requirement, the system can be partitioned in subsystems such that each subsystem contains the components involved in a specific service provision. One of the major advantage in this type of splitting is that the performance requirements at the system-level can be easily associated with the subsystem that implements the service undergoing a requirement. The subsystems obtained with this type of splitting will belong to the *type2* category.

Note, however, that in both the above cases we do not exclude that two subsystems overlap each other, i.e. that a component can belong to more than one subsystem. This situation is more frequent in case of *type2* partitioning, as it will be seen later.

Resource level - It represents the finest grain level for conducting a performance analysis. Indices that can be obtained at this level are associated to a specific component. We assume here a general definition of component, that is: an atomic part of a system (software or hardware), that has an internal behavior and an external interface, and cannot be further split. At this level of granularity, the major difference between the two resource types resides in the changes that can be made on them to satisfy the performance constraints. For example, a hardware resource like a CPU can be duplicated to improve the throughput, whereas the duplication of a software component might improve the performance only if the two instances can be allocated on separate machines. For an overloaded software component, it is rather better to split the services that it provides among other unoccupied components.

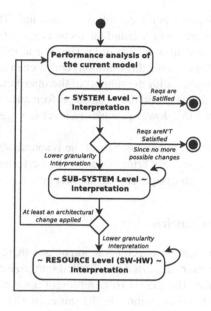

Fig. 1. Results interpretation and feedback generation process

2.2   Using Feedback for Architectural Refinements: A Thorough Process

Figure 1 shows an activity diagram representing the main flow of the whole process for interpretation of results and feedback generation. The iterative nature of the process is obviously related to the progressive refinements that are brought on the system architecture while the interpretation of performance indices progresses. The refinement steps are driven by the suggestions defined in special data structures that we call *interpretation matrices* and that will be described in more details in Section 2.3. One or more interpretation matrices are associated to each granularity level. In order to produce such suggestions the process also lays on the ability to recognize *antipatterns* in the architectural design. The concept of antipattern within the performance domain and some examples of them are provided in Section 2.4.

Our assumption is that one or more performance requirements have been formulated for the whole system. If any requirements only refers to a specific portion of the system, then this process can be applied only to that portion by considering the latter as a whole system.

A first performance model is built for the whole system. After results are obtained from the solution of the system-level performance model solution (i.e. topmost block in Figure 1), the first step consists in the interpretation of these results (i.e. SYSTEM level block in Figure 1). If all the requirements are satisfied then the process successfully stop without suggesting any change in the architecture. If some of the given requirements are not satisfied, then it is suggested to move to a lower granularity level that is, in this case, the subsystem level. The set of identified subsystems have to be sorted following a certain criterion that may depend on the application domain[1]. The performance indices of the various subsystems are observed, and the focus is given to the worst one.

Subsystems are examined in a certain order (i.e. the loop on the subsystem level interpretation in Figure 1 represents this iteration) and if changes can be made without ambiguity on some subsystem (with the support of the interpretation matrices) then the process goes back to the first step and the updated performance model has to be solved. Otherwise, a further move to a lower granularity level is suggested: in this case, the resource level.

Analogous behavior of the process occurs at the resource level. After this interpretation step in any case the process brings back to the performance model solution to check whether the performance requirements are met or not.

2.3   The Interpretation Matrices

In our approach, the identification and construction phases share a structured knowledge about the system that we have organized in so-called *interpretation matrices*. Such matrices have a 2×2 format. The matrix rows represent interval of values for a certain performance index, and matrix columns do the same. In a (i, j) cell we describe the performance scenario that is characterized from the corresponding interval of indices values. If it is needed, we also define in a cell the actions that should be taken to find alternative scenarios.

We have devised matrices for different levels of granularity, different splitting strategies of subsystems, and different types of components.

Figure 2 shows the matrix that we have built for system-level analysis (in [3] we present the other four matrices that we have defined). We assume that performance requirements at the system level must be formulated in terms of system throughput and response time ([2]). On the matrix rows we split the range of the system throughput in two intervals: the throughput values higher than the value Req_X specified in the requirement are associated to the upmost row of the matrix, whereas the lower values are associated to the bottommost row. On the matrix columns we represent the range of the system response time in two intervals: the values higher than the value Req_R specified in the requirement are associated to the leftmost column of the matrix, whereas the lower values are associated to the rightmost column.

In each cell of the matrix in Figure 2 we identify the performance scenario (in plain text), and we specify the next step (in italic text) to find an alternative scenario, if needed. For example, the lower leftmost cell represents the case of a low system-level throughput associated to a high response time. The matrix entry suggests to investigate at the subsystem level, and the designer has to choose one of the splitting strategies illustrated in Section 2.1. As opposite, the upper rightmost cell represents the case of a high system-level throughput associated to a low response time. The matrix entry

---

[1] The identification of subsystem is still a step that requires some human support, especially in case of flat requirement.

[2] We do not deal here with requirements on the utilization index, as it is quite rare to have such a requirement at the system and subsystem level. Utilization enters however in the picture at resource level of granularity.

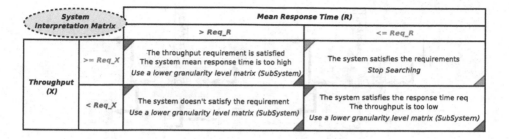

System Interpretation Matrix		Mean Response Time (R)	
		> Req_R	<= Req_R
Throughput (X)	>= Req_X	The throughput requirement is satisfied The system mean response time is too high *Use a lower granularity level matrix (SubSystem)*	The system satisfies the requirements *Stop Searching*
	< Req_X	The system doesn't satisfy the requirement *Use a lower granularity level matrix (SubSystem)*	The system satisfies the response time req The throughput is too low *Use a lower granularity level matrix (SubSystem)*

Fig. 2. System Level Interpretation Matrix

suggests to stop the analysis because all the system requirements have been satisfied (recall that we assume all requirements at the system level).

2.4 Supporting Structures: Some Classified Antipatterns

A quite crucial role in the interpretation matrices is played by *antipatterns*. Indeed, almost always at the subsystem level (and sometimes at the resource level) the action to be taken for result interpretation and to find alternative scenarios consists of searching in the subsystem for an antipattern, that we define here below.

A *design pattern* is a standard solution for a known problem. An antipattern is in practice a negative pattern, in that it is a pattern whose presence into a design has negative effects that should be avoided. In our case we consider performance antipatterns [10] that produce effects on the system performance. For each known performance antipattern a *refactoring* mechanism can be provided to overcome it. The refactoring consists of a sequence of transformations, from the original architectural model to a target model, that improve system performance while preserving the system functionalities [3].

Many antipatterns have been classified in literature [10,11,12]. In our work we have considered the ones that can feasibly applied, with appropriate tailoring, to software architectures for performance goals. In this section we provide evidence of two antipatterns that will be used in the example provided in Section 3. However, other classified antipatterns are available in [8].

The *Blob* antipattern reveals itself if a particular resource does the majority of the work in a software architecture while banishing the other ones to minor support roles. This situation is often easy to recognize looking at the performance results, because the "blobbing resource", that embeds many of the functionalities provided by the system, presents a very high utilization if compared to resources in its neighborhood. The left side of Figure 3 shows an example of such antipattern.

The density of lines within each resource indicates the intensity of the resource load. A poor distribution of the system intelligence evidently appears in Figure 3. In the right side of Figure 3 a refactoring has been made on the system by distributing the system logics over all the resources. A better performing pattern can be thus obtained.

---

[3] In the remainder of the paper we will call software performance antipatterns simply as antipatterns, with few exceptions where differently specified.

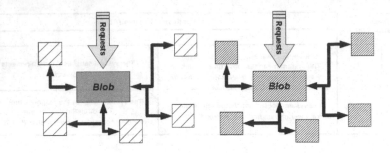

Fig. 3. An example of Blob antipattern

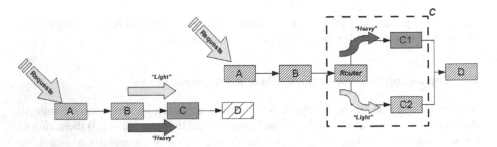

Fig. 4. An example of Unbalanced Extensive Processing antipattern

In the left side of Figure 4 the *Unbalanced Extensive Processing* antipattern is shown. It characterizes the scenario in which a specific class of requests generates a pattern of execution within the system that tends to overload a particular resource (or a set of resources). In other words the overloaded resource (i.e. typically the slowest one) will be executing a certain type of job very often, thus in practice damaging other classes of jobs that will experience very long waiting times and, in addition, leaving quite idle the following resources in the pattern. This scenario has negative effects on the mean response time of the whole system, especially for the requests that do not belong to the considered class, as well as on the whole system throughput.

The *Unbalanced Extensive Processing* antipattern can be recognized by observing the utilization of the resources along the pattern and the classes of jobs that they process. This antipattern can be refactored by introducing specific *fast-paths* for the service requests that do not overload the considered resource and/or that need a particularly fast service, as shown in the right side of Figure 4.

Obviously the positive effects of this refactoring will be more pronounced for the requests that will use the fast-path, while the positive effects on the whole system depend on the percentage of this request type overall the served requests.

3 Applying Our Approach

Our approach is not intended to be specific for a particular performance model, but for sake of experimental validation we need to choose a notation to instantiate the methodology and use it on a case of study. We have chosen the Layered Queued Networks [7,14].

The Layered Queuing Network (LQN) model is a canonical form for extended queueing networks with a layered structure. The layered structure arises from servers at one level making requests to servers at lower levels as a consequence of a request from a higher level. LQN was developed for modeling software systems, but it applies to any extended queueing network with multiple resource possession, in which multiple resources are held in a nested fashion.

The case study on which we have applied our approach represents a software architecture used for a small robot that can interact with the environment where it works and learns from its past experiences. The robot consists of three fundamental parts:

- *sensor machinery* - the robot makes use of sensors for visual perception, for measuring the environmental temperature and for communicating with other robots via wireless;
- *servosystems* - they enable the robot to move around and to interact, and possibly avoid, objects on its path;
- *computational engine* - this includes the intelligent and reactive components.

The main activity of the robot is to explore the whole environment around it and acquire knowledge for classifying events and sharing information with other robot-friends.

When an event happens either it is pointed out by the devices in the sensor machinery, or it is reported by one or more robot-friends that collaborate with the considered robot. The computational engine, using the acquired knowledge, establishes whether it is a potentially dangerous event or not and, in the latter case, it can be used to acquire new knowledge. The knowledge might also be acquired using the servosystems, for example by interacting with some objects on the ground. If an event is instead classified as dangerous, then the robot must quickly react by making suitable remarks and stopping itself before running into danger. An UML Sequence Diagram of a generic regular event handling is shown in [3].

We have modeled such system architecture in LQN, as shown in Figure 5. The *Environment* and *OtherROBOTS* tasks of Figure 5 are used only as request sources to generate the system workload and do not belong to the analyzed system.

Following the previous classification, the LQN tasks can be subdivided as:

- *sensor machinery*: Sensors, NetRX, NetTX;
- *servosystems*: Arms, Motors, MoveController;
- *computational engine*: StorageMemory, VolatileMemory, AI, Handler.

We assume that the number of sensors is fixed at 2 (i.e. visual and temperature input sensors) and the robot-friends number can instead vary from 1 up to 13. Besides, we defined the following performance requirements:

1. the robot must react in no more than 4.5 seconds from the moment in which an event is classified as dangerous;
2. the mean processing and reaction time for an event, from the moment in which it starts its path from the computational engine, must not exceed 11 seconds.

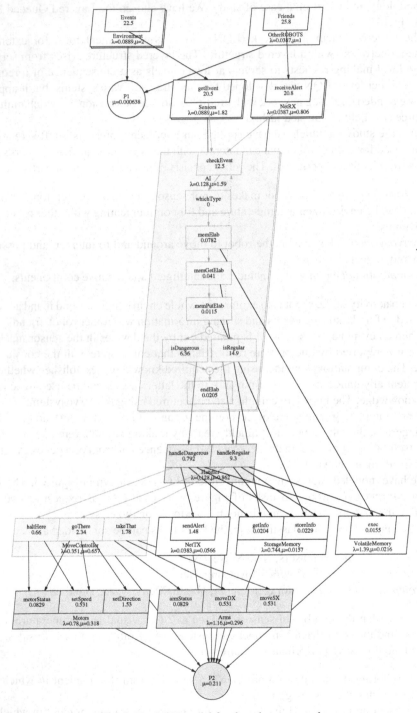

Fig. 5. The LQN model for the robot case study

Table 1. *Requirements and Performance Results - Iteration0*

	Target Value	Current Value
isDangerous (req1)	$\leq 4,5$	$\approx 9,25$
checkEvent (req2)	≤ 11	$\approx 15,5$

We associate the first requirement, in the LQN model, to the mean service time of the *isDangerous* entry. The second requirement is associated to the mean service time of the *checkEvent* entry. Both entries belong to the *AI* task.

In [3] all the parameters used for the initial LQN model are shown. The performance analysis of the initial model produces the results reported in Table 1. It is evident that the initial architecture does not satisfy the performance requirements. Our approach, basing on the system-level interpretation matrix of Figure 2, suggests to identify subsystems, in one of the previously described ways, for a finer grain performance analysis. In this case study we have both types of requirements, as classified in Section 2.1. The first one is service specific whereas the second one is related to the whole system (i.e. a flat requirement). At this point we have chosen to adopt a type2 system splitting, even though type1 could be used as well. Of course, depending on the type of splitting, the appropriate interpretation matrix has to be used in the next step.

SubS_dangerous is the first analyzed subsystem, and it is composed by all the system tasks with the exception of the *Arms* task.

The subsystem type2 interpretation matrix [3] has to be referred for actions to take.

In this case, high mean response time and a good throughput level ([4]) suggest to search for any known antipattern in the considered subsystem.

By observing the *Handler* task and the type of requests that run over the system, the "Unbalanced Extensive Processing" antipattern can be retrieved on it (see left side of Figure 6. In fact the considered task has a sufficiently high utilization level (i.e. about 86.2%) and it receives two different request types: one relates to the regular events processing (and consequently with potentially heavy environmental interactions), and the other one relates with the dangerous events which need a faster processing.

By applying the suggested solution to the retrieved antipattern, the refactored architecture, as shown in the right side of Figure 6, achieves the performance levels summarized in Table 2. Indices have been improved, the first requirement has been satisfied but the second one has still not been met.

The analysis should proceed with the goal of reducing the mean system response time for a generic event while considering that, in accordance with performance model parameters, the 70% of the captured events are classified as regular. Thus we will analyze the *SubS_regular* subsystem because its performance affects the global system performance more than the other subsystems.

In the new considered model the *Handler2* task belongs to the *SubS_dangerous* subsystem but the *Handler* task, that now does not offer any service for the dangerous events processing, only belongs to the *SubS_regular* subsystem, as shown in table 3.

---

[4] Note that no requirement has been imposed on the throughput, hence any value can be considered as feasible.

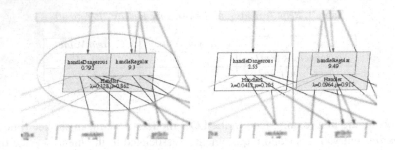

Fig. 6. Unbalanced Extensive Processing antipattern in robot system

Table 2. *Requirements and Performance Results - Iteration1*

	Target Value	Current Value	distance from the previous iteration
isDangerous (req1)	$\leq 4,5$	$\approx 3,3$	$-64,32\%$
checkEvent (req2)	≤ 11	$\approx 13,75$	$-11,29\%$

The subsystem type2 interpretation matrix used with the *SubS_regular* subsystem suggests to search for antipatterns in this case as well. Here the interactions among the tasks *MoveController*, *Motors* and *Arms* announce for a "Blob" antipattern, as shown in the left side of Figure 7.

The refactoring of the system due to the latter antipattern identification does not modify the model structure, but only the distribution of load, as shown in the right side of Figure 7.

This allows the software architecture to achieve the performance values summarized in Table 4.

The second requirement is still slightly over the desired level, so the analysis should make one more step. Now the subsystems do not contain any known antipattern, and the interpretation matrix suggests to go for a lower level of granularity and use the "software resource" interpretation matrix.

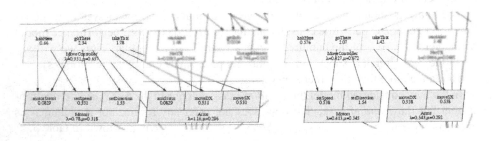

Fig. 7. Blob antipattern in robot system

Table 3. *SubSystems - Iteration2*

Software Resources	SubSystem SubS_dangerous	SubSystem SubS_regular
Sensors	√	√
NetRX	√	√
NetTX	√	
StorageMemory	√	√
VolatileMemory	√	√
AI	√	√
Handler		√
Handler2	√	
MoveController	√	√
Motors	√	√
Arms		√
SubSystem performance target	$R \leq 4,5$ (on isDangerous)	—
System performance target	$R \leq 11$ (on checkEvent)	

Table 4. *Requirements and Performance Results - Iteration2*

	Target Value	Current Value	distance from the previous iteration
isDangerous (req1)	$\leq 4,5$	$\approx 3,15$	$-4,54\%$
checkEvent (req2)	≤ 11	≈ 12	$-12,73\%$

The first analysis consists of examining the utilization level for the resources belonging to the considered subsystem to find the one in the worst state. As shown in the left side of Figure 8, the *Handler* resource has the highest utilization value and the "software resource" interpretation matrix suggests to clone it. Thus we have raised its resource multiplicity in the LQN model.

This change has positive effects on the generic event processing performance although it is not enough to satisfy the requirements. Thus we can consider the *AI* resource that is the current most used resource in the *SubS_regular* subsystem, as shown in the right side of Figure 8. However, the raise of its multiplicity has negative effects, very likely because the number of requests in the queues of other system resources becomes too high. For this reason, we did not apply this change.

Handler is the second highly used resource in the subsystem and its utilization level is over 80%, as shown in the right side of Figure 8. Raising its multiplicity, as suggested by the proper interpretation matrix, is in this case useless because the performance levels remain unchanged, so we did not apply this change either.

At this point, considering that the hardware (like CPU and memories) which is directly used by the software components can support the current workload with medium utilization levels, we can try to improve the hardware related with the servosystems, i.e. the *Motors* and *Arms* tasks that are the slowest components of the whole robot system.

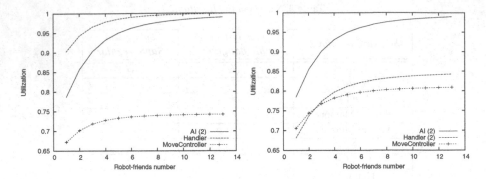

Fig. 8. Resource Utilization Graphs

Table 5. *Requirements Summary - Iteration3*

	Target Value	Current Value	distance from the previous iteration
isDangerous (req1)	$\leq 4, 5$	≈ 4	$+26, 98\%$
checkEvent (req2)	≤ 11	$\approx 10, 3$	$-14, 17\%$

Thus, basing on the hardware resource interpretation matrix, we decided to drop the delay of each servosystems activity by 0.1 seconds. This leads to a considerable performance increase. In fact, at the end of the process the performance goals are achieved, as shown in table 5.

4 Conclusions

We have presented an approach to interpret performance analysis results and generate architectural feedback on the basis of result interpretation. Using our approach, guidelines for interpretation and a thorough process can be followed to break the adversary design choices that negatively affect the system performance.

Although we have implemented a prototyped tool that may guide the developers along the whole process, it is still necessary some human experience in several steps. For example, the detection of antipatterns in a subsystem is a task whose complexity heavily depends on the structure of the subsystem and the definition of the antipattern itself. However, at the best of our knowledge, this is the first work that embeds in the same process the interpretation of performance results and the formulation of architectural alternatives. In addition, we have given a first (still preliminary) contribution to structuring the knowledge necessary for such task.

As future work we mainly intend to consolidate the antipattern definitions and retrieving. Consequently, we can improve the tool support to the whole process. Interpretation matrices are still too informal, thus more effort shall be dedicated to their refinement in order to apply our approach to more complex case studies. Besides, we plan to extend our approach by considering possible architectural constraints that may prevent from applying suggested changes (e.g. a certain load cannot be distributed on other components due to "narrow" connectors). The whole approach does not depend on the notation adopted to represent the performance model, however it will be interesting to experiment on other notations such as Petri Nets. As a long-term goal, we plan to introduce cost issues in the choice of architectural alternatives, exactly like CBAM process suggests [5].

References

1. Balsamo, S., Di Marco, A., Inverardi, P., Simeoni, M.: Model-based Performance Prediction in Software Development: A Survey. IEEE Trans. on Soft. Eng. 30(5), 295–331 (2004)
2. Barber, S., Graser, T., Holt, J.: Enabling Iterative Software Architecture Derivation Using Early Non-Functional Property Evaluation. In: Proc. of the 17th IEEE ASE conference. IEEE Computer Society Press, Los Alamitos (2002)
3. Cortellessa, V., Frittella, L.: A framework for automated generation of architectural feedback from software performance analysis, TRCS 007-2007, Technical Report, Dipartimento di Informatica, University of L'Aquila (2007), http://www.di.univaq.it/cortelle/docs/feedbackreport.pdf
4. Dobrzanski, L., Kuzniarz, L.: An Approach to Refactoring of Executable UML Models. In: Proc. of ACM SAC. ACM Press, New York (2006)
5. Kazman, R., et al.: Quantifying the Costs and Benefits of Architectural Decisions. In: Proc. of ICSE01 (2001)
6. Lazowska, E., et al.: Quantitative System Performance - Computer System Analysis Using Queueing Network Models. Prentice-Hall Inc., Englewood Cliffs (1984)
7. Franks, G., et al.: Layered Queueing Network Solver and Simulator User Manual. Tech. Report, Department of Systems and Computer Engineering, Carleton University (2005), http://www.sce.carleton.ca/rads
8. Frittella, L.: Feedback Architetturale Basato su Sistematica Interpretazione di Software Performance Analysis (in italian). Master Thesis, Universitá degli Studi dell'Aquila, Italy (2006), http://www.di.univaq.it/cortelle/docs/TesiLaurento.pdf
9. Sancho, P., Juiz, C., Puigjaner, R.: Automatic Performance Evaluation and Feedback for MASCOT designs. In: Proc. of the 5th ACM WOSP. ACM Press, New York (2005)
10. Smith, C., Williams, L.: Software Performance AntiPatterns. In: Proc. of 2nd ACM WOSP. ACM Press, New York (2000)
11. Smith, C., Williams, L.: New Software Performance AntiPatterns: More Way to Shoot Yourself in the Foot. In: Proc. of CMG international conference (2002)
12. Smith, C., Williams, L.: More New Software Performance AntiPatterns: Even More Ways to Shoot Yourself in the Foot. In: Proc. of CMG international conference (2003)
13. Williams, L., Smith, C.: PASA: An Architectural Approach to Fixing Software Performance Problems. In: Proc. of CMG international conference (2002)
14. Woodside, M., Franks, G.: Tutorial Introduction to Layered Modeling of Software Performance, Tech. Report, Department of Systems and Computer Engineering, Carleton University (2005), http://www.sce.carleton.ca/rads

Optimal Dynamic Server Allocation in Systems with On/Off Sources

Joris Slegers, Isi Mitrani, and Nigel Thomas

School of Computing Science, Newcastle University, NE1 7RU
{j.a.l.slegers,isi.mitrani,nigel.thomas}@ncl.ac.uk

Abstract. A system consisting of several servers, where demands of different types arrive in bursts, is examined. The servers can be dynamically reallocated to deal with the different requests, but these switches take time and incur a cost. The problem is to find the optimal dynamic allocation policy. To this end a Markov decision process is solved, using two different techniques. The effects of different solution methods and modeling decisions on the resulting solution are examined.

Keywords: Resource allocation, dynamic optimization, bursty arrival sources.

1 Introduction

Recent developments in distributed and grid computing allow the hosting of services on clusters of computers. The users of such a system do not have to specify the server on which their requests (or 'jobs') are going to be executed. The jobs are submitted to a central dispatcher which chooses an available server to execute them. These job streams tend to be bursty, i.e. they consist of alternating 'on' and 'off' periods, during which jobs of the corresponding type do and do not arrive.

The flexibility of the job execution can be combined with reallocation and reconfiguration of the available servers by the provider. This can be done in a reasonable (although in general non-zero) amount of time, allowing the provider to use his servers for several different services (or 'job types') by reconfiguring them when desirable. Finding a policy that efficiently decides when to reallocate (or 'switch') servers from one job type to another is non-trivial. The main benefit of switching servers from one job type to another is the increased efficiency with which the servers are used, particularly in the presence of bursty job arrivals. The main downside is the unavailability of servers during such a switch and the possible other costs incurred by this decision. An efficient policy should balance these issues carefully.

Earlier work examined the case without on/off periods (see [3]) or focussed on finding both the optimal static policy, i.e. the optimal policy when switching is not possible, as well as heuristics for the dynamic policy, where switching of servers is possible (see [4] and [5]). This paper takes the natural next step which is to look at the optimal dynamic policy. Computing this policy involves solving

K. Wolter (Ed.): EPEW 2007, LNCS 4748, pp. 186–199, 2007.

a continuous time Markov Decision Process (MDP). To make this tractable, we examined the equivalent discrete time MDP and limited the allowed queue size. This enabled the calculation of a solution which should be very close to optimal for some cases. The focus here is on comparing various methods of calculating this solution and comparing them for performance and closeness to optimality.

2   The Model

The system we examine is illustrated in Figure 1 and more formally described as follows. The system contains N servers, each of which may be allocated to the service of any of M job types. There is a separate unbounded queue for each type. Jobs of type i arrive according to an independent interrupted Poisson process with on-periods distributed exponentially with mean $1/\xi_i$, off-periods distributed exponentially with mean $1/\eta_i$ and arrival rate during on-periods λ_i ($i = 1, 2, ..., M$). The required service times for type i are distributed exponentially with mean $1/\mu_i$.

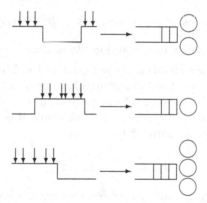

Fig. 1. Heterogeneous clusters with on/off sources

Any of queue i's servers may at any time be switched to queue j; the reconfiguration period, during which the server cannot serve jobs, is distributed exponentially with mean $1/\zeta_{i,j}$. If a service is preempted by the switch, it is eventually resumed from the point of interruption.

We denote the queue of job type i by j_i, the on/off state of job type i by $l_i = 0$ for a job type that is off and $l_i = 1$ for a job type that is on. The number of servers currently assigned to a job type is denoted by k_i and the number of servers currently being switched from type i to type j is denoted by m_{ij}.

Using this notation we can describe the state S of the system as:

$$S = (\mathbf{j}, \mathbf{l}, \mathbf{k}, \mathbf{m}) , \tag{1}$$

where $\mathbf{j}$, $\mathbf{l}$ and $\mathbf{k}$ are vectors of size M, and $\mathbf{m}$ is an $M \times M$ matrix. If no action is taken, the instantaneous transition rate $r(S, S')$ from state S to state S' is given by:

$$r(S, S') = \begin{cases} l_i \lambda_i & \text{if } \mathbf{j}' = \mathbf{j} + \mathbf{e_i} \\ \min(k_i, j_i)\mu_i & \text{if } \mathbf{j}' = \mathbf{j} - \mathbf{e_i} \\ m_{ij}\zeta_{ij} & \text{if } \mathbf{k}' = \mathbf{k} + \mathbf{e_i} \\ & \text{and } m'_{i,j} = m_{i,j} - 1 \\ l_i \xi_i & \text{if } l'_i = 0 \\ |1 - l_i|\eta_i & \text{if } l'_i = 1 \end{cases} \tag{2}$$

where $\mathbf{e_i}$ is the vector whose i-th element is 1 and all others are 0.

The above Markov process becomes a 'Markov decision process' by associating with each state, S, a set of actions, $\{a\}$, that may be taken in that state. An allowable action, a, consists of choosing a particular pair of job types, i and j, and switching a number of servers from type i to type j. If that number is k, then state S changes immediately to state S^a, where

$$k_i^a = k_i - k \; ; \; m_{ij}^a = m_{ij} + k \; ; \; k = 0, 1, \ldots, k_i \, . \tag{3}$$

The case $k = 0$ corresponds to the action 'do nothing'.

These immediate state changes are not part of the Markov transition structure. We say that S^a is the 'resulting' state of action a in state S. The transition rate of the Markov decision process from state S to state S', given that action a is taken in state S, is denoted $r_a(S, S')$. By definition, it is equal to the transition rate (2) from the resulting state S^a to state S':

$$r_a(S, S') = r(S^a, S') \, . \tag{4}$$

In order to apply existing Markov decision theory, it is convenient to transform the continuous time process into an equivalent discrete time one. This is done by means of a mechanism called 'uniformization' (see e.g. [6]), which introduces fictitious transitions from a state to itself, so that the average interval between consecutive transitions no longer depends on the state. A Markov chain is then embedded at these transition instants.

For this we need a uniformization constant, Λ, which is an upper bound for the transition rate out of each state, under all possible actions. Although the tightness of the bound does not matter in principle, the numerical properties of the solution are improved if the bound is tight. The uniformization constant we use is given by

$$\Lambda = \sum_{i=1}^{M} \lambda_i + N \max_i \mu_i + N \max_{i,j} \zeta_{i,j} + \sum_{i=1}^{M} \max(\xi_i, \eta_i) \, . \tag{5}$$

The one-step transition probabilities of the embedded Markov chain, in the absence of any actions, are denoted by $q(S, S')$ and are given by

$$q(S, S') = \begin{cases} l_i \lambda_i / \Lambda & \text{if } \mathbf{j'} = \mathbf{j} + \mathbf{e_i} \\ \min(k_i, j_i) \mu_i / \Lambda & \text{if } \mathbf{j'} = \mathbf{j} - \mathbf{e_i} \\ m_{i,j} \zeta_{i,j} / \Lambda & \text{if } \mathbf{k'} = \mathbf{k} + \mathbf{e_i} \\ & \text{and } m'_{i,j} = m_{i,j} - 1 \\ l_i \xi_i / \Lambda & \text{if } l'_i = 0 \\ |1 - l_i| \eta_i / \Lambda & \text{if } l'_i = 1 \\ 1 - \sum_{S' \neq S} q(S, S') & \text{if } S' = S \end{cases} . \tag{6}$$

Again, this Markov chain becomes a discrete time Markov decision process by associating actions a with state S. The one-step transition probability of that process from state S to state S', given that action a is taken in state S, is denoted by $q_a(S, S')$. By definition, it is equal to the transition probability (6) from the resulting state S^a to state S':

$$q_a(S, S') = q(S^a, S') . \tag{7}$$

An optimization problem is associated with the Markov decision process. Let c_i be the cost of keeping a type i job in the system per unit time ($i = 1, 2, ..., M$). These 'holding' costs reflect the relative importance, or willingness to wait, of the M job types. In addition, there may be a cost, c^a, associated with carrying out action a (this represents the monetary cost of switching servers from one job type to another). Then the total one-step cost, $c_a(S)$, incurred when the system is in state S and action a is taken, is given by:

$$c_a(S) = c^a + \sum_{i=1}^{M} c_i j_i . \tag{8}$$

The special case of $c^a = 0$ represents cost-free, but not necessarily instantaneous, switching.

A mapping, f, from states S to actions a is called a 'policy'. Moreover, f is said to be a 'stationary policy' if the action taken in state S is unique and depends only on S, not on the process history prior to entering that state.

Consider the average long-term cost incurred per step, when a stationary policy f is in operation. Denote by Q_f the one-step transition probability matrix of the Markov decision process under policy f. The elements of Q_f are given by (7), with actions specified by f. Then the nth power of Q_f, Q_f^n, contains the n-step transition probabilities of the process under policy f. By definition, Q_f^0 is the identity matrix.

Suppose that the process starts in state S and proceeds for n steps under policy f. The total average cost incurred over that period, $V_{f,n}(S)$, is equal to

$$V_{f,n}(S) = \sum_{t=0}^{n-1} \sum_{S'} q_f^t(S, S') c_f(S') , \tag{9}$$

where $q_f^t(S, S')$ is the (S, S') element of Q_f^t, i.e. the t-step transition probability from state S to state S'; $c_f(S')$ is the one-step cost (8) incurred in state S' with action specified by f.

The long-term average cost incurred per step under policy f, g_f, is defined as the limit

$$g_f = \lim_{n \to \infty} \frac{1}{n} V_{f,n}(S) . \tag{10}$$

For an irreducible process (which is our case), the right-hand side of (10) does not depend on the starting state S.

The optimization problem can now be stated as that of determining the minimum achievable average cost, $g = \min_f \{g_f\}$, together with a stationary policy, f, that achieves it. For this problem to be numerically tractable, the infinite-state Markov decision process must be truncated to a finite-state one. This is done by imposing bounds, $j_{i,\max}$, on all queue sizes. In other words, all one-step transition probabilities $q_a(S, S')$ where S' contains a queue size exceeding its bound, are set to 0. This will be referred to as the 'truncated model'. There are obvious trade-offs in setting the queue size bounds: the larger they are, the more accurate the truncated model, but also the more expensive to solve.

There is also a second way of looking for an optimal policy. Instead of aiming for the average cost criterion, one could try to minimize the total discounted cost over an infinite horizon. Using a discount factor $0 < \alpha < 1$, the n-step cost (9) becomes

$$V_{f,n}(S) = \sum_{t=0}^{n-1} \alpha^t \sum_{S'} q_f^t(S, S')c_f(S') , \tag{11}$$

and $V_{f,\infty}(S)$ is finite. It then makes sense to look for a policy f that, for each state S, minimizes the total future cost incurred when starting in that state. The advantage of discounted optimization is that the factor α speeds up numerical convergence. The disadvantage is that an optimal policy under a discounted cost criterion is not necessarily optimal under an average cost one (except in the limit $\alpha \to 1$, where the numerical advantage of α is lost). This second approach to finding an optimal solution will also be used in this paper.

A known result in Markov decision theory (see [7]) states that if there exist a set of numbers, $\{v_S\}$ (one for each state), and a number g, such that for every S,

$$v_S = \min_{a \in A(S)} \left\{ c_a(S) - g + \sum_{S'} q_a(S, S')v_{S'} \right\} , \tag{12}$$

where $A(S)$ is the set of all possible actions in state S, then

1. The actions achieving the minima in the right-hand side of (12) constitute an optimal stationary policy.
2. The long-term average cost achieved by that policy is g.

The numbers v_S are not actual incurred costs in various states, but may be thought of as 'relative costs'. Note that if a set of relative costs provides a solution to (12), then adding any fixed constant to all of them would also produce a solution. Hence, one of the relative costs can be fixed arbitrarily, e.g. $v_S = 0$ for some particular S.

3   Solution Method

There are two standard ways of solving (12) and computing the optimal policy: value iteration and policy improvement. Value iteration is quite straightforward but has some rather unappealing convergence properties. It lacks, for example, a stopping criterion that is guaranteed to give an optimal solution. Policy improvement on the other hand, has nice convergence properties but requires the solving of a large set of simultaneous equations, which is computationally expensive. We will first discuss the policy improvement algorithm and then address the value iteration algorithm. Both of these are discussed first in their discounted form and then in their undiscounted form.

3.1   Policy Improvement

The policy improvement algorithm is due to Howard [2] and has four steps.

Step 1. Choose an initial policy, f, i.e. allocate to every state S, an action a to be taken in it. For example, one could choose the policy that 'does nothing' in all states. Also, select the state whose relative cost will be 0.

Step 2. For the policy f, calculate the relative costs, v_S, and the average cost, g. This requires the solution of the set of simultaneous linear equations:

$$v_S = c_f(S) - g + \sum_{S'} q_f(S, S') v_{S'} . \tag{13}$$

There are as many equations here as unknowns, since we also set one of the v_S to 0.

Step 3. Find, for every state, the action a that achieves the minimum in

$$\min_{a \in A(S)} \left\{ c_a(S) - g + \sum_{S'} q_a(S, S') v_{S'} \right\}, \tag{14}$$

using the relative costs and g computed in step 2. This set of actions defines a policy, f', which is at least as good as f and possibly better.

Step 4. If f' and f are identical, terminate the algorithm and return f and g as the optimal policy and the minimal average cost. Otherwise set $f = f'$ and go to step 2.

The computational complexity of this algorithm tends to be dominated by step 2. It is convenient to rewrite this step in matrix and vector form:

$$\mathbf{V} = \mathbf{c}_f + A_f \mathbf{V} , \tag{15}$$

where $\mathbf{V} = (\mathbf{v}, g)$ is the vector of relative costs v_S and the average cost g; $A_f = [Q_f, -1]$ is the one-step transition probability matrix under policy f, extended with a column of (-1)s; the last equation (15) is the condition v_S, for the chosen S.

This equation can be rewritten in the standard form

$$(I - A_f)\mathbf{V} = \mathbf{c}_f .\tag{16}$$

There are many numerical methods for solving this type of equation. We have used the direct solution method provided by Matlab (and inherited from LA-PACK). This can sometimes suffer from numerical instabilities; it turns out to be better to solve yet another form of equations (16), namely:

$$(I - A_f)^*(I - A_f)\mathbf{V} = (I - A_f)^*\mathbf{c}_f ,\tag{17}$$

where B^* denotes the transpose of matrix B. This equivalent equation is more convenient, because for any non-singular matrix B, the matrix B^*B is positive definite. This greatly helps the numerical stability of most procedures, including the ones used by Matlab. The form (17) was therefore adopted.

This undiscounted policy improvement algorithm can easily be adapted to solve the discounted cost problem (11). We simply replace the equations (13) and (14) by their discounted forms:

$$v_S = c_f(S) - g + \sum_{S'} \alpha q_f(S, S')v_{S'} ,\tag{18}$$

and

$$\min_{a \in A(S)} \{c_a(S) - g + \sum_{S'} q_a(S, S')v_{S'}\} .\tag{19}$$

As mentioned before, this discounted problem has better convergence properties. The reason for this can be found in linear algebra. It is know (see e.g. [1]) that iterative solutions of the linear equations of the form $Ax = b$ converge at a geometric rate if the spectral radius $\rho(A) < 1$. Since A is a stochastic matrix, $\rho(A) = 1$. So if we use a discount factor $0 < \alpha < 1$, it is guaranteed that $\rho(\alpha A) < 1$ and we get geometric convergence. For $\rho(A) = 1$ the convergence is much more complicated in general but an exception can be made for matrices that are positive definite. This is the reason why we used form (17) over (16).

3.2   Value Iteration

The value iteration algorithm is due to White [8]. It too has four steps.
Step 1. Initialize the cost V_0 at step 0 of each state S to some value. Here we used the obvious choice of the holding cost as the selected starting cost:

$$V_0(S) = \sum_{i=1}^{M} c_i j_i .\tag{20}$$

Also initialize some termination accuracy ϵ.

Step 2. Choose a state S^*. Calculate the cost in that state as:

$$g_n = \min_{a \in A}[c_a(S^*) + \sum_{S'} q_a(S^*, S')V_{n-1}(S')] . \tag{21}$$

We use this as our normalizing cost.

Step 3. Given the $n-1$ step cost V_{n-1} for each state, calculate the n step cost $V_n(S)$ and n step optimal decision $a(S)$ in each state. We do this by finding the decision a that minimizes:

$$V_n(S) = \min_{a \in A}[c_a(S) - g_n + \sum_{S'} q_a(S, S')V_{n-1}(S')] . \tag{22}$$

and the cost $V_n(S)$ that results from this decision.

Step 4. Calculate the maximum M_n and minimum m_n change in cost as:

$$M_n = \max S[V_n(S) - V_{n-1}(S)] \text{ and } m_n = \min S[V_n(S) - V_{n-1}(S)] . \tag{23}$$

If the termination criterion:

$$M_n - m_n \leq \epsilon m_n , \tag{24}$$

is satisfied, we terminate with the decisions $a(S)$ as output. Otherwise we go to step 2.

Again this algorithm can be converted to solve the discounted cost problem (11). This can be done by just introducing the discount factor α in the relevant equations. But a more efficient method is to remove step 2 from the algorithm. This step was only introduced to counter the problems of the costs V_n tending to infinity in the undiscounted case. Having removed step 2, we replace equation (22) by:

$$V_n(S) = \min_{a \in A}[c_a(S) + \alpha \sum_{S'} q_a(S, S')V_{n-1}(S')] . \tag{25}$$

The rest of the algorithm is left unchanged.

4   Results

We used the two algorithms mentioned above, policy improvement and value iteration, to calculate the optimal solution for a set of systems. We varied both the truncation level and the discount factor, including setting it to 1, i.e. using the full cost. We then compared the different methods in terms of performance achieved (in terms of achieved cost) and time required to compute.

4.1   Example 1: Lightly Loaded System

The first case considers a system with just two job types and two servers, i.e. $N = 2$ and $M = 2$. The system is symmetrical in both job types, lightly loaded and each job type is 'on' half of the time. In terms of the parameters: $\lambda_1 = \lambda_2 =$

0.047, $\mu_1 = \mu_2 = 0.113$ and $\eta_1 = \eta_2 = \xi_1 = \xi_2 = 0.01$. The two job types are *not* symmetrical in cost assigned to them. The holding cost for job type 2 is twice that of job type 1, $c_1 = 1$, $c_2 = 2$. And finally switching is free but takes an average of one completion time to finish, i.e. $C_{sw} = 0$ and $\zeta_{1,2} = \zeta_{2,1} = 0.113$. We examine the effect of the chosen discount factor on this system for the policy improvement algorithm and fix the truncation levels of our system at queue length 20. The effect of the truncation level will be discussed in more detail later on and in other examples. Results generated by the value iteration algorithm will also be discussed in a later example.

Table 1 shows some of the actions the optimal policy makes, given various discount factors. An optimal policy is of course defined for every state and the table here only shows the actions made when one server is assigned to each of the two job types and both job types are in an 'on' period.

Table 1. Optimal actions for example 1 with various discount factors: ($\alpha = 0.9$, $\alpha = 0.99$, $\alpha = 0.999$). 1 denotes switching a server from job type 1 to job type 2 and -1 denotes the converse switch.

j1 j2	0	1	2	3	4	5	6	7	8	9	10
0			1,0,0	1,1,1	1,1,1	1,1,1	1,1,1	1,1,1	1,1,1	1,1,1	1,1,1
1								1,1,1	1,1,1	1,1,1	1,1,1
2								1,0,0	1,1,1	1,1,1	1,1,1
3								1,0,0	1,1,0	1,1,1	1,1,1
4								1,0,0	1,1,0	1,1,1	1,1,1
5	-1,-1,-1							1,0,0	1,0,0	1,1,1	1,1,1
6	-1,-1,-1							1,0,0	1,0,0	1,1,0	1,1,1
7	-1,-1,-1							1,0,0	1,0,0	1,1,0	1,1,1
8	-1,-1,-1								1,0,0	1,0,0	1,1,1
9	-1,-1,-1								1,0,0	1,0,0	1,1,0
10	-1,-1,-1								1,0,0	1,0,0	1,1,0

In the table the actions for queue lengths up to 10 are displayed. The first number denotes the action made by the optimal policy calculated with a discount factor of 0.9, the second for a discount factor of 0.99 and the third one for a discount factor of 0.999. Here 1 denotes the decision to switch a server from job type 1 to job type 2, -1 denotes the decision to switch a server from job type 2 to job type 1 and 0 denotes the decision not to switch. Where the table is left blank, all three optimal policies made the decision not to make any switch.

Recall that the job types are symmetrical but that job type 2 is twice as expensive. This explains the much higher willingness of all the optimal solution to switch a server to job type 2, rather than the other way round. The optimal solution is also less willing to switch when the discount factor is closer to 1, i.e. when future costs are discounted less. The explanation seems to be that although there is a short term benefit in reducing the current queue length by switching a server to a (relatively) heavily loaded system, there is also a longer-term disadvantage since the system is taken out of a stable state. This means that the other queue length will grow and the server will have to switched back at some point. Systems with a discount factor closer to 1 should penalize this behavior more heavily. Not shown in the table are the actions of the optimal policy when there is no discount, i.e. $\alpha = 1$. For the states in the table, these actions are identical to those generated by the $\alpha = 0.999$ discounted policy. In fact, the action is different in just 48 of the 17640 states considered here.

The next obvious question is how these different decisions affect the system in terms of the performance of the policy, expressed as a cost. It should be noted that the cost is derived from direct computation, not simulation. The idea is that, given the (optimal) decision $f(S)$ in each state S, we calculate the steady state distribution denoted π_f. The average cost of the system is then calculated as the product $g_f = \pi'_f \cdot V(S)$. There is a slight complication. Due to the policy some states can be unreachable. Those states are removed from the system in order to solve the steady state equations. All this is not necessary in the case of the optimal solution found by the non-discounted policy improvement algorithm, as the optimal cost g^* is actually outputted there.

The cost achieved by the optimal policy generated with a discount factor of $\alpha = 0.9$, $\alpha = 0.99$, $\alpha = 0.999$ and the undiscounted version, is 1.5095, 1.4250, 1.4249 and again 1.4249 respectively. In this example there is a clear benefit of setting the discount factor to at least 0.99, a very modest benefit to setting it to 0.999 and no noticeable benefit to calculating the undiscounted policy. The downside of setting a higher discount policy is the increased computation time it requires. There is no straight-forward formula for calculating the exact increase since it is not caused by an increase in state space, but by the ease with which the matrix equation (17) can be solved. In general this is harder (i.e. requires more iterations) if α is closer to 1. Indeed in this example it took about half an hour to calculate the policy with discount factor 0.9, 1 hour for $\alpha = 0.99$, 5 hours for $\alpha = 0.999$ and 7 hours for the undiscounted version.

It is difficult to draw any definitive conclusions from this example since the results are completely dependent on the parameters of the system. E.g. although here a discount factor of 0.99 seems to achieve a reasonable balance between performance and computational effort, it could very well be that for different system parameters the 'best' discount factor is entirely different. Indeed in the next few examples different values will be presented. But the trade-off is general: higher discount factors require significantly more computation time but offer better performance.

A second factor of interest is the effect of the truncation level on the policy. Table 2 shows the actions of two policies, both generated by the undiscounted policy improvement algorithm, one for a system truncated at maximum queue lengths of 10 and a second truncated at queue lengths 20. As mentioned before, the second actions are identical to those generated with $\alpha = 0.999$. The most striking differences in decisions between the two policies can be found where both queue lengths are big. Here the policy computed with the maximum queue length set at 10 makes seemingly odd decisions. E.g. if $j_1 = 10$ and $j_2 = 7$ it still decides to switch the server assigned to queue 1 to queue 2. The explanation is

Table 2. Example 1 continued: Optimal actions for different truncation levels (10,20)

j1 \ j2	0	1	2	3	4	5	6	7	8	9	10
0				1,1	1,1	1,1	1,1	1,1	1,1	1,1	1,1
1								1,0	1,1	1,1	1,1
2									1,1	1,1	1,1
3										1,1	1,1
4										1,1	1,1
5	-1,-1									1,0	1,1
6	-1,-1									1,0	1,1
7	-1,-1									1,0	1,1
8	-1,-1								1,0	1,0	1,0
9	-1,-1								1,0	1,0	1,0
10	-1,-1							1,0	1,0	1,0	1,0

that the system cannot get any worse with respect to job type 1 at that point, so it makes sense to try and decrease the more expensive queue 2 and not make any efforts towards reducing queue 1. While this is truly the optimal solution for the truncated system, it is obviously nonsensical if the system under consideration allows larger or even infinite queues. This makes the generalization of results for truncated systems to larger ones problematic.

4.2   Example 2: Medium Loaded System

The second example considers a system with very similar parameters to the previous one. The only change is in the load during an on period. Here these are $\lambda_1 = \lambda_2 = 0.1$, leading to a system that could be considered to experience medium load. The focus will be on the effect of truncation and discount factor on the performance of the policy, rather than on its form. There are also some results from the value iteration algorithm.

Table 3 shows the cost of the policy computed under various conditions. Horizontally we vary the allowed maximum queue length and vertically we consider several ways of computing the policy. Here 'QL' stands for the maximum allowed queue size of both job types, PI stands for the policy improvement algorithm, VI for the value iteration algorithm, the numbers 0.9, 0.99, 0.999 for the discount factors used and the addition 'full' indicates that the undiscounted policy was computed.

The cost increase with the maximum allowed queue size because the cost is computed for the system with the specified maximum queue length. I.e. if $QL = 20$ any job request arriving to a queue that already contains 20 jobs (including those being served), is rejected. There is no cost attached to this rejection. This makes the different policies somewhat more difficult to compare, but as noted previously, there is no clear cut way of generalizing a policy to allow for a system with higher queue lengths. Although some patterns are similar to ones noted earlier, one remarkable difference can be found in the effect of the discount factor. Where in the previous example a discount factor of 0.99

Table 3. Example 2: cost of policy computed with various queue lengths and discount factors

	QL=10	QL=20	QL=30	QL=40
PI, 0.9	4.1769	6.8937	11.003	16.77
PI, 0.99	4.0411	6.7794	10.745	16.201
PI, 0.999	3.961	5.8398	8.4187	13.644
PI, full	3.961	5.7952	8.2851	12.794
VI, 0.9	4.1769	6.8937	11.003	
VI, 0.99	4.0411	6.7794	10.745	
VI, full	3.961	5.8231		

seemed to generate reasonable results, here a big gain seems to be possible when using the higher 0.999 discount factor or even using an undiscounted cost. This effect is much more pronounced when the allowed maximum queue lengths are higher. This re-emphasizes the caution one must use when computing a discounted policy.

The results of the value iteration are very similar to those of the equivalent policy improvement algorithm. This is probably caused by the stopping criterion used. Recall that criterion mentioned in section 3.2 means the algorithm terminates when the biggest and the smallest change in values between two iterations are relatively (with some proportional factor ϵ) close. Here that factor was chosen as $\epsilon = 0.001$, a fairly strict criterion. To guarantee stopping in a reasonable amount of time, there was a second stopping criterion. If the number of iterations exceeded 10000 the algorithm terminated as well. For a maximum queue length of 10, both the 0.99 discounted and the undiscounted calculations terminated after less than 10000 iterations, meaning that the relative convergence criterion was achieved. This yields equivalent policies (and hence cost) to the guaranteed optimal solution generated by the policy improvement algorithm. For a maximum allowed queue length of 20, the 0.99 discounted computation also terminated on the ϵ criterion, after 1115 iterations. However the undiscounted version terminated due to reaching the 10000th iteration. As can be seen, this results in a suboptimal policy.

Table 4 shows some of the compute times and number of iterations required. The compute times are only an indication since they are dependent on the machine running the algorithm. In this case a 2.8 Ghz. desktop with 2 GB of RAM was used. The size of the state space is 4841 for a truncation level of 10 (implying 4841^2 possible transitions, although most of them are zero) and 17641, 38441, 67241 for truncation levels 20, 30 and 40 respectively. In general, for N servers, M job types and QL maximum queue length the size of the state space is:

$$|S| = (QL + 1)^M \cdot 2^M \cdot \binom{N + M^2 - 1}{M^2}.$$

It should be noted that the time to compute the policies using the value iteration algorithm, significantly exceeded that of the policy improvement algorithms. For the smaller or more heavily discounted systems, this could perhaps

Table 4. Example 2 continued: compute time and number of iterations required for various policies

	QL=10, time	iterations	QL=20 time	iter	QL=30 time	iter	QL=40 time	iter
PI, 0.9	2 minutes	5	27 minutes	5	3 hours	5	7 hours	5
PI, 0.99	3 minutes	7	45 minutes	8	3.5 hours	8	14 hours	10
PI, 0.999	3 minutes	8	45 minutes	8	3.5 hours	8	14.5 hours	10
PI, full	3 minutes	8	51 minutes	9	4.5 hours	10	15 hours	10
VI, 0.9	32 minutes	311	5.5 hours	328	23 hours	344		
VI, 0.99	2 hours	1115	1 day	1596	4.5 days	1789		
VI, full	14 hours	10000	5 days	10000				

be helped by setting a less stringent convergence criterion. But the case of the undiscounted value iteration algorithm with a maximum queue length of 20 provides an indication that this is not likely to consistently generate optimal results.

5   Conclusions and Future Research

We examined a server allocation problem in the presence of on/off sources. Both a value iteration and a policy improvement algorithm were used to calculate the optimal policy for some parameters of such a system. This calculation is not straight forward and requires several choices that balance the accuracy of the computed policy with the computational effort required. We examined this in some detail and showed the problems arising when using a more tractable computation.

For future research these phenomenon should be considered in much more detail. It is also interesting to compare the performance of these optimal dynamic policies with that of the optimal static allocation and the dynamic heuristic policies outlined in earlier work by the authors. One might hope to even get some insight into general (heuristic) policies that perform well.

References

1. Golub, G.H., Van Loan, C.F.: Matrix computations. Johns Hopkins University Press, Baltimore (1996)
2. Howard, R.A.: Dynamic Programming and Markov Processes. Wiley, New York (1960)
3. Palmer, J., Mitrani, I.: Optimal Server Allocation in Reconfigurable Clusters with Multiple Job Types. Journal of Parallel and Distributed Computing 65/10, 1204–1211 (2005)
4. Slegers, J., Mitrani, I., Thomas, N.: Server Allocation in Grid Systems with On/Off Sources. In: Min, G., Di Martino, B., Yang, L.T., Guo, M., Ruenger, G. (eds.) ISPA 2006 Workshops. LNCS, vol. 4331, pp. 897–906. Springer, Heidelberg (2006)

5. Slegers, J., Mitrani, I., Thomas, N.: Static and Dynamic Server Allocation in Systems with On/Off Sources, to appear in special issue of Annals of Operations Research, entitled Stochastic Performance Models for Resource Allocation in Communication Systems
6. de Souza e Silva, E., Gail, H.R.: The Uniformization Method in Performability Analysis. In: Haverkort, B.R., Marie, R., Rubino, G., Trivedi, K. (eds.) Performability Modelling, Wiley, Chichester (2001)
7. Tijms, H.C.: Stochastic Models. Wiley, New York (1994)
8. White, D.J.: Dynamic Programming, Markov Chains and the Method of Successive Approximations. J. Math Anal. and Appl. 6, 373–376 (1963)

Towards an Automatic Modeling Tool for Observed System Behavior

Thomas Begin[1], Alexandre Brandwajn[2], Bruno Baynat[1], Bernd E. Wolfinger[3], and Serge Fdida[1]

[1] Université Pierre et Marie Curie – Lab. LIP6 – CNRS, Paris, France
{Thomas.Begin, Bruno.Baynat, Serge.Fdida}@lip6.fr
[2] University of California Santa Cruz, Baskin School of Engineering, USA
alexb@soe.ucsc.edu
[3] Universitaet Hamburg, Dept. Informatik, Germany
Wolfinger@informatik.uni-hamburg.de

Abstract. Current computer systems and communication networks tend to be highly complex, and they typically hide their internal structure from their users. Thus, for selected aspects of capacity planning, overload control and related applications, it is useful to have a method allowing one to find good and relatively simple approximations for the observed system behavior. This paper investigates one such approach where we attempt to represent the latter by adequately selecting the parameters of a set of queueing models. We identify a limited number of queueing models that we use as Building Blocks in our procedure. The selected Building Blocks allow us to accurately approximate the measured behavior of a range of different systems. We propose an approach for selecting and combining suitable Building Blocks, as well as for their calibration. We are able to successfully validate our methodology for a number of case studies. Finally, we discuss the potential and the limitations of the proposed approach.

Keywords: High-Level Modeling, Automatic Tool, Constructive Modeling, Computer and Communication Systems, Model Calibration, Building Blocks, Performance, Measurements.

1 Introduction

1.1 Motivations

Analytic performance modeling of computer and communication systems has numerous applications throughout the life-cycle of such systems, from their design phase to the actual configuration, tuning and capacity planning [11]. A commonly used method, which we refer to as the constructive approach, is to attempt to reproduce in the mathematical model essential aspects of the system structure and operation. This constructive approach has its limits. First, important aspects of large and heterogeneous computer or communication systems, such as modern I/O controllers, or Internet Service Provider networks, may be largely unknown. Second, extensive knowledge

K. Wolter (Ed.): EPEW 2007, LNCS 4748, pp. 200–212, 2007.

and expertise that may simply not be available may be necessary to correctly identify key system components and features lest the resulting models become unrealistic or intractable in their complexity. These difficulties motivate in part our approach.

In our high-level modeling, we don't necessarily seek to "mimic" the structure of the system under study. Rather, we focus on the observable behavior of the system as given by measurements, and attempt to infer a possible high-level model structure capable of adequately reproducing the observed system. In doing so, we forego the detailed representation of the system in favor of the possibility that a relatively simple model, not necessarily related to the apparent structure of the system, might be able to capture the behavior of the system under consideration (e.g. certain priority systems, cf. Section 2.3). An obvious justification for our approach is that, even in a complex system, it is possible that a small number of components, or a single component, may be the critical bottleneck, effectively driving the system behavior. This idea is by no means novel, and has been frequently employed in the past, e.g. in the case of an Internet path [20, 2], disk arrays [22], time-sharing system [21] and a Web server [7].

Our approach has several objectives. First, it may help discover properties of the system not immediately apparent from the system structure. This may include both the fact that the system performance can be represented by a simple model, or, on the contrary, that no simple model (among the ones examined) will be able to adequately represent the system. As such, our approach can be viewed as helpful for and complementary to constructive system modeling. Second, our approach may provide the performance analyst with a ready-to-use model to generate reliable predictions for system performance at other workload levels, without the expense and the effort of obtaining additional measurements. Finally, for a subsystem embedded in a larger system (with the obvious proviso that measurements be available for the subsystem), our approach may be able to provide a model of the subsystem that can then be incorporated in the overall system model. This latter application has a clear connection with decomposition methods [4].

The advantage of the proposed approach is that it requires a priori little information about the system. Our contribution is to automate the process of model selection and to make it systematic by embedding it into a software tool with an optimization method. As a result, the approach requires no special modeling or queueing theory expertise from the end user.

1.2 Structure

The paper is structured as follows. Section 2 describes the general framework in which we cast our approach. We present a subset of the selected models (Building Blocks), as well as our general approach to determining the best set of model parameters and grading the goodness of fit for a given Building Block. Section 3 presents a few examples of application of our tool. All case studies in our paper use measurement data from real life systems. Finally, Section 4 summarizes the main contributions of our approach, as well as its limitations, and outlines possible extensions of our work.

2 General Framework

2.1 Terminology

Systems considered in our study may represent a whole computer or communication system, or specific components such as processors, a disk array, an Ethernet network or a WLAN, etc. We use the term requests to refer to the individual entities that are treated by the system, such as packets or frames in the case of networks, I/O requests in the case of storage systems, HTTP requests in the case of web servers, etc. The workload (offered load) includes all the requests that are submitted to the system for treatment. In our view, the system performance changes in response to the workload, and these changes are reflected in the corresponding measurements. More details on workloads for networks can be easily found (e.g. [24] and [8]).

2.2 Measurements of the Observed System's Behavior

Our approach relies on the availability of measurements of specific system perform-ance parameters. These parameters may include quantities such as the attained throughput of requests processed by the system per time unit, as well as measures of internal system congestion such as the number of requests inside the system. Typical measured performance parameters include throughput, loss probability, average re-sponse time and queue length, denoted by $\bar{X}_{mes}$, $\bar{L}_{mes}$, $\bar{R}_{mes}$, and $\bar{Q}_{mes}$, respectively. This is illustrated in Fig. 1. The throughput $\bar{X}_{mes}$ represents the average number of requests that leave the system per unit time (this quantity may differ from the offered workload if the system is subject to losses). $\bar{L}_{mes}$ gives the probability that an arriving request is rejected, i.e., denied entry to the system. $\bar{R}_{mes}$ defines the average sojourn time (waiting for and receiving service) experienced by a request inside the system. Finally, $\bar{Q}_{mes}$ represents the average number of requests in the system. Note that, by Little's law [15], $\bar{Q}_{mes} = \bar{X}_{mes}\bar{R}_{mes}$ so that it suffices to measure any two of these three quantities.

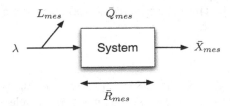

Fig. 1. Performance parameters

   In computer networks, typical performance parameters are the throughput at an in-terface, the time spent by packets inside the network and the packet loss ratio. In disk arrays, performance parameters may represent the I/O response time, I/O request throughput, device utilization, etc. Crovella and Krishnamurthy [10], as well as Pax-son [17] give additional useful information regarding network measurements.

Each measurement point corresponds to a set of performance parameters that have been measured at a particular state of the load (e.g. $(\overline{X}_{mes}, \overline{R}_{mes})$) and may in general also include input parameters such as the corresponding offered load. A total of n measurement points for the same system constitutes a set of measurements.

Note that in our high-level modeling approach, the measurement set must include measurement points for different load levels. Hence, methods that consist in fitting a model of discrete or continuous distribution to a sample of measurements for a single level of system load are clearly unsuitable for our approach [5].

2.3 Simple and Not So Simple Models

As discussed in Section 1, one of the premises of our approach is that a complex system may exhibit behavior that can be reproduced by a relatively simple queueing model. Consider for example an M/G/1 queue with preemptive-resume priority discipline and three priority levels where level 1 has the highest and level 3 the lowest priority. We denote by λ_i the rate of arrivals to priority level i, by $1/\mu_i$ the mean and by γ_i the coefficient of variation of the service time for level i. We look at the mean response time of the lowest priority level for a number of values of λ_3 with the workload of higher priority levels kept constant. The well-known solution of the M/G/1 priority queue (e.g. [1]) gives the performance curve represented in Fig. 2.

While the analytical formula used to generate this curve is manageable, it may not be obvious that the mean response time for the selected priority level is in fact that of a simple M/G/1 queue with a different (higher) coefficient of variation as shown in Fig. 2. It is interesting to note that, for the parameter values used in this example, a simple M/M/1 queue (as proposed in some approximations) cannot adequately represent the behavior of lower priority levels (cf. [12]).

Our simple Building Blocks include queues such as the M/M/C, M/M/C/K, M/G/1, M/G/1/K [6], as well as the M/G/C approximation [14]. Additionally, we have defined original Building Blocks whose service times are driven by the congestion parameters of an embedded model. These Building Blocks belong to models with load dependent service times, and are not presented in this paper due to lack of space. To represent the fact that, in some systems, the response time comprises a fixed overhead as an additive load-independent component, we expand our Building Blocks to include a fixed "offset" value. Note that this offset does not affect the congestion at the server, and the response time in our Building Blocks is simply the sum of the offset value and the response time at the server. This quantity can be viewed as an irreducible and load independent additive overhead in the response time. This constant offset value is denoted by *Off* in figures and formulas.

In the example shown in Fig. 2, to find an M/G/1 block that matches the behavior of a lower priority level in an M/G/1 priority queue, we need to determine the appropriate values for the first moment of the service time, its coefficient of variation, as well as the additional offset value. These three quantities are the parameters of this particular Building Block. We note that, in our approach we are unable to derive the values of its parameters directly from the underlying model, as would be the case in

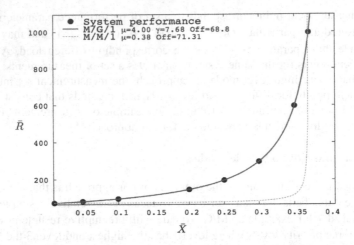

Fig. 2. Behavior of the lowest priority class in an M/G/1 priority system with $\mu_1 = 0.1, \gamma_1 = 2$, $\mu_2 = 0.5, \gamma_2 = 2$ and $\mu_3 = 1, \gamma_3 = 2$ with higher classes workload kept constant

constructive modeling. This limits the predictive power of our approach. However, the fact that an M/G/1 queue (in this example) is a good fit, and the M/M/1 is not, may be valuable in the search of a simple constructive model. Interestingly, several authors [21, 20] have contemplated the use of the M/G/1 queue to model general queueing networks.

2.4 Error Criterion

We need a way to measure the goodness of fit of a given model versus the measurement set. This is the role of the error criterion, referred to as ϕ. The goal of the function ϕ is to provide a convenient way to compare fairly various models. There are many reasonable ways to define such a function. In our implementation, we have selected the sum of the deviations between mean sojourn time obtained from measurements and the one obtained from the model for values of throughput equal to the measured throughput as illustrated by the Fig. 3. We use the subscript *th* to denote values obtained from a model. Thus, let $\bar{R}_{mes,i}, i = 1,...,n$ be the measured mean response time values, and $\bar{R}_{th,i}, i = 1,...,n$, the corresponding mean response times obtained from a model. ϕ can be formally expressed as:

$$\phi = \sum_{i=1}^{n} \left| \bar{R}_{th,i} - \bar{R}_{mes,i} \right| \tag{1}$$

It is worthwhile noting that using a different definition for the function ϕ may affect the results of our approach. In particular, the selected definition, while simple to implement, may introduce an undue bias for points near system saturation where a small visual distance between two curves may result in a very large error value (see Fig. 3). Some adjustments to the definition of ϕ are possible. As an example, one can take into account absolute and relative components for deviations.

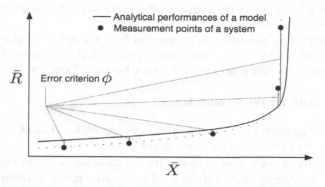

Fig. 3. Error criterion

2.5 Search for an Adequate Model Among the Building Blocks

Our high-level approach uses a set of generic models - the Building Blocks - that we attempt to automatically calibrate. By calibration of a Building Block we mean the search for a set of values of model parameters that minimizes the error criterion ϕ. In general, this leads to a non-linear numerical regression problem. Such a search must be efficient since it is repeated for each Building Block. Clearly, because of its inherent exponential complexity, we must exclude exhaustive search of the parameter space. Liu et. al. [16] propose an efficient and robust solution method based on a quadratic programming. Unfortunately, their method does not appear usable for our application since it is specifically tailored to open Kelly-type queueing networks [13], and it appears restricted to end-to-end delays and server utilization. We avoid as well algorithms based on derivatives of ϕ. In most cases, computing the derivative of ϕ, if at all possible, is time consuming and it is specific to each Building Block making the inclusion of new blocks difficult.

We cast the calibration of a Building Block as a numeric optimization problem, and we choose to employ an iterative descent technique in order to find a minimum of the error function. Our tool is based on Derivative Free Optimization (DFO) methods [18] and [9]. These methods have the advantage that no derivatives are invoked or estimated. They are not specific to a particular Building Block, so that the introduction of a new Building Block is an easy task. In our specific implementation, we use a local quadratic approximation, which implies a low computational cost while speeding up the convergence. A drawback of DFO methods is that they require that all parameters be continuous. To treat all Building Block parameters as continuous, we define intermediate models in which discrete parameters are replaced by their corresponding continuous extensions. These intermediate models coincide with "standard" models when their extension parameters have integer values.

We note in passing that for a given Building Block and a set of measurements, certain bounds on the values of the Building Block (such as related to the stability of an open queue) must be taken into account in the search procedure.

The results of our experiments indicate that the proposed search method tends to be robust and very fast for Building Blocks with a limited number of parameters (say, up to 5 or 6). With a larger number of parameters, the complexity of the method leads to excessive search times. There exist several other DFO methods, some of which might outperform the one we use.

In our search for an adequate model, we start by the simplest Building Blocks (in terms of the number of parameters and their computational complexity) and move on to more complex ones only if no good calibration has been found for a simpler model.

2.6 Requirements for the Methodology

Measurements represent a key component for our approach. To be of use, the sets of measurements must satisfy certain common sense conditions.

First, the different measurement points from a particular set must come from the same system, and correspond to varying load levels. As a result, it makes sense to require that key parameters of the system stay identical for every measurement point or vary in a "non-random" way as a function of the workload.

Second, in our view, the system resources can be shared by two types of traffic: the one directly captured in the available measurements (captured traffic) and the uncaptured or background traffic. In a large computer network, a significant part of the traffic may be processed without being directly captured by measurements. Since the background traffic competes for shared system resources, the common sense condition discussed above requires that the background traffic be either negligible, constant, or in a clear relationship to the captured (measured) traffic for all measurement points.

Third, the available measurement data must adequately capture the salient features of system behavior in the range of interest. Clearly, for instance, if the system response exhibits an inflection point and this inflection point is not present in the measurement data, there is little chance that the model proposed by our approach will correctly reproduce such a behavior.

3 Case Studies

3.1 Preliminaries

The proposed approach aims at finding a model, referred to as the laureate model, whose performance parameters match as closely as possible those known from system measurements (in terms of the error function described in Section 2.4). As discussed before, the laureate model is chosen from a set of pre-defined more or less simple Building Blocks.

In addition to simply matching the data points in the measurement set, we would want the laureate model to be able to correctly predict the performance of the system within some reasonable domain. Therefore, in the case studies that follow we deliberately remove one or more data points from the measurement sets. Having found the laureate model for a given data set, we then test the ability of this model to predict the system performance at the removed data points.

The data sets used in this paper have been measured in operational real-life systems such as wireless and Ethernet networks.

3.2 Broadband Wireless Network

We start by considering the high-speed wireless network for which Quintero et al. give in [19] a set of performance measurements. The measurement points, shown in Fig. 4, relate packet throughput to queueing delays experienced by packets in high load scenarios. As mentioned before, we remove some number of measurement points from the measurement set during the search for the laureate model. It is apparent from the shape of the delay time curve in Fig. 4 that, in this case, the point for the highest load level is likely to be most difficult to reproduce accurately. We elect to remove precisely this point from the measurement set in order to test the predictive capabilities of the laureate model.

Fig. 4 shows that a simple M/G/1 queue with adequate parameters determined by our approach, viz. $\mu = 20.03$, $\gamma = 5.5$ and $Off = 0.44$, closely approximates the observed performance for this system. We have also represented in Fig. 4 the results of the "best" (in terms of smallest error) M/M/C and M/M/C/K queues (these two curves are so close that they are difficult to tell apart). We notice that neither of these two queueing models is able to correctly reproduce the measured system behavior. The laureate M/G/1 model provides also a reasonable prediction for the removed point. When comparing the expected sojourn times for the throughput level of the removed point, we observe a relative error of 15%, while a comparison of expected throughputs at the same mean sojourn time for the removed point yields a relative difference of less than 1%. Given the steep slope of the performance curve in the vicinity of the removed point, we view the attained accuracy as more than reasonable. Not surprisingly, we note that the performance predictions of the M/M/C and M/M/C/K Building Blocks are poor. If we remove other, randomly selected points, and repeat the calibration procedure, we find that the laureate M/G/1 model yields predictions whose relative errors are all below 5%.

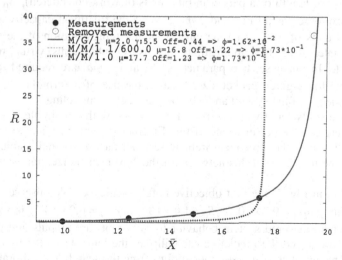

Fig. 4. Broadband Wireless Network

It may be of interest in building a constructive model of the average performance parameters for the wireless network considered that neither the M/M/1 (M/M/C) nor the M/M/1/K (M/M/C/K) models appear adequate. Our results show that even with the best possible combination of parameters these two Building Blocks fall short from matching the observed performance.

3.3 Ethernet Network

In this example, we consider the Ethernet network with a nominal rated capacity of 10 Mbps described and measured by Wang and Keshav [23]. The performance of this network has been measured for three packet sizes: 64, 512 and 1500 bytes. Thus we have three measurement sets, one per packet length. The data points in each set give the expected sojourn time and the corresponding average packet throughput in the network.

As could be expected, the behavior of the Ethernet network considered depends on the packet size. Since the service time of a packet in this network (such as in many other communication and computer systems) includes a fixed incompressible overhead, using shorter packets reduces the transfer time of a packet but also the achievable network throughput. This tradeoff between minimizing delay versus maximizing network throughput has been extensively studied.

Fig. 5 illustrates the results obtained for this Ethernet network with 64, 512 and 1500 byte blocks. Note that the throughput in Fig. 5 is expressed in requests per time unit and not in bits or bytes per time unit.

To represent the effect of the size of packets on the network behavior, we assume that the intrinsic service time in our Building Blocks $1/\mu$ can be expressed as

$$1/\mu = S_0 + U/capa \tag{2}$$

where U is the length of a packet in bits (units of work considered), S_0 is the fixed overhead expressed as a time, and $capa$ denotes the treatment capacity of the server in terms of units of work per time unit. A similar representation of the service time may be of interest in other applications such as I/O subsystems, virtual memory, file systems, etc. In our case, two parameters, S_0 and $capa$, are required to define the service-time for a given packet size. Clearly, the use of a formula like (2) implies some knowledge of the system and a bit of constructive modeling.

This case study has two objectives. First, we show that a simple model can adequately represent the performance of this Ethernet system. Second, we show that, if we use only two of the three measurement sets, our laureate model is able to correctly predict the performance of this network for the third packet size, not used to calibrate the laureate model.

As shown in Fig. 5, the first objective is fully achieved. We observe that a simple M/G/1 with ($capa = 9.7 \times 10^{+6}$, $S_0 = 1.4 \times 10^{-4}$ and $\gamma = 6.0 \times 10^{-1}$) is well suited to reproduce the measured system behavior for different throughputs and packet sizes. As before, we tested the predictive capability of the laureate model by randomly removing some number of measurement points from the search and calibration process. These results are not presented for the sake of clearness, but the laureate M/G/1 yielded accurate predictions for the removed data points.

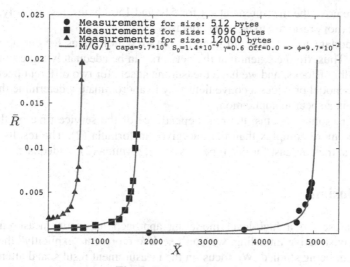

Fig. 5. Ethernet Network

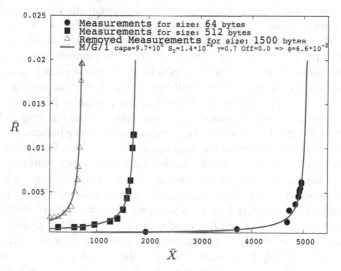

Fig. 6. Ethernet network – only sets for 64 and 512 bytes packets are used for calibration

To illustrate our second objective, we remove one of the data sets (corresponding to one of the packet sizes) from the model search and calibration procedure. As an example, we remove the measurement set for 1500 byte packets, and we search for the "best" model. We find the same laureate as before, viz. an M/G/1 queue with ($capa = 9.7 \times 10^{+6}$, $S_0 = 1.4 \times 10^{-4}$ and $\gamma = 5.3 \times 10^{-1}$). Therefore, it is not surprising that the laureate model correctly predicts the performance of the network for the "missing" packet size of 64 bytes. This is illustrated in Fig. 6. Similar experiments where we remove the measurement set for 512 and 1500 bytes, respectively, yield the same result (not presented to be more concise).

It is important to note that, in general, the execution times for our approach are quite short. Thus, (to the extent that the network can be adequately represented as one of the Building Blocks, and we have measurement sets for two different packet sizes), the laureate model provides a convenient way to approximately determine the optimal packet size in a specific application.

Clearly, in some systems, the real dependence of the service time on the request size may be more complex than the one given in formula (2). The results presented here, suggest that, at least for this type of system, formula (2) is adequate.

4 Conclusions

We have presented a high-level modeling approach based on measurement data. Unlike in constructive modeling, we don't seek to represent "explicitly" the structure of the system being studied. We focus on the measurement results, and attempt to discover a more or less elementary model that might correctly reproduce the observed behavior. We identify a few obvious classical queueing models as possible Building Blocks for our approach. Using several sets of measurements from real computer and communication systems, we have shown that our Building Blocks are not only able to reproduce the observed system behavior, but have also some predictive power.

We embed the search for a best fitting model in an efficient Derivative Free Optimization procedure. The speed and the efficiency of this approach allow us to automate the search for the best fitting Building Block. Note that, owing to the use of DFO methods, our approach is not limited to the particular performance measures used in this paper. Other performance measures could be used as long as the Building Blocks considered can be solved for the selected performance indices.

Our main contribution lies in the automation of the search for the laureate model. Since the search for a laureate model has been automated, performance analysts with a minimal queueing network background can use the resulting tool. It is worthwhile noting that, in addition to the laureate model, our tool can produce the next best candidate (from another Building Block), which may be of interest in some situations.

The laureate models obtained from our approach are useful to predict performance at workload levels for which measurements may not have been obtained. Hence, our approach may be of help in predicting whether the system considered fulfills or fails to fulfill a quality of service requirement. For instance, based on a projection of the growth in workload, the laureate model provides a quick answer whether a given allowed threshold-value for the average response time will be satisfied or not by the system. Unlike the "classical" constructive approach (such as a proposed framework for e-business applications [3] or disk arrays [22]), our approach reaches this goal without investigating the internal behavior of the system. The nature of the best-fitting Building Block may also be of help for constructive modeling of the system. Indeed, it may provide guidance in the search for simple approximations, by indicating which Building Block may and which ones may not work.

Our approach has several limitations. Since it is based on measurement data, the system considered (or a detailed constructive simulation model of the system) must exist, and there must be a sufficient number of measurement points to adequately capture the behavior of the system. In general, there is no guarantee that our approach will find an adequate model, and a failure of the approach does not necessarily imply that there is no adequate simple model for the given system.

As mentioned before, the laureate model determined by our approach may be a good starting point for constructive modeling or for a search for a good approximation. The potential drawback of our approach is that there is in general no clear readily seen relationship between the parameters of the laureate model and the "natural" parameters of the corresponding constructive model. This limits also the predictive application of the laureate model in that it is not typically clear how the parameters of the laureate should be modified to reflect a change in the characteristics of the system being modeled. However, we believe that, packaged as a ready-to-use tool, our approach can be of significant value both to the performance analyst in capacity planning situation, and to the performance modeler in general.

Acknowledgments. We would like to thank Safia Kedad and Francis Sourd from LIP6 for their valuable help in designing the specific Derivative Free Optimization method we implemented in our automatic model calibration tool.

References

1. Allen, A.O.: Probability, Statistics, and Queueing Theory with Computer Science Applications, 2nd edn. Academic Press, London (1990)
2. Alouf, S., Nain, P., Towlsey, D.F.: Inferring network characteristics via moment-based estimators. In: INFOCOM, pp. 1045–1054 (2001)
3. Bacigalupo, D.A., Turner, J.D., Graham, R.N., Dillenberger, D.N.: A dynamic predictive framework for e-business workload management. In: 7th World Multiconference on Systemics,Cybernetics and Informatics (SCI2003) Performance of Web Services Invited Session, Orlando, Florida, USA (2003)
4. Brandwajn, A.: Equivalence and decomposition in queueing systems- a unified approach. Performance Evaluation 1985, 175–186 (1985)
5. Burnham, K.P., Anderson, D.R.: Model Selection and Multi-Model Inference, 2nd edn. Springer, Heidelberg (2002)
6. Brandwajn, A., Wang, H.A.: Conditional Probability Approach to M/G/1-like Queues. Submitted for publication, available as a technical report (2006)
7. Cao, J., Andersson, M., Nyberg, C., Kihl, M.: Web server performance modeling using an M/G/1/K*PS queue. In: ICT'2003: 10th International Conference on Telecommunications, 2nd edn., pp. 1501–1506 (2005)
8. Cong, J., Wolfinger, B.E.: A unified load generator based on formal load specification and load transformation. In: Proceedings of ValueTools 2006: International Conference on Performance Evaluation Methodologies and Tools, Pisa, Italy (2006)
9. Conn, A.R., Scheinberg, K.K., Toint, P.L.: Recent progress in unconstrained nonlinear optimization without derivatives. Mathematical Programming 79, 397–414 (1997)
10. Crovella, M., Krishnamurthy, B.: Internet Measurement: Infrastructure, Traffic and Applications. John Wiley & Sons, Inc, Chichester (2006)
11. Heidelberger, P., Lavenberg, S.S.: Computer performance evaluation methodology. IEEE Trans. Computers 33, 1195–1220 (1984)

12. Kaufman, J.S.: Approximation Methods for Networks of Queues with Priorities. Performance Evaluation 4, 183–198 (1984)
13. Kelly, F.P.: Reversibility and Stochastic Networks. John Wiley & Sons, Chichester (1979)
14. Kimura, T.: Approximations for Multi-Server Queues: System Interpolations. Queueing Systems: Theory and Applications 17, 347–382 (1994)
15. Kleinrock, L.: Queueing Systems, Volume 1: Theory. John Wiley & Sons, Chichester (1975)
16. Liu, Z., Wynter, L., Xia, C.H., Zhang, F.: Parameter inference of queueing models for IT systems using end-to-end measurements. Performance Evaluation 63, 36–60 (2006)
17. Paxson, V.E.: Measurements and Analysis of End-To-End Internet Dynamics. Doctoral Thesis, University of California at Berkeley (1998)
18. Powell, M.J.D.: Unconstrained minimization algorithms without computation of derivatives. Bollettino della Unione Matematica Italiana 9, 60–69 (1974)
19. Quintero, A., Elalamy, Y., Pierre, S.: Performance evaluation of a broadband wireless access system subjected to heavy load. Computer Communications 27, 781–791 (2004)
20. Salamatian, K., Fdida, S.: A framework for interpreting measurement over Internet. In: Proceedings of the ACM SIGCOMM workshop on models, methods and tools for reproducible network research, Karlsruhe, Germany, pp. 87–94 (2003)
21. Scherr, A.: An Analysis of Time-Shared Computer Systems. MIT Press, Cambridge (1967)
22. Varki, E., Merchant, A., Xu, J., Qiu, X.: Issues and challenges in the performance analysis of real disk arrays. IEEE Trans. Parallel Distrib. Syst. 15, 559–574 (2004)
23. Wang, J., Keshav, S.: Efficient and accurate Ethernet simulation. In: 24th Annual IEEE International Conference on Local Computer Networks, Boston, MA, pp. 182–191. IEEE Computer Society Press, Los Alamitos (1999)
24. Wolfinger, B.E., Zaddach, M., Heidtmann, K.D., Bai, G.: Analytical modeling of primary and secondary load as induced by video applications using UDP/IP. Computer Communications 25, 1094–1102 (2002)

Censoring Markov Chains and Stochastic Bounds

J.-M. Fourneau[1,2], N. Pekergin[2,3,4], and S. Younès[2]

[1] INRIA Project MESCAL, Montbonnot, France
[2] PRiSM, University Versailles-Saint-Quentin, 45, Av. des Etats-Unis 78000 France
[3] Marin Mersenne Laboratory, University Paris 1, 90, Rue de Tolbiac, 75013 France
[4] LACL, 61 avenue Général de Gaulle 94010, Créteil, France
{jmf,nih,sayo}@prism.uvsq.fr

Abstract. We show how to combine censoring technique for Markov chain and strong stochastic comparison to obtain bounds on rewards and the first passage time. We present the main ideas of the method, the algorithms and their proofs. We obtain a substantial reduction of the state space due to the censoring technique. We also present some numerical results to illustrate the effectiveness of the method.

1 Introduction

Modeling systems with huge or infinite Markov chain is still a hard problem when the chain does not exhibit some regularity or symmetry which allow analytical techniques or lumping. An alternative approach is to compute bounds on the rewards we need to check against requirement. For instance we may obtain an upper bound on the loss probability and verify that this bound is smaller than the quality of service required by a network application. To compute bounds on rewards the usual way is to bound the steady-state or transient distribution at time t, define the elementary reward for state i and perform the summation of the product of the elementary rewards by the state probabilities. The last two parts are the easiest step of the method. The main difficulty is to obtain a bound of the steady state or transient distributions. Some rewards are also related to the first passage time or the absorbing time if the chain has some absorbing states. We must in that case compute the fundamental matrix of the chain, again a difficult problem when the state space is extremely large. The main idea is to derive a smaller chain which provides a bound. In the recent years, several algorithms have been published to obtain some stochastic bounds on Markov chains [18,7,10,3]. But most of these algorithms have used the lumpability approach to reduce the size of chain and only considered finite DTMC (Discrete Time Markov Chain). Here we show how we can compute stochastic bounds using the Censored Markov chain and how we can deal with large Markov chains.

Consider a discrete time Markov chain $\{X_t : t = 1, 2, \ldots\}$ with finite state space S. Suppose that $S = E \cup E^c$, $E \cap E^c = \emptyset$. Suppose that the successive

K. Wolter (Ed.): EPEW 2007, LNCS 4748, pp. 213–227, 2007.

visits of X_t to E take place at time epochs $0 < t_1 < t_2 < \ldots <$. Then the chain $\{X_u^E = X_{t_u}, u = 1, 2, \ldots\}$ is called the censored process (or chain) with censoring set E [19]. Let Q denote the transition matrix of chain X_t. Consider the partition of the state space to obtain a block description of Q:

$$Q = \begin{pmatrix} Q_E & Q_{EE^c} \\ Q_{E^cE} & Q_{E^c} \end{pmatrix} \begin{matrix} E \\ E^c \end{matrix} \qquad (1)$$

The censored chain only watches the chain when it is in E. Under some structural condition on the matrix, it can be proved [19] that the stochastic matrix of the censored chain is:

$$S_E = Q_E + Q_{EE^c} \left(\sum_{i=0}^{\infty} (Q_{E^c})^i \right) Q_{E^cE} \qquad (2)$$

Assume that (Q_{E^c}) does not contain any recurrent class, the fundamental matrix is $\sum_{i=0}^{\infty} (Q_{E^c})^i = (I - Q_{E^c})^{-1}$. Censored Markov chains have also been called restricted or watched Markov chains. When the chain is ergodic there are strong relations with the theory of stochastic complement [11]. Note that it is not necessary for censored Markov chains to be ergodic and we can study for instance the absorbing time. In many problems Q can be large and therefore it is difficult to compute $(I - Q_{E^c})^{-1}$ to finally get S_E. Deriving bounds of S_E from Q_E and some information on the other blocks without computing S_E is therefore an interesting alternative approach.

To the best of our knowledge this paper is the first approach to combine stochastic bounds and censored Markov chain, even if the stochastic complement approach was mentioned in a survey on algorithmic aspects of stochastic bounds [9]. However some of the methods already published for NCD (Nearly Completely Decomposable) chains may be applied to construct bounds. For instance in [17] Truffet has proposed a two-level algorithm for NCD chains by using aggregation and the stochastic ordering to compute bounding distributions. This method is different from the bounded aggregation method proposed by Courtois-Semal which uses polyhedra theory [4] to compute bounds. In [13], this approach has been extended by employing reordering to improve the accuracy and a better component-wise probability bounding algorithm. In these works, before employing the aggregation of blocks, the slack probabilities which are small due to the NCD structure are included in the last column for the upper bounding case and to the first column for the lower bounding case. In the case of general Markov chains, an algebraic approach has been recently proposed to dispatch slack probabilities [6].

In this work, we derive bounds on S_E, in a completely different way by applying graph algorithms. Indeed we propose to compute element-wise lower bounds on the second term of Eq. 2 by exploring some paths that return to partition E passing through partition E^c. We give some relations between element-wise lower bound on S_E and the derived stochastic bounds on it.

The following of the paper is as follows. In section 2 we present stochastic bounds and the basic algorithm to build a monotone upper bound for any stochastic matrix and we present the basic operator used to formally define this algorithm. We also give some necessary definitions and results for censored Markov chains. Section 3 is devoted to the main theoretical results of this paper: we show how we can obtain a stochastic upper bound of S_E from any element-wise lower bound of S_E. We also prove that the more accurate is the element-wise lower bound the more accurate is the stochastic upper bound. Clearly, Q_E is an element-wise lower bound of S_E. $Q_{EE^c} \left(\sum_{i=0}^{\infty} (Q_{E^c})^i \right) Q_{E^cE}$ represents all the paths entering E^c, staying in this set for an arbitrary number of transitions and finally returning to E. Thus if we only keep some paths in consideration we obtain again an element-wise lower bound of S_E. We develop this approach in section 4 using several graph techniques to obtain sets of paths and their probabilities. Finally in section 5 we present some examples and numerical results.

2 Theoretical Background

In this section, we present some preliminaries on the stochastic comparison method and on censored Markov chains. We refer to the books [14,15] for the theoretical issues for comparison of random variables and Markov chains. We study Discrete Time Markov chains (DTMC in the following) on finite or denumerable state space endowed with a total ordering. Let S be the state space.

2.1 Basic Algorithms to Bound a Markov Chain

Definition 1. *Let X and Y be random variables taking values on a totally ordered space S. Then X is said to be less than Y in the strong stochastic sense, $(X \preceq_{st} Y)$ if and only if $E[f(X)] \leq E[f(Y)]$ for all non decreasing functions $f : S \to R$, whenever the expectations exist.*

Indeed $\preceq_{st}$ ordering provides the comparison of the underlying probability distribution functions: $X \preceq_{st} Y \leftrightarrow Prob(X > a) \leq Prob(Y > a) \quad \forall a \in S$. Thus it is more probable for Y to take larger values than for X. Since the $\preceq_{st}$ ordering yields the comparison of sample-paths, it is also known as sample-path ordering. We give in the next proposition the $\preceq_{st}$ comparison in the case of finite state space.

Property 1. Let X, Y be random variables taking values on $\{1, 2, \cdots, n\}$ and p, q be probability vectors which are respectively denoting distributions of X and Y, $X \preceq_{st} Y$ iff $\sum_{j=i}^{n} p[j] \leq \sum_{j=i}^{n} q[j] \quad \forall i = \{n, n-1, \cdots, 1\}$. Remark that $X = Y$ implies that $X \preceq_{st} Y$.

The stochastic comparison of random variables has been extended to the comparison of Markov chains. It is shown in Theorem 5.2.11 of [14, p.186] that monotonicity and comparability of the probability transition matrices of time-homogeneous Markov chains yield sufficient conditions to compare stochastically the underlying chains. We first define the monotonicity and comparability of stochastic matrices and then state this theorem and some useful corollaries.

Definition 2. *Let P be a stochastic matrix. P is said to be stochastically st-monotone (monotone for short) if for any probability vectors p and q,*

$$p \preceq_{st} q \implies p\,P \preceq_{st} q\,P.$$

Definition 3. *Let P and Q be two stochastic matrices. Q is said to be an upper bounding matrix of P in the sense of the strong stochastic order $(P \preceq_{st} Q)$ iff*

$$P_{i,*} \preceq_{st} Q_{i,*}, \quad \forall i$$

where $P_{i,*}$ denotes the ith row of matrix P.

Theorem 1. *Let P (resp. Q) be the probability transition matrix of the time-homogeneous Markov chain $\{X_t, t \geq 0\}$ (resp. $\{Y_t, t \geq 0\}$). If*

- *$X_0 \preceq_{st} Y_0$,*
- *at least one of the probability transition matrices is monotone, that is, either P or Q is monotone,*
- *the transition matrices are comparable, (i.e. $P \preceq_{st} Q$).*

then $X_t \preceq_{st} Y_t \quad \forall t$.

Then the following corollary ([14]) lets us compare the steady-state distributions of Markov chains when they exist. And we can also compare absorption time if the chain has an absorbing state (see [2] for a proof).

Corollary 1. *Let Q be a monotone, upper bounding matrix for P for the st-ordering. If the steady-state distributions ($\Pi_\mathbf{P}$ and $\Pi_\mathbf{Q}$) exist, then $\Pi_\mathbf{P} \preceq_{st} \Pi_\mathbf{Q}$.*

Corollary 2 (proposition 2.9 in [2])). *Let $\{X_t, t \geq 0\}$ and $\{Y_t, t \geq 0\}$ be two Markov chains on the same finite state space. Assume that the last state (say n) is absorbing for both chains. Assume that $X_t \preceq_{st} Y_t, \forall t$ then $T_{i,n}(Y) \preceq_{st} T_{i,n}(X)$ where $T_{i,n}(X)$ is the absorption time in n for chain X when initial state is i.*

Stochastic comparison and monotonicity can be represented by linear inequalities. Once we have derived a set of equalities, instead of inequalities and ordered them we obtain a constructive way to design a monotone upper bounding stochastic matrix Q for an arbitrary stochastic matrix P.

$$\begin{cases} \sum_{k=j}^{n} Q_{1,k} = \sum_{k=j}^{n} P_{1,k} \\ \sum_{k=j}^{n} Q_{i+1,k} = max(\sum_{k=j}^{n} Q_{i,k}, \sum_{k=j}^{n} P_{i+1,k}) \end{cases} \quad \forall\, i, j \qquad (3)$$

This is the basic theory behind Vincent's algorithm [1]. We now present an operator description of this basic algorithm (see [9] for a survey of algorithmic aspects of stochastic bounds).

Definition 4. *Let P and Q be two positive matrices with the same size, $P \preceq_{el} Q$ iff $P[i,j] \leq Q[i,j]$ for all i and j.*

Definition 5. *Following the presentation in [5] we define two operators r and v for matrix of size $n \times n$ as follows:*

- r *is a summation operator:* $r(P)[i,j] = \sum_{k=j}^{n} P[i,k]$. *The inverse of r (denoted as r^{-1}) is:*

$$r^{-1}(P)[i,j] = \begin{cases} P[i,n] & \text{if } j = n \\ P[i,j] - P[i,j+1] & \text{if } j < n \end{cases}$$

- *Let v be the operator defined by:*

$$v(P)[i,j] = max_{m \leq i}\left(\sum_{k \geq j} P[m,k]\right) = max_{m \leq i} r(P)[m,j] \tag{4}$$

Property 2. Vincent's algorithm is simply operator $r^{-1}v$.

Example 1. Let P be a stochastic matrix. Vincent's algorithm gives:

$$P = \begin{bmatrix} 0.1 & 0.3 & 0.2 & 0.4 \\ 0.1 & 0.4 & 0.2 & 0.3 \\ 0.2 & 0.1 & 0.5 & 0.2 \\ 0.2 & 0 & 0.4 & 0.4 \end{bmatrix} \quad v(P) = \begin{bmatrix} 1 & 0.9 & 0.6 & 0.4 \\ 1 & 0.9 & 0.6 & 0.4 \\ 1 & 0.9 & 0.7 & 0.4 \\ 1 & 0.9 & 0.8 & 0.4 \end{bmatrix} \quad r^{-1}v(P) = \begin{bmatrix} 0.1 & 0.3 & 0.2 & 0.4 \\ 0.1 & 0.3 & 0.2 & 0.4 \\ 0.1 & 0.2 & 0.3 & 0.4 \\ 0.1 & 0.1 & 0.4 & 0.4 \end{bmatrix}$$

Property 3. Let P and Q two stochastic matrices with the same size, $P \preceq_{st} Q$ iff $r(P) \preceq_{el} r(Q)$.

And we define two new operators θ and γ which transform a sub-stochastic matrix P into stochastic matrix by adding the probability missing in P in the last (resp. the first) column.

$$\theta(P)[i,j] = \begin{cases} P[i,j] & \text{if } j < n \\ P[i,j] + \beta_i & \text{if } j = n \end{cases} \quad \gamma(P)[i,j] = \begin{cases} P[i,j] & \text{if } j > 1 \\ P[i,j] + \beta_i & \text{if } j = 1 \end{cases}$$

where $\beta_i = 1 - \sum_{j=1}^{n} P[i,j]$. Of course, if P is stochastic $\theta(P) = P = \gamma(P)$.

2.2   Censoring a Markov Chain

Let us go back to the definition and the fundamental results on censored chains.

Lemma 1 (Theorem 2 in [19]). *Let Q be the transition probability matrix of a DTMC $X(t)$. Consider a partition of the finite state space S into two subsets E and E^c.*

$$Q = \begin{pmatrix} Q_E & Q_{EE^c} \\ Q_{E^cE} & Q_{E^c} \end{pmatrix} \begin{matrix} E \\ E^c \end{matrix}$$

Then, the censored process $X_E(t)$ is a Markov chain and its transition probability matrix is given by:

$$S_E = Q_E + Q_{EE^c} \left(\sum_{i=0}^{\infty} (Q_{E^c})^i \right) Q_{E^c E} \tag{5}$$

When Q is irreducible the transition probability matrix of the censored chains is the stochastic complement matrix defined by Meyer and we have the following results [11]:

Theorem 2. *If Q is irreducible, with steady state distribution $\mathbf{\Pi}_Q = (\mathbf{\Pi}_E, \mathbf{\Pi}_{E^c})$ and transient distribution at discrete time epoch t, $\mathbf{\Pi}_Q^t = (\mathbf{\Pi}_E^t, \mathbf{\Pi}_{E^c}^t)$. Then the steady state distribution $\mathbf{\Pi}_{S_E}$ and the transient distribution at time t, $\mathbf{\Pi}_E^t$ of the censored matrix S_E are given by:*

$$\mathbf{\Pi}_{S_E} = \frac{\mathbf{\Pi}_E}{\sum_{i \in E} \mathbf{\Pi}_E(i)} \quad and \quad \mathbf{\Pi}_{S_E}^t = \frac{\mathbf{\Pi}_E^t}{\sum_{i \in E} \mathbf{\Pi}_E^t(i)} \tag{6}$$

The transition matrix of the censored chain can be decomposed into two parts. Q_E is an element-wise lower bound of S_E. $Q_{EE^c} \left(\sum_{i=0}^{\infty} (Q_{E^c})^i \right) Q_{E^c E}$ represents all the paths entering E^c, staying in this set for an arbitrary number of transitions and finally returning to E. Assuming that Q_{E^c} does not contain any recurrent class we have: $\sum_{i=0}^{\infty} (Q_{E^c})^i = (Id - Q_{E^c})^{-1}$. But the state space is so huge that this operation is too complex. Thus instead of computing S_E we advocate that we can obtain stochastic bounds of this matrix.

As $Q_{EE^c} \left(\sum_{i=0}^{\infty} (Q_{E^c})^i \right) Q_{E^c E}$ contains all the paths, we will only keep some of them in consideration and we obtain more accurate bounds of S_E. The main idea is that only some elements of Q_{E^c} are generated and stored during the construction of the Markov chain.

3   Bounds for Censored Chains

We first prove some technical lemmas and then give the theorems to provide bounds.

Lemma 2. *Let P and Q be two stochastic or sub-stochastic matrices of size $n \times n$. if $P \preceq_{el} Q$ then $\theta(Q) \preceq_{st} \theta(P)$.*

Proof. $\forall \ 1 \leq i \leq n$ and $\forall \ 1 \leq q \leq n$ we have:

$$\sum_{j=q}^{n} \theta(Q)[i,j] = 1 - \sum_{j<q} Q[i,j] \leq 1 - \sum_{j<q} P[i,j] = \sum_{j=q}^{n} \theta(P)[i,j]$$

Thus $\theta(Q) \preceq_{st} \theta(P)$.

Lemma 3. *Let P and Q be two stochastic matrices, if $P \preceq_{st} Q$ then $r^{-1}v(P) \preceq_{st} r^{-1}v(Q)$.*

Proof. It follows from Property 3 and Eq. 4 that if $P \preceq_{st} Q$ then $v(P) \leq_{el} v(Q)$. This implies following Property 3 that $r^{-1}v(P) \preceq_{st} r^{-1}v(Q)$.

We now present the two fundamental theorems which allow to bound a censored Markov chain. For both theorems, let $\{X_t, t \geq 0\}$ be a denumerable DTMC with transition matrix Q and E a finite subset of state space S. Let S_E be the matrix of the censored Markov chain and Q_E the block of Q restricted to states in E.

Theorem 3. *For all sub-stochastic matrix M such that $Q_E \preceq_{el} M \preceq_{el} S_E$, we have*

$$S_E \preceq_{st} r^{-1}v\theta(M) \tag{7}$$

Proof. We assume that $M \preceq_{el} S_E$. We apply Lemma 2 to obtain: $\theta(S_E) \preceq_{st} \theta(M)$. But S_E is a stochastic matrix. Thus $\theta(S_E) = S_E$ and we get: $S_E \preceq_{st} \theta(M)$. We now apply lemma 3 which implies that: $r^{-1}v(S_E) \preceq_{st} r^{-1}v\theta(M)$.

We finally remark that due to the definition of operators r and v we have $S_E \preceq_{st} r^{-1}v(S_E)$ and we obtain that $S_E \preceq_{st} r^{-1}v\theta(M)$ to complete the proof.

Similarly we can obtain a lower bound with operator γ and the modified version of Vincent's algorithm to obtain monotone lower bound. The following theorem explains how we can improve this bound. If we are able to improve the element-wise lower bound M, we also improve the stochastic upper bound for S_E. However remember that $X \preceq_{st} Y$ does not exclude that $X = Y$ and the improvement on the stochastic bound can be zero (see for instance the first part of the example in Section 4).

Theorem 4. *For all sub-stochastic matrices $M1$ and $M2$ such that $M1 \preceq_{el} M2 \preceq_{el} S_E$, we have:*

$$r^{-1}v\theta(M2) \preceq_{st} r^{-1}v\theta(M1) \tag{8}$$

Proof. As we assume that $M1 \preceq_{el} M2$ Lemma 2 shows that: $\theta(M2) \preceq_{st} \theta(M1)$. But $\theta(M1)$ and $\theta(M2)$ are stochastic matrices. We then apply Lemma 3 to obtain $r^{-1}v\theta(M2) \preceq_{st} r^{-1}v\theta(M1)$ to complete the proof.

So the algorithms mainly consist in computing an element-wise lower bound of S_E which is obtained by adding some probability to Q_E and then apply operators θ and Vincent's algorithm. We show in the next section how we can improve element-wise lower bounds of S_E. We now show that bounds on censored chains can provide bounds for some performances measures on the original chain. First we have a very simple property, the proof of which is a simple application of theorem 2.

Property 4. Let i and j be two states in S. If $i \in E$ and $j \in E^c$ then:

$$\mathbf{\Pi}_Q(i) \leq \mathbf{\Pi}_{S_E}(i) \quad and \quad \mathbf{\Pi}_Q(j) \leq \mathbf{\Pi}_{S_{E^c}}(j) \tag{9}$$

We can derive bounds for steady-state rewards, absorbing probabilities and absorbing time. Assume that we have derived two monotone stochastic matrices UE and LE such that: $LE \preceq_{st} S_E \preceq_{st} UE$.

Property 5 (Steady-state rewards). Let $w : S \to R$ be the reward function that assign to each state $i \in S$ a reward value $w(i)$. Assume that $w(i) \geq 0$ for all i. Let E be the set of states which has a positive reward. Assuming that we sort the states in E such that function w is non decreasing. We clearly have:

$$R = \sum_{i \in S} w(i) \mathbf{\Pi}_Q(i) = \sum_{i \in E} w(i) \mathbf{\Pi}_E(i) \leq \sum_{i \in E} w(i) \mathbf{\Pi}_{S_E}(i) \leq \sum_{i \in E} w(i) \mathbf{\Pi}_{UE}(i)$$

We obtain an upper bound on the reward.

Property 6 (Probability of Absorption). We consider a chain with a finite number of absorbing states. Assume that all these absorbing states are in E and assume that the initial state is in E. Assume also that the states which immediately precede absorbing states are also in E. Then the absorption probabilities in the initial chain and in the censored chain are the same.

Proof. Remember that when we have a block decomposition of a transition matrix with absorbing states equal to $\left[\begin{array}{c|c} Id & 0 \\ \hline F & H \end{array}\right]$, matrix $M = (Id - H)^{-1}$ exists and is called the fundamental matrix [16]. Furthermore the entry $[i, j]$ of the product matrix $M * F$ gives the absorption probability in j knowing that the initial state is i.

We assume that the absorbing states are gathered in the first part of set E. Thus we can describe the matrix of the chain by its block decomposition:

$$\left[\begin{array}{c|c|c} Id & 0 & 0 \\ \hline R & A & B \\ \hline 0 & C & D \end{array}\right]$$

According to lemma 1, the transition matrix of the censored chain is:

$$\left[\begin{array}{c|c} Id & 0 \\ \hline R & A \end{array}\right] + \left[\begin{array}{c} 0 \\ \hline B \end{array}\right] \sum_i [D]^i \left[0 | C\right]$$

which is finally equal to: $\left[\begin{array}{c|c} Id & 0 \\ \hline R & A + B \sum_i D^i C \end{array}\right]$. As D is transient, we have: $\sum_i D^i = (Id - D)^{-1}$. And the fundamental matrix of the censored chain is:

$$(Id - A - B(Id - D)^{-1}C)^{-1}.$$

The fundamental matrix of the initial chain is: $M = \left[\begin{array}{c|c} Id - A & B \\ \hline C & Id - D \end{array}\right]^{-1}$. To obtain the probability we must multiply by $\left[\begin{array}{c} R \\ \hline 0 \end{array}\right]$ and consider an initial state in E. Thus we only have to compute the upper-left block of F. According to [12] page 123, it is equal to:

$$(Id - A - B(Id - D)^{-1}C)^{-1}$$

if blocks $(Id - A)$ and its Schur complements are non singular. This is clearly true. So we have the same absorption probability in Q and in S_E and bounds for the censored chain will also be bounds for the initial chain.

Property 7 (Average Time for Absorption). We consider a chain X with several absorbing states and the same block decomposition. Let Y be the censored chain. Let i be an initial state in E, j an arbitrary state in S and k an absorbing state. Let $Z_X[i, j]$ be the average number of passages in j before absorption knowing that the initial state is i for chain X. We have:

1. $Z_X[i, j] = Z_Y[i, j]$ if j is in E.
2. $\mathbf{E}(T_{i,k}(Y)) \leq \mathbf{E}(T_{i,k}(X))$.

Proof. Again remember that the average number of visits in j when the initial state is i is entry $[i, j]$ of the fundamental matrix. The proof of the previous property states that the upper-left block of the fundamental matrix of X is equal to the fundamental matrix of Y. This equality implies the first part of the property. The second part is a consequence of the first part and of the average number of visits to states in E^c which are positive in X and equals to 0 in Y.

4   Algorithms

The algorithms must find some paths which are contained in the fundamental matrix $(Id - Q_{E^c})^{-1}$, thus there is clearly a trade-off between complexity and accuracy. So we have developed several algorithms and data structures to deal with paths exploration. The aim is to deal with chains which are so large that the transition matrix does not fit in memory.

The algorithms compute some paths leaving immediately state i in E and coming back to E in any state. The output of the algorithms is a row vector called q whose the jth entry contains the probability of the paths from i to j which have been selected. Thus if we add q to row i of Q_E we obtain a more accurate element-wise lower bound for row i of S_E : $Q_E[i, *] \leq_{el} Q_E[i, *] + q \leq_{el} S_E[i, *]$.

Note also that all the rows do not have the same importance for the computation of the bound. Due to the monotonicity constraints, the last rows are often completely modified by Vincent's algorithm. Thus it is much more efficient to try to improve the first rows of Q_E than the last ones. This is illustrated by the following example.

$$Q_E = \begin{bmatrix} 0.1 & 0.3 & 0.2 & 0.1 \\ 0.1 & 0.4 & 0.2 & 0 \\ 0.2 & 0.1 & 0.5 & 0.2 \\ 0.3 & 0 & 0.4 & 0 \end{bmatrix}$$

Truffet's approach gives:

$$\theta(Q_E) = \begin{bmatrix} 0.1 & 0.3 & 0.2 & 0.4 \\ 0.1 & 0.4 & 0.2 & 0.3 \\ 0.2 & 0.1 & 0.5 & 0.2 \\ 0.3 & 0 & 0.4 & 0.3 \end{bmatrix} \qquad r^{-1}v\theta(Q_E) = \begin{bmatrix} 0.1 & 0.3 & 0.2 & 0.4 \\ 0.1 & 0.3 & 0.2 & 0.4 \\ 0.1 & 0.2 & 0.3 & 0.4 \\ 0.1 & 0.2 & 0.3 & 0.4 \end{bmatrix}$$

Now suppose that one has computed the probability $[0.1, 0.1, 0, 0.1]$ of some paths leaving E from state 4 and entering again set E after a visit in E^c. This is a lower bound of the set of all paths beginning in state 4. Let M be the improved element-wise lower bound.

$$M = \begin{bmatrix} 0.1 & 0.3 & 0.2 & 0.1 \\ 0.1 & 0.4 & 0.2 & 0 \\ 0.2 & 0.1 & 0.5 & 0.2 \\ 0.4 & 0.1 & 0.4 & 0.1 \end{bmatrix} \quad \theta(M) = \begin{bmatrix} 0.1 & 0.3 & 0.2 & 0.4 \\ 0.1 & 0.4 & 0.2 & 0.3 \\ 0.2 & 0.1 & 0.5 & 0.2 \\ 0.4 & 0.1 & 0.4 & 0.1 \end{bmatrix} \quad r^{-1}v\theta(M) = \begin{bmatrix} 0.1 & 0.3 & 0.2 & 0.4 \\ 0.1 & 0.3 & 0.2 & 0.4 \\ 0.1 & 0.2 & 0.3 & 0.4 \\ 0.1 & 0.2 & 0.3 & 0.4 \end{bmatrix}$$

And the bound does not change despite the computation of paths beginning in state 4. Assume now one has improved the first row and we have got the same vector of probability for the paths:

$$M = \begin{bmatrix} 0.2 & 0.4 & 0.2 & 0.2 \\ 0.1 & 0.4 & 0.2 & 0 \\ 0.2 & 0.1 & 0.5 & 0.2 \\ 0.3 & 0 & 0.4 & 0 \end{bmatrix} \quad \theta(M) = \begin{bmatrix} 0.2 & 0.4 & 0.2 & 0.2 \\ 0.1 & 0.4 & 0.2 & 0.3 \\ 0.2 & 0.1 & 0.5 & 0.2 \\ 0.3 & 0 & 0.4 & 0.3 \end{bmatrix} \quad r^{-1}v\theta(M) = \begin{bmatrix} 0.2 & 0.4 & 0.2 & 0.2 \\ 0.1 & 0.4 & 0.2 & 0.3 \\ 0.1 & 0.2 & 0.4 & 0.3 \\ 0.1 & 0.2 & 0.4 & 0.3 \end{bmatrix}$$

Clearly this bound is now much better than the original one.

We consider the directed graph $G = (\mathcal{S}, DE)$ associated to the initial Markov chain where DE is the set of directed edges. If $Q(i, j) > 0$ then there exists an arc from i to j in G and arc (i, j) has probability $Q(i, j)$. The directed edges (or arcs) in the graph are labelled with a positive cost. A path $\mathcal{P}$ is an ordered list of consecutive arcs. The cost of path $\mathcal{P}$ is the sum of the cost of arcs which belong to $\mathcal{P}$ multiplied by their number of occurrences in $\mathcal{P}$. Indeed an arc may appear several times in a path. The probability of path $\mathcal{P}$ (denoted as $Pr(\mathcal{P})$) is the product of the probability of the arcs which belongs to $\mathcal{P}$. Again we must take into account the number of occurrence of the arcs in the path. The set of paths beginning in i a node of E, then jumping to a node in E^c, staying in E^c for an arbitrary number of jumps and finally entering again E in state j is denoted as $\mathcal{SP}_{i,j}$.

The main idea is to select paths with high probabilities and to perform this selection very quickly. We present here two type of algorithms: the Shortest Path approach and Breadth First search. The first one builds one path to every destination while the second builds all the paths whose lengths are smaller than a parameter Δ. We also show that we can take into account the self loops to obtain easily an infinite set of paths rather than a single one.

4.1   Shortest Path

We use Dijkstra's shortest path algorithm. The length taken into account in the algorithm is the cost $c()$ which is positive. The following property states how we first compute the cost to obtain the path with the highest probability.

Property 8. If for all arcs in DE, the cost is defined as $c(i, j) = -log(Q(i, j))$ then the shortest path according to cost c is also the path with maximum probability. Note that as $Q(i, j) < 1$ the cost is positive.

Proof. Let $\mathcal{P}1$ be this shortest path. Assume that there exists $\mathcal{P}2$, a path such that $Pr(\mathcal{P}2) > Pr(\mathcal{P}1)$. As function logarithm is increasing we have: $log(Pr(\mathcal{P}2)) > log(Pr(\mathcal{P}1))$. The probability of the path is the product of the probability of arcs. Thus:

$$\sum_{(i,j)\in\mathcal{P}2} log(Q(i,j)) > \sum_{(k,l)\in\mathcal{P}1} log(Q(k,l))$$

After substitution:

$$\sum_{(i,j)\in\mathcal{P}2} c(i,j) < \sum_{(k,l)\in\mathcal{P}1} c(k,l)$$

And $\mathcal{P}2$ is shorter than the shortest path; a contradiction.

Thus the algorithm searches the shortest path from state i in a graph where the costs are defined as the negative of the logarithm of transition probabilities and where the arcs from i to other nodes in E have been removed because we want to get a path from i which passes through E^c and comes back to E. The shortest path with the cost function may have a large number of arcs. Thus we must give a bound on the number of arcs in the shortest path to avoid very large number of iterations. Let Δ be this bound. The following algorithm computes the probability of the shortest path. In the algorithm, P is the set of generated vertices, $\Gamma(x)$ denotes the set of successors of node x and $p(x)$ is the probability to reach x from i in the selected paths.

Algorithm 1. Shortest path

Input   : vertex $i \in E$; Δ
Output : row vector q: q_j is the probability to return to $j \in E$ from i
$P = \varnothing$; $q_z = 0$, $z \in E$
foreach *vertex* $x \in \Gamma(i)$ *such that* $x \in E^c$ **do**
   p(x)=prob. of transition from i to x; put x in P
end
repeat
   Select a leaf $y \in P$ such that $p(y) = \max_{\text{leaf } x \in P}\{p(x)\}$
   foreach $z \in \Gamma(y)\backslash\{y\}$ **do**
      $p_2 =$(prob. of transition from y to z) $* p(y)$
      switch z **do**
         case $z \in E$: $q_z = q_z + p_2$
         case $z \notin P$: $p(z) = p_2$; put z in P
         case z *is a leaf and* $p(z) < p_2$: $p(z) = p_2$
      end
   end
until *number of iteration* $> \Delta$;

Note that as we only search for successors of a limited number of nodes, only a part of the transition matrix must be in memory. Even if the whole matrix does not fit in memory it is sufficient that the states we really use during the construction of the paths can be stored or generated.

4.2 Adding Self Loops

Once a path from i to j is selected it is possible to build an infinite set of paths from i to j and to sum their probabilities in a closed-form formula. We just have to use the directed cycles. The proofs of following properties are quite simple and they are omitted here due to the limitation on the size of the paper.

Property 9. Let i and j be two arbitrary vertices in E. Let $\mathcal{P}$ be a path in $\mathcal{SP}_{i,j}$ with a probability p. Let k be a vertex which belongs to $\mathcal{P}$ and E^c such that there exists a directed cycle using nodes of E^c going through k. Let q be the product of the probabilities of the arcs in this directed cycle. Then the path $\mathcal{P}_k$ built with $\mathcal{P}$ and k times the directed cycle is also in $\mathcal{SP}_{i,j}$ and its probability is $p\ q^k$. Considering all these paths $\mathcal{P}_k$ for all values of k, we finally obtain a probability equals to $\frac{p}{1-q}$.

Computing a directed cycle may be difficult but it is quite simple to take into account the self loops during the visits. Indeed self loops are directed cycles and finding them does not require any new computational effort.

Property 10. Let $\mathcal{P} = (i, k_1, k_2, \ldots, k_l, j)$ be an arbitrary elementary path in $\mathcal{SP}_{i,j}$. Suppose that every vertex k_m in the path has a self loop with probability q_{k_m}. If there is no loop in k_m we simply have $q_{k_m} = 0$. Then all the path obtained from $\mathcal{P}$ and an arbitrary number of visits in each loop is also in $\mathcal{SP}_{i,j}$. And the resulting probability for all these paths is $p \prod_{m=0}^{l} \frac{1}{1-q_m}$.

4.3 Breadth First Search

We just build all paths of length smaller than Δ using a Breadth First search technique and computing their probabilities. Some of these paths return to a node in E at step $k \leq \Delta$. We use in the algorithm the same notation for data structure as in Shortest Path Algorithm and we finally denote by $InE[y, z]$ the probability to enter E through z leaving from $y \in E^c$.

5 Examples and Numerical Results

Due to the limitation on the size of the paper, it is not possible to present here a real example. We have just designed an abstract model to test our algorithms and show some numerical experiments. We consider a set of N resources: they can be operational or faulty. In the considered model we distinguish two types of faults: hard and soft, that we denote respectively by h and s. The fault arrivals of (h and s) follow independent Poisson processes with rate respectively λ_h and λ_s. The distribution of times to fix a fault are exponential with rate μ_h and μ_s except when all the resources are faulty. In that case, the repairman can speed up the fixing and with rate μ all the resources are repaired. Under these Markovian arrival hypothesis, the considered system can be modelled as a CTMC with state space $S = \{(n_s, n_h), C = n_s + n_h \leq N\}$ where C represents the total number of

---

Algorithm 2. Breadth-First search

Input   : vertex $i \in E$; Δ
Output : row vector q such that q_z is the probability to return to $z \in E$
$P = \varnothing$;
foreach $x \in \Gamma(i)$ *such that* $x \in E^c$ **do**
    p(x)=prob. of transition i to x; put x in P
end
$P_{last} = P$;
repeat
    $P_2^{last} = \varnothing$
    foreach *vertex* $x \in P_{last}$ **do**
        foreach *vertex* $y \in \Gamma(x)$ **do**
            switch y **do**
                case $y \in E$: $InE[x,y]$ =prob. of transition from x to y
                case $y \notin P$: $p(y) = p(x)*$(prob. of transition from x to y); put y
                in P and in P_2^{last}
                case $y \in P$: $p(y) = p(y) + p(x)*$(prob. of transition from x to y);
                put y in P_2^{last}
            end
        end
    end
    $P_{last} = P_2^{last}$
until *number of iteration* $> \Delta$;
foreach $y \in P$ **do**   **foreach** $z \in E$ **do** $q_z = p(y) * InE[y,z]$

---

faulty resources, n_s (resp. n_h) represents the number of faulty resources caused by soft (resp. hard) error. The size of the underlying chain is $\frac{(N+1)(N+2)}{2}$. Note that the considered chain is not NCD because of the numerical values of rate μ we have considered in the examples.

We present in Table 1, the conditional probability p to have the N resources operational and the upper bound on this probability. The censored state space contains states with no faulty hardware components. The states are ordered according to the decreasing number of software faulty components. The second step is to determine an element-wise lower bound to S_E. We apply the shortest path algorithm presented previously in subsection 4.1 with considering self loops. Remind that we have to fix the maximum number of arcs of shortest paths Δ and the number of first rows R in which we will apply the algorithm to simplify the computation of the bound. In the following table we present results for different values of Δ and R that represent parameters of the algorithm given in column *algorithm parameters*. Numerical Results are computed in a 3.2 GHz Intel Pentium 4 CPU with 1.5 Go of memory under Linux 2.6.8 kernel system. We also report computation time T (in *second*) needed to obtain the exact and bounding probability. We can see obviously that computation times are drastically reduced using the proposed bounding approach. It also provides results when the exact analysis fails ($N = 10000$). Moreover, obtained results confirm that it is not necessary to apply proposed algorithms to all rows. For

Table 1. $\lambda_s = 0.5$, $\lambda_h = 0.0001$, $\mu_s = \mu = 1$, $\mu_h = 0.02$

model size		Exact		algorithm parameters		Bound	
N	space size	p	T	Δ	R	p	T
100	5151	3.622e-6	1.57	2	$N/4$	4.14361e-6	.06
					N	4.14351e-6	.08
				10	$N/4$	4.12148e-6	.07
					N	4.12111e-6	.17
300	45451	1.224e-6	32.56	2	$N/4$	1.408871e-6	.16
					N	1.40884e-6	.22
				10	$N/4$	1.40141e-6	.23
					N	1.40127e-6	.51
500	125751	7.528e-7	168.47	2	$N/4$	8.76306e-7	.27
					N	8.76287e-7	.39
				10	$N/4$	8.71677e-7	.38
					N	8.71588e-7	.91
1000	501501	4.013e-7	603.14	2	$N/4$	4.82768e-7	.78
					N	4.82757e-7	1.01
				10	$N/4$	4.80213e-7	1.08
					N	4.80164e-7	2.31
10000	50015001	-	-	2	$N/4$	2.90822e-7	55.98
					N	2.90815e-7	55.10
				10	$N/4$	2.89280e-7	71.02
					N	2.89250e-7	123.01

this example we do not remark a notable difference between bounds obtained by considering all rows $R = N$ or ($R = N/4$). We can therefore decrease the complexity of the computation of the bounds by considering only some rows.

6   Concluding Remarks

We have proposed a new method to numerically obtain simple stochastic bounds. This method may also help to find lower bound on the absorption time if the chain is absorbing. The chain may be very large. We are still working to improve this approach to infinite DTMC. Indeed, we must correctly define ordering and censoring for transient and ergodic infinite DTMC. We only require that set E must be finite and that the absorbing states must be observed. The method only samples some paths in the non-observed part of the chain. This allows several tradeoffs between accuracy and computation time. We proved that if we add a new path in the samples the new bound we obtain is stochastically smaller than the previous one when we compute upper bound. We hope that this new approach will open new perspectives to study very large Markov chains.

References

1. Abu-Amsha, O., Vincent, J.M.: An algorithm to bound functionals of Markov chains with large state space. In: 4th INFORMS Conference on Telecommunications, Boca Raton, Florida (1998)
2. Benmammoun, M., Busic, A., Fourneau, J.M., Pekergin, N.: Increasing convex monotone Markov chains: theory, algorithms and applications. In: Markov Anniversary Meeting, pp. 189–210. Boson Books (2006)
3. Busic, A., Fourneau, J.M.: Bounds for Point and Steady-State Availability: An Algorithmic Approach Based on Lumpability and Stochastic Ordering. In: Bravetti, M., Kloul, L., Zavattaro, G. (eds.) EPEW, WS-FM 2005. LNCS, vol. 3670, pp. 94–108. Springer, Heidelberg (2005)
4. Courtois, P., Semal, P.: Bounds for the positive eigenvectors of nonnegative matrices and for their approximations by decomposition. J. of ACM 31, 804–825 (1984)
5. Dayar, T., Fourneau, J.M., Pekergin, N.: Transforming stochastic matrices for stochastic comparison with the st-order. RAIRO-RO 37, 85–97 (2003)
6. Dayar, T., Pekergin, N., Younes, S.: Conditional Steady-State Bounds for a Subset of States in Markov Chains. In: SMCTools, Pisa,Italy (2006)
7. Fourneau, J.M., Le Coz, M., Quessette, F.: Algorithms for an irreducible and lumpable strong stochastic bound. Linear Algebra and Applications 386, 167–186 (2004)
8. Fourneau, J.M., Le Coz, M., Pekergin, N., Quessette, F.: An open tool to compute stochastic bounds on steady-state distributions and rewards. In: IEEE Mascots 03, Orlando, USA (2003)
9. Fourneau, J.M., Pekergin, N.: An algorithmic approach to stochastic bounds. In: Calzarossa, M.C., Tucci, S. (eds.) Performance 2002. LNCS, vol. 2459, pp. 64–88. Springer, Heidelberg (2002)
10. Haddad, S., Moreaux, P.: Sub-stochastic matrix analysis for bounds computation-Theoretical results. Eur. Jour. of Operational. Res. 176, 999–1015 (2007)
11. Meyer, C.D.: Stochastic complementation, uncoupling Markov chains, and the theory of nearly reducible systems. SIAM Review 31(2), 240–272 (1989)
12. Meyer, C.D.: Matrix Analysis and Applied Linear Algebra. SIAM (2000)
13. Pekergin, N., Dayar, T., Alparslan, D.: Compenent-wise bounds for nearly completely decomposable Markov chains using stochastic comparison and reordering. Eur. Jour. of Op. Res. 165, 810–825 (2005)
14. Muller, A., Stoyan, D.: Comparison Methods for Stochastic Models and Risks. Wiley, New York (2002)
15. Shaked, M., Shantikumar, J.G.: Stochastic Orders and Their Applications. Academic Press, San Diago (1994)
16. Trivedi, K.S.: Probability and Statistic with Reliability, Queueing and Computer Science Applications. Second Edition, Wiley (2002)
17. Truffet, L.: Near Complete Decomposability: Bounding the error by a Stochastic Comparison Method. App. Prob. 29, 830–855 (1997)
18. Truffet, L.: Reduction Technique For Discrete Time Markov Chains on Totally Ordered State Space Using Stochastic Comparisons. Journal of Applied Probability 37(3) (2000)
19. Zhao, Y.Q., Liu, D.: The Censored Markov chain and the Best Augmentation. Jour. of App. Prob. 33, 623–629 (1996)

Workload Characterization of the SPECjms2007 Benchmark

Kai Sachs[1], Samuel Kounev[1,2], Jean Bacon[2], and Alejandro Buchmann[1]

[1] Databases and Distributed Systems Group, TU Darmstadt, Germany
[2] Computer Laboratory, University of Cambridge, UK

Abstract. Message-oriented middleware (MOM) is at the core of a vast number of financial services and telco applications, and is gaining increasing traction in other industries, such as manufacturing, transportation, health-care and supply chain management. There is a strong interest in the end user and analyst communities for a standardized benchmark suite for evaluating the performance and scalability of MOM. In this paper, we present a workload characterization of the SPECjms2007 benchmark which is the world's first industry-standard benchmark specialized for MOM. In addition to providing standard workload and metrics for MOM performance, the benchmark provides a flexible performance analysis framework that allows users to customize the workload according to their requirements. The workload characterization presented in this paper serves two purposes i) to help users understand the internal components of the SPECjms2007 workload and the way they are scaled, ii) to show how the workload can be customized to exercise and evaluate selected aspects of MOM performance. We discuss how the various features supported by the benchmark can be exploited for in-depth performance analysis of MOM infrastructures.

1 Introduction

Message-oriented middleware (MOM) is increasingly adopted as an enabling technology for modern event-driven applications like stock trading, event-based supply chain management, air traffic control and online auctions to name just a few. Novel messaging applications, however, pose some serious performance and scalability challenges. For example, the next generation of event-driven supply chain management based on RFID technology [6] (for instance SAP's AutoID infrastructure [3]) will be highly reliant on scalable and efficient backend systems to support the processing of acquired real-time data and its integration with enterprise applications and business processes [12]. Large retailers, like Wal-Mart, Metro or Tesco, are expected to have throughput rates of about 60 billion messages per annum [2]. The performance and scalability of the underlying MOM platforms used to process these messages will be of crucial importance for the successful adoption of such applications in the industry.

To guarantee that applications meet their Quality of Service (QoS) requirements, it is essential that the platforms on which they are built are tested using

K. Wolter (Ed.): EPEW 2007, LNCS 4748, pp. 228–244, 2007.

benchmarks to measure and validate their performance and scalability. However, if a benchmark is to be useful and reliable, it must fulfill several fundamental requirements [9]. First of all, it must be designed to stress platforms in a manner representative of real-world messaging applications. It must exercise all critical services provided by platforms and must provide a level playing field for performance comparisons. Finally, to be reliable, a benchmark must generate reproducible results and must not have any inherent scalability limitations. While a number of proprietary benchmarks for MOM servers (for example [14,7,1,8]) have been developed and used in the industry for performance testing and product comparisons (see [5,11,4]), these benchmarks do not meet the above requirements. The reason is that most of them use artificial workloads that do not reflect any real-world application scenario. Furthermore, they typically concentrate on stressing individual MOM features in isolation and do not provide a comprehensive and representative workload for evaluating the overall MOM server performance. To address these concerns, in September 2005 we launched a project at the Standard Performance Evaluation Corporation (SPEC) with the goal to develop a standard benchmark for evaluating the performance and scalability of MOM products. The new benchmark was called SPECjms2007 and it was developed at SPEC's OSG-Java Subcommittee with the participation of TU-Darmstadt, IBM, Sun, BEA, Sybase, Apache, Oracle and JBoss. SPECjms2007 exercises messaging products through the JMS (Java Message Service) [15] standard interface which is supported by all major MOM vendors.

In this paper, we introduce the SPECjms2007 benchmark and provide a comprehensive characterization of its workload. We start with a brief overview of the benchmark goals and then present the business scenario it models and discuss the way it was implemented. An important advantage of SPECjms2007 is that it allows users to customize the workload to their needs by configuring it to stress selected features of the MOM infrastructure in a way that resembles a given target customer workload. However, in order to exploit this, users need to understand the way the workload is decomposed into components and which performance aspects are exercised by these components. To this end, after discussing the benchmark scenario and its implementation, we present a detailed characterization of the benchmark workload. This characterization, on the one hand, aims to help users gain an in-depth understanding of the SPECjms2007 workload, so that they can interpret the benchmark results correctly. On the other hand, it provides the information needed to enable users to tailor the workload to their own requirements.

The rest of the paper is organized as follows. In Section 2, we briefly discuss the goals of SPECjms2007 and then introduce the business scenario and interactions it models. Following this, in Section 3, we present an in-depth characterization of the SPECjms2007 workload in terms of the number and types of destinations, the interaction mix, the message types, the message sizes and the message delivery modes. We show how the workload can be customized to stress selected performance aspects and discuss two standard strategies for scaling the workload. The paper is wrapped up in Section 4.

2   The SPECjms2007 Benchmark

2.1   Requirements and Goals

The aim of the SPECjms2007 benchmark is to provide a standard workload and metrics for measuring and evaluating the performance and scalability of MOM platforms. To achieve this the SPECjms2007 workload must fulfill several important requirements. First of all, it must be based on a representative workload scenario that reflects the way platform services are exercised in real-life systems. The goal is to allow users to relate the observed behavior to their own applications and environments. Second, the workload should be comprehensive in that it should exercise all platform features typically used in MOM applications including both point-to-point (P2P) and publish/subscribe (pub/sub) messaging. The features and services stressed should be weighted according to their usage in real-life systems. The third requirement is that the workload should be focused on measuring the performance and scalability of the MOM server's software and hardware components. It should minimize the impact of other components and services that are typically used in the chosen application scenario. For example, if a database would be used to store business data and manage the application state, it could easily become the limiting factor of the benchmark as experience with other benchmarks shows [10]. Finally, the SPECjms2007 workload must not have any inherent scalability limitations. The user should be able to scale the workload both by increasing the number of destinations (queues and topics) as well as the message traffic pushed through a destination.

Producing and publishing standard results for marketing purposes will be just one usage scenario for SPECjms2007. Many users will be interested in using the benchmark to tune and optimize their platforms or to analyze the performance of certain specific MOM features. Others could use the benchmark for research purposes in academic environments where, for example, one might be interested in evaluating the performance and scalability of novel methods and techniques for building high-performance MOM servers. All these usage scenarios require that the benchmark framework allows the user to precisely configure the workload and transaction mix to be generated. Providing this configurability is a great challenge because it requires that interactions are designed and implemented in such a way that one could run them in different combinations depending on the desired transaction mix.

2.2   Workload Scenario

The workload scenario chosen for SPECjms2007 models the supply chain of a supermarket company. The participants involved are the supermarket company, its stores, its distribution centers and its suppliers. The scenario offers an excellent basis for defining interactions that stress different subsets of the functionality offered by MOM servers. Moreover, it offers a natural way to scale the workload. The participants involved in the scenario can be grouped into the following four roles:

Company Headquarters (HQ). The company's corporate headquarters are responsible for managing the accounting of the company, managing information about the goods and products offered in the supermarket stores, managing selling prices and monitoring the flow of goods and money in the supply chain.

Distribution Centers (DCs). The distribution centers supply the supermarket stores. Every distribution center is responsible for a set of stores in a given area. The distribution centers in turn are supplied by external suppliers. The distribution centers are involved in the following activities: taking orders from supermarkets, ordering goods from suppliers, delivering goods to supermarkets and providing sales statistics to the HQ (e.g. for data mining).

Supermarkets (SMs). The supermarkets sell goods to end customers. The scenario focuses on the management of the inventory of supermarkets including their warehouses. Some supermarkets are smaller than others, so that they do not have enough room for all products, others may be specialized for some product groups like certain types of food. We assume that every supermarket is supplied by exactly one of the distribution centers.

Suppliers (SPs). The suppliers deliver goods to the distribution centers of the supermarket company. Different suppliers are specialized for different sets of products and they deliver goods on demand, i.e. they must receive an order from the supermarket company to send a shipment.

2.3 Modeled Interactions

SPECjms2007 implements seven interactions between the participants in the supermarket supply chain.

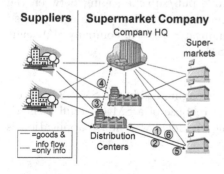

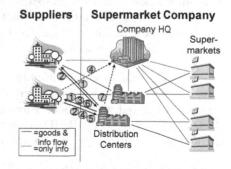

Fig. 1. Interaction 1 - Communication between SM and DC

Fig. 2. Interaction 2 - Communication between SP and DC

Interaction 1: Order/Shipment Handling between SM and DC
This interaction exercises persistent P2P messaging between the SMs and DCs. The interaction is triggered when goods in the warehouse of a SM are depleted and the SM has to order from its DC to refill stock. The following steps are followed as illustrated in Figure 1:

1. A SM sends an order to its DC.
2. The DC sends a confirmation to the SM and ships the ordered goods.
3. Goods are registered by RFID readers upon leaving the DC warehouse.
4. The DC sends information about the transaction to the HQ (sales statistics).
5. The shipment arrives at the SM and is registered by RFID readers upon entering the SM warehouse.
6. A confirmation is sent to the DC.

Interaction 2: Order/Shipment Handling between DC and SP
This interaction exercises persistent P2P and pub/sub (durable) messaging between the DCs and SPs. The interaction is triggered when goods in a DC are depleted and the DC has to order from a SP to refill stock. The following steps are followed as illustrated in Figure 2:

1. A DC sends a call for offers to all SPs that supply the types of goods that need to be ordered.
2. SPs that can deliver the goods send offers to the DC.
3. Based on the offers, the DC selects a SP and sends a purchase order to it.
4. The SP sends a confirmation to the DC and an invoice to the HQ. It then ships the ordered goods.
5. The shipment arrives at the DC and is registered by RFID readers upon entering the DC's warehouse.
6. The DC sends a delivery confirmation to the SP.
7. The DC sends transaction statistics to the HQ.

Interaction 3: Price Updates
This interaction exercises persistent, durable pub/sub messaging between the HQ and the SMs. The interaction is triggered when selling prices are changed by the company administration. To communicate this, the company HQ sends messages with pricing information to the SMs.

Interaction 4: SM Inventory Management
This interaction exercises persistent P2P messaging inside the SMs. The interaction is triggered when goods leave the warehouse of a SM (to refill a shelf). Goods are registered by RFID readers and the local warehouse application is notified so that inventory can be updated.

Interaction 5: Sales Statistics Collection
This interaction exercises non-persistent P2P messaging between the SMs and the HQ. The interaction is triggered when a SM sends sales statistics to the HQ. HQ can use this data as a basis for data mining in order to study customer behavior and provide useful information to marketing.

Interaction 6: New Product Announcements
This interaction exercises non-persistent, non-durable pub/sub messaging between the HQ and the SMs. The interaction is triggered when new products are announced by the company administration. To communicate this, the HQ sends messages with product information to the SMs selling the respective product types.

Interaction 7: Credit Card Hot Lists
This interaction exercises non-persistent, non-durable pub/sub messaging between the HQ and the SMs. The interaction is triggered when the HQ sends credit card hot lists to the SMs (complete list once every hour and incremental updates as required).

2.4 Benchmark Implementation

Event Handlers and Agents. SPECjms2007 is implemented as a Java application comprising multiple JVMs and threads distributed across a set of *client nodes*. For every destination (queue or topic), there is a separate Java class called *Event Handler (EH)* that encapsulates the application logic executed to process messages sent to that destination. Event handlers register as listeners for the queue/topic and receive call backs from the messaging infrastructure as new messages arrive. For maximal performance and scalability, multiple instances of each event handler executed in separate threads can exist and they can be distributed over multiple physical nodes. Event handlers can be grouped according to the physical location (e.g. HQ, SM, DC or SP) they pertain to in the business scenario. In addition to the event handlers, for every physical location, a set of threads is launched to drive the benchmark interactions that are logically started at that location. These are called *driver threads*. The set of all event handlers and driver threads pertaining to a given physical location is referred to as *agent*. For example, each DC agent is comprised of a set of event handlers for the various destinations inside the DC and a set of driver threads used to drive Interaction 2, which is the only interaction with logical starting point at DCs.

Workload Configurability. An important goal of SPECjms2007 that we discussed in Section 2.1 was to provide a flexible framework for performance analysis of MOM servers that allows users to configure and customize the workload according to their requirements. To achieve this goal, the interactions have been implemented in such a way that one could run them in different combinations depending on the desired transaction mix. SPECjms2007 offers three different ways of structuring the workload: horizontal, vertical and freeform. The latter are referred to as *workload topologies* and they correspond to three different modes of running the benchmark offering different level of configurability. The horizontal topology is meant to exercise the ability of the system to handle increasing number of destinations. To this end, the workload is scaled by increasing the number of physical locations (SMs, DCs, etc.) while keeping the traffic per location constant. The vertical topology, on the other hand, is meant to exercise the ability of the system to handle increasing message traffic through a fixed set of destinations. Therefore, a fixed set of physical locations is used and the workload is scaled by increasing the rate at which interactions are run. Finally, the freeform topology allows the user to use the seven SPECjms2007 interactions as building blocks to design his own workload scenario which can be scaled in an arbitrary manner by increasing the number of physical locations and/or the rates at which interactions are run. The user can configure the number of physical locations emulated, the number of message producers and consumers, the message size disributions, the message delivery modes, etc. Most importantly, the user can selectively turn off interactions or change the rate at which they are run to shape the workload according to his requirements. At the same time, when running the horizontal or vertical topology, the benchmark behaves as if the interactions were interrelated according to their dependencies in the real-life application scenario. For further details on the benchmark implementation, the reader is referred to [13].

3   SPECjms2007 Workload Characterization

3.1   Message Traffic Analysis

We start with a detailed analysis of the message traffic produced by the benchmark workload in terms of the number and type of messages generated and their sizes. We consider the workload parameters that can be configured in the most general freeform topology and show how they affect the resulting message traffic. The different types of messages and destinations used in the various interactions are detailed in Table 1.

Messages Sizes. The sizes of the messages generated as part of each interaction can be configured by setting an interaction-specific message sizing parameter (for example, "number of order lines sent to DC" for Interaction 1). Each sizing parameter can be assigned three possible values with respective probabilities (discrete probability distribution). The message sizing parameters used for the different interactions are listed in Table 2, along with some data that can be used to compute the resulting message sizes in KBytes. This data is based on measurements we took using a deployment of SPECjms2007 on a major JMS server platform[1]. The exact message sizes may be slightly different on different platforms, as MOM servers add their own platform-specific message headers. The measurements provided here were compared against measurements on a second popular JMS server and the differences were negligible. Based on the data in Table 2, the message sizes in KBytes for Interactions 1, 2, 4, 6 and 7 can be computed as $\vartheta = m_1 \cdot x + b$ where x is the interaction's message sizing parameter and m_1 and b are set to their respective values from Table 2. The `priceUpdate` messages of Interaction 3 have constant size that cannot be changed by the user. The size of the `statInfoSM` messages used in Interaction 5 is configured using two sizing parameters as follows $\vartheta = x \cdot (m_1 + m_2 \cdot y) + b$ where x and y are

---

[1] Due to product license restrictions, the specific configuration used cannot be disclosed.

Table 1. Message Types Used in The Interactions - (N)P=(Non-)Persistent; (N)T=(Non-)Transactional; (N)D=(Non-)Durable

Intr.	Message	Destination	Type	Prop.	Description
1	order	Queue (DC)	ObjectMsg	P, T	Order sent from SM to DC.
	orderConf	Queue (SM)	ObjectMsg	P, T	Order confirmation sent from DC to SM.
	shipDep	Queue (DC)	TextMsg	P, T	Shipment registered by RFID readers upon leaving DC.
	statInfo-OrderDC	Queue (HQ)	StreamMsg	NP, NT	Sales statistics sent from DC to HQ.
	shipInfo	Queue (SM)	TextMsg	P, T	Shipment from DC registered by RFID readers upon arrival at SM.
	shipConf	Queue (DC)	ObjectMsg	P, T	Shipment confirmation sent from SM to DC.
2	callForOffers	Topic (HQ)	TextMsg	P, T, D	Call for offers sent from DC to SPs (XML).
	offer	Queue (DC)	TextMsg	P, T	Offer sent from SP to DC (XML).
	pOrder	Queue (SP)	TextMsg	P, T	Order sent from DC to SP (XML).
	pOrderConf	Queue (DC)	TextMsg	P, T	Order confirmation sent from SP to DC (XML).
	invoice	Queue (HQ)	TextMsg	P, T	Order invoice sent from SP to HQ (XML).
	pShipInfo	Queue (DC)	TextMsg	P, T	Shipment from SP registered by RFID readers upon arrival at DC.
	pShipConf	Queue (SP)	TextMsg	P, T	Shipment confirmation sent from DC to SP (XML).
	statInfo-ShipDC	Queue (HQ)	StreamMsg	NP, NT	Purchase statistics sent from DC to HQ.
3	priceUpdate	Topic (HQ)	MapMsg	P, T, D	Price update sent from HQ to SMs.
4	inventoryInfo	Queue (SM)	TextMsg	P, T	Item movement registered by RFID readers in the warehouse of SM.
5	statInfoSM	Queue (HQ)	ObjectMsg	NP, NT	Sales statistics sent from SM to HQ.
6	product-Announcement	Topic (HQ)	StreamMsg	NP, NT, ND	New product announcements sent from HQ to SMs.
7	creditCardHL	Topic (HQ)	StreamMsg	NP, NT, ND	Credit card hotlist sent from HQ to SMs.

the two sizing parameters (i.e. "number of SM cash desks" and "number of sales lines") and m_1, m_2 and b are set to their respective values from Table 2. Based on the above two formulas and the data in Table 2, the user can configure the benchmark to use message sizes that match the user's own target workload.

Message Throughput. We now characterize the message throughput first on a per interaction basis and then on a per location basis. The two most important sets of workload parameters that determine the message throughput are the number of locations of each type and the interaction rates. We denote the sets of physical locations as follows:

$$\Psi_{SM} = \{SM_1, SM_2, \ldots, SM_{|\Psi_{SM}|}\} \qquad \Psi_{DC} = \{DC_1, DC_2, \ldots, DC_{|\Psi_{DC}|}\}$$
$$\Psi_{SP} = \{SP_1, SP_2, \ldots, SP_{|\Psi_{SP}|}\} \qquad \Psi_{HQ} = \{HQ_1, HQ_2, \ldots, HQ_{|\Psi_{HQ}|}\}$$

Note that although the modeled scenario has a single physical HQ location, the benchmark allows multiple HQ instances to exist each with its own set of queues. The goal is to avoid the HQ queues becoming a bottleneck when scaling

Table 2. Parameters for Message Size Calculation

Intr.	Message Sizing Parameters	Message	m_1	m_2	b
1	No of order lines sent to DC	orderConf	0.0565	na	1.7374
		statInfoOrderDC	0.0153	na	0.1463
		shipInfo	0.0787	na	0.8912
		shipDep	0.0787	na	0.7222
		order	0.0565	na	1.4534
		shipConf	0.0202	na	0.7140
2	No of purchase order lines sent to SP	callForOffers	0.1785	na	0.8094
		offer	0.2489	na	0.9414
		pOrder	0.2498	na	1.1076
		pShipConf	0.0827	na	0.7612
		statInfoShipDC	0.0831	na	0.7681
		pOrderConf	0.2410	na	1.3494
		invoice	0.1942	na	1.1211
		pShipInfo	0.0827	na	0.7279
3	*Message has fixed size*	priceUpdate	na	na	0.2310
4	No of registered items leaving warehouse	inventoryInfo	0.0970	na	0.5137
5	No of cash desks & sales lines	statInfoSM	0.0139	0.3650	0.9813
6	No of new products announced	productAnnouncement	0.0103	na	0.1754
7	No of credit cards in hot list	creditCardHL	0.0166	na	0.1846

the number of SMs, DCs and SPs. It is assumed that messages sent to the HQ are distributed evenly among the HQ instances. Multiple HQ instances are considered as separate servers within the same physical location.

For each interaction, the *interaction rate* specifies the rate at which the interaction is initiated by every physical instance of its initiating location, SM for Interaction 1, DC for Interaction 2, etc. We denote the interaction rates as $\lambda_i, 1 \le i \le 7$. Since multiple HQ instances are not considered as separate physical locations, it follows that the rates of Interactions 3, 6 and 7 which are initiated by the HQ are interpreted as rates over all HQ instances as opposed to rates per HQ instance. Interaction 2 uses a set of topics representing the different product families offered by suppliers. These topics help to distribute the `callForOffers` messages sent by DCs. Suppliers subscribe to all topics corresponding to groups of products they offer so that they receive all relevant `callForOffers` messages. We denote the set of product families as $\Pi = \{PF_1, PF_2, PF_3, \ldots, PF_{|\Pi|}\}$.

The probability that a SP offers products from a given product family $PF_i \in \Pi$ is a configurable workload parameter and will be denoted as ρ. Every SP subscribes to $\rho \cdot |\Pi|$ product families and thus $|\Psi_{SP}| \cdot \rho \cdot |\Pi|$ subscriptions exist overall. The number of subscribers that subscribe to a given product family is denoted as $\zeta = |\Psi_{SP}| \cdot \rho$.

In the following, we show how the message throughput, in terms of the number of messages sent and received per unit of time, can be broken down according

Table 3. Message Groups

Group	a	b	c	d
Type	Pub/Sub	Pub/Sub	P2P	P2P
Properties	NP NT ND	P T D	NP NT	P T

to the type of messaging (P2P vs. pub/sub) and the message delivery mode (persistent vs. non-persistent, transactional vs. non-transactional, durable vs. non-durable). To this end, we group messages as shown in Table 3. Further, we define the following sets:

$\Gamma = \{a, b, c, d\}$: Message groups as defined in Table 3.
$\Omega = \{se, re\}$: Messages sent vs. messages received.
$\Lambda = \{SM, SP, DC, HQ\}$: Types of physical locations.

3.1a). Message Throughput per Interaction
We first analyze the message throughput on a per interaction basis. We will use the following notation:

$\xi_{i,k}^{j}$ for $j \in \Omega, 1 \leq i \leq 7$ and $k \in \Gamma$
   No of messages of group k sent/received per sec as part of Interaction i.
$\xi_i^j = \sum_{k \in \Gamma} \xi_{i,k}^j$ for $1 \leq i \leq 7, j \in \Omega$
   Total no of messages sent/received per sec as part of Interaction i.
$\xi^j = \sum_{i=1}^{7} \xi_i^j$ for $j \in \Omega$
   Total no of messages sent/received per sec over all interactions.

Based on the information provided in the previous sections and analysis of the benchmark design, the following equations are derived characterizing the message throughput of each interaction:

Interaction 1: $\quad \xi_{1,c}^{se} = \xi_{1,c}^{re} = \lambda_1 \cdot |\Psi_{SM}| \qquad \xi_{1,d}^{se} = \xi_{1,d}^{re} = 5 \cdot \lambda_1 \cdot |\Psi_{SM}|$
$$\xi_{1,k}^{j} = 0, \quad \forall k \in \{a, b\} \wedge j \in \Omega$$

Interaction 2: $\qquad \xi_{2,a}^{j} = 0, \; \forall j \in \Omega \qquad \xi_{2,c}^{se} = \xi_{2,c}^{re} = \lambda_2 \cdot |\Psi_{DC}|$
$$\xi_{2,b}^{se} = \lambda_2 \cdot |\Psi_{DC}| \qquad \xi_{2,d}^{se} = \xi_{2,d}^{re} = (\zeta + 5) \cdot \lambda_2 \cdot |\Psi_{DC}|$$
$$\xi_{2,b}^{re} = \zeta \cdot \lambda_2 \cdot |\Psi_{DC}|$$

Interaction 3: $\qquad \xi_{3,b}^{se} = \lambda_3 \qquad \xi_{3,k}^{j} = 0, \; \forall k \in \Gamma, k \neq b \wedge j \in \Omega$
$$\xi_{3,b}^{re} = \lambda_3 \cdot |\Psi_{SM}|$$

Interaction 4: $\quad \xi_{4,d}^{se} = \xi_{4,d}^{re} = \lambda_4 \cdot |\Psi_{SM}| \quad \xi_{4,k}^{j} = 0, \; \forall k \in \Gamma, k \neq d \wedge j \in \Omega$

Interaction 5: $\quad \xi_{5,d}^{se} = \xi_{5,d}^{re} = \lambda_5 \cdot |\Psi_{SM}| \quad \xi_{5,k}^{j} = 0, \; \forall k \in \Gamma, k \neq d \wedge j \in \Omega$

Interaction 6: $\qquad \xi_{6,a}^{se} = \lambda_6 \qquad \xi_{6,k}^{j} = 0, \; \forall k \in \Gamma, k \neq a \wedge j \in \Omega$
$$\xi_{6,a}^{re} = \lambda_6 \cdot |\Psi_{SM}|$$

Interaction 7: $\qquad \xi_{7,a}^{se} = \lambda_7 \qquad \xi_{7,k}^{j} = 0, \; \forall k \in \Gamma, k \neq a \wedge j \in \Omega$
$$\xi_{7,a}^{re} = \lambda_7 \cdot |\Psi_{SM}|$$

3.1b). Message Throughput per Location

We now analyze the message throughput on a per location basis. The following notation will be used:

$\chi_{l,k}^{j}$ for $j \in \Omega, l \in \Lambda, k \in \Gamma$

No of messages of group k sent/received per sec by a location of type l.

$\chi_{l}^{j} = \sum_{k \in \Gamma} \xi_{l,k}^{j}$ for $j \in \Omega, l \in \Lambda$

Total no of messages sent/received per sec by a location of type l.

SMs participate in all interactions apart from Interaction 2. The following equations characterize the message throughput of each SM:

$$\chi_{SM,a}^{se} = \chi_{SM,b}^{se} = \chi_{SM,c}^{re} = 0 \qquad\qquad \chi_{SM,c}^{se} = \lambda_5$$
$$\chi_{SM,a}^{re} = \lambda_6 + \lambda_7 \qquad\qquad\qquad\quad \chi_{SM,d}^{se} = 2\lambda_1 + \lambda_4$$
$$\chi_{SM,b}^{re} = \lambda_3 \qquad\qquad\qquad\qquad\quad \chi_{SM,d}^{re} = 2\lambda_1 + \lambda_4$$

SPs participate only in Interaction 2. Overall $\lambda_2 \cdot |\Psi_{DC}|$ callForOffers messages are sent by the DCs per sec. Therefore, every SP receives $\rho \cdot \lambda_2 \cdot |\Psi_{DC}|$ messages and for each of them it sends an offer to the respective DC. The probability that an offer is accepted is $\frac{1}{\zeta}$ and hence the number of SP offers accepted per sec is given by:

$$\frac{\rho \cdot \lambda_2 \cdot |\Psi_{DC}|}{\zeta} = \frac{\lambda_2 \cdot |\Psi_{DC}|}{|\Psi_{SP}|}$$

The following equations characterize the message throughput of each SP:

$$\chi_{SP,a}^{se} = \chi_{SP,a}^{re} = \chi_{SP,b}^{se} = \chi_{SP,c}^{se} = \chi_{SP,c}^{re} = 0$$
$$\chi_{SP,b}^{re} = \rho \cdot \lambda_2 \cdot |\Psi_{DC}|$$
$$\chi_{SP,d}^{se} = \rho \cdot \lambda_2 \cdot |\Psi_{DC}| + \frac{3\lambda_2 \cdot |\Psi_{DC}|}{|\Psi_{SP}|}$$
$$\chi_{SP,d}^{re} = \frac{2\lambda_2 \cdot |\Psi_{DC}|}{|\Psi_{SP}|}$$

DCs participate in Interactions 1 and 2 both as producers and consumers of messages. The number of SMs supplied by each DC is given by $\delta = \frac{|\Psi_{SM}|}{|\Psi_{DC}|}$.

The following equations characterize the message throughput of each DC:

$$\chi_{DC,a}^{se} = \chi_{DC,a}^{re} = \chi_{DC,b}^{re} = \chi_{DC,c}^{re} = 0$$
$$\chi_{DC,b}^{se} = \lambda_2$$
$$\chi_{DC,c}^{se} = \delta \cdot \lambda_1 + \lambda_2$$
$$\chi_{DC,d}^{se} = 3\lambda_1 \cdot \delta + 2\lambda_2$$
$$\chi_{DC,d}^{re} = 3\lambda_1 \cdot \delta + \lambda_2(\zeta + 2)$$

The HQ participate in Interactions 1, 2, and 5 as message consumer and in Interactions 3, 6, and 7 as message producer. The following equations characterize the message throughput of the HQ:

$$\chi^{re}_{HQ,a} = \chi^{re}_{HQ,b} = \chi^{se}_{HQ,c} = \chi^{se}_{HQ,d} = 0$$
$$\chi^{se}_{HQ,a} = \lambda_6 + \lambda_7$$
$$\chi^{se}_{HQ,b} = \lambda_3$$
$$\chi^{re}_{HQ,c} = \lambda_1 \cdot |\Psi_{SM}| + \lambda_2 \cdot |\Psi_{DC}| + \lambda_5 \cdot |\Psi_{SM}|$$
$$\chi^{re}_{HQ,d} = \lambda_2 \cdot |\Psi_{DC}|$$

The detailed message throughput analysis presented above serves two main purposes. First, using the throughput equations, the user can assemble a workload configuration (in terms of number of locations and interaction rates) that stresses specific types of messaging under given scaling conditions. As a very basic example, the user might be interested in evaluating the performance and scalability of non-persistent pub/sub messaging under increasing number of subscribers. In this case, a mix of Interactions 6 and 7 can be used with increasing number of SMs. Second, the characterization of the message traffic on a per location basis can help users to find optimal deployment topology of the agents representing the different locations such that the load is evenly distributed among client nodes and there are no client-side bottlenecks. This is especially important for a messaging benchmark where the server acts as mediator in interactions and significant amount of processing is executed on the client side.

3.2   Horizontal Topology

As mentioned earlier, the goal of the horizontal topology is to exercise the ability of the system to handle increasing number of destinations. To achieve this, the workload is scaled by increasing the number of physical locations (SMs, DCs, etc) while keeping the traffic per location constant. A scaling parameter BASE is introduced and the following rules are enforced:

1. $|\Psi_{SM}| = \text{BASE}$
2. $|\Psi_{DC}| = \lceil \frac{|\Psi_{SM}|}{5} \rceil$
3. $|\Psi_{SP}| = \lceil 0.4 \cdot |\Psi_{SM}| \rceil$
4. $|\Psi_{HQ}| = \lceil \frac{|\Psi_{SM}|}{20} \rceil$

5. $|\Pi| = |\Psi_{SM}|$
6. $\rho = \frac{5}{|\Pi|}$
7. $\lambda_i, 1 \le i \le 7$ are fixed

Figure 3 shows how the number of locations of each type is scaled as the BASE parameter is increased. The rates λ_i at which interactions are initiated by participants are fixed so that the traffic per location (and therefore also per destination) remains constant. The relative weights of the interactions are set based on a detailed business model of the supermarket supply chain which captures the interaction interdependencies. This model has several input parameters (e.g. total number of product types, size of supermarkets, average number of items sold per week) whose values are chosen in such a way that the following overall target messaging mix is achieved as close as possible:

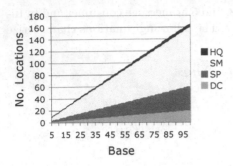

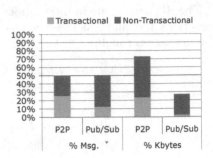

Fig. 3. # Locations for Horiz. Topology   **Fig. 4.** Horiz. Topology Message Mix

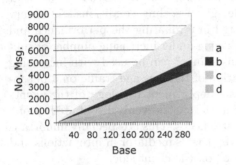

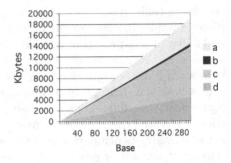

Fig. 5. Horizontal Topology: # msg   **Fig. 6.** Message traffic in Kbytes

- 50% P2P messages and 50% pub/sub
- 50% of P2P messages persistent, 50% non-persistent
- 25% of pub/sub messages persistent, 75% non-persistent

The goal is to put equal weight on P2P and pub/sub messaging. Within each group the target relative weights of persistent vs. non-persistent messaging have been set according to the relative usage of these messaging styles in real-life applications. Table 5(a) shows the achieved message mix in the horizontal topology. Figure 4 presents the same data in graphical form. Figures 5 and 6 show how the number of messages of each type and the bandwidth they use are scaled as a function of the BASE parameter. As evident from the figure, when scaling the workload the proportions of the different types of messages remain constant. This is expected since the relative weights of the various messaging styles used by the workload should not depend on the scaling factor.

The sizes of the messages used in the various interactions have been chosen to reflect typical message sizes in real-life MOM applications. Pub/sub messages are generally much smaller than P2P messages due to the decoupled nature of the delivery mechanism. For every type of message, SPECjms2007 generates messages with sizes chosen from a discrete distribution with three possible values as shown in Table 4. There are two exceptions, the priceUpdate message used

Table 4. Message Sizes in KByte

Intr.	Message *Probability*	Size 1 *95 %*	Size 2 *4 %*	Size 3 *1 %*	Avg. Size
1	orderConf	2.02	7.39	41.29	2.63
	statInfoOrderDC	0.22	1.67	10.83	0.39
	shipInfo	1.28	8.76	55.95	2.13
	shipDep	1.12	8.59	55.79	1.96
	order	1.74	7.10	41.01	2.34
	shipConf	0.81	2.73	14.83	1.03
2	callForOffers	1.35	7.06	36.52	1.93
	offer	1.69	9.65	50.71	2.50
	pOrder	1.86	9.85	51.07	2.67
	pShipConf	1.01	3.65	17.29	1.28
	statInfoShipDC	1.02	3.68	17.38	1.29
	pOrderConf	2.07	9.79	49.56	2.86
	invoice	1.70	7.92	39.95	2.33
	pShipInfo	0.98	3.62	17.26	1.24
3	priceUpdate	0.24	0.24	0.24	0.24
4	inventoryInfo	1.48	10.22	49.03	2.31
5	statInfoSM		*na*		5.27
6	productAnnouncement	1.21	0.28	10.51	1.26
7	creditCardHL	1.01	8.49	50.00	1.80

in Interaction 4 and the `statInfoSM` message used in Interaction 5. The former has a fixed size, while the latter has size between 4.7 and 24.78 KB with an average of 5.27 KB. Since `statInfoSM` messages contain sales statistics, their size is determined by the rate at which items are sold in supermarkets which depends on the number of customers visiting a supermarket per day and the average number of items sold per customer.

Table 5. Topology Message Mix

(a) Horizontal

Message Group	Message Count Target	Achieved	Bandwidth Used
a	37.50%	37.46%	24.66%
b	12.50%	12.45%	2.41%
c	25.00%	24.55%	49.19%
d	25.00%	25.55%	23.74%

(b) Vertical

Message Group	Message Count Target	Achieved	Bandwidth Used
a	15.00%	14.19%	7.19%
b	5.00%	5.99%	2.25%
c	40.00%	39.09%	61.03%
d	40.00%	40.74%	29.52%

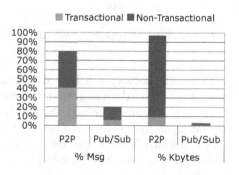

Fig. 7. Vert. Topology Message Mix

3.3 Vertical Topology

The goal of the vertical topology is to exercise the ability of the system to handle increasing message traffic through a fixed set of destinations. Therefore, a fixed set of physical locations is used and the workload is scaled by increasing the rate at which interactions are executed. Similar to the horizontal case, a single parameter BASE is used as a scaling factor. The following rules are enforced:

1. $|\Psi_{SM}| = 10$
2. $|\Psi_{DC}| = 2$
3. $|\Psi_{SP}| = 5$
4. $|\Psi_{HQ}| = 1$

5. $|\Pi| = 100$
6. $\rho = 50\%$
7. $\lambda_i = c_i \cdot$ BASE, where c_i is a fixed factor and $1 \leq i \leq 7$

Again, the relative weights of the interactions are set based on the business model of the supply chain scenario. Unlike the horizontal topology, however, the vertical topology places the emphasis on P2P messaging which accounts for 80% of the total message traffic. The aim is to exercise the ability of the system to handle increasing traffic through a destination by processing messages in parallel. This aspect of MOM server performance is more relevant for P2P messaging (queues) than for pub/sub messaging where the message throughput is inherently limited by the speed at which subscribers can process incoming messages.

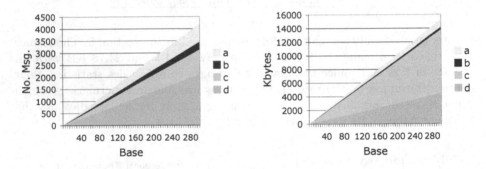

Fig. 8. Vertical Topology: # msg   **Fig. 9.** Message traffic in Kbytes

Table 5(b) shows the achieved message mix in the vertical topology. Figure 7 presents the same data in graphical form. Figures 8 and 9 shows how the number of messages of each type and the bandwidth they use are scaled as a function of the BASE parameter. Again, when scaling the workload the message mix remains constant which is the expected behavior. The sizes of the messages used in the various interactions are computed in the same way as for the horizontal topology (see Table 4).

4   Concluding Remarks

We presented a comprehensive workload characterization of the SPECjms2007 benchmark which is the world's first industry standard benchmark specialized for MOM. SPECjms2007 provides a flexible and robust tool that can be used for in-depth performance evaluation of MOM servers. However, in order to take advantage of this, users need to understand the way the workload is decomposed into components and which performance aspects are exercised by these components. The workload characterization presented in this paper is meant to help users gain an in-depth understanding of the SPECjms2007 workload and how it can be configured and customized. Our extensive analysis of the message traffic produced by the benchmark considered the following dimensions, i) message types and destinations, ii) message sizes, iii) message throughput and iv) message delivery modes. We characterized the message traffic both on a per interaction and location basis. The results we presented can be used to define a workload configuration that stresses selected features of the MOM infrastructure in a way that resembles a given target customer workload. Moreover, the traffic equations are essential for finding an optimal deployment topology with a uniform load distribution and no client-side bottlenecks. After considering the general freeform topology, we looked at the more specific horizontal and vertical topologies. We discussed their goals and characterized the interaction and message mixes they are based on and the way they are scaled. Our analysis not only helps to better understand and interpret official benchmark results, but also provides an example of how to define a scalable workload configuration for evaluating selected performance and scalability aspects of MOM.

Acknowledgments

This work was partially funded by the German Research Foundation. We acknowledge the contributions of the members of the SPECjms Working Group to the specification and development of SPECjms2007, in particular Marc Carter and Tim Dunn from IBM, George Tharakan from Sun Microsystems, Tom Barnes and Russell Raymundo from BEA, Evan Ireland from Sybase, and Adrian Co from Apache. We are also especially thankful to Lawrence Cullen, Robert Berry, Alan Adamson and John Stecher from IBM, Steve Realmuto from BEA and Ricardo Morin from Intel for their continued support of the SPECjms project.

References

1. ActiveMQ. JMeter performance test (2006),
   http://incubator.apache.org/activemq/jmeter-performance-tests.html
2. Alexander, K., Gillian, T., Gramling, K., Kindy, M., Moogimane, D., Schultz, M., Woods, M.: IBM Business Consulting Services - Focus on the Supply Chain: Applying Auto-ID within the Distribution Center. White paper IBM-AUTOID-BC-002 (2003)
3. Bornhövd, C., Lin, T., Haller, S., Schaper, J.: Integrating Automatic Data Acquisition with Business Processes - Experiences with SAP's Auto-ID Infrastructure. In: Proceedings of VLDB'04 (2004)
4. Carter, M.: JMS Performance with WebSphere MQ for Windows V6.0 (2005),
   http://www-1.ibm.com/support/docview.wss?rs=171\&uid=swg24010028

5. Crimson Consulting Group. High-Performance JMS Messaging - A Benchmark Comparison of Sun Java System Message Queue and IBM WebSphere MQ (2003)
6. Finkenzeller, K.: RFID Handbook: Fundamentals and Applications in Contactless Smart Cards and Identification, 2nd edn. John Wiley & Sons, Chichester (May 2003)
7. IBM Hursley. Performance Harness for Java Message Service (2005), http://www.alphaworks.ibm.com/tech/perfharness
8. JBoss. JBoss JMS New Performance Benchmark (2006), http://wiki.jboss.org/wiki/Wiki.jsp?page=JBossJMSNewPerformanceBenchmark
9. Kounev, S.: Performance Engineering of Distributed Component-Based Systems - Benchmarking, Modeling and Performance Prediction. Shaker Verlag (Dec 2005), ISBN: 3832247130
10. Kounev, S., Buchmann, A.: Improving Data Access of J2EE Applications by Exploiting Asynchronous Processing and Caching Services. In: Proceedings of VLDB'02 (2002)
11. Krissoft Solutions. JMS Performance Comparison (2006), http://www.fiorano.com/comp-analysis/jms_perf_report.htm
12. Sachs, K.: Evaluation of Performance Aspects of the SAP Auto-ID Infrastructure. Master's thesis, Department of Computer Science, Darmstadt University of Technology (2004)
13. Sachs, K., Kounev, S., Carter, M., Buchmann, A.: Designing a Workload Scenario for Benchmarking Message-Oriented Middleware. In: Proceedings of the 2007 SPEC Benchmark Workshop. SPEC (January 2007)
14. Sonic Software Corporation. SonicMQ Test Harness (2005)
15. Sun Microsystems Inc. Java Message Service (JMS) Specification Version 1.1(2002), http://java.sun.com/products/jms/docs.html

Resource Sharing in Performance Models

Vlastimil Babka, Martin Děcký, and Petr Tůma

Department of Software Engineering
Faculty of Mathematics and Physics, Charles University
Malostranské náměstí 25, Prague 1, 118 00, Czech Republic
{vlastimil.babka,martin.decky,petr.tuma}@dsrg.mff.cuni.cz

Abstract. In software systems, individual components interact not only through explicit function invocations, but also through implicit resource sharing. The use of shared resources significantly influences the duration of the invoked functions. For resources that are heavily shared, capturing this influence can lead to performance models that have a large number of elements and a large number of dependencies. We introduce an approach that can model resource sharing separately from function invocations, keeping the performance model reasonably simple while still describing many of the effects of resource sharing on the duration of function invocations. The approach has been tested on the CoCoME component application modeling example.

Keywords: enterprise systems, performance modeling, resource sharing.

1 Introduction

Our work focuses on performance models of software systems that describe the interaction of individual software components in terms of atomic actions, and that derive the duration of the atomic actions from the implementation of the components [15, 16, 17, 18, 26, 27, 29]. The duration of the atomic actions, needed to solve the performance model, is typically chosen to reflect the duration of function invocations on individual software components.

The duration of function invocations is typically determined by benchmarking. This, however, cannot be done by benchmarking the entire software system − if the entire software system were readily available and easily benchmarked, performance modeling would not be of much use. The individual components of the software system are thus benchmarked mostly in isolation and the average duration of function invocations determined by benchmarking applies to this isolated execution.

Unfortunately, the duration of a function invocation typically depends on the resources the function uses. When such resources are shared within a software system, the duration of the function invocation is likely to differ from the duration of the function invocation observed during the relatively isolated execution of benchmarks. Unless resource sharing is described in the performance model, this naturally impacts the performance model precision.

K. Wolter (Ed.): EPEW 2007, LNCS 4748, pp. 245–259, 2007.

Resource sharing is very common and in some cases, such as sharing of processor caches, physical memory, or disk caches, concerns many components. Describing these resources in a performance model increases the complexity of the model both in the number of elements and in the number of dependencies between elements. This is probably why even recent work on performance modeling of software systems often tends to omit some heavily shared resources [16, 17, 18, 26, 27, 29] or points out the high cost of solving the performance model when heavily shared resources are present [15]. Both intuition and evidence, however, suggest that these resources need to be modeled [13, 14].

To remedy the difficulties associated with describing heavily shared resources in performance modeling of software systems, we present an approach where resource sharing can be modeled separately from function invocations. Our combined model consists of the *resource model*, which describes how resources are used, and the *performance model*, which describes how functions are invoked.

The resource model and the performance model complement each other. To solve the resource model, knowledge of the interactions between the individual components and of the degree of parallelism inside the individual components is needed – and is provided by the performance model. Similarly, to solve the performance model, knowledge of the duration of the atomic actions is needed – and is provided by the resource model. The two models are solved iteratively.

We test our approach by modeling the performance of the architecture provided by CoCoME [5]. This architecture describes an enterprise information system responsible for tracking the stocks and sales of products in multiple stores. Its prototype implementation relies on contemporary middleware technologies such as ActiveMQ [1], Apache Derby [2] and Hibernate [11], and can be considered a reasonably realistic example of a software system for the purposes of performance modeling.

To describe our approach in detail, we first illustrate on examples of two heavily shared resources why we believe such resource sharing to be difficult to describe in performance models. We proceed by detailing the concept of separating the resource model and the performance model and explaining the complementary character of the two models. The test of our approach follows, with due evaluation and conclusion.

2   Resource Sharing

In the context of performance modeling, our definition of a resource includes any shared entity that individual components rely on in their execution. Typical resources are physical memory, processor with its various caches, disk with its caches and queues, and even entire file systems and network connections. The duration of function invocations, represented by the duration of atomic actions in performance models, naturally depends on the use of resources. The exact nature of this dependency is affected by the resource kind and by the way it is used. We select two common examples for a more detailed look.

2.1 Sharing Processor Cache

Processor cache is a resource that is shared inherently by any code running on the same processor. To illustrate how sharing of processor cache can change the duration of method invocation, we use two simple experiments with a Fast Fourier Transform library, FFT for short.

When processing data in a memory buffer, FFT will naturally perform faster if the memory buffer is cached. In our first experiment, we model a situation where FFT is one in a pipe of functions competing for the data cache. In detail, we fill the memory buffer with input data, simulate the competing functions by reading a set number of random addresses outside the buffer, and finally perform the FFT.[1] Figure 1 shows the dependence of the FFT duration on the number of the random addresses. As expected, increasing the portion of the buffer evicted from the cache by competing functions decreases the FFT performance.

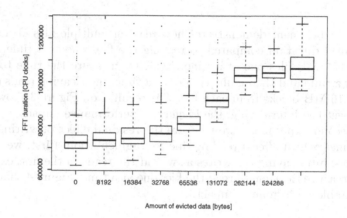

Fig. 1. Data cache sharing in FFT, one 128 KB buffer

As our second experiment, we show that the results can also be surprisingly different from expectations. The experiment is similar to the first one except in that it uses separate input and output buffers and runs on a different hardware[2] Figure 2 shows that the negative impact of data cache sharing is limited and that even a positive impact can be observed.

2.2 Sharing File System

File system is another frequently shared resource, or, rather, a complex of related resources whose sharing exhibits even residual effects, potentially affecting future operations. We illustrate two sharing effects via experiments.

---

[1] Intel Pentium 4 Northwood 2.2 GHz, 8 KB data L1, 12 KB code L1, 512 KB unified L2, Fedora Core 6. FFTW 3.1.1 *fftw_plan_dft_1d* [7].

[2] AMD Athlon 64 3000+ Venice DH7-CG 1.8 GHz, 64 KB data L1, 64 KB code L1, 512 KB unified L2.

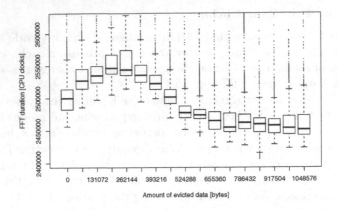

Fig. 2. Unusual effects of data cache sharing in FFT, two 320 KB buffers

The first experiment demonstrates how reading multiple files at a time prolongs the read duration compared to reading the files one at a time. First, we write four 256 MB files one at a time. Next, we measure the time to read the files one at a time and then multiple files at a time, interleaving reads of 32 KB, 1 MB and 16 MB blocks from each file. The results[3] on Figure 3 show that the more frequent the interleaving, the bigger the performance impact.

In the second experiment, we measure the residual effect of writing multiple files at a time, which affects reading due to fragmentation. First, we write four 256 MB files, interleaving the writes as we did the reads in the first experiment. Next, we measure the time to read the files one at a time. Figure 4 shows a small but measurable performance impact.

Block size	Read slowdown
32 KB	2.60 ± 0.32
1 MB	1.33 ± 0.04
16 MB	1.03 ± 0.04

Block size	Read slowdown
32 KB	1.06 ± 0.03
1 MB	1.05 ± 0.03
16 MB	1.02 ± 0.03

Fig. 3. Effect of interleaved reading

Fig. 4. Effect of interleaved writing

2.3   Describing Sharing

The common denominator of these two and other examples of resource sharing is that they are difficult to model precisely. When a performance model of a resource does exist, it typically focuses on a specific feature of the resource – for example, the cache models in [3,12] would not cover the processor cache example presented here simply because they did not focus on the interaction of multiple cache hierarchies, and the storage models in [6, 19] would not cover the file

---

[3] Intel Pentium 4 2.2 GHz, 512 MB RAM, Hitachi 250 GB ATA, Fedora Core 5, *ext3*.

system example presented here simply because they did not focus on interleaving and fragmentation. Furthermore, the performance models of resources can be based on a different formalism than the performance model of a software system, making their integration difficult.

Another observation is that often, the general knowledge of how a resource performs when shared is based on measurement rather than modeling. Instead of using modeling to predict performance issues, we use measurement to discover and understand performance issues and revert to modeling to confirm our understanding. The fact that even this method of arriving at understanding requires considerable amount of work [10, 20] underscores our argument that heavily shared resources are inherently difficult to describe in performance models.

We believe that one approach to tackling the complexity of describing resource sharing is separating the resource model and the performance model for heavily shared resources as described next.

3   Combined Performance Model

To explain the concept of separating the resource model and the performance model, let us first consider a performance model of a software system that omits some heavily shared resources and that describes the interaction of the individual components in terms of atomic actions whose average durations are known. These average durations have been determined by measuring the durations of corresponding function invocations in a benchmark experiment.

Since function invocations use the omitted resources, we can only expect the performance model to provide a good approximation of the software system when the benchmark experiment that provided the average durations of atomic actions used a good approximation of the resource usage. In the examples from Section 2, if we were to model software that frequently evicts data from processor caches, we would have to frequently evict data from processor caches in the benchmark. Similarly, if we were to model software that uses heavily fragmented files, we would have to use heavily fragmented files in the benchmark.

The question that we need to ask is therefore how well we can approximate resource usage in the benchmark experiment. For further discussion, we describe resource usage as consisting of two related factors, *mode* of resource usage and *degree* of resource usage.

3.1   Mode of Resource Usage

The mode of resource usage describes in which way the resource is used – this concerns details such as access patterns, strategies, interleaving, etc. On our examples of the processor cache and file system resources, mode of resource usage boils down to issues including strong or weak locality of memory references, sequential or random character of file accesses, ratio of file reads to writes, etc.

These issues are not only specific to each resource, but also difficult to formalize and quantify. Fortunately, we can avoid the need for formalizing and quantifying the mode of resource usage by designing the benchmark experiment so that it resembles the scenario we are modeling. This is routinely done by many benchmarks, such as TPC [23], which resembles transaction processing applications, or RUBiS [21], which resembles an on-line bidding application.

We can conclude that as far as the mode of resource usage goes, benchmarks that provide the average durations to the performance model can be designed to resemble the scenarios we want to model and therefore approximate the mode of resource usage in these scenarios. Note, however, that this does not yet guarantee that the benchmarks will provide useful average durations, a simultaneous approximation of the degree of resource usage is needed for that as well.

3.2   Degree of Resource Usage

The degree of resource usage describes how much the resource is used – this concerns details such as capacity, size or rate of requests and replies, parallelism, etc. On our examples of the processor cache and file system resources, degree of resource usage boils down to issues including cache and working set sizes, number of threads and rate of context switches, number of concurrent file readers and writers, etc.

Compared to the mode of resource usage, these issues are relatively easy to quantify. Unlike the mode of resource usage, however, we cannot approximate the degree of resource usage by designing the benchmark experiment so that it resembles the scenario we are modeling. The mode of resource usage is typically an input to performance modeling, but the degree of resource usage is related to the output of performance modeling and therefore not available when designing the benchmark experiment.

To illustrate the argument, consider the examples of the TPC and RUBiS benchmarks. When designing a benchmark experiment that would approximate the database usage in these benchmarks, we can easily approximate the mode of usage, because the specification of the benchmarks includes the types and ratios of queries and updates to be executed. We cannot, however, approximate the degree of usage, because the specification of the benchmarks does not say how frequently the queries and updates are executed or how many queries or updates are executed in parallel. This information is what would be the output of the benchmarks – or the output of performance modeling, if we were to model rather than execute the benchmarks.

3.3   Iterating Between Models

As outlined, we are faced with a situation where we could expect the performance model to give us good results, if only we could feed it with good approximations of the average durations of atomic actions – and we could use benchmark experiments to provide us with good approximations of the average durations, if only we could design the experiments knowing what degree of resource usage to approximate – or, in other words, knowing the results of the performance model. In principle, this situation can be solved by starting with a sensible degree of resource usage and then iterating between using the benchmark experiments to obtain the average durations of atomic actions for the current degree of resource usage and solving the performance model to obtain an updated degree of resource usage. If and when the iteration stabilizes, the results will be based on good approximations of the average durations of atomic actions.

Generally, benchmark experiments tend to be cumbersome and expensive, which is why, as a final step of our approach, we replace them in the iteration by performance models of resources. Together, the performance models of heavily shared resources form a *resource model*, which complements the *performance model* of the software system. In light of the arguments from Section 2, we note that the resource model remains separate from the performance model, giving us freedom in the choice of formalisms and even allowing us to arbitrarily combine the resource model with benchmark experiments when our knowledge of how a resource performs is not sufficient to construct a precise model – as would be the case with examples from Sections 2.1 and 2.2.

An obvious question is whether the iteration between the two models ever converges. As there are no constraints on either of the two models, convergence is generally impossible to guarantee – in fact, for all but trivial cases, a resource model or a performance model that prevents the iteration from converging can be constructed. We can, however, argue that the iteration between the resource model and the performance model that describes certain workload resembles initial behavior of the software system when put under that workload – as the iteration adjusts the resource usage and thus the average durations of atomic actions, so does the software system react to the workload by changing the average durations of function invocations. An oscillation or divergence in the iteration can therefore suggest a tendency towards similar behavior in the software system.

Finally, we should point out that the iteration does not accumulate error. For a given degree of resource usage, the resource model outputs the average durations of function invocations with an error inherent only to that model. The same is respectively true for the performance model. The errors therefore bear influence on the progress of the iteration, but when the iteration stabilizes, the results are precise up to the errors introduced in the last cycle only.

4   Proof of Concept Example

We have chosen the Common Component Modeling Example, or CoCoME [5] for short, as a proof of concept platform for our combined model. CoCoME describes an enterprise information system that keeps track of *products* sold by a chain of *stores*. When stocked by a store, a product is represented by a *stock item* that has a bar code, a price and an amount as its important attributes. Sale of an item is done at one of the *cash desks* of a store, which locates the item by its bar code, shows its price and, when the sale completes, decrements its amount in the stock.

CoCoME has been created with emphasis on practical usability. The architecture is reasonably large and comes with a reference implementation in Java. This prototype implementation uses contemporary middleware technologies such as ActiveMQ [1], Apache Derby [2] and Hibernate [11], which makes it similar to the platforms modeled recently for example in [16, 17, 18, 24, 26, 27, 29].

When creating our combined model, we have further relied on the fact that the CoCoME architecture has been described within the SOFA component framework [22]. This description includes the deployment plan, which provides us with information on the placement of individual components of the application on the nodes that run it, and the behavior model, which provides us with information on the interactions between individual components. This information is used to construct the resource model.

4.1 Performance Model

The obvious performance related question in CoCoME is how many concurrent sales it can handle. To answer this question, we build our performance model by identifying the activities that make up the sale or that interfere with the sale and representing them explicitly in the performance model. Each sale consists of scanning the bar codes of the items being sold – a scan is followed by a query of the stock item in the database – and of booking the sale – a booking is done by an update of the amounts of stock items in the database. This activity is at the core of our performance model.

Other activities described by the CoCoME architecture, such as handling of customers that do not have enough money to pay for the sale, have been omitted from the performance model. These activities have no impact on how many concurrent sales can be handled, and their omission allows us to keep the model reasonably simple.

We have also decided to simplify activities of the components that are deployed on embedded devices and are unlikely to represent performance bottlenecks – for example, we do not model the bar code scanner or the cash desk display components separately as they are always serving only a single sale and there is little chance that the sale would progress at a speed that the bar code scanner or the cash desk display cannot handle. As a result, each cash desk is modeled by a single component that calls atomic actions at the rate that corresponds to the time elapsing between scans of individual items.

For the formalism of the performance model, we have decided to adopt LQN [28] – the feedback from LQN to the resource model will take the form of queue length and processor utilization values. Another choice would be adopting SPN [9] – the feedback from SPN to the resource model would take the form of numbers of tokens in selected places. Both LQN and SPN were reported to achieve good results when modeling enterprise information systems [4].

The CoCoME specification defines the rates of requests, size of sales and other properties necessary to seed the performance model with proper constants. Where defined using tabulated distribution functions, we have used averages instead.

4.2   Resource Model

The performance model needs the resource model to provide the average durations of two atomic actions, namely the stock item query and the sale booking update. Benchmarking experiments with the middleware used by the CoCoME reference implementation suggest that these durations are most sensitive to the use of system memory and to the use of database cache, which is why we describe these two resources in our model.

The model of the database cache assumes that the query and the update operations either use cached data or fetch data from disk and that the probability of the two alternatives depends on the relative size of the cache with respect to the size of the database. Similarly, the model of the system memory assumes that the query and the update operations access some resident pages and some swapped out pages and that the frequency of swapping depends on the relative usage of memory with respect to the total amount of available memory.

We therefore start the construction of the resource model by determining the average durations of the two alternatives of the query and update operations by benchmark experiments, see Figure 5. Similarly, we get the additive unit overhead of swapping, which is 162 ms.

Operation	Query time (ms)	Update time (ms)
cached	5.53	75
fetched	8.31	169

Fig. 5. Average durations of the atomic operations

To determine what is the probability of each variant of the atomic operations, we need to calculate the degree of resource usage in the resource model, which depends on the particular implementation of the resources.

The implementation uses Hibernate for persistent representation of stock items in the database. Hibernate caches data separately for each transaction. The memory usage therefore grows linearly (i) with the number of transactions executing simultaneously and (ii) with the size of the data fetched in each transaction. The number of transactions executing simultaneously is not bounded, the size of the fetched data is bounded by the size of the database.

The database is Apache Derby, which keeps separate context for each connection and caches pages for all transactions together. Its memory usage therefore grows linearly (i) with the number of connections opened simultaneously and (ii) with the size of the data cached for all transactions. The number of simultaneous connections is bounded by the size of the Hibernate connection pool, the cache size is bounded by a configurable maximum cache size.

Considering the configurable maximum cache size with the default value of 10000 pages ($pages_{available}$), 4096 bytes each ($size_{page}$), and a single stock item occupying 460 bytes ($size_{stockitem}$), the probability that a query or an update is cached can be computed as the equation (4.1) suggests.

$$pages_{used} = \frac{size_{page}}{size_{stockitem}} \cdot products \cdot stores$$

$$P_{cached} = \min\left(1, \frac{pages_{available}}{pages_{used}}\right) \tag{4.1}$$

Considering a node with 512 MB of physical memory, of which 451 MB was available for applications ($memory_{available}$), the degree of memory usage is determined by two constituents listed in equation (4.4) – the memory occupied by the code and static data of the components from equation (4.3) (memory shared by the running virtual machines, memory private to each virtual machine, memory private to the database) – and the memory consumed by the concurrent activities from equation (4.2) (memory consumed per database connection, memory consumed per query).

$$usage_{concurrency} = \lceil concurrency \rceil \cdot usage_{connection} \tag{4.2}$$

$$usage_{components} = usage_{shared} + stores \cdot usage_{store} + usage_{database} \tag{4.3}$$

Given the degree of memory usage, the probability that a query or an update does not require swapping can be very roughly approximated by equation (4.5). Note that a rough approximation suffices since swapping should not occur during normal mode of operation, whose performance modeling is of interest.

$$memory_{used} = usage_{components} + usage_{concurrency} \tag{4.4}$$

$$P_{resident} = \min\left(1, \frac{memory_{available}}{memory_{used}}\right) \tag{4.5}$$

Concurrency represents the number of concurrent queries. During iteration, it is provided by the performance model, except for the initial value, which is taken to be zero. The solution of the performance model consists of the throughput and the observed service times of the atomic operations, the number of concurrent queries corresponds to the length of the queue of requests on the database component and is calculated using equation (4.6).

$$concurrency = queue_{length} = \sum_{m \in ops} throughput_m \cdot time_m \tag{4.6}$$

The value of *concurrency* is used by the resource model to recalculate the total memory usage $usage_{concurrency}$ and the probability $P_{resident}$ – the probability P_{cached} does not depend on *concurrency*. The iteration is repeated until the results converge, using a simple ϵ stability criterion.

4.3   Results

The results provided by our combined model in the form of an average throughput in stock items processed per second and an average time spent on each sale

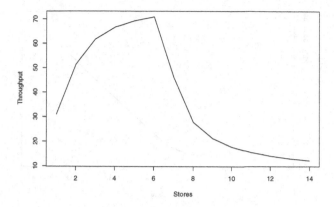

Fig. 6. Throughput calculated from the combined model (8 cash desks per store)

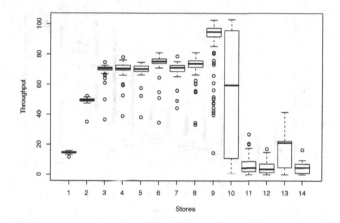

Fig. 7. Throughput benchmarked on the prototype (8 cash desks per store)

are displayed on Figures 6 and 8. The figures plot dependency of the throughput and round-trip values on the number of cash desks per store and the number of stores per enterprise as the scalability factors.

On average, the combined model needed only three iterations to converge. This is because the memory consumption per query is relatively low compared to the total memory consumption. The value of the *concurrency* variable at the end of the iteration was approximately 1.24 for a single store with 8 cash desks, 5.16 for two stores, 11.57 for three stores and growing rapidly. We can therefore conclude that the effect of memory consumption per query is not negligible.

For comparison, the results of a real benchmark of the CoCoME reference implementation are on Figures 7 and 9. The benchmark, as well as the benchmark experiments used to obtain the average durations of the atomic actions, have used an Intel Pentium 4 Xeon 2.2 GHz machine with 512 MB RAM running Fedora Core 6 and the database cache of 10000 pages for the server machine,

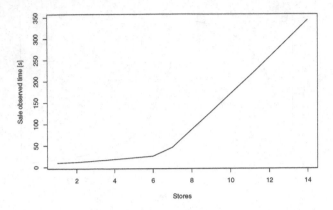

Fig. 8. Round-trip calculated from the combined model (8 cash desks per store)

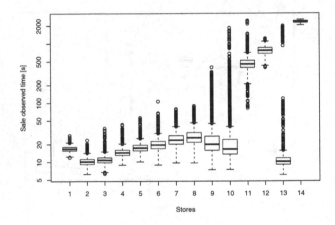

Fig. 9. Round-trip benchmarked on the prototype (8 cash desks per store)

and a dual Intel Core 2 Quad Xeon 1.8 GHz machine with 8 GB RAM running Fedora Core 6 for the client machine. The relatively low amount of memory on the server machine was used deliberately to allow the manifestation of swapping with a reasonably small number of cash desks and stores.

5   Evaluation

One approach to evaluating our method is comparing the results predicted by the combined model on Figures 6 and 8 with the results measured by the real benchmark on Figures 7 and 9. This comparison suggests that the approach is reasonably precise – the maximum throughput predicted by the model is 71 stock items per second, the maximum throughput measured by the benchmark is 74 stock items per second. Similarly, the duration of a sale predicted by the model is 10 seconds for one store (with 8 cash desks) and grows to around 26 seconds before the server starts swapping, the duration of a sale measured by the benchmark is 17 seconds for one store and grows to around 25 seconds before the server starts swapping. If a better precision were desired, the usual calibration of the model could be employed as in [24, 26].

As stated in the introduction, however, our goal is not predicting the exact values of round-trip and throughput, but predicting how the values of round-trip and throughput change when the scale of the application changes. Comparing the results, we see that our approach predicted getting within 10% of the maximum throughput around 2 stores, when the measurement shows this happening around 3 stores. Our approach also predicts the onset of swapping and the associated degradation in throughput around 8 stores, when the measurement shows this happening around 10 stores. The difference can be explained by our inability to determine the precise memory requirements of the individual components, something that is difficult to do with current tools.

When comparing our results to the results of other researchers, we did not achieve that good a precision in predicting the values of round-trip and throughput. We believe that this is not inherent to our approach but specific to the proof of concept performance model, which has been kept intentionally simple – our approach allows us to easily reuse performance models such as those in [24, 26].

We note, however, that of the models of similar platforms in [16, 17, 18, 24, 26, 27, 29], none is able to predict the onset of swapping and the associated degradation of performance due to resource sharing of computer memory. We believe that this is a result of practical importance in performance modeling.

Finally, we should point out that early work recognizing the importance of resource models in addition to performance models exists, such as [25]. There, complexity functions in workload models are introduced to provide the contention model, which corresponds to the performance model in our terminology, with information on resource usage. The work, however, still expects that resource sharing will be described together with component interaction inside the contention model, which is something that we argue is too complex.

The idea of iterating between the resource model and the performance model can also be seen as an extension of earlier iterative approaches to solving the performance models. For illustration, [15] describes solving the performance model iteratively in initialization and simulation phases, with the initialization phase calculating service times and routing probabilities based on an assumed value that the simulation phase adjusts. The work, however, gives no details on this value and views the entire iteration as an unfortunate consequence of the performance model complexity.

6   Conclusion

We have described an approach to performance modeling of software systems based on creating a combined model, in which a resource model and a performance model complement each other in an iterative calculation. The advantage of the approach is that it allows modeling heavily shared resources separately from other concerns, keeping the combined model reasonably simple.

We use an example of an enterprise information system to show that even with very simple resource and performance models, the effects of resource sharing can be predicted. We use the average durations of only four variants of two atomic actions determined by benchmarking experiments for the resource model, and only six tasks in the performance model. With that, we predict the effects of both database cache sharing and system memory sharing, including the conditions of resource exhaustion, which are rarely modeled elsewhere.

Our approach is based on the assumption that resource usage can be described as consisting of two factors – mode of usage and degree of usage, where the mode is determined by the scenario we are modeling and captured by the resource model, and the degree is determined by the performance of the system we are modeling and provided by the performance model. We believe that our approach has a potential to work for heavily shared resources such as physical memory or file systems, where long periods of stable execution are considered. In these situations, the effects of resource sharing can often be modeled relatively simply in the resource model, without cluttering the performance model.

An obvious requirement of our approach is being able to model the behavior of individual resources. In this aspect, our approach retains the options of using benchmark experiments to measure the resource, using a separate performance model to model the resource, or modeling the resource as a part of the integrated performance model of the entire software system. We should therefore always be better off than approaches that only have one integrated performance model.

Acknowledgments. The authors would like to thank the team working on the SOFA model of the CoCoME architecture for providing a supporting framework, especially the deployment plan and the behavior model. This work was partially supported by the Grant Agency of the Czech Republic project GD201/05/H014 and by the Czech Academy of Sciences project 1ET400300504.

References

1. ActiveMQ, http://activemq.apache.org
2. Apache Derby, http://db.apache.org/derby
3. Agarwal, A., Hennessy, J., Horowitz, M.: An Analytical Cache Model. In: TOCS, vol. 7(2), ACM Press, New York (1989)
4. Balsamo, S., DiMarco, A., Inverardi, P., Simeoni, M.: Model-Based Performance Prediction in Software Development. In: TSE, IEEE Computer Society Press, Los Alamitos (2004)
5. CoCoME, http://agrausch.informatik.uni-kl.de/CoCoME
6. Drakopoulos, E., Merges, M.J.: Performance Analysis of Client-Server Storage Systems. In: TC, IEEE Computer Society Press, Los Alamitos (1992)
7. Frigo, M., Johnson, S.G.: FFTW, http://www.fftw.org
8. Ghosh, A., Givargis, T.: Cache Optimization for Embedded Processor Cores: An Analytical Approach. In: TODAES, vol. 9(4), ACM Press, New York (2004)

9. Haas, P.J.: Stochastic Petri Nets: Modelling, stability, simulation. Springer, Heidelberg (2002)
10. Hauswirth, M., Diwan, A., Sweeney, P.F., Mozer, M.C.: Automating Vertical Profiling. In: OOPSLA'05, ACM Press, New York (2005)
11. Hibernate, http://www.hibernate.org
12. Hossain, A., Pease, D.J.: An Analytical Model for Trace Cache Instruction Fetch Performance. In: ICCD'01, IEEE Computer Society Press, Los Alamitos (2001)
13. Kalibera, T., Bulej, L., Tuma, P.: Benchmark Precision and Random Initial State. In: SPECTS'05, SCS (2005)
14. Kannan, H., Guo, F., Zhao, L., Illikkal, R., Iyer, R., Newell, D., Solihin, Y., Kozyrakis, C.: From Chaos to QoS: Case Studies in CMP Resource Management. In: SIGARCH CAN, vol. 35(1), ACM Press, New York (2007)
15. Kant, K., Sundaram, C.R.M.: A Server Performance Model for Static Web Workloads. In: ISPASS'00, IEEE Computer Society Press, Los Alamitos (2000)
16. Kounev, S., Buchmann, A.: Performance Modeling of Distributed E-Business Applications using Queuing Petri Nets. In: ISPASS'03, IEEE Computer Society Press, Los Alamitos (2003)
17. Liu, Y., Gorton, I.: Performance Prediction of J2EE Applications Using Messaging Protocols. In: Heineman, G.T., Crnković, I., Schmidt, H.W., Stafford, J.A., Szyperski, C.A., Wallnau, K. (eds.) CBSE 2005. LNCS, vol. 3489, Springer, Heidelberg (2005)
18. Liu, Y., Fekete, A., Gorton, I.: Predicting the Performance of Middleware-Based Applications at the Design Level. In: WOSP'04, ACM Press, New York (2004)
19. Pentakalos, O.I., Menasce, D.A., Halem, M., Yesha, Y.: An Approximate Performance Model of a Unitree Mass Storage System. In: MSS'95, IEEE Computer Society Press, Los Alamitos (1995)
20. Pimentel, A.D., Thompson, M., Polstra, S., Erbas, C.: On the Calibration of Abstract Performance Models for System-Level Design Space Exploration. In: SAMOS'06, IEEE Computer Society Press, Los Alamitos (2006)
21. RUBiS, http://rubis.objectweb.org
22. SOFA Component Model, http://dsrg.mff.cuni.cz/sofa
23. TPC Benchmarks, http://www.tpc.org/information/benchmarks.asp
24. Ufimtsev, A., Murphy, L.: Performance Modeling of a JavaEE Component Application using Layered Queuing Networks: Revised Approach and a Case Study. In: SAVCBS'06, ACM Press, New York (2006)
25. Vetland, V.: Measurement-Based Composite Computational Work Modelling of Software, Doctoral thesis, University of Trondheim (1993)
26. Xu, J., Oufimtsev, A., Woodside, C.M., Murphy, L.: Performance Modeling and Prediction of Enterprise JavaBeans with Layered Queuing Network Templates. In: SIGSOFT SEN, vol. 31(2), ACM, New York (2006)
27. Xu, J., Woodside, C.M.: Template-Driven Performance Modeling of Enterprise Java Beans. In: MWS'05, IEEE Computer Society Press, Los Alamitos (2005)
28. Woodside, C.M., Neron, E., Ho, E.D.S., Mondoux, B.: An Active-Server Model for the Performance of Parallel Programs Written Using Rendezvous. In: JSS, vol. 6(1-2), Elsevier, Amsterdam (1986)
29. Wu, X.P., Woodside, C.M.: Performance Modeling from Software Components. In: WOSP'04, ACM Press, New York (2004)

Exploiting Commodity Hard-Disk Geometry to Efficiently Preserve Data Consistency

Alessandro Di Marco

DISI, Università di Genova
Via Dodecaneso, 35
16146 Genova, Italy
dmr@disi.unige.it

Abstract. In the last couple of years, hard-disk technology has experienced an unjustified progressive boost of the built-in cache size, affecting both the power consumption and the reliability of stored data. Large built-in caches offer limited benefits in terms of performance with respect to the smaller ones. Moreover, they need to be kept in write-through mode to preserve data in case of a power failure in mission-critical systems. This implies severe repercussions on the disk write performance, due to the role of the built-in cache itself, mainly acting as a write scheduler, rather than just a mere I/O buffer, as its ever increasing size would suggest.

In this scenario, an exact hard-disk characterization can provide the upper layers enough information to compensate the performance loss produced by the write-through policy. File-systems and device-drivers can in fact obviate most of these issues via proper data layouts, depending on a detailed knowledge of the hard-disks geometry.

This paper introduces the chunk skew layout, a novel data layout strategy targeted to improve the performance of commodity hard-disks in mission-critical systems. For this purpose we also analyze the differences in terms of geometry and performance in a batch of identical commodity hard-disks, discovering an unexpected and more complex scenario where most of the assumptions made so far on hard-disk technology do not hold anymore.

Keywords: disk drives, performance, rotational latency reduction, data layout, disk characterization, measurement techniques.

1 Introduction

For decades magnetic disk drives have been the preferred components for secondary data storage. This induced a sustained innovation in the hard-drive industry, providing an incredible speedup in terms of both performance and capacity of the disks at any price-range. Unfortunately, although disk storage densities starting from the beginning of the 90s have improved at the amazing rate of nearly 178 percent per year[1], in the same period performance has improved

---

[1] Which rises to 181 percent per year, considering the platter densities.

K. Wolter (Ed.): EPEW 2007, LNCS 4748, pp. 260–274, 2007.

about 135 percent per year. As a result, performance became a dominant factor in overall disk system behavior.

The performance speedup of modern hard-disks with respect to the older ones is mainly due to the presence of an internal buffer, also called *built-in cache*. In the past this buffer has grown with the disk size, up to the dramatical size of the latest SCSI drives that can reach more than 16MB. Built-in cache contributes significantly to the efficient hard-disk management, acting as *read cache, read-ahead cache* and *write cache* [1,2,3]. Its improvements are quite evident. For example, disabling one of these features in a modern hard-disk could easily lead to a performance drop up to 80 percent. Nevertheless there is some concern regarding the real advantages in equipping hard-disks with such large buffers, affecting both the power consumption and the reliability of stored data. Moreover, research showed that caches larger than 512KB are of little impact on performance [4].

The built-in cache of commodity hard-disks is usually made of ordinary RAM, losing its content in case of power failure. To see how this can impact on reliability of stored data, consider that built-in cache can be used for writing either in *write-back* or *write-through* mode. The first case is the faster, as write requests are considered completed as soon as all their data have been transferred to the cache, but not necessarily to the disk media [5]. This has the effect of drastically reducing the write latency, but also exposes to the risk of data loss in case of power shortage [6,1]. Obviously, the larger the cache is, the higher are the chances of losing some important data.

There are quite few solutions to this problem, one of them consists in employing high-end SCSI hard-disks. These not-so-cheap devices in fact are equipped with a battery backed-up built-in cache, which effectively protects against these risks [1]. A second possibility pursued by some hardware manufacturers in the attempt to use cheaper commodity hard-disks in mission-critical environments, consists in adopting special RAID [7] controllers equipped with built-in battery backed caches [8,9]. This lets hard-disks provide the maximum throughput in write-back mode, yet with the guarantee that data are safely retained by the controller cache in case of power loss. A third possibility consists in employing SATA-II hard-disks. These latest generation commodity hard-disks provide Native Command Queuing (NCQ), a powerful interface/disc technology designed to increase performance by allowing the drive to internally optimize the execution order of workloads [10]. As a consequence, under some assumptions NCQ-powered hard-disks can reach their maximum speed also in write-through mode.

Nevertheless, all these solutions do not completely solve the problem. There are cases, in fact, where they cannot be adopted. In software RAIDs, for example, neither is there space for pricey high-end hard-disks nor would it be viable to equip each participating workstation with a battery backed RAID controller. Furthermore, the NCQ performance advantage can only be realized by queuing a number of write operations in the drive [10]. This poses at least two problems. First, a large number of applications still perform synchronous I/O. Second, asynchronous I/O applications would be subjected to data consistency problems in case of power failure, due to the potential write operation reordering produced by the NCQ technology within the drive's internal command queue.

In these cases, the only feasible solution to guarantee the data consistency seems to resort to the legacy write-through mode [6,5,1], where requests are considered completed only when they are physically on-disk and no implicit command reordering is performed. Unfortunately, this operative way constitutes a serious performance bottle-neck that makes it unaffordable in data intensive contexts.

This paper describes the *chunk skew layout*, a novel data layout that can be effectively exploited to improve the streaming disk performance in write-through mode. As we will discuss, the effectiveness of this layout is highly location-dependent, and therefore an appropriate software has been developed to automatically tune-up its parameters during the deployment phase. As Section 4 reports, this layout proved to be really effective, scoring up to 400 percent of performance speedup with respect to the legacy disk layout for sequential write operations. For a thorough evaluation of this layout, different workloads characteristics should be also taken into account; a successive version of this paper will contain a complete analysis in such sense.

The balance of the paper is as follows: Section 2 provides basic details on hard-disks functioning, Section 3 covers the hard-disks characterization problem, Section 4 analyzes the chunk skew layout. Finally, Section 5 concludes this work discussing the effectiveness of the proposed layout.

2 Hard-Disk Basics

This section covers the basic details to introduce the reader to the techniques involved in the paper; please refer to [1,11] for a thorough analysis on hard-disks functioning.

Hard-disks are essentially composed of two parts: an *interface* and a *disk-head assembly*. The interface has a dual role, consisting both in communicating with the clients and in managing the disk-head compound. The latter involves complex work, usually carried out by a programmable micro-controller, rather than dedicated electronic components. The micro-controller can also use a built-in buffer to speedup the operations. All the requests that are not directly satisfiable by the built-in buffer are directed to the disk-head assembly. A hard-disk is usually formed by multiple platters, each one surrounded by two heads (one per surface) attached to a bar called *arm*. Each platter is then split into *tracks*, concentric rings ranging from the outer to the internal border of the platter. A set of tracks (one per platter), all with the same distance from the center, is called a *cylinder*. Cylinders are a direct consequence of the fact that the arms are all tied together, so switching between tracks on the same cylinder requires theoretically less time than switching between tracks on different ones. Unfortunately, this is no longer true on modern hard-disks for short head displacements [1]. In other words, a disk contains as many cylinders as tracks in any of its platters. Finally, each track is then divided into a certain number of fixed length *sectors* (usually 512 bytes).

Older hard-disk models were characterized by uniform sized tracks. This choice was quite expensive in terms of storage efficiency. Outer tracks were in fact longer than the inner ones, and in the last few years hard-disk manufacturers have decided to adopt *variable sized tracks*. The disk surface has been therefore split into *zones*, each characterized by a different track density. Clearly this implies a greater controller complexity, due to its central role in translating a given Logical Block Address (LBA) to the corresponding head, cylinder and sector coordinates. In legacy LBA scheme, a disk is seen as a big mono-dimensional array of sectors, numbered starting from zero. The absolute sector number is the logical block address.

Once the target sectors have been identified on disk, the micro-controller can start issuing proper signals to the disk-head assembly to fulfill the request. It starts switching to the desired head, moving simultaneously the heads on the right cylinder (seek action). This is probably the most complex hard-disk activity, so it has been divided in four phases [1]: *speedup, coast, slowdown* and *settle*. Firstly, the arm is accelerated until it reaches half of the seek distance or a fixed maximum velocity (speedup). Only with the longest seeks the arm is allowed to move at the maximum speed for a while (coast). Then the arm is brought to remain close to the desired cylinder (slowdown) and finally the micro-controller can adjust the head to access the desired location (settle). Clearly, in case of short seeks the time spent in this last phase (settle time) dominates over the other ones. At the end of the settle phase the head is guaranteed to be on the correct track, so that the micro-controller has only to wait that the requested sectors run under the head. When the disk's head moves, the time spent between the beginning of the speedup and the end of the settle phases is called *seek latency*, whereas the time wasted between the end of the settle phase and the start of the data transfer is called *rotational latency*.

In the worst case, rotational latencies can last for several milliseconds, corresponding to a whole disk revolution. As a consequence, the overall disk performance could degrade if the interface does not carefully handle the I/O requests. Clearly this does not affect only random accesses, but also the sequential ones, when the disk's head has to move from the end of a track to the start of the next one. In such cases, once the disk's head reaches the last sector of the first track, the micro-controller triggers a seek action that, due to the extreme proximity of the target, lasts roughly as much as the settle time. Being directly proportional to the disk's track density [1,11], this time is non-negligible on the high-density hard-disks of the last generation[2]. As a consequence, keeping aligned the start sectors of the disk tracks entails a rotational latency per seek. Older hard-disks relied upon two different approaches to prevent rotational latencies in seek actions, namely, *head skew* and *cylinder skew*. These consisted in a way to compensate the seek latency by shifting ahead the start sector of the next track of a certain amount. However, this distinction is no more true for latest generation

---

[2] One fifth of the rotational latency at least.

hard-disks anymore (i.e. head and cylinder skews are pretty much the same), so we will refer to both with the more general *track skew* term. The track skew accounts for the track switch delay to maximize streaming bandwidth.

Carefully calculated track skews can keep the rotational latencies out from the sequential transfers. Unfortunately this is not enough to gather the maximum throughput out of a hard-disk. A central role in this case is held by the built-in buffer. At first it accumulates requests in order to eliminate the *host transfer delay*[3] [14]. Without the built-in buffer, the disk would in fact accept a single request at a time, spending a non-negligible amount of time in idle between the notification of the end of a request and the arrival of the next one. Clearly, the built-in buffer latencies are far lower than the host transfer delay, and therefore the client experiences a substantial performance improvement. As a secondary effect, the built-in cache also guarantees prolonged sequential data transfers at the maximum speed. This is due to the fact that a single request encompasses only a limited amount of data. As a consequence, in the time the host transfers the next request, the disk's head has already run beyond the right starting sector, introducing an extra disk's revolution delay between adjacent write requests on the same track. Instead, thanks to the negligible latency of the built-in buffer accumulating the write requests, the disk is able to promptly serve them without extra delays.

From the above discussion, host transfer delay and rotational latency turn out to be the main reasons for the poor performance provided by hard-disks when their built-in buffers work in write-through mode. Rotational latency results far more penalizing than the other (nearly 70% of performance drop off). Therefore, addressing it would provide a significant performance improvement for the streaming write operations in write-through mode. Our contribution in this sense consists in the chunk skew layout, a novel way to displace groups of sectors, called *chunks*, in a way similar to the tracks one. This is quite different from other well known approaches, which attempt to maximize the disk's performance by preserving the track alignment (see [13] for example). On the opposite, our approach is targeted to synchronize the disk's head position with the stored data in order to avoid rotational delays. The track-to-track switch time is negligible if compared with rotational latency. As a consequence, it produces only a minimal slow-down in the disk's performance that anyway can be readily overcome in the chunk skew layout via extra chunks displacements, targeted to avoid that a given chunk spans over adjacent tracks. On the other hand, without proper hardware support (e.g. a FIFO buffer), we can only rely on synchronous write operations in write-through mode: a given request has to wait for the completion of the previous one before being sent out to the disk. This leaves little room to address at the software level the host transfer delay, roughly accounting for 30 percent of the transfer time in our testbed (see Section 3).

As discussed in Section 4, our testbed showed that skewing 13 percent of the track size is enough to avoid rotational delays between adjacent chunks

---

[3] Time elapsed between the generation of a request and its receipt on the disk's interface (also known as *host delay* [12] or *bus transfer time* [13]).

in 90 percent of the cases, providing a substantial speedup of the disk's I/O performance in write-through mode. Better results can be further gained by fine-tuning this value based on the disk's properties. Chunk skew layout is in fact highly dependent on parameters such as *disk rotation speed, seek latency, tracks size*, and so on.

3   Hard-Disks Characterization

Several hard-disk characterization papers have been published [15,16,17,18], all sharing the same basic approach[4]. It consists in measuring the access time for a plurality of sectors on the disk drive, performing alternately the following steps. First, (in the order) accessing an *anchor sector* and a *successive sector* of the disk drive. Second, measuring the *completion time* of the accesses.

For example, in order to measure the disk rotational latency we can subtract the completion times of two successive accesses to the *same* disk sector [15].

The parameters related to the data layout geometry of the disk drive are inferred from the measured completion times. Clearly this must be done without resorting to the built-in buffer, in order to avoid measuring its latency in place of the sought rotational latency. A second method, that does not suffer from the built-in buffer activity consists in accessing two adjacent sectors in reverse order, causing a slightly minor precision.

We started measuring the rotational latency on a testbed of 29 Maxtor ATA/133 80GB hard-disks, sharing the same model number (6Y080P0) and firmware revision (YAR41BW0). We modified the 2.6.20.1 version of the Linux kernel to measure the completion time of any given I/O request directly in the IDE driver, respectively before and after the DMA activity. This gives far more accurate measurements than the usual queue-level approach commonly adopted by hard-disk benchmarks. Moreover, for the maximum accuracy we rely on the rdtscll() function to sample the clock cycles counter, containing the number of clock cycles elapsed since the CPU powered on. These values are then converted into milliseconds via a simple division by the CPU clock rate.

With the above instrumentation we obtained estimations of the rotational delay in accordance with the Maxtor's specifications (7200 RPM +/- 1%) for every hard-disk in the testbed. On the other end, some problems arose with the zones measurements. From Section 2, a zone consists in bunch of tracks all having the same size. The track size can be defined in terms of consecutive *skew-points*[5] distance, which are in turn identified by track skews. Therefore, we can precisely characterize the zones boundaries of a disk simply traversing its skew-points via fast, binary search-based algorithms [15,18]. Exploiting the tracks uniformity in each hard-disk zone, these approaches quickly sweep the disk surface, backtracking to find the exact zone boundary when they detect a track size change. Notwithstanding, all these advanced techniques failed to

---

[4] A second approach based on *drives mode pages* is possible only on high-end SCSI drives [12].

[5] The last sector of a track.

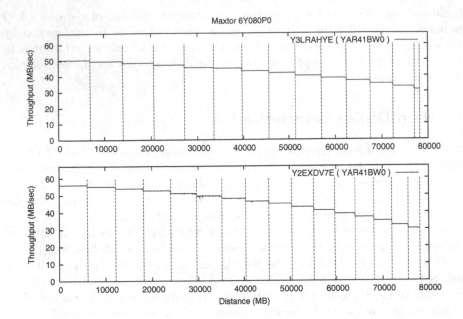

Fig. 1. Reference hard-disks with 14/16 zones

determine the zones boundaries in our testbed due to the presence of zones with non uniform track size. As a consequence, we resorted to a more accurate yet less efficient method to characterize the hard-disks in our testbed.

3.1 A More Accurate Approach

We started isolating the disk's zones boundaries through a method already extensively adopted in many hard-disk reviews, consisting in a uniform sampling of the disk throughput. From the variable zones sector density and the constant disk rotation speed follows that outer disk zones are able to provide greater throughput than inner ones. Figure 1 reports the throughput of two reference disks in function of the distance from the outer border. Easily recognizable as descending throughput steps and clearly separated by vertical lines, these disks present respectively 14 and 16 zones. All the other disks in the testbed match either of these results, so we started from the middle of each respective zone to calculate the track size via a variant of the basic approach of Section 3.

When the built-in buffer is turned off, the completion time difference of two adjacent accesses is equal to the rotational latency. The only exception occurs when the two accesses are on adjacent tracks, namely, when a track skew is located between them. In such cases the difference of the completion times should drop to the settle time, since the track skew should take care of the rotational latency. In our approach we issue a stream of consecutive one-sector disk accesses starting from a given logical block address. This required the inhibition of the

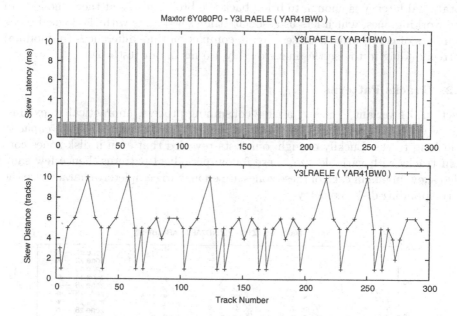

Fig. 2. Track-to-track switch times and distance in tracks between broken skews

elevator system[6], since there is no way on stock Linux kernels that two adjacent single-sector requests can reach the disk device driver independently (i.e. not merged). Measuring the differences in completion times for adjacent requests would expect a periodical drop in correspondence to skew-points. However we found that not all the skew-points are actually able to compensate the track-to-track switch time.

The upper graph of Figure 2 depicts the measured difference between the completion times of two accesses straddling a track, i.e. accessing the last sector of a track and the first sector of the next one. It reports the values measured in correspondence to the first 600 tracks of one of the disks in our testbed (all the other disks showed similar results as well). Moreover, it clearly shows that some of these values are affected by an unexpected full rotational delay (around 8.3 ms). This could be due to several factors, such as either wrong track or cylinder skews, as well as defects on the disk surface. Anyway, we found that the placement of these "broken" skew-points on the disk surface follows a regular pattern, ruling out most of the hypotheses. The lower graph of Figure 2 reports the distance between successive "broken" skew-points in function of the track number, which clearly reveals the cited pattern. The analysis of the hard-disks in our testbed revealed a number of different patterns. As reported to the end of Section 3.2, we presuppose that their presence is strictly related to the length of the disk tracks. At the moment, scaling the completion times down to the modulo of the

---

[6] Linux kernel component that is responsible of merging different I/O requests into a single larger one before the transmission to the underlying disk device driver.

rotational latency is enough to bring back the broken skews at the same level of the working ones, which lets us associate the skew-points with the logical block numbers of consecutive accesses having completion time differences (in modulo) corresponding to the settle time (roughly 1.5 ms in our testbed).

3.2 Tracks Patterns

Section 3.1 variant is clearly a time-consuming process, unpractical to exhaustively enumerate all the skew-points in modern hard-disks with huge capacity and long tracks. Luckily enough, our tests revealed that even if disk zones contain tracks with variable size, these follow periodical patterns, hence few sampled skew-points in each of these zones are enough to completely characterize the corresponding disk geometry.

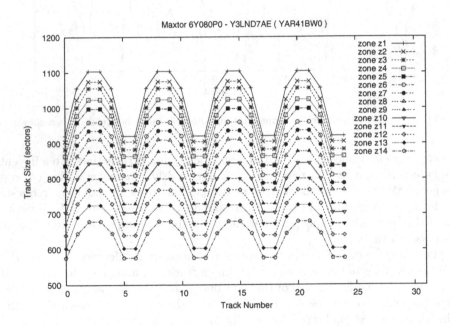

Fig. 3. Track size patterns in hard-disk zones

Figures 3 and 4 report the size of 25 adjacent tracks, sampled starting from the middle of the respective zones in two selected hard-disks of our testbed. The lower is the zone number, the more external is the zone itself. As usual, the track sizes diminish as the zone number increases. Anyway, what is unexpectedly new here, is the odd sequence of tracks with different sizes in each zone. Nearly all disks in our testbed exhibit different track patterns (see [19] for a complete review of these patterns). Moreover, from preliminary data collected on several other models (also from different brands) we noticed analogous phenomena, suggesting that every relatively recent hard-disk on the market is subjected to a non negligible chance to be unique.

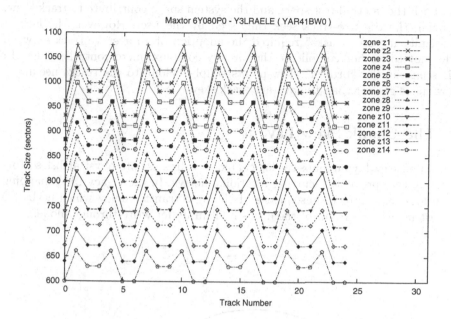

Fig. 4. Track size patterns in hard-disk zones

In our opinion these patterns are a direct consequence of the intrinsic complexity level reached by hard-disk technology in these last years. These hard-disk characterization techniques simply do not have anymore access to the whole disk addressing range to obtain the real track size. In fact, modern hard-disks usually split the entire storage area in three data spaces [20,21]. The first, the *user space*, is a storage area for user data. The second, the *internal test space*, is a reserved area for diagnostic purposes. The third, the *system space*, is an area for exclusive use of hard-disks themselves.

Whilst the user space allows the user to access directly data through the logical block addressing system, both the internal test space and the system space are reserved to the system, and therefore they cannot be directly accessed. They are accessed exclusively by the hard-disk self-diagnostics tests and at hard-disk power-on, respectively. However, hard-disks allocate cylinders to each of these spaces. Spare areas for defective sectors are for example "immersed" in the user space. Several sectors in the last track of a cylinder and the last cylinder in the zone are usually allocated as spare areas. All these factors contribute to obfuscate the real hard-disk geometry, as also suggested by the presence of the same scaled pattern in all the zones of each analyzed hard-disk. Nevertheless, hard-disk analytical models and optimized data layouts operate in user space area, so hardly they can neglect track patterns in order to effectively improve the hard-disk performance.

These patterns also offer a possible explanation for the "broken" skews above. Hard-disk manufacturers calibrated the track skews on the user space. In this way both the internal test space and the system space contribute to track skew, reducing the track-to-track seek time seen by the user. However, the lack of uniformity in "user tracks" required the adoption of an average track skew, in order not to further complicate the already complex micro-controller logic. In this scenario, the "broken" skew-points simply belong to the tracks needing a skew space greater than the average track skew.

4 The Chunk Skew Layout

The chunk skew layout maps the logical block addresses onto physical disk sectors in a way that prevents incurring rotational delays. In the legacy LBA mapping these arise as a direct consequence of the host transfer delay which each I/O request incurs as a result of the disk's built-in buffer write-through mode.

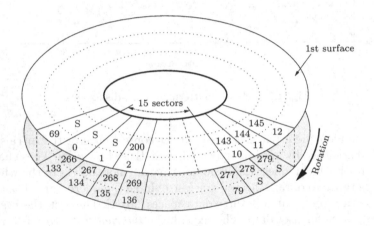

Fig. 5. Chunk skewed logical block address mapping onto physical disk sectors

Figure 5 depicts an example of the chunk skew layout for a disk drive having 100 sectors per track, two media surfaces, 6 sectors track skew, 10 sectors chunks and constant chunk skew of 5 sectors. Logical blocks are assigned to the outer track of the first surface, the outer track of the second surface, the second track of the first surface, and so on. The track skew accounts for the track switch delay, as well as the chunk skews account for the host transfer delay in order to maximize streaming bandwidth. In the depicted layout, chunks are separated by a skew of six sectors (sectors labeled with S in the Figure), except for the 7th (60 → 69 LBA), the 14th (130 → 139 LBA) and the 21st (200 → 209 LBA) chunks requiring no skew space at all. The existing track skew between the 7th and the 8th, between the 14th and the 15th, and between the 21st and the 22nd chunk is in fact enough to compensate the host transfer delay in these cases, without the need of further displacements. Therefore, each track contains 7 chunks, corresponding to 70 free data sectors, while the remaining 30 sectors are **S**-sectors. For example, the Figure depicts the last sector of the first track (69 LBA, belonging to the 7th chunk) followed 6 + 9 sectors away by last sector of the second track's first chunk (79 LBA, belonging to the 8th chunk). We urge to stress how the six S-sectors separating these two chunks are completely ignored by the chunk skew layout. In fact, they are used as mere spacers to preserve hard-disk's head synchronization. This does not prevent a hypothetical chunk skewed file-system to accommodate smaller files in S-sectors of course, since these files would not benefit of the speed-up provided by the chunk skew layout anyway.

Please note that the values involved in the examples above are not related with those measured in our testbed at all, and have been appositely chosen to simplify the drawing. In fact, the unexpected results of Section 3.2 complicate a lot the deployment of the chunk skew layout. The presence of variable track size makes the analytical estimation of the chunk skews difficult, whereas the presence of "broken" skew-points scattered all over the disk surface or potentially relocated defective blocks introduces another level of complexity. Therefore, as a first approximation we directed our interest to discover how much this layout was dependent on variable tracks sizes. For this purpose we empirically experimented with progressively increasing chunk skews on several chunk sizes, ranging from 8 to 256 sectors. These are hard-limits imposed by the hard-disks in our testbed, since the Maxtor's DMA interface refuses to transfer more than 128KB per I/O operation.

For each couple of values[7] we tested the corresponding chunk skew layout on a large write operation (500 MB), starting from the outer disk track. This is in fact the highest performance area in hard-disks and therefore the most penalized by the legacy disk layout.

Figure 6 reports the average performance measured on a reference hard-disk in write-through mode in function of the chunk offset. The six curves correspond to different values of the chunk size.

Each curve shows an *optimal chunk skew* of approximately 128 sectors, providing the maximum throughput for the given chunk size. For values lower than the optimal chunk skew, the write performance remains substantially similar to the legacy LBA mapping case, represented with the zero chunk skew case at the left hand of the graph. This value corresponds to the number of sectors flowed under the disk's head during the host transfer delay, so it diminishes as the head moves towards the center of the platters. More interestingly, the optimal chunk skew remains practically constant in all the hard-disks of our testbed, emphasizing the good tolerance of the chunk skew layout to track pattern variations.

Switching to the read side, the optimal chunk skew performance remains substantially the same. Read operations do not involve data consistency problems, so we leave the read-ahead cache turned on. Anyway, as the left graph in Figure 7 shows, its contribution was confined to regularize rather than improve the performance. Most of the built-in buffer's benefits are in this case diminished by the continuous seek produced by the chunk skews.

---

[7] Chunk size varies in 2^n sectors steps just for drawing precision.

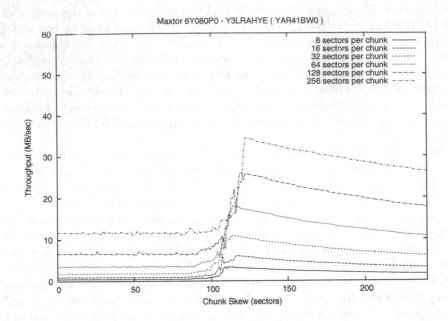

Fig. 6. Performance of the chunk skew layout

Figure 7 reports the "instantaneous" throughput of this layout, measured respectively using read and write operations. At this purpose we grouped several chunks in a *batch* (more precisely, 16 subsequent 256 sectors chunks spaced out by 128 sectors), afterward we measured the disk's submission and response time per batch. Each point in the figure reports the average batch speed for several different batches, identified by the offsets (in sectors) of their starting chunk. The plots has been limited to few samples just to reveal the regularization effect produced by the disk's read-ahead (see the left graph of Figure 7). At a first look, these graphs also show how the measured throughput follows a periodical pattern, essentially due to the presence of variable track size. For example, referring to the left graph in Figure 7 we can see how the first few sampled batches of chunks score 42 MBytes/sec, corresponding roughly to the maximum disk performance[8]. For the successive samples, the instantaneous throughput progressively diminishes down to 24 MBytes/sec due to the rotational latencies involved, and next raises again up to the maximum speed allowed by the host transfer delay. This behavior suggests that there is room for a certain degree of improvement in the chunk skew layout. In particular, the depicted samples are partitioned in three main clusters located at different performance levels, suggesting a still not perfect chunks synchronization. This is plausible considering that for this basic approach we adopted regular chunk skews, whereas the disks present extremely variable characteristics. A more geometry-oriented approach, targeted to bring

---

[8] When I/O operations are affected by the host transfer delay.

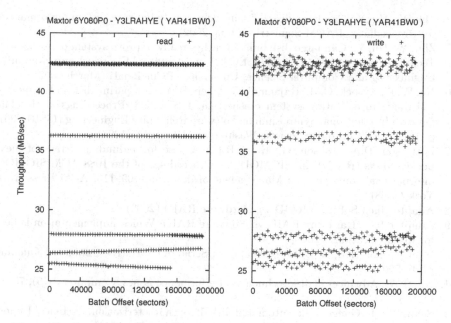

Fig. 7. Instantaneous performance of the chunk skew layout (128 sectors skew)

the lower two clusters up to the same performance level of the third one, is at the moment still under investigation.

5   Conclusions

In this paper we have tackled the problem of preserving data consistency still providing reasonable disk performance in commodity hard-disks. It has also been shown that hard-disks often present unexpected characteristics as a direct consequence of an intrinsic complexity targeted to squeeze performance. Chunk skew layout has proved to effectively alleviate the performance loss which hard-disks incur when their built-in buffer is operated in write-through mode. Comforted by these encouraging results, our efforts will now be directed to refine this layout, adapting it to the new complexities which dominate the latest hard-disk technology to develop a reliable yet efficient storage solution for the commodity hard-disks.

References

1. Ruemmler, C., Wilkes, J.: An introduction to disk drive modeling. IEEE Computer 27(3), 17–28 (1994)
2. Ruemmler, C., Wilkes, J.: Modeling disks. Technical Report HPL-93-68, Hewlett-Packard Laboratories (1993)
3. Ruemmler, C., Wilkes, J.: UNIX disk access patterns. In: Usenix Conference. 405–420 (Winter 1993)

4. Zhu, Y., Hu, Y.: Can large disk built-in caches really improve system performance? In: Proceedings of ACM Sigmetrics (June 2002)
5. Zhu, Y., Hu, Y.: Can large disk built-in caches really improve system performance? Technical Report TR259/03/02ECECS, Department of Electrical and Computer Engineering and Computer Science, University of Cincinnati (March 2002)
6. Ng, W.T., Aycock, C.M., Rajamani, G., Chen, P.M.: Comparing disk and memory's resistance to operating system crashes. In: ISSRE '96: Proceedings of the The Seventh International Symposium on Software Reliability Engineering (ISSRE '96), p. 182. IEEE Computer Society, Washington, DC, USA (1996)
7. Patterson, D.A., Gibson, G., Katz, R.H.: A case for redundant arrays of inexpensive disks (RAID). In: SIGMOD '88: Proceedings of the 1988 ACM SIGMOD international conference on Management of data, pp. 109–116. ACM Press, New York (1988)
8. Adaptec Inc.: Software RAID vs. Hardware RAID (2002)
9. Adaptec Inc.: Hardware RAID vs. Software RAID: Which implementation is best for my application? (2006)
10. Intel Corporation, Seagate Technology: Serial ATA Native Command Queuing (July 2003)
11. Ng, S.W.: Advances in disk technology: Performance issues. Computer 31(5), 75–81 (1998)
12. Schindler, J., Ganger, G.: Automated disk drive characterization. Technical Report CMU-CS-99-176, Carnegie Mellon University (November 1999)
13. Schindler, J., Griffin, J.L., Lumb, C.R., Ganger, G.R.: Track-aligned extents: Matching access patterns to disk drive characteristics. In: FAST '02: Proceedings of the Conference on File and Storage Technologies. USENIX Association, Berkeley, CA, USA, pp. 259–274 (2002)
14. Aboutabl, M., Agrawala, A.K., Decotignie, J.D.: Temporally determinate disk access: An experimental approach (extended abstract). In: Measurement and Modeling of Computer Systems, 280–281 (1998)
15. Mesut, O., Lambert, N.: HDD characterization for A/V streaming applications. IEEE Transactions on Consumer Electronics 48(3), 802–807 (2002)
16. Talagala, N., Arpaci-Dusseau, R.H., Patterson, D.: Microbenchmark-based extraction of local and global disk characteristics. Technical report, UC Berkeley Technical Report (1999)
17. Worthington, B.L., Ganger, G.R., Patt, Y.N., Wilkes, J.: On-line extraction of SCSI disk drive parameters. Technical Report CSE-TR-323-96 (19 1996)
18. Zedlewski, J., Sobti, S., Garg, N., Zheng, F., Krishnamurthy, A., Wang, R.: Modeling hard-disk power consumption. In: Proceedings of the 2nd USENIX Conference on File and Storage Technologies (FAST '03), pp. 217–230 (March 2003)
19. Di Marco, A.: The geometry of commodity hard-disks. Technical Report DISI-TR-07-07, DISI - Università di Genova (July 2007)
20. Fujitsu: C141-E103-02EN: MAH3182MC/MP series, MAH3091MC/MP series, MAJ3364MC/MP series, MAJ3182MC/MP series, MAJ3091MC/MP series disk drives product/maintenance manual (December 2000)
21. IBM: S31L-8989-06: Hard disk drive specifications, Ultrastar 36LZX, 3.5 inch SCSI hard disk drive, models: DDYS-T36950, DDYS-T18350, DDYS-T09170 (June 2000)

An Efficient Counter-Based Broadcast Scheme for Mobile Ad Hoc Networks

Aminu Mohammed, Mohamed Ould-Khaoua, and Lewis Mackenzie

Department of Computing Science, University of Glasgow, G12 8RZ,
Glasgow, United Kingdom
{maminuus,mohamed,lewis}@dcs.gla.ac.uk

Abstract. In mobile ad hoc networks (MANETs), broadcasting plays a fundamental role, diffusing a message from a given source node to all the other nodes in the network. Flooding is the simplest and commonly used mechanism for broadcasting in MANETs, where each node retransmits every uniquely received message exactly once. Despite its simplicity, it however generates redundant rebroadcast messages which results in high contention and collision in the network, a phenomenon referred to as *broadcast storm problem*. Pure probabilistic approaches have been proposed to mitigate this problem inherent with flooding, where mobile nodes rebroadcast a message with a probability p which can be fixed or computed based on the local density. However, these approaches reduce the number of rebroadcasts at the expense of reachability. On the other hand, counter-based approaches inhibit a node from broadcasting a packet based on the number of copies of the broadcast packet received by the node within a random access delay time. These schemes achieve better throughput and reachability, but suffer from relatively longer delay. In this paper, we propose an efficient broadcasting scheme that combines the advantages of pure probabilistic and counter-based schemes to yield a significant performance improvement. Simulation results reveal that the new scheme achieves superior performance in terms of saved-rebroadcast, reachability and latency.

Keywords: MANETs, Flooding, Broadcast storm problem, Saved-rebroadcast, Reachability, Latency.

1 Introduction

Broadcasting is a means of diffusing a message from a given source node to all other nodes in the network. It is a fundamental operation in MANETs and a building block for most other network layer protocols. Several unicast routing protocols such as Dynamic Source Routing (DSR), Ad Hoc on Demand Distance Vector (AODV), Zone Routing Protocol (ZRP), and Location Aided Routing (LAR), as well as multicast protocols employ broadcasting to detect and maintain routes in a dynamic environment. Currently, these protocols typically rely on simplistic form of broadcasting called *simple flooding*, in which each mobile node retransmits every unique received packet exactly once. Although flooding is simple and easy to

K. Wolter (Ed.): EPEW 2007, LNCS 4748, pp. 275–283, 2007.

implement, it often causes unproductive and harmful bandwidth congestion, a phenomenon referred to as the *broadcast storm problem* [1], [2], [3].

Several broadcast schemes have been proposed that mitigate the broadcast storms problem. The performance of these schemes is measured in terms of *reachability*, which is the fraction of the total nodes that receive the broadcast messages, the *saved-rebroadcast*, that is the fraction of the total nodes that does not rebroadcast the messages, and the *latency*, that is the time between the first and the last instant that the broadcast message is transmitted [4]. These schemes are usually divided into two categories [4], [5]: *deterministic schemes* and *probabilistic* schemes. Deterministic schemes require global topological information of the network and are guaranteed a reachability of 1 considering an ideal MAC layer. However, they incur large overhead in terms of time and message complexity for maintaining the global knowledge requirements due to the inherent dynamic topology of MANETs. On the other hand, probabilistic schemes do not require global topological information of the network to make a rebroadcast decision. As such every node is allowed to rebroadcast a message based on a predetermined *forwarding probability p*. As a consequence, these schemes incur a smaller overhead and demonstrate superior adaptability in dynamic environment when compared to deterministic schemes [6]. However, they typically sacrifice reachability as a trade-off against overhead.

Among the probabilistic schemes that have been proposed are *probability-based* and *counter-based schemes* [1], [2], [3]. In probability-based schemes, a mobile node rebroadcasts a message according to certain probability *p* which can be fixed or computed based on the local density. Current probabilistic schemes assume a fixed probability value and it is shown [1], [4], [7] that the optimal rebroadcast probability is around 0.65. However, these approaches reduce the number of rebroadcast at the expense of reachability [2]. In contrast, messages are rebroadcast only when the number of copies of the message received at a node is less than a threshold value in counter-based schemes. This lead to better throughput and reachability, but suffer from relatively longer delay [3], [4].

In this paper, we proposed an efficient counter-based scheme that combines the advantages of probabilistic and counter-based schemes. We set a rebroadcast probability at each node (as in [1], [4] and [7]) if the packet counter is less than the threshold value rather than rebroadcasting the message automatically. This is because the packet counter is not exactly equal to the node number of neighbors. Otherwise we drop the message. We compare this scheme with simple flooding, fixed probability and counter-based scheme. Simulation results reveal that this simple adaptation can lead to a significant performance improvement.

The rest of the paper is organized as follows: In Section 2, we introduce the related work on probabilistic and counter-based schemes. The description of our scheme is presented in Section 3. We evaluate the performance of our scheme and present the simulation results in Section 4. Finally, concluding remarks are presented in Section 5.

2 Related Work

This section sheds some light on the research work related to probabilistic and counter-based broadcasting schemes.

Ni *et al* [2] proposed a probability-based scheme to reduce redundant rebroadcast by differentiating the timing of rebroadcast to avoid collision. The scheme is similar to flooding, except that nodes only rebroadcast with a predetermined probability P. Each mobile node is assigned the same forwarding probability regardless of its local topological information. In the same work, counter-based scheme is proposed after analysing the additional coverage of each rebroadcast when receiving n copies of the same packet.

Cartigny and Simplot [8] have proposed an adaptive probabilistic scheme. The probability p for a node to rebroadcast a packet is determined by the local node density and a fixed value k for the efficiency parameter to achieve the reachability of the broadcast. However, the critical question thus becomes how to optimally select k, since k is independent of the network topology.

In Ni *et al* follow-on work [3], the authors have proposed an adaptive counter-based scheme in which each node dynamically adjusts its threshold value C based on its number of neighbors. Specifically, they extend the fixed threshold C to a function $C(n)$, where n is the number of neighbors of the node. In this approach there should be a neighbor discovery mechanism to estimate the current value of n. This can be achieved through periodic exchange of 'HELLO' packets among mobile nodes.

Recently, Zhang and Agrawal [9] have described a dynamic probabilistic broadcast scheme which is a combination of the probabilistic and counter-based approaches. The scheme is implemented for route discovery process using AODV as base routing protocol. The rebroadcast probability P is dynamically adjusted according to the value of the local packet counter at each mobile node. Therefore, the value of P changes when the node moves to a different neighborhood; for example, in sparser areas, the rebroadcast probability is large compared to denser areas. To suppress the effect of using packet counter as density estimates, two constant values d and d_l are used to increment or decrement the rebroadcast probability. However, the critical question is how to determine the optimal value of the constants d and d_l.

In this paper, we propose an efficient counter-based scheme which combines the merits of probability-based and counter-based algorithms to yield a significant performance improvement in terms of saved rebroadcast, reachability and end-to-end delay which are simple enough for easy implementation. The detail of the scheme is described in the next section.

3 Efficient Counter-Based Scheme (ECS)

In this section, we present the efficient counter-based scheme that aims to mitigate the broadcast storm problem associated with flooding. The use of ECS for broadcasting enables mobile nodes to make localized rebroadcast decisions on whether or not to rebroadcast a message based on both counter threshold and forwarding probability values. Essentially, this adaptation provides a more efficient broadcast solution in sparse and dense networks.

In ECS, a node upon reception of a previously unseen packet initiates a counter c that will record the number of times a node receives the same packet. Such a counter is maintained by each node for each broadcast packet. After waiting for a random assessment delay (RAD, which is randomly chosen between 0 and T_{max} seconds), if c

reaches a predefined threshold C, we inhibit the node from this packet rebroadcast. Otherwise, if c is less than the predefined threshold, C, the packet is rebroadcast with a probability P as against automatically rebroadcasting the message in counter-based scheme. The use of a rebroadcast probability stem from the fact that packet counter value does not necessarily correspond to the exact number of neighbours of a node, since some of its neighbours may have suppressed their rebroadcast according to their local rebroadcast probability. Thus, the selection of an optimal forwarding probability is vital to the performance of our scheme. Based on [1], [4], and [7], we opt for a rebroadcast probability of 0.65. A snapshot of our algorithm is presented in figure 1.

4 Performance Analysis

This section studies the performance of our scheme, counter-based, fixed probability and flooding in terms of reachability, saved-rebroadcast and latency. In order to isolate the effects of various design choices of the broadcast algorithms on performance we do not simulate other protocol layers such as the MAC and physical layers. Our performance analysis is based on the assumptions widely used in literature [11], [12], [17].

i.   All nodes participate fully in the protocol of the network. In particular each participating node should be willing to forward packets to other nodes in the network.

Algorithm : Efficient Counter-Based Scheme

On hearing a broadcast message m at a node X
- initialize the counter c = 1;
- set and wait for RAD to expire;
- for every duplicate message m received within RAD
  - o increment c, c = c +1;
  - o *if* (c < C) (counter threshold-value) {
    - wait for RAD to expires;
    - rebroadcast probability $P = P_1$; }
    else{ //where $P_1 = 0.65$
    - stop waiting
    - Drop the message *}*
- Generate a random number *RN* over [0, 1]
- *If* $RN \le P$
  - o Rebroadcast the message;
  else
  - o Drop the message

Fig. 1. A snapshot of efficient counter-based scheme algorithm

ii.   Packet may be corrupted or lost in the wireless transmission medium during propagation. A node has the capability of detecting a corrupted received packet and can discard it.

iii.   All mobile nodes are homogeneous. The wireless transmission range and the interface card are the same. Likewise the wireless channel is shared by all nodes and can be accessed by any node at random time. Therefore, collision is a possible phenomenon with the channel.

4.1 Simulation Setup

We use ns-2 packet level simulator (v.2.29) [10] to simulate a square 600m by 600m area populated with 25, 50, 75, ..., 150 mobile nodes that are uniformly distributed in the region, each with a circular radio transmission range of radius 100m. This corresponds to networks consisting of multi-hops radio across while the selected mobile nodes represent the various network densities ranging from sparse to high density network. The radio propagation model used in this study is the ns-2 default, which uses characteristic similar to a commercial radio interface, Lucent's WaveLAN card with a 2Mbps bit rate [13]. The distributed coordination function (DCF) of the IEEE 802.11 protocol [14] is utilized as MAC layer protocol while random waypoint model [15] is used as the mobility model. Because it takes time for the random way point model to reach a stable distribution of mobile nodes [16], the modified random waypoint mobility model [15] used take care of this node distribution problem. The simulation is allowed to run for 900 seconds for each simulation scenario. Other simulation parameters that have been used in our experiment are shown in Table 1.

Table 1. Simulation Parameters

Simulation Parameter	Value
Simulator	NS 2 (v.2.29)
Transmission range	100 meters
Bandwidth	2 Mbps
Interface queue length	50
Packet size	512 byte
Traffic type	CBR
Packet rate	10 packets/sec
Topology size	600 x 600 m^2
Number of nodes	25, 50, ..., 150
Number of trials	30
Simulation time	900 sec
Maximum speed	20 m/s
Counter threshold (C)	4
RAD Tmax	0.01 seconds

Each data point represents an average of 30 different randomly generated mobility models with 95% confidence interval. Likewise, the maximum speed used is the ns-2 default which characterise a high mobility network.

4.2 Simulation Results

In this section, we present the performance results of ECS (efficient counter-based broadcast scheme) side by side with counter-based, fixed probability and flooding. The simulation output is collected using replication mean method where each data point represents an average of 30 different randomly generated mobility models with 95% confidence intervals. Our main focus is to mitigate the broadcast storm problem therefore reducing the contention in the network and decreasing the probability of packet collisions. As a result, end-to-end delay can be reduced, and the percentage of saved rebroadcast can be improved.

4.2.1 Saved Rebroadcast (SRB)
Figure 2 shows the performance comparisons of fixed probability, counter-based, flooding and ECS in terms of SRB with varying network density. The four schemes achieve different SRB percentages with increasing network density.   The figure demonstrates that ECS can significantly mitigate the contentions and collisions incur during broadcasting especially in dense networks with node moving at 20 m/s. In sparse networks, ECS has superior SRB of 46% and about 56% in medium and high dense networks. Under the same network conditions, the SRB achieved by the other algorithms are as follows: fixed probability has 39% and 35%; counter-based has 22% and 32%; and flooding has 4% and 1% for sparse and medium – high dense network respectively. Thus, ECS has superior SRB performance in various network densities. As shown in Figure 2, ECS can substantially reduce the number of rebroadcast because nodes rebroadcast a packet with a certain probability value (0.65) rather than automatically rebroadcasting every received packet. However, sending too few rebroadcast can result in broadcast packet not reaching all the nodes in the network.

4.2.2 Reachability
Figure 3 shows that reachability increases when network density increases regardless of which scheme is used. Flooding has best performance in terms of reachability, reaching about 100% of the nodes. The performance of ECS scheme shows that the reachability is about 95% in sparse networks and above 98% in medium and high density network. In high density networks, very similar and comparable results are obtained for all the four schemes.   However, in the case of low density networks (specifically 25 nodes), flooding and counter-based schemes achieved better reachability performance than ECS.   As redundant rebroadcasts also contribute to chances of packet collisions which may eventually cause packet drops, thus negatively affecting the reachability. Depending on the value of the probability, ECS may have lower reachability compared to flooding and counter-based schemes. However, by choosing appropriate probability value, we can achieve acceptable reachability. ECS 's inferior reachability performance in sparse network is due to fact that the network might be partition and thus increasing the likelihood of more broadcast packets not reaching all the nodes in the network.

4.2.3 Latency
In this section we measure the end-to-end delay of the broadcast packet that has been received by all nodes in the network.   The results in figure 4 show the effects of

network density on the latency of broadcast packets. When node density increases, more broadcast packets fail to reach all the nodes due to high probability of packet collision and channel contention caused by excessive redundant retransmission of broadcast packets. Therefore the waiting time of packets in the interface queues increases. As shown in figure 4, ECS exhibits lower latency than counter-based, fixed probability and flooding. Since rebroadcast packets collide and content for channel with each other, and the ECS incurs the lowest number of rebroadcasts (highest saved-rebroadcast), it should have the lowest latency.

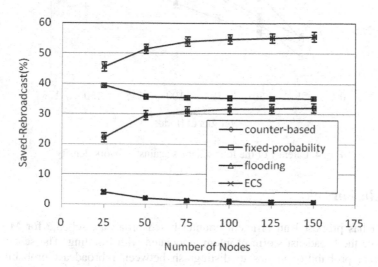

Fig. 2. Saved-Rebroadcast of the four schemes against network density

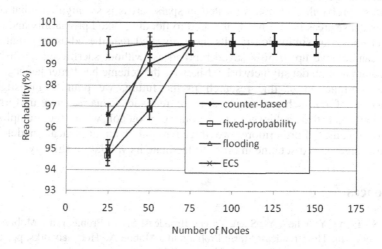

Fig. 3. Reachability of the four schemes against network density

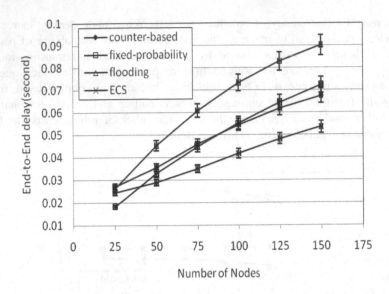

Fig. 4. Latency of the four schemes against network density

5 Conclusion

This paper has proposed an efficient counter-based broadcast scheme for MANETs that mitigate the broadcast storm problem associated with flooding. The scheme uses two different probability values to distinguish between rebroadcast probability for nodes in sparse network and that of a dense network. In order to reduce the broadcast overhead and without sacrificing the network connectivity in dense networks, the rebroadcast probability of nodes located in sparse areas is set high and that of nodes located in dense areas is set low. Compared to flooding, fixed probability and counter-based schemes, our simulation results have revealed that the adjusted counter-based scheme can achieve up to 56% saved rebroadcast without sacrificing reachability in both medium to high density networks. Likewise the scheme has better latency.

As a continuation of this research in the future, we plan to investigate the performance of our scheme under a more realistic scenario (non uniform node distribution) and that achieved by a routing protocol when they employ ECS broadcast schemes. Furthermore, we intend to build an analytical model for our efficient counter-based scheme in order to facilitate its validation strategy.

References

1. Ni, S., Tseng, Y., Chen, Y., Sheu, J.: The Broadcast Storm Problem in a Mobile Ad Hoc Networks. In: The Broadcast Storm Problem in a Mobile Ad Hoc Networks, pp. 151–162. IEEE Computer Society Press, Los Alamitos (1999)
2. Tseng, Y.-C., Ni, S.-Y., Chen, Y.-S., Sheu, J.-P.: The Broadcast Storm Problem in a Mobile Ad Hoc Network. Wireless Networks. 8, 153–167 (2002)

3. Tseng, Y.-C., Ni, S.-Y., Shih, E.-Y.: Adaptive Approaches to Relieving Broadcast Storms in a Wireless Multihop Ad Hoc Networks. IEEE Transactions on Computers. 52, 545–557 (2003)
4. Williams, B., Camp, T.: Comparison of Broadcasting Techniques for Mobile Ad Hoc Networks. In: Williams, B., Camp, T. (eds.) Proceeding MOBIHOC., pp. 194–205. Lausanne, Switzerland (2002)
5. Lou, W., Wu, J.: Localized Broadcasting in Mobile Ad Hoc Networks Using Neighbour Designation. CRC Press, Boca Raton, USA (2003)
6. Alireza, K-H., Vinay, R., Rudolf, R.: Color-Based Broadcasting for Ad Hoc Networks. 4th International Symposium on Modeling and Optimization in Mobile, Ad Hoc, and Wireless Networks, pp. 1–10 (2006)
7. Haas, Z.J., Halpern, J.Y., Li, L.: Gossip-based ad hoc routing. In: Proceeding of IEEE INFOCOM, IEEE Computer Society Press, Los Alamitos (2002)
8. Cartigny, J., Simplot, D.: Border node retransmission based probabilistic broadcast protocols in ad hoc networks. Telecommunication Systems. 22, 189–204 (2003)
9. Zhang, Q., Agrawal, D.P.: Dynamic Probabilistic Broadcasting in MANETs. Parallel and Distributed Computing. 65, 220–233 (2005)
10. The Network Simulator ns-2, http://www.isi.edu/nsnam/ns/
11. Perkins, C.E., Moyer, E.M.: Ad-hoc on-demand distance vector routing. In: Proceedings of 2nd IEEE Workshop on Mobile Computing Systems and Applications, pp. 90–100. IEEE Computer Society Press, Los Alamitos (1999)
12. Johnson, D.B., Maltz, D.A.: Dynamic source routing in ad hoc wireless networks. Mobile Computing, pp. 153–181. Dordrecht Academic Publishers, The Netherlands (1996)
13. IEEE802.11 WaveLAN PC Card - User's Guide, A-1
14. Internet Standard Comm: Wireless LAN medium access control (MAC) and physical layer (PHY) specifications. IEEE standard 802.11-1997. IEEE, New York (1997)
15. Navidi, W., Camp, T., Bauer, N.: Improving the accuracy of random waypoint simulation through steady-state initialization. In: Proceedings of the 15th International Conference on Modeling and Simulation (MS'04), Marina Del Rey, Califonia, USA (2004)
16. Camp, T., Boleng, J., Davies, V.: A survey of mobility models for ad hoc network research. Wireless Communication and Mobile Computing (WCMC), vol. 2 (2002)
17. Colagrosso, M.D.: Intelligent broadcasting in mobile ad hoc networks: Three classes of adaptive protocols. EURASIP Journal on Wireless Communication and Networking. 2007, p. 16 (2007)

The Effect of Mobility on Local Service Discovery in the Ahoy Ad-Hoc Network System*

Patrick Goering, Geert Heijenk, Boudewijn Haverkort, and Robbert Haarman

Faculty of EEMCS / DACS
University of Twente
P.O. Box 217, 7500 AE Enschede, The Netherlands
patrick.goering@utwente.nl, geert.heijenk@utwente.nl,
brh@ewi.utwente.nl, rhaarman@inglorion.net

Abstract. Ahoy, a protocol to perform local service discovery in ad-hoc networks is described in this paper. The protocol has been implemented in a discrete-event simulator to study its performance in case of a multihop mobile ad-hoc network. Especially the effect of mobility on the network load and the probability of finding services is investigated. Experiments show that the load caused by advertisement messages is very low, even when the mobility is increasing. For low speeds the percentage of found services is close to the maximum possible, while even at high speeds the probability of finding a service is still reasonable.

1 Introduction

Ad-hoc networks are used to enable wireless communication between mobile nodes without making use of any infrastructure. Users of these networks want to interconnect their devices, make use of services provided by other devices, and have the possibility to offer their own services to other devices. In many cases it is useful to be able to find the nearest available service, also called service discovery, such as a printer or scanner. In such an ad-hoc network environment we want to be able to find services that are located nearby, while keeping in mind the limited power and network capacity.

In [1] we described a simple local service discovery protocol and presented experiments in a static situation, without node mobility. In this paper, we introduce a keep_alive mechanism to the protocol to save bandwidth. We use keep_alive messages instead of larger advertisement messages where possible. We implemented this new protocol, now named Ahoy, in a discrete-event simulator. Furthermore, in this paper we study the effect of mobility, the amount of bandwidth it takes to keep information about local services up-to-date, and the effect on the success probability of queries; this has not been done before.

The organization of this paper is as follows. Section 2 describes other research related to service discovery in ad-hoc networks. Section 3 discusses our service discovery solution using attenuated Bloom filters; the hash functions we use, the effect of mobility on the protocol, and the impact of false positives. Section 4 describes the simulation setup and Sect. 5 gives simulation results of the protocol when there is mobility. Finally, Sect. 6 presents the conclusions and future work.

---

* This work is supported by the Dutch Ministry of Economic Affairs under the Innovation Oriented Research Program (IOP GenCom, QoS for Personal networks at Home).

K. Wolter (Ed.): EPEW 2007, LNCS 4748, pp. 284–300, 2007.

2   Related Work

Several service discovery protocols have been developed for computer networks. We look at the suitability of some of them for local service discovery in a mobile ad-hoc network (MANET). One distinction we can make is between centralized and distributed solutions. An example of a centralized service discovery system, with a directory server that stores all available services is SLP [2]. All devices in the network have to communicate with this directory server, which is a disadvantage for mobile ad-hoc networks, as there is limited network capacity and this server might not always be reachable.

A distributed solution has some advantages in a mobile ad-hoc network [3]; it can be proactive or reactive. A proactive solution forwards advertisements of available services to all nodes when there are any changes, whereas in a reactive solution query messages are forwarded through the network at the time a service is needed. A proactive solution has the advantage of services being available quicker at the cost of some bandwidth. An example of such an approach is Zeroconf [4], e.g., implemented as Apple Bonjour, an IETF protocol that enables the discovery of services on a local area network. A usable IP network is automatically created without the need for configuration or special servers, but it is limited to a single subnet. Bonjour does allow service discovery outside a single subnet, but this requires special DNS configuration and a connection to an infrastructure network. Thus in a multihop ad-hoc network Apple Bonjour cannot be used for local service discovery. In [5] the newscast epidemic protocol is used to provide a robust overlay network that adapts to (large) changes in a dynamic network. It uses quite some bandwidth to accomplish this, which makes it not suitable for wireless networks. Another approach was taken with HESED [6], where query messages are multicasted to all nodes. Selective edge nodes are used to reduce the number of multicast packets. Matching servers multicast their information to all nodes as well. Clients cache this information and use it to reduce the number of query messages.

For service discovery in ad-hoc networks, where we want to discover services located nearby, we need a fully distributed solution, suitable for multihop networks. Many nodes in ad-hoc networks will be mobile with a wireless network interface. Furthermore, such an approach should work as soon as a new node arrives, without the need to pre-establish a cluster or group. The Group-based Service Discovery Protocol (GSD) [7] is a distributed protocol for MANETs. In GSD, advertisements are limited to nodes within a maximum number of hops and services are grouped to allow selective forwarding of queries. The grouping of services is based on the semantics of the service descriptions and is predefined. Queries are forwarded to a node that has advertised services in the same group as the service might be available near this node. GSD does allow users to find a service within a maximum number of hops, but not necessarily the nearest service. Furthermore, groups need to be predefined and services classified in these groups to make use of selective forwarding of queries. Proximity Discovery Service (PDS) [8] also provides proximity based service discovery. This solution relies on the availability of the real geographic location by using a GPS satellite receiver, which we don't consider as a requirement for our protocol.

Attenuated Bloom filters have been used in [9] for context discovery. There, an analysis is done on the false positive probability and the size and depth of the used Bloom filters. Optimum values are found for several parameters to make efficient use of bandwidth. Here, we extend the service discovery protocol with a keep-alive mechanism to minimize the bandwidth usage further. Also, the impact of mobility on service discovery with respect to bandwidth usage and reachability of services is evaluated.

The Ahoy protocol is a combination of a proactive and a reactive approach; a summary of available services is forwarded between neighbors upto a certain number of hops and queries are selectively forwarded using the information in the summary. The work presented in this paper further evaluates the idea of using attenuated Bloom filters for service discovery, especially in the presence of mobility.

3   The Ahoy Service Discovery Protocol

The Ahoy service discovery protocol is described in this section. Firstly, an overview is given of the protocol and the usage of Bloom filters. Secondly, the advertising and querying algorithms used in the protocol are explained. Then we discuss the hash functions used, the effect of mobility on the protocol, and the impact of false positives.

3.1   Overview

A Bloom filter [10] can be used to describe the membership of objects in a set, with a small chance of false positives. It consists of an array of w bits, initially all set to 0. A number of b independent hash functions over the range $[1,w]$ is used to map a text string to the Bloom filter. A total number of b bits are set in the Bloom filter, one for each hash result. Some of the bits might be overlapping, that is, two different text strings might partially map to the same bits. A service, represented by a text string, is considered to be represented in a Bloom filter when all bits corresponding to the b hashes of this text string are set. For local service discovery in ad-hoc networks we propose to use attenuated Bloom filters [11]. They were introduced as a method to optimize the performance of location mechanisms especially when objects to be found are located nearby. We use Bloom filters in our service discovery protocol, because they can highly compress service availability information and thus reduce the bandwidth usage of the protocol.

An attenuated Bloom filter is a stack of standard Bloom filters of depth d. Every row in the filter represents objects at a different distance, indicated by the number of hops. Nodes maintain a separate attenuated Bloom filter for every link to a direct neighbor. This enables to select a link where an object most likely can be found, a so-called matching link. Periodically, an advertisement packet is broadcasted to all direct neighbors. The packet contains an attenuated Bloom filter, which represents the services reachable through the sending node. The attenuated Bloom filter is created by combining, a simple OR operation, all attenuated Bloom filters from all available links. This result is shifted down one layer and then combined with the node's own Bloom filter. See below for more details of the advertisement procedure.

When a client wants to find a specific service it will check whether the service is available locally. If this is not the case the client will check its attenuated Bloom filters and send a query packet to any link with a matching Bloom filter. A node receiving such a query again will check for local availability of the service, check its attenuated Bloom filters, and forward the query to any link with a matching Bloom filter. A node that does provide the service will send a response packet back along the path the queries followed (in reverse order), as will be explained later. When the client receives the response packet it can call upon the service, although there is a possibility it does not exist.

3.2 Advertising

Algorithm 1 shows the actions taken by each node independently when packets related to advertisements arrive in a node.

```
1  switch received packet do
2      case keep_alive
3          if BC_ID != previous_BC_ID then
4              send (request_update packet to originating link);
5          update cleanup timer for neighbor;
6      case advertisement
7          if BC_ID != previous_BC_ID then
8              store received attenuated Bloom filter;
9              store BC_ID;
10             foreach layer do
11                 combine attenuated Bloom filters from links;
12             if advertisement packet != previous advertisement packet then
13                 send (advertisement packet to all links);
14         update cleanup timer for neighbor
15     case request_update packet
16         send (advertisement packet to originating link);
```

Algorithm 1. Advertisement (Run by Each Node Independently)

Advertisement messages include the attenuated Bloom filter as well as a broadcast identification field (BC_ID) that uniquely identifies the advertisement packets per neighbor. Keep_alive messages are broadcasted to all direct neighbors every *period* seconds. This *period* consists of a fixed part and a random part. The random part is added to desynchronize the keep_alive messages from all nodes. It also prevents peaks in bandwidth used by keep_alive messages. The keep_alive messages include the BC_ID value from the last sent advertisement packet. Because the size of the keep_alive messages is small compared to the size of the advertisements, the bandwidth usage is lower than in the case where we would send advertisement messages periodically. This also means we can send more keep_alive messages for the same network load and thus be able to detect changes in the network, like a new neighbor with new services, quicker. Sending one UDP packet in an ad-hoc network also involves MAC, IP and UDP header overhead, where part of the MAC header is transmitted at a lower speed. Thus the number of messages we can send more does not only depend on the time it takes to send advertisement and keep_alive messages of a specific size, but also on the time it takes to transmit the overhead. Receiving a keep_alive packet (line 2) with a specific BC_ID signifies all neighboring nodes that the services announced with the advertisement packet with the same BC_ID from the same neighbor are still valid. The only action a node takes when the BC_ID matches is postponing the clean up procedure as explained below. When the BC_ID does not match (line 3), this signifies that the node has old information and should request an update of the available services reachable through the neighbor that sent the keep_alive packet. This situation could occur when an advertisement packet is lost, e.g., caused by interference in the radio link or by a new node moving into range. A request update packet is then sent directly to the neighbor, there is no need to broadcast this packet.

When an advertisement message is received (line 6) and the BC_ID differs from the BC_ID in the last advertisements from the same neighbor (line 7), the BC_ID and attenuated Bloom filter in the message are stored. All attenuated Bloom filters from all neighbors are combined (line 10). In case the newly constructed advertisement differs from the last advertisement sent (line 12), an advertisement message with the combined attenuated Bloom filter is broadcasted to all direct neighbors.

Upon receipt of a request update packet (line 15) a node will send an advertisement packet containing a full attenuated Bloom filter directly to the requesting neighbor.

A clean up procedure removes information of services reachable through a neighbor when this neighbor is out of reach of a node for a certain amount of time. A node is considered to be out of reach when the keep_alive messages are no longer received from this node. As packets can get lost in a wireless environment, a certain number of consecutive keep_alive messages should be allowed to be missed before the clean up procedure is started. After this number of keep_alive messages are missing, detected by not receiving a keep_alive packet for a number of keep_alive periods, the node will construct a new attenuated Bloom filter that represents the services reachable through this nodes at this specific time, i.e., without the services of the node that got out of reach. An advertisement packet containing this Bloom filter is transmitted to all neighbors when it contains information that is different from the previous advertisement.

Advertisements are not transmitted immediately after receiving new information from a neighbor for two reasons. Firstly, several nodes might receive an updated advertisement at the same time. Sending an advertisement immediately would result, with high probability, in collisions of the advertisement packets in the wireless network. Secondly, sending an update will likely trigger a neighbor to also send an updated advertisement. Randomization by adding a delay here allows to incorporate the information from this advertisement and will limit the number of messages per second nodes will send.

3.3 Querying

Algorithm 2 shows the query algorithm as it is run by each node independently.

Query messages contain a query identification (Q_ID), a maximum number of hops the message should be forwarded as well as a Bloom filter representing the queried service. The Q_ID together with the address of the originating node of the query is used to detect duplicates. When a node receives a query (line 2) with a Q_ID it has seen before, it can discard this query. In case the Q_ID is new (line 3), the maximum hops value is decremented by one. As the initial maximum hops value is d, up to a maximum of d hops away all services that match the query can be found. When the received query matches a Bloom filter previously received from any neighbor (line 7,8), the Q_ID value is stored together with the link the message was received from and the source address of the originating node. This information is used to send the response back along the

```
1  switch received packet do
2     case query
3        if not originating node and Q_ID match previous query then
4           maximum_hops -= 1;
5           if service matches Bloom filter locally then
6              send (response packet to originating link);
7           foreach link L do
8              if service matches Bloom filter for link L upto maximum_hops then
9                 send (query packet to L);
10                store Q_ID and link Q query was received from;
11    case response
12       if Q_ID matches previous query then
13          send (response packet to link Q);
```

Algorithm 2. Query (Run by Each Node Independently)

path the query traveled. The query is then forwarded to all neighbors with a matching Bloom filter. The destination of the query, a node with a matching service, will send a response back to the node the query was received from first. Upon receipt of a response packet (line 11), a response packet is send to the neighbor the query was received from (line 12), as known from the previously stored Q_ID. All nodes repeat this process until the query arrives at the originating node.

3.4 Hash Functions

For our protocol we need a number of hash functions, which distribute the bits set uniformly over the entire Bloom filter for the service being hashed. This is to make the probability of false positives as low as possible with a given Bloom filter width. In essence, we can tolerate some false positives, so this can be one of the criteria for the size of the Bloom filters being used. We use universal hashing [12]. These hash functions have the property that for any two distinct inputs the probability of a collision between those two inputs is the same as if we where using a uniform random function. In our service discovery protocol different nodes use hash functions to generate a number of bits to be set in a Bloom filter for announcing services as well as for querying for these services. Therefore, every node must use the same set of hash functions to be able to find services. The number of hash functions needed is determined by the number of bits that need to be set for every service that has to be represented in a Bloom filter. For the bandwidth usage of the protocol to be minimized, about half the bits need to be set in a Bloom filter [10]. In that case the false positive probability is low, while the width of the Bloom filters is not too high. The Bloom filters of d layers still have to fit in a single IP packet, to avoid the overhead of sending multiple IP packets for a single advertisement message.

3.5 False Positives

False positives affect the service discovery as follows: a service can appear to be available through a specific neighbor due to a false positive. False positives can show up as an effect of the combining of Bloom filters. When this happens in the lowest layer, only this node is affected, all other neighbors will not have the false positive. However, when it happens in layer d-1, all neighbors will have the same false positive in layer d, due to the way the advertisement procedure works. A query for such a service will be forwarded until it reaches a node where the false positive does not occur; the query along this path would then be silently dropped.

Generally, more nodes can be reached as the distance, and thus the maximum number of hops, increases. The lower layers of an attenuated Bloom filter will then contain more services, which means more bits are set. Thus, the probability of a false positive is higher in the lower layers than in the higher layers of an attenuated Bloom filter.

3.6 Mobility

In a situation, without node movement and without changes of services, results for queries are returned in the time it takes to forward and process the query messages for a maximum of d hops and sending back a response message. The bandwidth used by the protocol in this situation comes from sending keep-alive messages as well as the queries and responses themselves. A more challenging situation for a service discovery protocol appears when mobile nodes are moving around, so that there are changes in the services reachable. The frequency of the keep-alive messages determines how quick an update for a change in reachable neighbors and thus the update for the change in reachable services is propagated. When one node has a change in any of its services, potentially all nodes in a radius of d hops will exchange advertisement messages to notify all nodes in their range about the change.

4   Simulation Setup

The protocol described in the previous section has been implemented in the discrete-event simulator OPNET Modeler, version 11.5 [13]. The manet_station_adv model from the OPNET model library was used as a basis for our protocol implementation. In the following experiments mobile nodes are placed in a simulation area. The nodes have one wireless network interface that supports the IEEE 802.11b [14] standard for communicating with each other. The modified OPNET model was set to IEEE802.11b mode with a bitrate of 11 Mbps. Packets are always sent at 11 Mbps, there is no rate adaptation. For the moment the transmission range is limited to 300 meters. When a node is within a radius of 300 meters the free space path-loss propagation model, receiver sensitivity and transmission power are used to determine whether the transmission is successful or there is packet loss, i.e., packet transmissions may fail due to collisions or radio conditions. When a node moves out of this 300 meter radius of a sending node there is no interference with this sending node. We do not use a routing protocol in these experiments; from client to service the attenuated Bloom filters determine where packets are sent. The response messages from service back to the client follow the reverse path. Every simulation run is done with different seeds for the random number generator. The random number generator is used for all randomness in the standard OPNET models, as well as the random times in our model. Also both the advertised strings and the query strings are picked randomly using this random number generator, unless stated otherwise. More specifically, every node advertises one service. We select 10 random ASCII characters as input for the hash function for every service and for every simulation run. The clean up period is set to 40 seconds and the keep_alive *period* is 15 seconds plus a random time, drawn every time a message is sent, uniformly distributed between 0 and 2 seconds. All protocol messages are sent over IP version 4 and UDP, thus for every message there is an overhead of an IP and a UDP header. The total message size further depends on the width and depth of the Bloom filter. Table 1 shows the values of the parameters used in the experiments.

5   Experiments

Four different experiments have been selected to study the behaviour of our protocol in varying degrees of mobility. The first two experiments examine a mostly static situation, where all nodes are fixed in a grid structure. One node moves through this grid at different speeds and we examine the effect of the advertisement delay parameter, as introduced in Sect. 3.2. Experiment 2 extends this experiment by investigating the effect the delay has on reachability of services. The last two experiments introduce more mobility; all nodes are moving randomly in the simulation area. Experiment 3 focuses on the advertisement load depending on the average speed of the nodes and the maximum Bloom filter depth d. Experiment 4 investigates the percentage of successful queries achieved by our protocol compared to the maximum possible as determined by the transmission range and the position of the nodes.

5.1   Limited Mobility Experiments

We consider the situation where our service discovery protocol is used in an ad-hoc network in which the nodes are relatively static. This scenario shows the effect of a single node traveling through an area, where many stationary ad-hoc nodes provide services. We position 61 nodes in a grid structure, which will stay stationary during the experiments. The grid structure was chosen for basic understanding of the interaction between nodes. Here one extra node (node_62) with a starting position outside the reach of any other node starts moving after 20 minutes simulation time. In these 20 minutes all other nodes learn each others services and then send keep_alive messages periodically. As the keep_alive messages for all nodes will be transmitted at random times, they will not be synchronized to each other. The mobile node moves with a constant speed from the bottom left to the top right in a straight line, as illustrated in Fig. 1. The spacing between all nodes is 300 meter, so that the mobile node will be in reachable distance of at least one node as long as it is in the center area (for about 2500 m).

The speed of this node is varied from 0 to 100 km/hr (27.8 m/s) in steps of 10 km/hr and for each speed 20 simulation runs are done. We let the simulation run long enough to allow the mobile node move through the entire network, until it is out of reach of any node again. The travel time depends on the actual speed of the node, the higher the speed the shorter the required simulation time. Node_62 starts learning about available services and the Bloom filters are updated as it moves through the simulation area. The depth of the attenuated Bloom filters d is 5. Note that since the radius of the network is also 5, services of the center node are propagated to the edge of the network.

Table 1. Parameters

parameter	exp1,2	exp3,4
advertisement delay	0-2 + unif[0,0.5] s	2 + unif[0,0.5] s
d	5	1-5
w	512 bits	
b	8	
$period$	15 s + unif[0,2] s	
range	300 m	

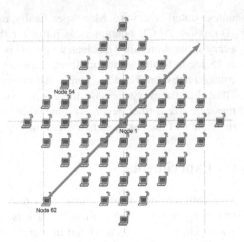

Fig. 1. Node movement

They would not propagate any further for a larger radius of the network. We selected the number of bits $b = 8$ and the Bloom filter width $w = 512$ bits. The size of one advertisement message, including MAC, IP, and UDP headers is then 384 bytes.

Experiment 1. In this experiment we measure the number of advertisement messages sent by the moving node (node_62), the center node (node_1), and the average for all nodes in the network. We do this while the moving node is within range of at least one of the static nodes of the network, i.e., we count all messages from the time the moving node comes within reach of the network until this node leaves the area where the other nodes are. The node is considered to be in range of one of the other nodes as long as it has neighbors for which it keeps an attenuated Bloom filter. After the last neighbor information has been removed through a clean up operation, we consider the node to be out of reach. We use the advertisement delay as a parameter for these experiments. The advertisement delay consists of a fixed and a random part. We always choose the random delay uniformly between 0 and 0.5 seconds, but vary the fixed delay. For different speeds the time we do the measurements will be different.

Figure 2 shows the number of advertisement messages per second per node averaged over all nodes during the simulation runs. We can observe that the advertisement load increases linearly with the speed of the mobile node. As the speed of the mobile node approaches zero, we see no advertisement messages at all. Nodes only send keep_alive messages to inform each other that there are no changes. As the speed of the mobile node increases, the number of advertisement messages per second increases as well, to keep all nodes up-to-date of the changed services. As the speed is increased to 100 km/hr (27.8 m/s) advertisement load increases to approximately 0.07 message per second. On average, nodes then use 215 bps ($\approx 0.002\%$ of 11 Mbps) for sending advertisement messages. As a reference: the AODV [15] routing protocol sends 608 bps of HELLO messages when a node is part of an active route. Note that in this graph the influence of the advertisement delay parameter is hardly visible.

When we look at the number of sent advertisements per second for two specific nodes some interesting phenomena can be observed. Both the mobile node (see Fig. 3) and the center node (see Fig. 4) exhibit the same linear increase of the advertisement load as the speed of the mobile node increases. In both figures the average number of advertisement messages from Fig. 2 is included for reference. However, the load of the center node, and especially of the mobile node increases much steeper than the load of an average node. At 100 km/hr (27.8 m/s) the load of the center node is almost twice the load of an average node, the load of the mobile node is approximately four times that value. This can be explained by the fact that the center node is on the trajectory of the mobile node, so most of the time, changes in reachability of services (from the mobile node) occur within $d=5$ hops. Of course the reachability of services from the mobile node changes continuously, so that the mobile node has an even higher advertisement load. Note however that the absolute value of the advertisement load is still very low.

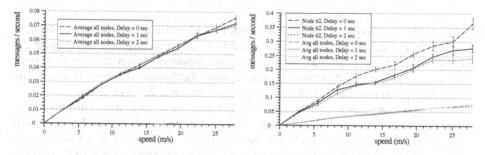

Fig. 2. Average number of advertisement messages from all nodes

Fig. 3. Advertisement messages from node_62

Let us now consider the influence of the advertisement delay parameter on the advertisement load. From Fig. 2, it can be observed that the parameter hardly has any effect for an average node, although at higher speeds of the mobile node, some influence starts to be visible. For the mobile node itself, the impact of the advertisement delay is more pronounced (see Fig. 3). Even at moderate speed, significant savings in the advertisement load can be achieved by delaying advertisements for 1 or 2 seconds. For the center node (Fig. 4) the effect of the parameter is less straightforward. There appear to be non-linear increases of the load for certain delay values, especially for the center node, but also for the mobile node. Below, we will give an explanation for these deviations.

When we look at the mobile node moving from the bottom left to the top right through the area, as shown in Fig. 5, we see that the mobile node will get in range of the nodes A and C as soon as it reaches the position of node D. From this moment on, nodes A and C can receive the keep_alive messages sent by the mobile node, and the mobile node can receive the keep_alive messages sent by nodes A and C. Keep_alive messages are sent periodically, so some time will elapse before either node A or C receives one from the mobile node, or the mobile node receives one from node A or C. Let us assume that the mobile node is the first node to receive a keep_alive message, and it receives it when it is exactly on the border of the outer shaded area. This will trigger the exchange of a request_update message and a subsequent unicast advertisement message, because

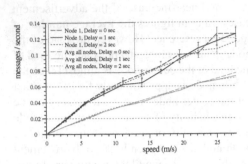

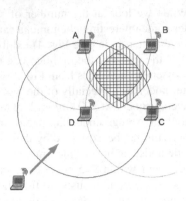

Fig. 4. Advertisement messages from node_1   **Fig. 5.** Effect of delay

the keep_alive message will refer to an unknown advertisement. Taking into account that this advertisement will contain as yet unknown services, its receipt will trigger the mobile node to broadcasting a new advertisement message. However, the mobile node will only broadcast the advertisement after waiting for the advertisement delay, during which the mobile node can travel to the border of the inner shaded area.

If the mobile node is within the inner shaded area when broadcasting its new advertisement to nodes A and C, the broadcast will also be received by node B, which will save the transmission of an extra broadcast message. It can be seen that this saving only occurs when the time of waiting for a keep_alive message from node A or C, plus the advertisement delay (plus the time for exchanging some messages) is sufficient for the mobile node to travel from the point where it gets in reach of nodes A and C to the point where it also gets in reach of node D. Note that a similar, yet slightly different effect occurs if either node A or C is the first node to receive a keep_alive message from the mobile node.

So, the speed of the mobile node influences the advertisement load in two different ways. If the speed increases, more changes in reachable services are detected, and hence more advertisements are sent in the same time period. On the other hand, if the speed increases, savings in the number of broadcasts to send can be made. The latter effect depends on the advertisement delay, among others, and is not continuous. Note that the same effect can also be observed for random topologies, although in a less deterministic way.

Experiment 2. For the same network as in the above experiment, we now want to know when a service can be found as long as the mobile node (node_62) is moving through the grid. We let node_54 try to find one of node_62's services. At the same time we also let the mobile node try to find a service advertised by the center node, node_1. Both node_1 and node_62 advertise a static, not randomly determined, service. When there is no match in any of the layers of the attenuated Bloom filter, nothing is done. When a match is found in one of the layers of the attenuated Bloom filter, a query is sent in that direction and forwarded as long as a match can be found and until it reaches node_62. At some points the location of the target node is not where it should be according to the apparently outdated information in the Bloom filters. We want to find how often the service is still found and a reply is sent back to and received by the originating node. After 20 minutes, the time the mobile node starts moving, we start querying for the services. The time between query tries on both nodes is exponentially distributed with a mean value of one second. In the optimal case a service can be found when a network path of at most d hops exists between the client and the service. In our regular grid network we know when such a network path exists and thus we can normalise the number of successful queries to the maximum number of queries that could be successful in this scenario.

We see in Fig. 6 that at low speeds the service is almost always found, it approaches 100% when the speed is low. When there is no mobility the service will always be found as long as a path of at most d hops exists. For increasing speeds the percentage of found services decreases and is also more dependent on the delay parameter. We can also see nonlinear behaviour in the percentage of successful queries for different speeds, caused by the deviations in the number of advertisement messages found in the previous experiment. When for a certain speed there are less advertisement messages, this means there is less information of available services. On average the probability of success to find a service will be lower as well for this specific speed. When we look at the effect of the delay parameter, we see that for smaller delays the service is more often found, because all nodes in the path between client and service will know about changes quicker. This comes at the price of more bandwidth usage when changes are detected.

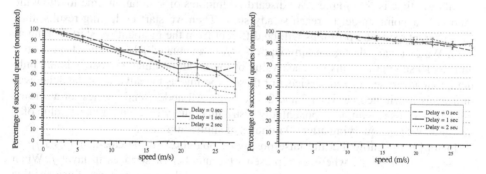

Fig. 6. Reachability of mobile node's services from node_54

Fig. 7. Reachability of center node's services from mobile node

When we also compare the percentage of successful queries from the mobile node to the center node, see Fig. 7, we see a difference. At higher speeds the percentage of found services decreases more for node_54 than for node_62. This can be explained by the distance or number of hops between client and service. The number of hops is always large from node_54 to node_62, namely the maximum depth $d = 5$ at which the service still can be found. Especially in this case a higher delay causes the number of found services to be lower, as there are more nodes in the path between client and service that need time, proportional to the advertisement delay value, to update their neighbors with new information. The percentage of successful queries from node_62 to node_1 is less dependent on the speed and delay, because here client and service are always moving towards each other or away from each other. As the position of the mobile node changes there is always a node within one hop distance, that knows a correct path less than a total of $d = 5$ hops to the service. Thus only a small part of the path between client and service needs to be updated to be able to keep finding the service.

5.2 Full Mobility Experiments

The following experiments investigate a more mobile situation, where a number of users move through an area. There are 25 nodes in a simulation area of 1500×1500 meters, which gives the same node density as in the limited mobility experiments. The nodes are all moving according to a random waypoint pattern. The starting positions of the nodes are uniformly spread over the simulation area and the nodes start moving as soon as the simulation starts. For all nodes a destination is chosen distributed uniformly over the simulation area. Nodes move towards their destination with a random speed and pause at their destination for a random amount of time. After the pause a new destination is chosen for the node with a new random speed. To prevent nodes getting trapped at low speeds, as shown in [16], in our simulations we use a minimum speed of 0.1 m/s. The maximum speed varies from 1 to 20 m/s and the wait time is uniformly distributed between 0 and 30 seconds. A higher maximum speed means a higher average level of mobility for the nodes in our simulation. All simulation runs use the same start positions for the nodes, but we use 10 different random waypoint patterns per speed. The total simulation time is 60 minutes. We discard 20 minutes of simulation time to allow the random waypoint model to reach steady state. Then we start collecting results, thus for different seeds the positions will be different from the moment we start looking as well. We then vary the maximum depth d of the attenuated Bloom filter from 1 to 5 and do 10 simulation runs for each value of the depth parameter. Node_1 is the only node that advertises a fixed service. For these experiments the advertisement delay was uniformly distributed between 2 and 2.5 seconds. All nodes send queries for a service node_1 advertises with an exponentially distributed query rate with a mean value of 5 seconds. We start querying after 20 minutes of simulation time.

From [9] we know that the false positive probability can be calculated as $P_{fp} \approx (1 - (1 - 1/w)^{bx_j})^b$, where x_j represents the number of services in layer j. When using the simulation parameters from experiments 3 and 4, the worst case false positive probability occurs when all nodes are reachable in the lowest layer: $P_{fp} \approx 0.012\%$. Then for every query the probability of a false positive in layer d of the attenuated Bloom filter is approximately 0.012%. However, at the next hop the number of services represented in layer d-1 and thus the false positive probability is significantly lower. In most cases a query message due to a false positive is forwarded only one hop and then it will be discarded.

Experiment 3. In this experiment we study the effect of mobility on the number of advertisement and query messages in the network respectively.

First, Fig. 8 shows for different maximum depths d and increasing mobility the increase in the average number of advertisement messages per node. For low speeds doubling the maximum depth of the attenuated Bloom filter from one to two causes an almost twice as high number of advertisement messages, but going from a maximum depth d of four to five has a smaller effect. When we first look at increasing the maximum depth d from one to two, we see the difference in the absolute number of advertisement messages increase as the maximum speed increases. However, proportionally seen there is a decrease. When we increase the maximum depth d more the influence on the number of advertisement messages gets smaller. Also increasing the speed any further does not result in an increase in the number of advertisement messages anymore. Thus at some point adding more mobility to the network does not give a higher advertisement load anymore. Nevertheless, this does have an effect on the probability of finding a service as we describe below. The average number of advertisement messages in both cases is limited by the keep_alive *period*, changes in the network cannot be detected any quicker anymore. This means a higher maximum depth d does not result in more advertisement messages. Off course the size of the advertisement packets is larger as information from an extra layer in the attenuated Bloom filter has to be transmitted, so there is still a cost involved when choosing the maximum depth d for a specific situation. Without mobility the number of advertisement messages is 0 for all depths. For a depth $d = 5$, the number of advertisement messages increases to 0.16 messages per second as the speed is increased to 20 m/s, which is still a low absolute value.

Second, we examine the average query load experienced by the mobile nodes. Figure 9 shows that for increasing depth d of the attenuated Bloom filter the average number of queries increases more. For nodes located further away, there are more possible paths from client to service over which queries are sent. When increasing the speed of the mobile nodes, there is first a decrease in the query load at 3 m/s. From speeds from 5 to 10 m/s the number of messages increases again. Speeds above 15 m/s result in a faster increase which is more pronounced for larger depths d of the Bloom filters. There are two effects that play a role, first, in a low mobility situation all Bloom filters are almost always up-to-date. When, somewhere on the path from client to service, a connection is broken due to mobility, this results in fewer query messages. Queries are no longer forwarded from that point on. Second, for higher speeds, the clean up period causes more nodes to be listed as direct neighbor. During this clean up period the information from the old neighbors is still kept, while new neighbors are being discovered. This explains the overall increase as more direct neighbors results in more queries. The maximum number of query message occurs at a speed of 20 m/s for depth $d=5$, where we observe 6.3 query messages per second. Note that, the effect of false positives as calculated in Sect. 5.2 is negligible in these results.

Experiment 4. We finally study the effect of mobility and the maximum depth d of the attenuated Bloom filter on the probability to find a service. As the nodes are sending queries when they find a match in their Bloom filters, we count the number of successfully found services, that is, a reply came back to the originating node. This is a measure for the reachability of the service with our protocol for different mobility patterns and varying maximum depth of the attenuated Bloom filters.

Figure 10 shows the percentage of successful queries for different levels of mobility and different values of the maximum depth d. As d increases, more layers are added tot the attenuated Bloom filters, the number of successfully found services increases

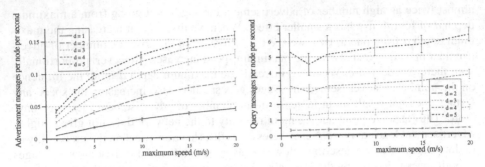

Fig. 8. Advertisement load   **Fig. 9.** Query load

as well. As the number of layers present gets higher, adding another layer does not give a large increase in the number of successfully found services anymore. Adding layers 4 and 5 gives us a slightly higher percentage of successful queries while increasing the advertisement cost. For $d = 5$, the percentage of successful queries is 73%. As the average speed of the nodes increases, the number of successful queries decreases, resulting in 55% success for $d = 5$. Propagating the changes in available services takes time, for a depth of $d = 5$ we have a maximum total delay of five times the advertisement delay before all nodes know about the changes in the network. Thus for a higher maximum depth d this effect is bigger, because there is a longer path of nodes between client and service that needs to know about changes in the topology. More mobility makes it more difficult to find services a larger number of hops away. There is a slight increase above 15 m/s, caused by the limited size of the area. A node forgets about neighbors after a fixed interval determined by the cleanup period. When there is more mobility nodes learn faster about more new neighbors, in effect, increasing the amount of information in the Bloom filters. More often a query is sent based on outdated information, but nodes along the path towards the service might already have new information, resulting in a successful query.

We can distinguish two main reasons for queries being unsuccessful; due to the properties of the protocol or due to the radio range combined with the location of the nodes during the simulation runs. To determine the efficiency of our protocol, we need to look at the maximum number of successful queries possible only. For a maximum depth of one, a range of r meters, and an area of aXa meters the maximum percentage of successful queries S_{max} can be approximated by dividing the area in range of node_1 with the total surface area: $S_{max} = \pi r^2 / a^2$. To get such a maximum percentage of successful queries for all depths d we calculated the number of nodes within d hops from the random waypoint patterns used in the simulation runs. Figure 11 shows the percentage of successful queries normalized to the maximum possible due to network limitations. Generally the percentage is lower when the maximum number of hops increases. For low speeds the percentage of successful queries achieved by the protocol is around 99%. As speed increases towards 20 m/s the number of successful queries decreases to 91% in case $d = 5$.

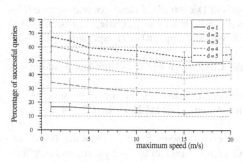
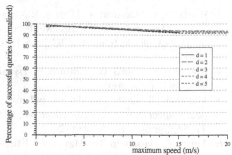

Fig. 10. Successfull queries depending on the speed

Fig. 11. Maximum reachability depending on the speed

6 Conclusions and Further Work

In this paper we have studied the lookup capabilities of a new service discovery protocol using Bloom filters in several scenarios. We thereby focused on the impact of node mobility on the performance of the protocol.

Attenuated Bloom filters can be used for local service discovery in ad-hoc networks where nodes may be mobile. To keep the information about available services in the vicinity up-to-date, advertisement messages need to be transmitted to neighbors. A delay between the time new information is received and an advertisement is sent helps to keep the bandwidth usage low. However, with a high delay the probability of finding services is lower, especially when there is more mobility in the ad-hoc network. The load of advertisement messages in a situation where nodes are moving randomly increases when there is more mobility, but is still quite low. For situations with higher mobility, the number of advertisement messages stabilizes to a maximum. For low mobility situations our protocol can find services close to 100% of the maximum possible as determined by the location and the transmission range of the nodes. With increased mobility still in a large number of cases (91% in experiment 4) services can be successfully found.

The Ahoy service discovery protocol has been implemented in a prototype [17]. In this MSc thesis, the feasibility of using Bloom filters for service discovery in ad-hoc networks is shown, and some alternative choices where investigated.

Further work includes adding more optimizations to the protocol to support node mobility even better. For instance, the number of advertisement messages can be further reduced by limiting the maximum number of hops a query can be propagated depending on the distance to the nearest service as found from the information in the attenuated Bloom filter.

References

1. Goering, P.T.H., Heijenk, G.J.: Service Discovery Using Bloom Filters In Ad-Hoc Networks. In: Participants Proceedings of the Dutch PhD Network on Computing and Imaging, June 2006, pp. 219–227 (2006)
2. Veizades, J., Guttman, E., Perkins, C., Kaplan, S.: Service Location protocol. RFC 2165 (June 1997)

3. Hoebeke, J., Moerman, I., Dhoedt, B.: Analysis of Decentralized Resource and Service Discovery Mechanisms in Wireless Multi-hop Networks. In: Braun, T., Carle, G., Koucheryavy, Y., Tsaoussidis, V. (eds.) WWIC 2005. LNCS, vol. 3510, pp. 181–191. Springer, Heidelberg (2005)
4. Cheshire, S., Aboba, B., Guttman, E.: Dynamic Configuration of IPv4 Link-Local Addresses. RFC 3927 (May 2005)
5. Voulgaris, S., van Steen, M.: An epidemic protocol for managing routing tables in very large peer-to-peer networks. In: Brunner, M., Keller, A. (eds.) DSOM 2003. LNCS, vol. 2867, pp. 41–54. Springer, Heidelberg (2003)
6. Yang, Y., Hassanein, H., Mawji, A.: Efficient service discovery for wireless mobile ad hoc networks. In: 4th ACS/IEEE International Conference on Computer Systems and Applications, pp. 571–578. IEEE Computer Society Press, Los Alamitos (2006)
7. Chakraborty, D., Joshi, A., Finin, T., Yesha, Y.: GSD: a Novel Group-based Service Discovery Protocol for MANETs. In: 4th IEEE Conference on Mobile and Wireless Communication Networks (MWCN), pp. 140–144. IEEE Computer Society Press, Los Alamitos (2002)
8. Meier, R., Cahill, V., Nedos, A., Clarke, S.: Proximity-based service discovery in mobile ad hoc networks. In: Kutvonen, L., Alonistioti, N. (eds.) DAIS 2005. LNCS, vol. 3543, pp. 115–129. Springer, Heidelberg (2005)
9. Liu, F., Heijenk, G.J.: Context discovery using attenuated bloom filters in ad-hoc networks. Journal of Internet Engineering (2007)
10. Bloom, B.H.: Space/Time Trade-offs in Hash Coding with Allowable Errors. Communications of the ACM 13(7), 422–426 (1970)
11. Rhea, S.C., Kubiatowicz, J.: Probabilistic location and routing. In: Proc. of INFOCOM 2002, vol. 3, pp. 1248–1257 (2002)
12. Carter, J.L., Wegman, M.N.: Universal classes of hash functions. In: Proc. 9th annual ACM symposium on Theory of computing, pp. 106–112. ACM Press, New York (1977)
13. OPNET modeler software, available: http://www.opnet.com/products/modeler
14. LAN MAN Standards Committee of the IEEE Computer Society: Wireless LAN Medium Access Control (MAC) and Physical Layer (PHY) Specifications. IEEE std. 802.11b (1999)
15. Perkins, C., Belding-Royer, E., Das, S.: Ad hoc on-demand distance vector (aodv) routing. RFC 3561 (July 2003)
16. Yoon, J., Liu, M., Noble, B.: Random Waypoint Considered Harmful. In: Proceedings of IEEE INFOCOM., vol. 2, pp. 1312–1321. IEEE Computer Society Press, Los Alamitos (2003)
17. Haarman, R.: Ahoy: A Proximity-Based Discovery Protocol. Master's thesis, Computer Science, University of Twente (January 2007)

Author Index

Ardaiz, Oscar   141

Babka, Vlastimil   245
Bacon, Jean   228
Baynat, Bruno   200
Begin, Thomas   200
Bell, Alexander   2
Brandwajn, Alexandre   200
Brunner, Rene   141
Buchmann, Alejandro   228
Bušić, Ana   33

Chacin, Pablo   141
Chao, Isaac   141
Cortellessa, Vittorio   171

Děcký, Martin   245

Fdida, Serge   200
Fourneau, Jean-Michel   213
Freitag, Felix   141
Frittella, Laurento   171

Goering, Patrick   284

Haarman, Robbert   284
Haverkort, Boudewijn R.   2, 80,
    154, 284
Heijenk, Geert   284
Horváth, Gábor   48

Kounev, Samuel   125, 228
Kuntz, Matthias   80

López, Natalia   63

Mackenzie, Lewis   275
Marco, Alessandro Di   260
Markovski, Jasen   18
Mello, Emerson Ribeiro de   112
Merayo, Mercedes G.   97
Mitrani, Isi   1, 186
Mohammed, Aminu   275
Moorsel, Aad van   112

Navarro, Leandro   141
Nou, Ramon   125
Núñez, Manuel   63, 97

Ould-Khaoua, Mohamed   275

Pekergin, Nihal   33, 213

Reinelt, Patrick   154
Rodríguez, Ismael   63, 97

Sachs, Kai   228
Sadre, Ramin   154
Silva Fraga, Joni da   112
Slegers, Joris   186
Sokolova, Ana   18

Telek, Miklós   48
Thomas, Nigel   186
Torres, Jordi   125
Trčka, Nikola   18
Tůma, Petr   245

Vink, Erik P. de   18

Wolfinger, Bernd E.   200

Younès, Sana   213

Lecture Notes in Computer Science

Sublibrary 2: Programming and Software Engineering

For information about Vols. 1– 4063
please contact your bookseller or Springer

Vol. 4753: E. Duval, R. Klamma, M. Wolpers (Eds.), Creating New Learning Experiences on a Global Scale. XII, 518 pages. 2007.

Vol. 4749: B.J. Krämer, K.-J. Lin, P. Narasimhan (Eds.), Service-Oriented Computing – ICSOC 2007. XIX, 629 pages. 2007.

Vol. 4748: K. Wolter (Ed.), Formal Methods and Stochastic Models for Performance Evaluation. X, 301 pages. 2007.

Vol. 4741: C. Bessière (Ed.), Principles and Practice of Constraint Programming – CP 2007. XV, 890 pages. 2007.

Vol. 4680: F. Saglietti, N. Oster (Eds.), Computer Safety, Reliability, and Security. XV, 548 pages. 2007.

Vol. 4670: V. Dahl, I. Niemelä (Eds.), Logic Programming. XII, 470 pages. 2007.

Vol. 4634: H. Riis Nielson, G. Filé (Eds.), Static Analysis. XI, 469 pages. 2007.

Vol. 4615: R. de Lemos, C. Gacek, A. Romanovsky (Eds.), Architecting Dependable Systems IV. XIV, 435 pages. 2007.

Vol. 4610: B. Xiao, L.T. Yang, J. Ma, C. Muller-Schloer, Y. Hua (Eds.), Autonomic and Trusted Computing. XVIII, 571 pages. 2007.

Vol. 4609: E. Ernst (Ed.), ECOOP 2007 – Object-Oriented Programming. XIII, 625 pages. 2007.

Vol. 4608: H.W. Schmidt, I. Crnković, G.T. Heineman, J.A. Stafford (Eds.), Component-Based Software Engineering. XII, 283 pages. 2007.

Vol. 4591: J. Davies, J. Gibbons (Eds.), Integrated Formal Methods. IX, 660 pages. 2007.

Vol. 4589: J. Münch, P. Abrahamsson (Eds.), Product-Focused Software Process Improvement. XII, 414 pages. 2007.

Vol. 4574: J. Derrick, J. Vain (Eds.), Formal Techniques for Networked and Distributed Systems – FORTE 2007. XI, 375 pages. 2007.

Vol. 4556: C. Stephanidis (Ed.), Universal Access in Human-Computer Interaction, Part III. XXII, 1020 pages. 2007.

Vol. 4555: C. Stephanidis (Ed.), Universal Access in Human-Computer Interaction, Part II. XXII, 1066 pages. 2007.

Vol. 4554: C. Stephanidis (Ed.), Universal Acess in Human Computer Interaction, Part I. XXII, 1054 pages. 2007.

Vol. 4553: J.A. Jacko (Ed.), Human-Computer Interaction, Part IV. XXIV, 1225 pages. 2007.

Vol. 4552: J.A. Jacko (Ed.), Human-Computer Interaction, Part III. XXI, 1038 pages. 2007.

Vol. 4551: J.A. Jacko (Ed.), Human-Computer Interaction, Part II. XXIII, 1253 pages. 2007.

Vol. 4550: J.A. Jacko (Ed.), Human-Computer Interaction, Part I. XXIII, 1240 pages. 2007.

Vol. 4542: P. Sawyer, B. Paech, P. Heymans (Eds.), Requirements Engineering: Foundation for Software Quality. IX, 384 pages. 2007.

Vol. 4536: G. Concas, E. Damiani, M. Scotto, G. Succi (Eds.), Agile Processes in Software Engineering and Extreme Programming. XV, 276 pages. 2007.

Vol. 4530: D.H. Akehurst, R. Vogel, R.F. Paige (Eds.), Model Driven Architecture - Foundations and Applications. X, 219 pages. 2007.

Vol. 4523: Y.-H. Lee, H.-N. Kim, J. Kim, Y.W. Park, L.T. Yang, S.W. Kim (Eds.), Embedded Software and Systems. XIX, 829 pages. 2007.

Vol. 4498: N. Abdennahder, F. Kordon (Eds.), Reliable Software Technologies - Ada-Europe 2007. XII, 247 pages. 2007.

Vol. 4486: M. Bernardo, J. Hillston (Eds.), Formal Methods for Performance Evaluation. VII, 469 pages. 2007.

Vol. 4470: Q. Wang, D. Pfahl, D.M. Raffo (Eds.), Software Process Dynamics and Agility. XI, 346 pages. 2007.

Vol. 4468: M.M. Bonsangue, E.B. Johnsen (Eds.), Formal Methods for Open Object-Based Distributed Systems. X, 317 pages. 2007.

Vol. 4467: A.L. Murphy, J. Vitek (Eds.), Coordination Models and Languages. X, 325 pages. 2007.

Vol. 4454: Y. Gurevich, B. Meyer (Eds.), Tests and Proofs. IX, 217 pages. 2007.

Vol. 4444: T. Reps, M. Sagiv, J. Bauer (Eds.), Program Analysis and Compilation, Theory and Practice. X, 361 pages. 2007.

Vol. 4440: B. Liblit, Cooperative Bug Isolation. XV, 101 pages. 2007.

Vol. 4408: R. Choren, A. Garcia, H. Giese, H.-f. Leung, C. Lucena, A. Romanovsky (Eds.), Software Engineering for Multi-Agent Systems V. XII, 233 pages. 2007.

Vol. 4406: W. De Meuter (Ed.), Advances in Smalltalk. VII, 157 pages. 2007.

Vol. 4405: L. Padgham, F. Zambonelli (Eds.), Agent-Oriented Software Engineering VII. XII, 225 pages. 2007.

Vol. 4401: N. Guelfi, D. Buchs (Eds.), Rapid Integration of Software Engineering Techniques. IX, 177 pages. 2007.

Vol. 4385: K. Coninx, K. Luyten, K.A. Schneider (Eds.), Task Models and Diagrams for Users Interface Design. XI, 355 pages. 2007.

Vol. 4383: E. Bin, A. Ziv, S. Ur (Eds.), Hardware and Software, Verification and Testing. XII, 235 pages. 2007.

Vol. 4379: M. Südholt, C. Consel (Eds.), Object-Oriented Technology. VIII, 157 pages. 2007.

Vol. 4364: T. Kühne (Ed.), Models in Software Engineering. XI, 332 pages. 2007.

Vol. 4355: J. Julliand, O. Kouchnarenko (Eds.), B 2007: Formal Specification and Development in B. XIII, 293 pages. 2006.

Vol. 4354: M. Hanus (Ed.), Practical Aspects of Declarative Languages. X, 335 pages. 2006.

Vol. 4350: M. Clavel, F. Durán, S. Eker, P. Lincoln, N. Martí-Oliet, J. Meseguer, C. Talcott, All About Maude - A High-Performance Logical Framework. XXII, 797 pages. 2007.

Vol. 4348: S. Tucker Taft, R.A. Duff, R.L. Brukardt, E. Plödereder, P. Leroy, Ada 2005 Reference Manual. XXII, 765 pages. 2006.

Vol. 4346: L. Brim, B. Haverkort, M. Leucker, J. van de Pol (Eds.), Formal Methods: Applications and Technology. X, 363 pages. 2007.

Vol. 4344: V. Gruhn, F. Oquendo (Eds.), Software Architecture. X, 245 pages. 2006.

Vol. 4340: R. Prodan, T. Fahringer, Grid Computing. XXIII, 317 pages. 2007.

Vol. 4336: V.R. Basili, D. Rombach, K. Schneider, B. Kitchenham, D. Pfahl, R.W. Selby (Eds.), Empirical Software Engineering Issues. XVII, 193 pages. 2007.

Vol. 4326: S. Göbel, R. Malkewitz, I. Iurgel (Eds.), Technologies for Interactive Digital Storytelling and Entertainment. X, 384 pages. 2006.

Vol. 4323: G. Doherty, A. Blandford (Eds.), Interactive Systems. XI, 269 pages. 2007.

Vol. 4322: F. Kordon, J. Sztipanovits (Eds.), Reliable Systems on Unreliable Networked Platforms. XIV, 317 pages. 2007.

Vol. 4309: P. Inverardi, M. Jazayeri (Eds.), Software Engineering Education in the Modern Age. VIII, 207 pages. 2006.

Vol. 4294: A. Dan, W. Lamersdorf (Eds.), Service-Oriented Computing – ICSOC 2006. XIX, 653 pages. 2006.

Vol. 4290: M. van Steen, M. Henning (Eds.), Middleware 2006. XIII, 425 pages. 2006.

Vol. 4279: N. Kobayashi (Ed.), Programming Languages and Systems. XI, 423 pages. 2006.

Vol. 4262: K. Havelund, M. Núñez, G. Roşu, B. Wolff (Eds.), Formal Approaches to Software Testing and Runtime Verification. VIII, 255 pages. 2006.

Vol. 4260: Z. Liu, J. He (Eds.), Formal Methods and Software Engineering. XII, 778 pages. 2006.

Vol. 4257: I. Richardson, P. Runeson, R. Messnarz (Eds.), Software Process Improvement. XI, 219 pages. 2006.

Vol. 4242: A. Rashid, M. Aksit (Eds.), Transactions on Aspect-Oriented Software Development II. IX, 289 pages. 2006.

Vol. 4229: E. Najm, J.-F. Pradat-Peyre, V.V. Donzeau-Gouge (Eds.), Formal Techniques for Networked and Distributed Systems - FORTE 2006. X, 486 pages. 2006.

Vol. 4227: W. Nejdl, K. Tochtermann (Eds.), Innovative Approaches for Learning and Knowledge Sharing. XVII, 721 pages. 2006.

Vol. 4218: S. Graf, W. Zhang (Eds.), Automated Technology for Verification and Analysis. XIV, 540 pages. 2006.

Vol. 4214: C. Hofmeister, I. Crnković, R. Reussner (Eds.), Quality of Software Architectures. X, 215 pages. 2006.

Vol. 4204: F. Benhamou (Ed.), Principles and Practice of Constraint Programming - CP 2006. XVIII, 774 pages. 2006.

Vol. 4199: O. Nierstrasz, J. Whittle, D. Harel, G. Reggio (Eds.), Model Driven Engineering Languages and Systems. XVI, 798 pages. 2006.

Vol. 4192: B. Mohr, J.L. Träff, J. Worringen, J.J. Dongarra (Eds.), Recent Advances in Parallel Virtual Machine and Message Passing Interface. XVI, 414 pages. 2006.

Vol. 4184: M. Bravetti, M. Núñez, G. Zavattaro (Eds.), Web Services and Formal Methods. X, 289 pages. 2006.

Vol. 4166: J. Górski (Ed.), Computer Safety, Reliability, and Security. XIV, 440 pages. 2006.

Vol. 4158: L.T. Yang, H. Jin, J. Ma, T. Ungerer (Eds.), Autonomic and Trusted Computing. XIV, 613 pages. 2006.

Vol. 4157: M. Butler, C. Jones, A. Romanovsky, E. Troubitsyna (Eds.), Rigorous Development of Complex Fault-Tolerant Systems. X, 403 pages. 2006.

Vol. 4143: R. Lämmel, J. Saraiva, J. Visser (Eds.), Generative and Transformational Techniques in Software Engineering. X, 471 pages. 2006.

Vol. 4134: K. Yi (Ed.), Static Analysis. XIII, 443 pages. 2006.

Vol. 4119: C. Dony, J.L. Knudsen, A. Romanovsky, A.R. Tripathi (Eds.), Advanced Topics in Exception Handling Techniques. X, 302 pages. 2006.

Vol. 4111: F.S. de Boer, M.M. Bonsangue, S. Graf, W.-P. de Roever (Eds.), Formal Methods for Components and Objects. VIII, 447 pages. 2006.

Vol. 4089: W. Löwe, M. Südholt (Eds.), Software Composition. X, 339 pages. 2006.

Vol. 4085: J. Misra, T. Nipkow, E. Sekerinski (Eds.), FM 2006: Formal Methods. XV, 620 pages. 2006.

Vol. 4079: S. Etalle, M. Truszczyński (Eds.), Logic Programming. XIV, 474 pages. 2006.

Vol. 4067: D. Thomas (Ed.), ECOOP 2006 – Object-Oriented Programming. XIV, 527 pages. 2006.

Vol. 4066: A. Rensink, J. Warmer (Eds.), Model Driven Architecture – Foundations and Applications. XII, 392 pages. 2006.